D1542033

THE 50 GREATEST PLAYERS IN NEW YORK/SAN FRANCISCO GIANTS HISTORY

THE 50 GREATEST PLAYERS IN NEW YORK/SAN FRANCISCO GIANTS HISTORY

ROBERT W. COHEN

SPORTS
PUBLISHING

Sports Publishing books may be purchased in bulk at special discounts for sales promotion, corporate gifts, fund-raising, or educational purposes. Special editions can also be created to specifications. For details, contact the Special Sales Department, Sports Publishing, 307 West 36th Street, 11th Floor, New York, NY 10018 or sportspubbooks@skyhorsepublishing.com.

Sports Publishing® is a registered trademark of Skyhorse Publishing, Inc.®, a Delaware corporation.

Visit our website at www.sportspubbooks.com.

10 9 8 7 6 5 4 3 2 1

Library of Congress Cataloging-in-Publication Data is available on file.

Cover design by Tom Lau
Cover photo credits: Front cover (top): MEARSOnlineAuctions; (bottom left): Aaron Frutman of DGA Productions; (bottom right): Dirk Hansen; Back cover (top left): RMYAuctions; (top right): Library of Congress; (bottom left): Library of Congress; (bottom right): LegendaryAuctions

ISBN: 978-1-61321-999-7
Ebook ISBN: 978-1-68358-003-4

Printed in the United States of America

This book is for my beloved Lucky, who passed away during its writing.

CONTENTS

INTRODUCTION

The Giant Legacy

Comprised largely of members of the defunct Troy Trojans, who disbanded at the conclusion of the 1882 campaign, the New York Gothams joined the ranks of National League baseball teams in 1883. Founded by millionaire tobacco manufacturer John B. Day, who also owned the American Association's New York Metropolitans, the Gothams spent their first two seasons toiling in mediocrity before Day began transferring some of the Metropolitans' best players to his more profitable N.L. franchise. Led by slugging first baseman Roger Connor, versatile catcher Buck Ewing, and co-staff aces Mickey Welch and Tim Keefe, the Gothams soon became perennial contenders for the N.L. pennant, capturing league championship honors in 1888 and 1889, and winning their first two world championships both years in an early incarnation of the World Series.

Spending their first few seasons playing their home games at the original Polo Grounds, located north of Central Park, adjacent to Fifth and Sixth Avenues and 110th and 112th Streets, in upper Manhattan's Harlem, the Gothams became more commonly known as the "Giants" during this period after team manager Jim Mutrie stormed into the dressing room after a particularly satisfying victory and exclaimed, "My big fellows! My Giants!" The new moniker followed them when they moved farther north at the conclusion of the 1891 campaign to the second version of the Polo Grounds—an oddly configured ballpark situated between 155th and 159th Streets in Harlem and Washington Heights, which subsequently served as home to the Giants until they relocated to San Francisco in 1958.

In 1891, financial difficulties forced Day to sell controlling interest of the team to wealthy businessman Edward Talcott, who sold the club just four years later to Andrew Freedman, a real estate developer with ties to the Tammany Hall political machine running New York City. Abrasive and argumentative, Freedman ran the Giants into the ground, making a series of disastrous moves that enabled them to finish as high as third just once in his eight years in charge. Nevertheless, even in mediocrity, the Giants continued to feature a number of exceptional players, including future Hall of Fame shortstop George Davis, star outfielders Mike Tiernan and George Van Haltren, and ace right-hander Amos Rusie, who won more than 30 games four straight times, throwing the first no-hitter in franchise history along the way.

Things finally began to turn around for the Giants in 1903, shortly after new owner John T. Brush hired former Baltimore Orioles player-manager John McGraw to fulfill the same role in New York. Brush, who maintained control of the team until he passed away in 1912, also lured away from the rival American League several standout players, including star pitcher "Iron Man" Joe McGinnity and catcher Roger Bresnahan. Under McGraw's leadership, the Giants developed into the National League's most successful franchise, capturing 10 pennants, winning three World Series, and finishing lower than third just five times over the course of the next 30 years, even as ownership passed from Brush to financier and racehorse fancier Charles A. Stoneham. Particularly dominant during McGraw's first 11 years at the helm, the Giants won four N.L. pennants between 1903 and 1913, defeating the Philadelphia Athletics in the 1905 World Series, one year after the combative Giants' skipper showed his disdain for the American League by refusing to meet Boston in the 1904 Fall Classic. After a five-year hiatus, the Giants returned to the World Series for the first of three straight times in 1911—the same year that a fire destroyed the wooden stands at the Polo Grounds, prompting Brush to rebuild the stadium in concrete. Unfortunately, the Giants lost all three of those World Series, dropping the 1911 Fall Classic to the A's in six games, before falling to the Red Sox in seven games the following year and the A's again in 1913, this time in five games. Although several outstanding players graced the Giants' roster during this period, the team's dominant performer proved to be Christy Mathewson, who established himself as the greatest pitcher of his era. En route to winning a remarkable 373 games over the course of his Hall of Fame career, Mathewson surpassed 30 victories on four occasions, winning at least 20 games nine other times. Meanwhile, his 1905 World Series feat of throwing three straight complete-game shutouts is generally considered to be the greatest performance in the history of the Fall Classic.

After losing the 1917 World Series to the Chicago White Sox in six games, the Giants began a string of four straight Series appearances a few years later, defeating the Yankees in the 1921 and 1922 Fall Classics, before suffering a six-game defeat at the hands of their crosstown rivals in 1923. They subsequently dropped a seven-game decision to the Washington Senators in 1924, before failing to advance to the postseason in any of McGraw's final eight seasons at the helm. The Giants teams of the early 1920s featured five future Hall of Famers, with slugging first baseman George "High Pockets" Kelly, middle infielders Frankie Frisch and Dave Bancroft, third baseman Freddie Lindstrom, and outfielder Ross Youngs all eventually gaining admittance to Cooperstown.

Weary and frustrated over his inability to guide the Giants to the National League pennant in any of the previous seven seasons, McGraw chose to relinquish his managerial duties to star first baseman Bill Terry early in 1932. Under Terry's leadership, the Giants captured three more pennants over the course of the next 10 seasons, defeating Washington in five games in the 1933 World Series, before losing to the Yankees in the 1936 and 1937 Fall Classics. Hard-hitting outfielder Mel Ott and southpaw hurler Carl Hubbell established themselves as dominant players under Terry, with Ott setting numerous N.L. slugging records by the time he retired and Hubbell becoming the first pitcher to win league MVP honors twice.

Terry continued to manage the Giants through 1941, some five years after Horace Stoneham assumed the club presidency following the death of his father. With Terry choosing to step down prior to the start of the 1942 campaign after leading the team to two consecutive losing seasons, Ott took over as manager, piloting New York to six straight mediocre finishes before turning over the reins to Leo Durocher midway through the 1948 campaign. Durocher, who previously managed the hated Brooklyn Dodgers, remained in New York through 1955, leading the Giants to pennants in 1951 and 1954, and to a stunning four-game sweep of heavily favored Cleveland in the 1954 World Series. Durocher bore witness to two of baseball's most memorable moments while serving as Giants skipper, watching from the third base coaching box when Bobby Thomson hit his "Shot Heard 'Round the World" against the Dodgers in Game 3 of the 1951 playoffs, and observing first-hand when Willie Mays made his remarkable over-the-shoulder catch against the Indians in Game 1 of the 1954 Fall Classic. In addition to Mays and Thomson, other outstanding performers of the period included shortstop Alvin Dark, outfielder Monte Irvin, and pitchers Sal Maglie and Larry Jansen.

Mays remained the face of the Giants long after Bill Rigney replaced Durocher as manager in 1956, thrilling fans of the team with his tremendous hitting, superb base-running, and exceptional defense. Yet, in spite of Mays' greatness, attendance continued to dwindle at the crumbling Polo Grounds, convincing Horace Stoneham to join Dodgers' owner Walter O'Malley in relocating his team to the West Coast following the conclusion of the 1957 campaign. After moving to San Francisco, the Giants spent their first two seasons playing at Seals Stadium, a ballpark situated at 16th and Bryant Streets that had long served as home to the Pacific Coast League's San Francisco Seals. The Giants moved to Candlestick Park in 1960, a stadium built on Candlestick Point in San Francisco's southeast corner overlooking San Francisco Bay. Cold and windy, the Giants' new ballpark proved to be challenging for players and fans alike, prompting sluggers such as Mays to alter their swings somewhat to compensate for the swirling winds that blew in directly from left field, while causing attendance to gradually diminish over the years.

While National League fans in the city of New York lamented the loss of their beloved Giants, San Francisco fans welcomed their new team with open arms. And, although they initially had a difficult time accepting Mays as one of their own, preferring instead to dote on younger stars such as Orlando Cepeda, Willie McCovey, and Juan Marichal, each of whom joined the team after it arrived in the City by the Bay, they nevertheless found themselves marveling at the Say Hey Kid's extraordinary all-around ability that has prompted many baseball historians to refer to him as the most complete player in the history of the game.

The Giants possessed a considerable amount of talent during the 1960s, featuring, in addition to the aforementioned players, stars such as slugging third baseman Jim Ray Hart, right-handed pitcher Gaylord Perry, and five-tool outfielder Bobby Bonds. Yet, even though they remained contenders throughout the decade, compiling a winning record each season and posting five consecutive second-place finishes at one point, they advanced to the postseason just once, capturing the N.L. pennant in 1962, before losing to the Yankees in seven games in the World Series.

Following the institution of divisional play in 1969, the Giants returned to the playoffs under first-year manager Charlie Fox in 1971, only to lose the NLCS to the eventual world champion Pittsburgh Pirates, three-games-to-one. Featuring a host of mediocre ball clubs, the Giants failed to win their division again until 1987, 11 years after San Francisco realtor Bob Lurie saved the team from being moved to Toronto by purchasing it. Managed by second-year skipper Roger Craig, the Giants came up short once again in the 1987 NLCS, this time losing to the Cardinals in seven games. Their next wait didn't prove to be nearly as long, though, as, led by Will Clark and Kevin Mitchell, who captured league MVP honors, the Giants advanced to the postseason under Craig again just two years later, finishing first in the N.L. West with a record of 92–70. They subsequently won their first league championship in 27 years by defeating the Chicago Cubs in five games in the NLCS, before being swept by a powerful Oakland Athletics team in the "Bay Bridge Series" that is best remembered for the October 17, 1989, Loma Prieta earthquake that struck San Francisco at 5:04 PM, just before the scheduled start of Game 3 at Candlestick Park.

Three mostly uneventful seasons followed, after which Lurie sold the Giants to an ownership group headed by managing general partner Peter Magowan, former CEO of the supermarket chain, Safeway. In his first significant act after assuming control of the team, Magowan signed free agent superstar Barry Bonds away from the Pittsburgh Pirates. Bonds, a two-time N.L. MVP winner as a member of the Pirates, gave instant credibility to a Giants team that finished the previous campaign fifth in the N.L. West with a record of just 72–90. Reaping immediate benefits from the acquisition of Bonds, who captured league MVP honors in his first year in San Francisco, the Giants compiled a record of 103–59 under first-year manager Dusty Baker in 1993. Nevertheless, they ended up finishing second in the N.L. West, one game behind the division-winning Atlanta Braves.

The Giants didn't fare nearly as well in any of the next three seasons, compiling a losing record each year despite being paced on offense by Bonds and hard-hitting third baseman Matt Williams. In response, team management hired Brian Sabean to replace Bob Quinn as general manager prior to the start of the 1997 campaign. Numerous player personnel changes followed, with Sabean acquiring slick-fielding first baseman J. T. Snow from Anaheim and slugging second baseman Jeff Kent and a host of other players from Cleveland in exchange for Williams.

Fueled by the infusion of new talent, and led by Bonds, who continued to post extraordinary numbers year after year, the Giants began an extremely successful run in 1997 that saw them win in excess of 90 games in six of the next eight seasons, advancing to the playoffs four times and capturing one N.L. pennant during that time. The Giants made their first World Series appearance in 13 years in 2002, eventually losing to the A.L. champion Anaheim Angel in seven games after earlier holding a three-games-to-two advantage and leading by a score of 5–0 in the 7th inning of Game 6.

As the fortunes of the Giants changed, the team ushered in a new era, bidding farewell to Candlestick Park in 2000 and moving into a brand new, privately financed stadium situated in downtown San Francisco on that part of the shoreline of China Basin known to Giants fans as "McCovey Cove." Serving as home to the Giants since the turn of the century, AT&T Park, as it has since come to be known, is located at the corner of 3rd and King Streets, with an official address of 24 Willie Mays Plaza.

Although less than two decades old, AT&T Park has already hosted a number of historic events. In addition to serving as the backdrop for Barry Bonds's single-season record-setting 71st, 72nd, and 73rd home runs in 2001 and his record-breaking 756th career homer in 2007, the ballpark has hosted three World Series, each of which the Giants won. Employing a simple formula in which they predicate much of their success on clutch hitting, a strong bullpen, and exceptional starting pitching, the Giants have emerged as baseball's model franchise the past few years, winning three of the last seven World Series. After defeating the Texas Rangers in five games in the 2010 Fall Classic, they swept the Detroit Tigers in four straight games two years later. The Giants again reached the pinnacle of their sport in 2014 when they defeated the Kansas City Royals in seven games in the World Series. Standouts during this latest period of excellence have included catcher Buster Posey, third baseman Pablo Sandoval, and pitchers Tim Lincecum and Madison Bumgarner.

The Giants' last three world championships give them a total of 10, placing them second only to the St. Louis Cardinals (11) in National League history. Meanwhile, their 23 pennants rank as the highest total in the history of the Senior Circuit, placing them second only to the New York Yankees in baseball annals. Furthermore, as one of the longest-established professional baseball teams, the Giants have won more games as a franchise than any other team in the history of Major League Baseball.

In addition to the level of success the Giants have reached as a team over the years, a significant number of players have attained notable individual honors while wearing a Giants uniform. The franchise boasts 14 MVP winners, placing them second in the National League, behind only the St. Louis Cardinals. The Giants have also featured three Cy Young Award winners, 27 home-run champions, and eight batting champions. Meanwhile, a record 45 members of the Baseball Hall of Fame spent at least one full season playing for the Giants, 30 of whom had most of their finest seasons as members of the team.

Factors Used To Determine Rankings

It should come as no surprise that selecting the 50 greatest players ever to perform for a team with the rich history of the Giants presented a difficult and daunting task. Even after I narrowed the field down to a mere 50 men, I found myself faced with the challenge of ranking the elite players that remained. Certainly, the names of Willie Mays, Willie McCovey, Barry Bonds, Juan Marichal, Christy Mathewson, and Mel Ott would appear at, or near, the top of virtually everyone's list, although the order might vary somewhat from one person to the next. Several other outstanding performers have gained general recognition through the years as being among the greatest players ever to wear a Giants uniform. Bill Terry, Carl Hubbell, Orlando Cepeda, and Jeff Kent head the list of other Giant icons. But, how does one differentiate between the all-around brilliance of Willie Mays and the offensive dominance of Barry Bonds; or the pitching greatness of Juan Marichal and the exceptional slugging ability of Willie McCovey? After initially deciding who to include on my list, I then needed to determine what criteria to use when formulating my final rankings.

The first thing I decided to examine was the level of dominance a player attained during his time in New York or San Francisco. How often did he lead the National League in some major offensive or pitching statistical category? How did he fare in the annual MVP and/or Cy Young voting? How many times did he make the All-Star Team?

I also needed to weigh the level of statistical compilation a player achieved while wearing a Giants uniform. Where does a batter rank in team annals in the major offensive categories? How high on the all-time list of Giant hurlers does a pitcher rank in wins, ERA, complete games, innings pitched, shutouts, and saves? Of course, I also needed to consider the era in which the player performed when evaluating his overall numbers. For example, modern-day starting pitchers such as Tim Lincecum and Madison Bumgarner are not likely to throw nearly as many complete games or shutouts as either Carl Hubbell or Juan Marichal, who anchored the Giants' starting rotation during the 1930s and 1960s, respectively. Meanwhile, Mel Ott had a distinct advantage over Willie McCovey in that he competed during an era that was far more conducive to posting huge offensive numbers. And Deadball Era stars such as Larry Doyle and George Burns were not likely to hit nearly as many home runs as the players who performed for the team after the Major Leagues began using a livelier ball.

Other important factors I needed to consider were the overall contributions a player made to the success of the team, the degree to which he improved the fortunes of the ball club during his time in New York or San Francisco, the manner in which he impacted the team, both on and off the field, and the degree to which he added to the Giant legacy of winning. While the number of pennants the Giants won during a particular player's years with the ball club certainly entered into the equation, I chose not to deny a top performer his rightful place on the list if his years in New York or San Francisco happened to coincide with a lack of overall success by the team. As a result, the names of players such as Johnny Mize and Jack Clark will appear in these rankings.

There are two other things I wish to mention. First, I only considered a player's performance while playing for the Giants when formulating my rankings. That being the case, the names of exceptional players such as Gaylord Perry and Monte Irvin, both of whom had many of their best years while playing for other teams, may appear lower on this list than one might expect. In addition, since several of the rules that governed 19th-century baseball (including permitting batters to dictate the location of pitches until 1887, situating the pitcher's mound only 50 feet from home plate until 1893, and crediting a stolen base to a runner any time he advanced from first to third base on a hit) differed dramatically from those to which we have become accustomed, I elected to include only those players who competed after 1900, which is generally considered to be the beginning of baseball's "modern era." Doing so eliminated from consideration 19th-century standouts such as Roger Connor, Buck Ewing, George Davis, Tim Keefe, Mickey Welch, and Amos Rusie.

Having established the guidelines to be used throughout this book, we are ready to take a look at the 50 greatest players in Giants history, starting with number one and working our way down to number 50.

1 WILLIE MAYS

Willie Mays is considered by many to be the greatest all-around player in the history of the game. *(Courtesy of LegendaryAuctions.com)*

As great a pitcher as Christy Mathewson proved to be over the course of his career, Willie Mays and Barry Bonds ended up being the only two serious contenders for the number one spot in these rankings. Supporters of Bonds will argue that he reached a level of dominance as a hitter during his time in San Francisco that even the great *Say Hey Kid* failed to attain. They will point to the five MVP trophies Bonds won as a member of the Giants, as well as the vastly superior on-base and slugging percentages he compiled that gave him a significantly higher OPS than Mays (1.143 to .949). They also will argue that Bonds hit only 60 fewer home runs (586 to 646), knocked in just 419 fewer runs (1,440 to 1,859), and scored only 456 fewer times (1,555 to 2,011) than Mays did, in nearly 3,700 fewer plate appearances as a member of the team.

However, Bonds amassed his astounding numbers under a cloud of suspicion, compiling many of them with the aid of performance-enhancing drugs. Although he excelled as a player from the time he first joined the Giants as a free agent in 1993, Bonds never approached the figures he tallied later in his career until he began using steroids right around the turn of the century. Bonds averaged 38 home runs per season and batted over .320 just once in his first seven years in San Francisco. Over the course of the next five seasons, which took place after Bonds celebrated his 36th birthday, he averaged 52 homers and batted over .320 four times, topping the .340-mark on three separate occasions.

Having stated the above, the feeling here is that Willie Mays represented the only possible choice for the top spot here. Not only were the numbers Mays compiled over the course of his career legitimate in every way, but he amassed them during an era that was far less conducive to posting huge offensive totals. Furthermore, Mays was simply a better all-around player than Bonds, who lacked the former's defensive skills and powerful throwing arm. Mays also possessed more natural power than Bonds, who came close to hitting 50 home runs just once before he began using performance-enhancing drugs. As a result, Bonds must take a backseat to Mays as the greatest player in Giants history.

Considered to be the greatest all-around player in the history of the sport by many baseball historians, Willie Mays excelled in every aspect of the game. A consummate "five-tool" player, Mays hit for average and power, ran extremely well, played exceptional defense, and possessed one of baseball's strongest throwing arms. In addition to accumulating more outfield putouts than anyone else in MLB history, Mays ranks among the all-time leaders in home runs, RBIs, runs scored, hits, extra-base hits, and total bases. En route to earning 24 All-Star selections and two N.L. MVP Awards, the *Say Hey Kid* topped the Senior Circuit in a major offensive statistical category a total of 31 times, leading the league at different times in home runs, runs scored, batting average, hits, triples, stolen bases, total bases, on-base percentage, and slugging percentage. Placing in the top five in the N.L. MVP voting a remarkable nine times, Mays also won 12 Gold Gloves, establishing himself as arguably the finest defensive center-fielder ever to man the position. In the process of doing so, Mays played the game with unbridled enthusiasm and a certain flair that made him one of the most charismatic players in baseball history.

Born in Westfield, Alabama, on May 6, 1931, Willie Howard Mays attended Fairfield Industrial High School, where he starred in baseball, football, and basketball. Mays began his career in professional baseball while still in high school, playing briefly with the Chattanooga Choo-Choos in the summer of 1947, before joining the Birmingham Black Barons of the Negro American League. Mays spent the next two years patrolling center-field for the Black Barons, after which he signed with the New York Giants as an amateur free agent when he graduated from Fairfield in 1950.

Subsequently assigned to the Giants' minor-league affiliate in Trenton, New Jersey, Mays had an exceptional 1950 campaign in which he compiled a batting average of .353. Promoted to the Class AAA Minneapolis Millers of the American Association the following year, Mays earned a May 1951 call-up to New York by batting .477 in 35 games with the Millers.

Having previously succeeded at every level of competition, the 20-year-old Mays experienced his first bit of adversity after he joined the Giants, failing to get a hit in his first 23 at-bats. His confidence shattered, Mays found himself turning to roommate Monte Irvin for consolation, crying himself to sleep at night in the arms of the veteran outfielder and former Negro League star. However, after hitting a tremendous home run against future Hall of Famer Warren Spahn in his 24th at-bat, Mays eventually righted himself, finishing the year with 20 home runs, 68 runs batted in, and a .274 batting average, earning in the process N.L. Rookie of the Year honors. His contributions during the season's second half helped the Giants overcome a 13 ½ game deficit to the Dodgers, thereby forcing a three-game playoff between the bitter rivals that resulted in a Giants victory.

After being drafted into the United States Army during the early stages of the 1952 campaign, Mays missed virtually all of the next two years, appearing in a total of only 34 games during that time. Spending much of his time in the service playing baseball at Fort Eustis, Virginia, Mays learned his signature basket catch from a fellow Fort Eustis outfielder, Al Fortunato. Returning to the Giants in 1954, Mays led his team to the pennant and world championship, earning N.L. MVP and Major League Player of the Year honors by hitting 41 home runs, driving in 110 runs, scoring 119 times, and topping the Senior Circuit with 13 triples, a .345 batting average, a .667 slugging percentage, and an OPS of 1.078. He punctuated his great season by making one of the most famous catches in World Series history during New York's four-game sweep of the Indians—a spectacular over-the-shoulder grab of a ball hit some 450 feet by Cleveland slugger Vic Wertz.

Mays had another superb year in 1955, batting .319, knocking in 127 runs, scoring 123 times, stealing 24 bases, and leading the league with 51 home runs, 13 triples, 382 total bases, and an OPS of 1.059, while also finishing first among players at his position with 400 putouts and a career-high 23 outfield assists. The center fielder's brilliant all-around performance earned him a fourth-place finish in the N.L. MVP balloting and All-Star honors for the second of 20 consecutive seasons.

Although the Giants finished well out of contention in each of the next two years, Mays continued to post outstanding numbers, concluding the 1956 campaign with 36 homers, 84 RBIs, 101 runs scored, a .296 batting average, and a league-leading 40 stolen bases, before hitting 35 home runs, driving in 97 runs, scoring 112 times, batting .333, and topping the circuit with 20 triples, 38 steals, and a .626 slugging percentage the following season, en route to earning another fourth-place finish in the MVP voting. By amassing 35 homers, 20 triples, 26 doubles, and 38 stolen bases in the second of those campaigns, Mays became one of just a handful of players in the history of the game to surpass the 20-mark in all four categories in the same season. He also won the first of his 12 straight Gold Gloves that year.

With attendance falling off dramatically at New York's Polo Grounds and the West Coast beckoning, team owner Horace Stoneham decided to relocate the Giants to the city of San Francisco at the conclusion of the 1957 campaign. The move left Mays feeling disconsolate and dejected, since New York had become his adopted home. Possessing the enthusiasm of a young boy and an unmatched love of the game, Mays often played stickball on the streets of New York with the neighborhood children when he returned home at the end of the day. Yet, heartbroken as he was, Mays joined his teammates when they journeyed west at the start of the 1958 season.

Even though Mays continued to play exceptionally well after the Giants moved to San Francisco, the hometown fans initially treated him with indifference since they considered him to be very much a New Yorker. They also resented the favorable comparisons being made of Mays to Bay Area legend Joe DiMaggio, who reached iconic-like status while playing for the San Francisco Seals of the Pacific Coast League before he joined the Yankees in 1936. Local fans scoffed at the notion that anyone could be as good as DiMaggio, and they correspondingly reacted unfavorably to Mays. On the other hand, they immediately adopted as one of their own 1958 N.L. Rookie of the Year Orlando Cepeda, choosing to welcome him with open arms, while simultaneously displaying little in the way of affection towards Mays. Nevertheless, Willie remained one of the finest all-around players in the game, having superb years in both 1958 and 1959. After hitting 29 home runs, knocking in 96 runs, batting a career-high .347, and leading the league with 121 runs scored, 31 stolen bases, and an OPS of 1.002 in the first of those campaigns, Mays hit 34 homers, drove in 104 runs, scored 125 times, batted .313, stole a league-leading 27 bases, and collected a career-high 43 doubles in 1959.

The Giants spent their first two years in San Francisco playing in old Seals Stadium, the same ballpark in which Joe DiMaggio made a name for himself some 25 years earlier. In 1960, they moved to Candlestick Park, which remained their home until well after Mays retired. With its cold, swirling winds, Candlestick presented a new challenge to Mays, who not only had to learn to perform under extremely adverse conditions, but also needed to adapt his swing to accommodate his new surroundings. The gusty winds at Candlestick generally tended to blow in from left field, and out towards right. That being the case, the right-handed-hitting Mays, who previously had been predominantly a pull hitter, had to learn how to drive the ball more to the opposite field. Mays ended up hitting the ball to right field with great regularity in subsequent seasons, slugging a significant number of home runs over Candlestick's right-field fence.

After batting .319, driving in 103 runs, scoring 107 times, leading the league with 190 hits, and hitting "only" 29 homers in his first year at his new home ballpark, Mays went on to have some of the greatest seasons of his career while playing at Candlestick Park, averaging 44 home runs, 116 RBIs, and 119 runs scored from 1961 to 1966, while posting a composite batting average of .305 during that time. Here are the numbers he compiled in each of those six seasons, with the figures typed in bold indicating that he led the league in that category:

1961: 40 HR, 123 RBIs, **129** Runs Scored, .308 AVG., .393 OBP, .584 SLG, .977 OPS

1962: **49** HR, 141 RBIs, 130 Runs Scored, .304 AVG., .384 OBP, .615 SLG, .999 OPS

1963: 38 HR, 103 RBIs, 115 Runs Scored, .314 AVG., .380 OBP, .582 SLG, .962 OPS

1964: **47** HR, 111 RBIs, 121 Runs Scored, .296 AVG., .383 OBP, **.607** SLG, **.990** OPS

1965: **52** HR, 112 RBIs, 118 Runs Scored, .317 AVG., **.398** OBP, **.645** SLG, **1.043** OPS

1966: 37 HR, 103 RBIs, 99 Runs Scored, .288 AVG., .368 OBP, .556 SLG, .924 OPS

(Numbers printed in bold throughout the book signify that the player led the league in that particular statistical category that year.)

In addition to leading the league in home runs three times, runs scored once, on-base percentage once, and slugging percentage and OPS two times each during that period, Mays topped the Senior Circuit in total bases twice. He also earned three more top-five finishes in the N.L. MVP voting, never finishing any lower than sixth in the balloting. By hitting 52 home runs in 1965 en route to earning league MVP honors, Mays became the only player in baseball history to post two 50-homer campaigns more than a decade apart.

As Mays continued to thrill fans of the game with his all-around brilliance year after year, he received his just due from many of the sport's notables, with Sandy Koufax commenting, "I can't believe that Babe Ruth was a better player than Willie Mays. Ruth is to baseball what Arnold Palmer is to golf. He got the game moving. But I can't believe he could run as well as Mays, and I can't believe he was any better an outfielder."

Former Dodger great Gil Hodges, who competed against Mays during his playing career, later returned to New York to manage the Mets. In discussing the managerial strategy he employed whenever his team faced Mays, Hodges stated, "I can't very well tell my batters don't hit it to him. Wherever they hit it, he's there anyway."

Meanwhile, Cincinnati Reds slugger Ted Kluszewski said, "I'm not sure what the hell charisma is, but I get the feeling it's Willie Mays."

The 1966 season turned out to be the last great year for Mays. After celebrating his 36th birthday during the early stages of the 1967 campaign, Mays finally began to show signs of aging, experiencing a precipitous drop-off in offensive production in subsequent seasons. Yet, he remained a productive player the next five years, averaging 21 homers, 70 runs batted in, and 81 runs scored from 1967 to 1971, while batting over .280 in three of those seasons. Mays had his best season during that period in 1970, when he hit 28 home runs, knocked in 83 runs, scored 94 times, and batted .291. He followed that up by stealing 23 bases at 40 years of age in 1971, while also leading the league in walks (112) and on-base percentage (.429).

Strictly a part-time player by 1972, Mays returned to New York early that year when the Giants traded him to the Mets for pitcher Charlie Williams and $50,000. He spent his final two years in New York, ending his magnificent career in the same city in which it first began some 22 years earlier. Mays retired from the game with 660 home runs, 1,903 runs batted in, 2,062 runs scored, 3,283 hits, 140 triples, 523 doubles, 338 stolen bases, a .302 batting average, a .384 on-base percentage, and a .557 slugging percentage, compiling virtually all those numbers while playing for the Giants. He continues to hold numerous franchise records, including most home runs (646), runs scored (2,011), hits (3,187), extra-base hits (1,289), doubles (504), and total bases (5,907). Mays also ranks second in team history with 1,859 RBIs, 139 triples, a .564 slugging percentage, and an OPS of .949. In addition to reaching the 50-homer plateau twice, Mays surpassed 40 home runs on four other occasions. He also knocked in more than 100 runs and batted over .300 ten times each, scored more than 100 runs 12 times, and stole more than 30 bases on three separate occasions.

Following his retirement as an active player, Mays remained in the New York Mets organization as their hitting instructor until the end of the 1979 season. He returned to the Giants in 1986, since which time he has served as Special Assistant to the President of the team. In addition to retiring his number 24, the Giants have since honored Mays by naming the plot of land on which AT&T Park is situated *24 Willie Mays Plaza*.

Mays' greatness as an all-around player has continued to live on in baseball lore through the years, with the totality of his game prompting many knowledgeable people to call him the most complete player in the history of the sport. Giants' president Peter Magowan stated, "He would routinely do things you never saw anyone else do. He'd score from first base on a single. He'd take two bases on a pop-up. He'd throw somebody out at the plate on one bounce. And the bigger the game, the better he played."

Hall of Fame pitcher Gaylord Perry commented, "I played with who I thought was the greatest player I ever saw play. I never saw Mickey Mantle and DiMaggio play, but the greatest guy I saw, and I had him for 10 years in center-field, was Willie Mays. He was awesome. He did not have to dive after the ball. He got such a quick jump."

Reflecting back on his earliest days as Mays' teammate, Monte Irvin recalled, "Leo Durocher was our manager, and he brought Willie up to me and said, 'This is Willie Mays and he's your new roommate.' You could see right away that this young man was a natural. He had those real big hands, great power and speed, and would catch everything hit in his direction. He's the best center-fielder that ever lived, no question."

Irvin added, "I think anybody who saw him will tell you that Willie Mays was the greatest player who ever lived."

Leo Durocher, who managed the Giants Mays' first few years with the club, agreed with Irvin's assessment, once stating, "If somebody came up and hit .450, stole 100 bases, and performed a miracle in the field every day, I'd still look you in the eye and say Willie was better. He could do the five things you have to do to be a superstar: hit, hit with power, run, throw, and field. And he had that other magic ingredient that turns a superstar into a super superstar. He lit up the room. He was a joy to be around."

Giant Career Highlights:

Best Season: There are so many great seasons from which to choose, with Mays' 1954, 1955, 1957, 1962, 1964, and 1965 campaigns heading the list. Although any of those seasons would have made a good choice, I ultimately decided to go with 1954. En route to leading the Giants to the world championship for the only time in his career, Mays captured N.L. MVP honors by topping the Senior Circuit with 13 triples, a .345 batting average, a .667 slugging percentage, and a career-high OPS of 1.078. He also knocked in 110 runs and finished either second or third in the league with 41 home runs, 119 runs scored, 195 hits, and 377 total bases. Furthermore, Mays led all N.L. outfielders with 9 double plays and finished second among players at his position with 13 assists, a .985 fielding percentage, and 448 putouts, which represented the highest total of his career.

Memorable Moments/Greatest Performances: With a major-league record 22 extra-inning home runs to his credit, Mays delivered a number of memorable game-winning blows over the course of his career. On June 22, 1951, the 20-year-old Mays gave the Giants a 9–6 win over the Cubs by hitting a three-run homer in the top of the 10th inning. Less than two weeks later, on July 3, Mays' solo shot in the bottom of the 13th gave the Giants a 9–8 win over Philadelphia. Mays again came up big in the clutch on April 30, 1954, when his two-run homer in the top of the 14th gave Sal Maglie and the Giants a 4–2 victory over the Cubs. Mays again delivered the game's decisive blow against Chicago on July 14, 1957, hitting a two-run blast in the bottom of the 12th inning, to give the Giants an 8–6 victory over the Cubs.

Mays continued his late-inning heroics after the Giants moved to San Francisco, giving the Giants a 2–1 win over the Cubs on June 13, 1963, by belting a solo homer off Chicago's Dick Ellsworth in the bottom of the 10th inning. On August 12, 1966, Mays ended a pitcher's duel between Gaylord Perry and Houston's Mike Cuellar by driving in the game's only run with a leadoff homer in the bottom of the 9th inning. Mays hit the only extra-inning grand slam of his career on June 13, 1967, when he homered off Astros starter Dave Giusti with the bases loaded in the top of the 10th inning, to give the Giants a 6–2 victory over Houston. Mays, though, hit the most memorable extra-inning home run of his career on July 2, 1963, when his solo shot in the bottom of the 16th inning brought to an end a classic pitcher's duel between Milwaukee's Warren Spahn and San Francisco's Juan Marichal. Both hurlers worked all 16 innings, with Spahn allowing 9 hits and just that one run over 15 ⅓ innings, while Marichal worked 16 scoreless frames, surrendering just 8 hits to the hard-hitting Braves.

Mays scored 5 runs in one game on three separate occasions, doing so for the first time during a lopsided 21–4 victory over the Pittsburgh Pirates on May 25, 1954, when he went 3-for-4, with a triple and a pair of walks. He accomplished the feat again on April 24, 1964, when he went 3-for-3, with a homer, 2 walks, and 2 RBIs during a 15–5 win over Cincinnati. Mays again tallied 5 runs in one game later in the year, going 2-for-3, with a homer, a pair of walks, and 2 RBIs during a 13–4 victory over Pittsburgh on September 19.

Mays defeated the Dodgers almost single-handedly on June 29, 1955, knocking in all 6 Giants runs by going 3-for-4, with a pair of homers, during a 6–1 victory over Brooklyn. Mays again drove in 6 runs on May 13, 1961, when he hit a grand slam homer and a two-run shot, in leading the Giants to an 8–5 win over Milwaukee.

Mays stole a career-high 4 bases during a 5–4 victory over the Cardinals on May 6, 1956, recording 2 steals of second and another 2 of third.

Mays led the Giants to a 16–9 victory over the Dodgers on May 13, 1958, by going 5-for-5, with 2 homers, 2 triples, 4 RBIs, and 4 runs scored. Mays had another perfect 5-for-5 day at the plate against the Phillies on August 2,

1962, leading the Giants to a 9–2 win by homering twice and driving in 5 runs.

Mays had a huge game against the Braves on September 17, 1959, going 4-for-4, with a homer, 5 RBIs, and 2 runs scored, during a 13–6 Giants win.

Mays displayed his all-around brilliance in leading the Giants to a 5–3 win over Cincinnati on June 24, 1960, going 3-for-4 at the plate, with a pair of homers and 3 RBIs, scoring 3 times, stealing home, and recording 10 outfield putouts. During an 11-inning, 8–6 win over the Phillies later in the year, on September 15, Mays collected 5 hits, including 3 triples, tying in the process the modern major-league record for the most three-baggers in one game.

Mays, though, turned in his most dominant hitting performance on April 30, 1961, when he led the Giants to a 14–4 win over Milwaukee by becoming the ninth player in MLB history to hit 4 home runs in one game. Willie also knocked in a career-high 8 runs during the contest.

Mays also homered three times in one game twice, doing so for the first time later that same year, on June 29, 1961, when he reached the seats three times during a 4-for-5, 5-RBI performance against the Phillies. Mays' last homer of the contest—a solo shot in the top of the 10th inning—proved to be the decisive blow of an 8–7 Giants' win. He again homered three times in one game on June 2, 1963, leading the Giants to a 6–4 victory over St. Louis in the process.

Mays reached several milestones during his time with the Giants, hitting the 500th home run of his career against Houston's Don Nottebart during a 5–1 Giants' win on September 13, 1965. Nearly one year later, on August 17, 1966, Mays moved into second place on the all-time home-run list when he reached the seats for the 535th time during a 4–3 victory over the Cardinals. On September 22, 1969, Mays became just the second player in MLB history to reach the 600-homer plateau when he hit a pinch-hit home run during a 4–2 win over the San Diego Padres. The following year, on July 18, 1970, Mays became a member of the 3,000-hit club when he singled off Montreal's Wike Wegener during a 10–1 victory over the Expos.

Yet, in spite of the many outstanding batting feats Mays recorded over the course of his career, he is equally remembered for his defensive brilliance. Mays made one of his greatest fielding plays during a 3–1 victory over the Dodgers on August 15, 1951, when he raced deep into the gap in right center field to snare a drive hit by Carl Furillo, spun 360 degrees counterclockwise, and threw the ball on a 325-foot line to home plate to nail Billy Cox trying to score from third base. Following the contest, Brooklyn manager Charlie Dressen commented, "I won't believe that play until I see him do it again."

Still, the most iconic moment of Mays' career arguably took place in the 8th inning of Game 1 of the 1954 World Series. With the Giants and Indians tied at 2–2 in the top of the frame, Cleveland slugger Vic Wertz stepped into the batter's box with runners on first and second and nobody out. Wertz proceeded to drive the ball some 450 feet to deep center-field, where Mays made a remarkable over-the-shoulder grab that subsequently became known simply as "The Catch." Mays then whirled and fired the ball to the infield, to keep the lead runner, Larry Doby, from scoring. Doby ended up being stranded at third base, after which the Giants won the contest by a score of 5–2 when Dusty Rhodes delivered a pinch-hit three-run homer in the bottom of the 10th inning. The Giants went on to sweep the Series in four games, with Mays' astonishing play remaining the most indelible image of that year's Fall Classic.

Notable Achievements:

Hit more than 30 home runs 11 times, surpassing 40 homers six times and 50 homers twice. Knocked in more than 100 runs 10 times, topping 120 RBIs three times and 140 RBIs once (141 in 1962).

Scored more than 100 runs 12 times, surpassing 120 runs scored on six occasions.

Batted over .300 10 times, surpassing the .330-mark on three occasions.

Topped 200 hits once (208 in 1958).

Finished in double-digits in triples five times, reaching the 20-mark once (20 in 1957).

Surpassed 30 doubles six times, topping 40 two-baggers once (43 in 1959).

Stole more than 20 bases seven times, surpassing 30 thefts on three occasions.

Walked more than 100 times once (112 in 1971).

Compiled on-base percentage in excess of .400 five times.

Posted slugging percentage in excess of .500 14 times, topping the .600-mark six times.

Compiled OPS in excess of 1.000 five times.

Surpassed 30 home runs and 30 stolen bases in same season twice (1956 & 1957).

One of only four players in MLB history to surpass 20 home runs, 20 triples, 20 doubles, and 20 stolen bases in the same season (1957).

Led N.L. in: home runs four times; runs scored twice; batting average once; hits once; triples three times; total bases three times; stolen bases four times; walks once; on-base percentage twice; slugging percentage five times; and OPS five times.

Led N.L. outfielders in: putouts once; assists once; and double plays four times.

Led N.L. center-fielders in: putouts twice; assists three times; and double plays five times.

Second player in MLB history to hit 600 home runs.

Member of 3,000-hit club.

Ranks among MLB all-time leaders in: home runs (5th); RBIs (11th); runs scored (7th); hits (12th); extra-base hits (5th); and total bases (3rd).

Holds MLB record for most putouts by an outfielder (7,095).

Holds MLB record for most games played in center-field (2,829).

Ranks among MLB all-time leaders in assists (5th) and double plays (2nd) by a center-fielder.

Holds Giants career records for most: home runs (646); runs scored (2,011); hits (3,187); extra-base hits (1,289); doubles (504); total bases (5,907); games played (2,857); plate appearances (12,015); and at-bats (10,477).

Ranks among Giants career leaders in: RBIs (2nd); triples (2nd); slugging percentage (2nd); OPS (2nd); stolen bases (3rd); and bases on balls (3rd).

Hit four home runs in one game vs. Milwaukee Braves on April 30, 1961.

Hit three home runs in one game twice.

Holds share of modern MLB record by tripling three times in one game (vs. Philadelphia on September 15, 1960).

1951 N.L. Rookie of the Year.

1954 Major League Player of the Year.

Two-time N.L. MVP (1954 & 1965).

Finished in top five of N.L. MVP voting a total of nine times.

Two-time All-Star Game MVP (1963 & 1968).

11-time *Sporting News* All-Star selection (1954, 1957, 1958, 1959, 1960, 1961, 1962, 1963, 1964, 1965 & 1966).

24-time N.L. All-Star (1954–1973, including twice each from 1959 to 1962).

12-time Gold Glove winner (1957–1968).

1971 Roberto Clemente Award winner.

Four-time N.L. Player of the Month.

Member of Major League Baseball's All-Century Team.

Number 2 on *The Sporting News'* 1999 list of Baseball's 100 Greatest Players.

The Sporting News' 1960s Player of the Decade.

Two-time N.L. champion (1951 & 1954).

1954 world champion.

Elected to Baseball Hall of Fame by members of BBWAA in 1979.

2 BARRY BONDS

Barry Bonds hit more home runs than any other player in Major League history.
(Courtesy of Aaron Frutman of DGA Productions)

Arguably the finest all-around player of his generation, Barry Bonds earned
12 Silver Sluggers, eight Gold Gloves, and a major-league record seven MVP
Awards over the course of his career, which he split between the Giants and
Pittsburgh Pirates. After spending his first seven seasons in Pittsburgh, Bonds
joined the Giants as a free agent in 1993, beginning in the process a lengthy
15-year stay in San Francisco during which he performed at such a high level
that he came to rival his godfather, Willie Mays, as the greatest player in franchise history. Bonds finished in the top five in the N.L. MVP voting nine
times as a member of the Giants, winning the award on five separate occasions. He also won nine Silver Sluggers and five Gold Gloves, topped the
Senior Circuit in a major offensive statistical category a total of 36 times,

and reached a level of dominance that only a select few in the history of the game have attained. En route to becoming one of only two players in MLB history to surpass 30 home-runs 13 straight times, Bonds established new single-season and career home run records. He also set numerous other marks, including most career walks (2,558), most walks in a season (232), highest single-season on-base percentage (.609), and highest single-season slugging percentage (.863). Yet, in spite of his numerous achievements, Bonds found himself steeped in controversy throughout much of his time in San Francisco, with his surly disposition, egotistical nature, and involvement with steroids garnering him a significant amount of negative publicity.

Born in Riverside, California, on July 24, 1964, Barry Lamar Bonds grew up some 420 miles northwest, in the city of San Carlos. Excelling in baseball, football, and basketball while attending Junipero Serra High School in nearby San Mateo, Bonds earned prep All-American honors on the diamond as a senior by compiling a .467 batting average. The son of former major-league outfielder Bobby Bonds, who began his professional career with the Giants, Barry seemed destined to follow in his father's footsteps when the Giants selected him in the second round of the 1982 MLB draft following his graduation from Junipero Serra. However, when contract negotiations between the two parties stalled, Bonds instead elected to enroll at Arizona State University.

Bonds spent the next three years starring in the outfield for the Sun Devils, making an extremely strong impression on everyone associated with the team. Former teammate Mike Devereaux recalled years later, "Barry did things that were amazing. He would hit a ball with topspin over the fence that would be incredible. A ball that would usually drop in front of the outfielder, but, instead, his went over the fences."

Selected by Pittsburgh with the sixth overall pick of the 1985 amateur draft, Bonds spent less than one full season in the minor leagues before making his debut with the Pirates on May 30, 1986. Struggling somewhat at the plate as a rookie, Bonds batted just .223 and struck out a career-high 102 times, although he managed to hit 16 homers, knock in 48 runs, score 72 times, and steal 36 bases in the 113 games in which he appeared. After being shifted from center-field to left the following year, Bonds posted relatively modest numbers on offense the next three seasons, averaging 23 home runs, 58 RBIs, 97 runs scored, and 27 stolen bases from 1987 to 1989, while compiling batting averages of .261, .283, and .248.

The 26-year-old Bonds finally emerged as an elite player in 1990, when he led the Pirates to the N.L. East title for the first of three straight times by hitting 33 homers, driving in 114 runs, scoring 104 times, stealing 52 bases, batting .301, compiling a .406 on-base percentage, and topping the Senior Circuit with a .565 slugging percentage and a .970 OPS. He also led all N.L. left-fielders in putouts and assists for the second straight time, earning in the process his first Gold Glove, his initial All-Star selection, and league MVP honors. Bonds followed that up with two more stellar seasons for the Pirates, performing particularly well in 1992 when he won his second MVP trophy by hitting 34 homers, knocking in 103 runs, stealing 39 bases, batting .311, and leading the league with 109 runs scored, 127 bases on balls, a .456 on-base percentage, and a .624 slugging percentage. Bonds' exceptional all-around play prompted Pirates' teammate R. J. Reynolds to prophetically proclaim, "One day, he will put up numbers no one can believe." Meanwhile, Cincinnati Reds right-hander Jose Rijo stated, "Barry Bonds is the best player I've ever seen. He can be pitched to, but very carefully."

In spite of the tremendous amount of success Bonds experienced during his time in Pittsburgh, he gradually developed a reputation as a self-absorbed individual who cared little about the feelings of others. In discussing his godson, Willie Mays, who remained close to Bonds throughout the latter's career, said, "Sometimes he says things before he thinks. That's why I'm here—to remind him other people have feelings too." Nevertheless, former Pirates manager Jim Leyland, who clashed with the star outfielder on more than one occasion, looked back favorably on the time the two men spent together, explaining years later in a Bonds biography written by Carrie Muskat:

> Most guys who talk about what they're going to do, they usually set themselves up to get humbled. Barry Bonds was like Joe Namath or Muhammed Ali. He could make a statement and go out and back it up. Not a lot of guys can do that. In fact, managers usually cringe when guys make statements about what they're going to do. In Barry's case, I liked it. I think he did it on purpose to motivate himself. In a lot of ways, it's easy for Barry. I think he needs a little controversy around him.

A free agent at the conclusion of the 1992 campaign, Bonds chose to leave Pittsburgh when the Giants offered him a six-year deal worth a then-record

$43.75 million. The contract enabled Bonds to fulfill his lifelong dream of playing for the Giants, with whom his father spent his first seven big-league seasons.

Bonds performed magnificently his first year in San Francisco, winning his third N.L. MVP Award by leading the Giants to within one game of the N.L. West title. Establishing new career highs in virtually every offensive category, Bonds concluded the 1993 campaign with 129 runs scored, 181 hits, 38 doubles, a .336 batting average, and a league-leading 46 homers, 123 RBIs, 365 total bases, .458 on-base percentage, and .677 slugging percentage. Giants' owner Peter Magowan preferred to focus on the other aspects of Bonds' game, though, telling the *Boston Globe*:

> Where Barry has truly affected the entire team is the way he has fun just practicing the game. He truly loves to play. And his defense is contagious. In one game, he made a game-saving catch and cut three sure doubles off at the line and held them to singles; in a couple of cases, his plays saved what would have been runs. He's made everyone in the field more aggressive. Defense is the most contagious aspect of baseball, and Barry has dramatically affected the way the Giants play the game.

After subsequently hitting 37 homers, driving in 81 runs, scoring 89 times, and batting .312 during the strike-shortened 1994 season, Bonds had another extremely productive year in 1995, hitting 33 homers, knocking in 104 runs, scoring 109 times, batting .294, and leading the league with 120 bases on balls, a .431 on-base percentage, and an OPS of 1.009. Commenting on his teammate's exceptional performance his first few years with the club, Matt Williams suggested, "He's the one guy in our league I would pay to watch."

Even though Bonds generated a great deal of power at the plate, his keen batting eye and short, compact swing made him a difficult batter for opposing pitchers to fool, preventing him from ever placing anywhere near the top of the league rankings in strikeouts. In discussing his hitting style, Bonds said, "I think of myself as 'catching' the ball with my bat and letting the pitcher supply the power." At the same time, he displayed his boastful tendencies by stating, "It's called talent. I just have it. I can't explain it. You either have it or you don't."

Bonds earned a fifth-place finish in the N.L. MVP voting in both 1996 and 1997, totaling 82 home runs, 230 RBIs, 245 runs scored, and 77 stolen bases over the course of those two seasons, while compiling batting averages of .308 and .291, respectively. By hitting 42 homers and stealing 40 bases in the first of those campaigns, he became just the second player in MLB history to reach the 40-mark in both categories in the same season (Jose Canseco was the first). Yet, in spite of his outstanding accomplishment, Bonds ended up alienating virtually everyone in the Giants' clubhouse by announcing at one point during the season that his teammates failed to give him the support he needed to reach his ultimate goal of winning the World Series.

Bonds had another excellent season in 1998, finishing the year with 37 home runs, 122 RBIs, 120 runs scored, a career-high 44 doubles, a .303 batting average, a .438 on-base percentage, and a .609 slugging percentage. However, he grew increasingly frustrated and envious over the course of the campaign as he watched lesser players Mark McGwire and Sammy Sosa become the darlings of the fans and media as they drew inexorably closer to Roger Maris's long-standing single-season home-run record through the use of steroids. Subsequently choosing to enhance his own performance by artificial means, Bonds spent the next two years transforming his previously sinewy 6'1", 200-pound frame into one of monstrous proportions, gradually building himself up to a muscular 240 pounds.

Limited by injuries to only 102 games in 1999, Bonds hit 34 homers, knocked in just 83 runs, scored only 91 times, and batted just .262. Returning to the Giants fully healthy and 15 pounds heavier the following year, Bonds earned a runner-up finish to teammate Jeff Kent in the N.L. MVP balloting by hitting 49 homers, driving in 106 runs, scoring 129 times, batting .306, compiling an OPS of 1.127, and topping the circuit with 117 bases on balls. Having added another 25 pounds of muscle onto his frame by the start of the ensuing campaign, Bonds subsequently began an extraordinary four-year run during which time he established himself as arguably the most dominant offensive force in the history of the game. Here are the numbers he posted from 2001 to 2004:

2001: **73** HR, 137 RBIs, 129 Runs, **177** BB, .328 AVG, **.515** OBP, **.863** SLG, **1.379** OPS
2002: 46 HR, 110 RBIs, 117 Runs, **198** BB, .370 AVG, **.582** OBP, **.799** SLG, **1.381** OPS
2003: 45 HR, 90 RBIs, 111 Runs, **148** BB, .341 AVG, **.529** OBP, **.749** SLG, **1.278** OPS
2004: 45 HR, 101 RBIs, 129 Runs, **232** BB, **.362** AVG, **.609** OBP, **.812** SLG, **1.422** OPS

Bonds compiled those outstanding home-run and RBI totals in spite of the fact that opposing pitchers rarely gave him anything good to hit. In addition to hitting an MLB record 73 homers in 2001, Bonds twice established new single-season marks for most walks, highest on-base percentage, and highest OPS during the period. His .863 slugging percentage in 2001 also set a new single-season record. Meanwhile, Bonds' batting averages of .370 in 2002 and .362 in 2004 earned him the only two batting titles of his career. He also earned All-Star, Silver Slugger, and N.L. MVP honors all four years.

Bonds's incredible performance over the course of those four seasons prompted several notable baseball people to sing his praises. Giants shortstop Rich Aurilia commented, "The rest of us play in the major leagues. He's at another level." Teammate Benito Santiago added, "The rest of us should spend all of our time in the dugout bowing to him."

Hall of Fame pitcher Greg Maddux suggested, "You walk Barry. Just walk him." He then added, "He's always been the best player in the game. Is he the best ever? What do I know? I only know what happened in the nineties. He's always been a complete player. He didn't have to hit 30 extra home runs to convince me of that."

Dodgers Manager Jim Tracy noted, "He's beginning to make a case for himself as arguably being maybe the greatest player to ever play the game." Florida Marlins skipper Jack McKeon expressed even more conviction on the matter, stating, "You can't tell me the Babe was any better than this guy. You can't tell me this guy isn't the best player in the history of the game."

Bonds never again posted such outlandish numbers for the Giants. After missing virtually all of the 2005 campaign with injuries, he totaled just 54 homers over the course of the next two seasons. However, during that time he established himself as MLB's all-time leader in home runs, bases on balls, and intentional bases on balls. After the Giants chose not to re-sign him when he became a free agent at the end of the 2007 season, no other team elected to pursue him, leaving the 43-year-old slugger no choice but to retire. In addition to ending his playing career with more home runs (762), walks (2,558), and intentional walks (688) than any other player in baseball history, Bonds posted a lifetime batting average of .298, amassed 2,935 hits, 77 triples, 601 doubles, and 514 stolen bases, and finished among the all-time leaders with 1,996 RBIs (4th), 2,227 runs scored (3rd), 5,976 total bases (4th), a .444 on-base percentage (6th), a .607 slugging percentage (5th), and a 1.051 OPS (4th). During his time in San Francisco, he hit 586 homers, knocked in

1,440 runs, scored 1,555 times, accumulated 1,951 hits, 41 triples, and 381 doubles, stole 263 bases, walked 1,947 times, batted .312, compiled an on-base percentage of .477, and posted a slugging percentage of .666. Bonds earned 12 of his 14 All-Star selections, two of his three Major League Player of the Year nominations, and five of his record seven MVP Awards while playing for the Giants.

Yet, in spite of his amazing list of accomplishments, Bonds has failed to gain induction into the Baseball Hall of Fame since his name first appeared on the list of eligible candidates in 2013 due to his involvement with steroids, which the 2006 book *Game of Shadows* described in detail. Written by Lance Williams and Mark Fainaru-Wada, the work alleges that Bonds enhanced his performance by using stanozolol and a host of other steroids that he received from his personal trainer, who worked for the Bay Area Laboratory Co-operative (BALCO)—a known provider of performance-enhancing drugs. Although Bonds initially declared his innocence, attributing his changed physique and increased power at the plate to a strict regimen of bodybuilding, diet, and legitimate supplements, it later surfaced that he admitted during 2003 grand jury testimony that Anderson supplied him with a clear substance and a cream that Bonds claimed he believed to be the nutritional supplement flaxseed oil and a rubbing balm for arthritis. Eventually indicted on four counts of perjury and one count of obstruction of justice, Bonds was convicted on April 13, 2011, on the obstruction of justice charge, for giving an evasive answer to a question under oath. However, after a three-judge panel of the U.S. Court of Appeals for the Ninth Circuit initially upheld the conviction, a larger panel of the court overturned it on April 22, 2015.

The question of how Bonds's involvement with steroids impacts his place in history will have to be answered separately by each individual. There are those who have expressed the belief that they consider Bonds to be among the handful of greatest players of all time. Certainly, his teammates, peers, most members of the media, and the vast majority of Giants fans seemed to care little about his illicit activities as he continued to etch his name into the record books, with many of them declaring him to be the greatest player of all time. However, the feeling here is that more restraint needs to be shown before making such declarations. There is little doubt that Bonds was a truly great player, with or without steroids. Yet, it must be remembered that he failed to earn a spot on Baseball's All-Century Team when the selections were announced in 1999. And, prior to the turn of the century, most baseball historians would have ranked him behind such all-time greats as Ruth, Mays, Aaron, Cobb, Wagner, Williams, Musial, and Gehrig. And many others would have placed Mantle, DiMaggio, and his contemporary, Ken Griffey Jr., ahead of him. All those factors must be considered when evaluating Bonds's place among the baseball immortals.

Giant Career Highlights:

Best Season: Bonds posted extraordinary numbers from 2001 to 2004, a period during which he established himself as perhaps the greatest offensive threat in the history of the game. Particularly dominant in 2001 and 2004, Bonds set new single-season MLB records for most home runs (73) and highest slugging percentage (.863) in the first of those campaigns. He also drove in a career-high 137 runs, scored 129 times, batted .328, amassed a career-best 411 total bases, and led the league with 177 walks, a .515 on-base percentage, and a 1.379 OPS. Three years later, Bonds homered 45 times in only 373 official at-bats, knocked in 101 runs, again scored 129 times, and topped the Senior Circuit with a .362 batting average, an .812 slugging percentage, 232 walks, a .609 on-base percentage, and an OPS of 1.422, establishing new major-league marks in each of the last three categories. He also amazingly struck out just 41 times, becoming in the process one of the few players in history to accumulate more home runs than strikeouts in a season.

Still, the fact that Bonds used performance-enhancing drugs to compile those astonishing numbers prevented me from identifying either of those campaigns as his greatest season. Instead, I opted for 1993—his first season with the Giants. En route to earning N.L. MVP honors for the third of seven times, Bonds scored 129 runs, stole 29 bases, collected a career-high 181 hits, batted .336, drew 126 bases on balls, and led the league with 46 home runs, 123 RBIs, 365 total bases, a .458 on-base percentage, and a .677 slugging percentage. He also won the fourth Gold Glove of his career, with his brilliant all-around performance bringing the Giants to within one game of the N.L. West title with a record of 103–59.

Memorable Moments/Greatest Performances: Bonds hit a number of game-winning home runs during his time in San Francisco, with his first such blast coming on August 15, 1993, when his one-out solo homer in the top of the 11th inning proved to be the decisive blow in a 9–7 victory over the Chicago Cubs.

Bonds hit his first walk-off homer as a member of the Giants on June 30, 1995, when his two-run shot off Trevor Hoffman with 2 men out in the bottom of the 9th inning gave the Giants a 7–6 win over the Padres. Bonds's blast—his second of the game—punctuated an exceptional 4-for-5, 5-RBI performance.

Bonds again came through in the clutch on May 26, 1997, when he concluded a 3-for-4 afternoon by hitting a leadoff homer in the bottom of the 9th inning that gave the Giants a 4–3 win over Houston. Bonds delivered another walk-off homer on August 30, 1999, giving the Giants a 6–4 victory over the Philadelphia Phillies with a two-run blast in the bottom of the 10th inning. Bonds gave the Giants another walk-off win on April 5, 2002, when his two-run shot in the bottom of the 10th resulted in a 3–1 victory over the San Diego Padres.

Bonds had several memorable days at the plate for the Giants, with one of those coming on July 8, 1993, when he collected 3 hits, homered twice, scored 3 times, and knocked in 6 runs during a 13–2 pounding of the Phillies in Philadelphia. Nearly six weeks later, on August 18, he led the Giants to a 9–6 win over Pittsburgh by going 4-for-5, with a pair of homers, a double, 4 RBIs, and 3 runs scored. Although the Giants came up one game short in their quest to capture the division title that year, Bonds did everything within his power to lead them into the playoffs, driving in a career-high 7 runs, with 2 homers and a double, during an 8–7 victory over the Dodgers in the final series of the 1993 campaign.

Bonds had one of the biggest games of his record-setting 2001 season on July 26, when he led the Giants to a lopsided 11–3 win over Arizona by homering twice, knocking in 5 runs, and scoring 3 times. The following year, he picked up right where he left off in 2001, hitting a pair of homers and driving in 5 runs during a 9–2 victory over the Dodgers on Opening Day.

Although the Giants lost their April 18, 2004, matchup with the Dodgers by a score of 7–6, Bonds had a huge game, knocking in 5 of his team's 6 runs with 4 hits, including a double and 2 homers. Later in the year, on August 29, Bonds led the Giants to a 9–5 win over the Braves by going 4-for-5, with a pair of homers and 6 RBIs.

Bonds twice scored a franchise record 5 runs in one game, accomplishing the feat for the first time during an 11–10 extra-inning loss to the Padres on August 4, 1993. Bonds duplicated his earlier effort on April 18, 2000, when he crossed the plate five times during a 13–9 victory over Cincinnati.

Bonds homered three times in one game on four separate occasions during his time in San Francisco, doing so during a 9–7 loss to Cincinnati on August 2, 1994, a 6–3 victory over Atlanta on May 19, 2001, a 9–4 win over Colorado on September 9, 2001, and a 7–4 victory over the Rockies on August 27, 2002.

After struggling terribly at the plate in each of his five previous postseason appearances, Bonds put on a performance for the ages in the 2002 playoffs and World Series, hitting 8 homers, driving in 16 runs, scoring 18 times, and batting .356 in the Giants' 17 postseason contests. Particularly effective against the Angels in the Fall Classic, Bonds homered 4 times, knocked in 6 runs, scored 8 times, drew 13 bases on balls, batted .471, compiled an on-base percentage of .700, and posted a slugging percentage of 1.294. His 8 postseason home runs tied an MLB record.

Bonds also reached several milestones while playing for the Giants, joining the 500-home-run club on April 17, 2001, when he homered during a 3–2 victory over the Dodgers. Later that year, on September 6, he became the fifth player in MLB history to hit 60 home runs in a season when he reached the seats during a 9–5 win over the Diamondbacks. Nearly one month later, on October 4, Bonds tied Mark McGwire's single-season record when he hit his 70th homer during a 10–2 victory over Houston. Bonds established a new mark the very next night when he went deep twice during a heartbreaking 11–10 loss to the Dodgers, delivering his record-setting 71st blast in the first inning against Chan Ho Park.

On August 9, 2002, Bonds joined Hank Aaron, Babe Ruth, and Willie Mays as the only players ever to reach the 600-homer plateau when he homered during a 4–3 loss to the Pirates. On April 13, 2004, he moved ahead of his godfather, Willie Mays, into third place on the all-time home run list when he went deep for the 661st time in his career during a 4–2 win over the Astros. Some five months later, on September 17, Bonds became a member of the select 700-home-run club when he homered off Jake Peavy during a 4–1 victory over the Padres.

Bonds tied Babe Ruth for second place on the all-time home run list on May 20, 2006, when he hit his 714th round-tripper during a 4–2 win over Oakland. He moved ahead of the Babe eight days later, when he reached the seats during a 6–3 loss to the Rockies. Bonds hit his record-setting 756th career home run during an 8–6 loss to the Washington Nationals on August 7, 2007, surpassing in the process Hank Aaron, who had held the Major League mark for 33 years. Bonds's blast, which he hit off Washington pitcher Mike Bacsik, came at 8:51 PM PDT.

Notable Achievements:

Hit more than 30 home runs 12 straight times, surpassing 40 homers eight times and 70 homers once (73 in 2001).

Knocked in more than 100 runs nine times, topping 120 RBIs on four occasions.

Scored more than 100 runs 10 times, surpassing 120 runs scored on seven occasions.

Batted over .300 nine times, topping the .320-mark on five occasions, and surpassing .360 twice.

Surpassed 30 doubles five times, topping 40 two-baggers once (44 in 1998).

Stole more than 20 bases six times, swiping more than 30 bags on three occasions.

Drew more than 100 bases on balls 12 times, surpassing 200 walks once (232 in 2004).

Compiled on-base percentage in excess of .400 14 times, topping the .500-mark four times, and surpassing .600 once (.609 in 2004).

Posted slugging percentage in excess of .600 11 times, topping the .700-mark four times, and surpassing .800 twice.

Compiled OPS in excess of 1.000 14 times, surpassing 1.300 on three occasions.

Surpassed 400 total bases once (411 in 2001).

One of only four players in MLB history to surpass 40 home runs and 40 steals in the same season (1996).

Led N.L. in: home runs twice; RBIs once; batting average twice; total bases once; walks 11 times; on-base percentage eight times; slugging percentage five times; and OPS six times.

Led N.L. left-fielders in: putouts three times; assists three times; and double plays once.

Holds MLB career records for most: home runs (762); bases on balls (2,558); and intentional bases on balls (688).

Ranks among MLB career leaders in: runs scored (3rd); RBIs (5th); extra-base hits (2nd); total bases (4th); on-base percentage (6th); slugging percentage (5th); and OPS (4th).

Holds MLB career record for most putouts by a left-fielder (5,225).

Ranks second in MLB history in games played in the outfield (2,874).

Holds MLB single-season records for: most home runs (73 in 2001); most bases on balls (232 in 2004); most intentional bases on balls (120 in 2004); highest on-base percentage (.609 in 2004); and highest slugging percentage (.863 in 2001).

Holds Giants career records for: most bases on balls (1,947); highest on-base percentage (.477); highest slugging percentage (.666); and highest OPS (1.143).

Ranks among Giants career leaders in: home runs (2nd); RBIs (3rd); runs scored (3rd); batting average (10th); hits (5th); doubles (3rd); total bases (3rd); stolen bases (tied-10th); games played (4th); plate appearances (4th); and at-bats (5th).

Holds Giants single-season records for: most home runs (73); most extra-base hits (107); most total bases (411); most bases on balls (232); highest on-base percentage (.609); highest slugging percentage (.863); and highest OPS (1.422).

2001 Associated Press Male Athlete of the Year.

Two-time Major League Player of the Year (2001 & 2004).

Five-time N.L. MVP (1993, 2001, 2002, 2003 & 2004).

Nine-time N.L. Player of the Month.

Three-time N.L. Hank Aaron Award winner (2001, 2002 & 2004).

Five-time Gold Glove winner (1993, 1994, 1996, 1997 & 1998).

Nine-time Silver Slugger winner (1993, 1994, 1996, 1997, 2000, 2001, 2002, 2003 & 2004).

Nine-time *Sporting News* All-Star selection (1993, 1994, 1996, 1997, 2000, 2001, 2002, 2003 & 2004).

Twelve-time N.L. All-Star (1993–98, 2000–2004 & 2007).

Number 34 on *The Sporting News'* 1999 list of Baseball's 100 Greatest Players.

Number 6 on *The Sporting News'* 2005 list of Baseball's 100 Greatest Players.

2002 N.L. champion.

3 CHRISTY MATHEWSON

Christy Mathewson amassed a National League record 373 victories over the course of his Hall of Fame career. *(Courtesy of Library of Congress)*

Considered by many baseball historians to be the greatest pitcher in National League history, Christy Mathewson won 373 games over the course of his career, tying him with Grover Cleveland Alexander for the most wins ever in the Senior Circuit. Notching all but one of those victories as a member of the Giants, Mathewson won at least 20 games 13 times, surpassing 30 wins on four separate occasions. Along the way, the Hall of Fame right-hander established virtually every franchise record for pitchers, tossed two no-hitters, won two pitching Triple Crowns, and led the Giants to five pennants and one world championship. A member of Major League Baseball's All-Century Team, Mathewson also brought a level of respectability to the national pastime with his wholesome image and intellectual approach to his craft.

Born in Factoryville, Pennsylvania, on August 12, 1880, Christy Mathewson proved to be a rare breed of baseball player in the early days of the 20th century. A clean-cut, well-spoken college graduate, Mathewson stood in stark contrast to the vast majority of players he competed with and against, conducting himself in a far more sophisticated and gentlemanly manner. While still attending Bucknell University, where he served as class president and played on the school's football and baseball teams, Mathewson began pitching professionally for Taunton of the New England League in 1899. He spent the following year with the Norfolk team of the Virginia-North Carolina League, for whom he compiled a 20–2 record. The New York Giants purchased Mathewson's contract from Norfolk for $1,500 in July of 1900, after which the 6'1", 195-pound right-hander appeared in only six games for them before being returned to the minors. The Cincinnati Reds subsequently plucked Mathewson off the Norfolk roster, but they elected to trade him back to the Giants shortly thereafter for pitcher Amos Rusie.

Joining the Giants for good at the start of the 1901 campaign, Mathewson experienced a moderate amount of success over the course of his first two full seasons, pitching well in New York despite compiling an overall record of just 34–34. In addition to placing among the league leaders in ERA, strikeouts, complete games, and innings pitched both years, Mathewson led all N.L. hurlers with 8 shutouts in 1902. "Big Six," as he came to be known due to his relatively tall stature, took his game to the next level in 1903 when, employing a good fastball, exceptional control, and a new pitch he called the "fadeaway" (later known as the "screwball"), he emerged as a truly dominant pitcher. Teaming up with fellow Hall of Famer "Iron Man" Joe McGinnity to give the Giants baseball's best one-two punch, Mathewson compiled a record of 30–13, along with a 2.26 ERA, 37 complete games, 366 ⅓ innings pitched, and a league-leading 267 strikeouts. He followed that up by surpassing 30 victories in each of the next two seasons as well, concluding the 1904 campaign with a record of 33–12, an ERA of 2.03, 33 complete games, 367 ⅔ innings pitched, and a league-leading 212 strikeouts, before capturing the pitcher's version of the Triple Crown the following year by going 31–9, with a 1.28 ERA and 206 strikeouts. Mathewson capped off his brilliant 1905 season with a magnificent performance against Philadelphia in the World Series, leading the Giants to the world championship by tossing three complete-game shut-outs over a six-day period.

Hampered by an early-season diagnosis of diphtheria, Mathewson subse-quently suffered through a subpar 1906 campaign in which he finished "just" 22–12, with a rather pedestrian 2.97 ERA. However, fully recovered by the start of 1907, "Big Six" reestablished himself as baseball's greatest pitcher, con-tinuing his string of 12 consecutive seasons with more than 20 wins by posting a league-leading 24 victories, against 12 losses, while also compiling an ERA of 2.00 and topping the circuit with 8 shutouts and 178 strikeouts. Mathewson then put together two of his finest seasons, winning his second pitcher's Triple Crown in 1908 by going 37–11, with a 1.43 ERA and 259 strikeouts, before finishing 25–6, with a league-leading and career-best 1.14 ERA the following year. He performed magnificently in each of the next four seasons as well, aver-aging 25 victories during that period, while also tossing more than 300 innings and 25 complete games each year and leading the league in ERA twice.

Mathewson's greatest weapons during his period of dominance proved to be his intelligence, composure, and remarkable control. Issuing only 1.3 walks per game over the course of his career, Mathewson established a strikeouts-to-walks ratio of nearly 3-to-1 that ranks as the third-best in Giants history. Amazingly, he threw more than 300 innings and walked fewer than 50 batters on five separate occasions, issuing fewer than 30 bases on balls three times, and surrendering only 42 walks in 1908, when he worked a career-high 390 ⅔ innings. At one point during the 1913 campaign, he pitched 68 consecu-tive innings without issuing a walk. In discussing Mathewson's impeccable control, Hall of Fame second baseman Johnny Evers suggested, "He could pitch into a tin cup."

Meanwhile, Mathewson became known as "a thinking man's pitcher," espousing in his 1912 book, *Pitching in a Pinch: Baseball from the Inside,* his theory of using brain as well as brawn to navigate one's way past opposing lineups when he suggested, "To be a successful pitcher in the Big Leagues, a man must have the head and the arm." Knowing that opposing batters expected him to rely heavily on his much-publicized "fadeaway" to get them out, Mathewson rarely threw more than a dozen a game, expertly mixing it in with his other pitches. Asked on one occasion what he considered his best pitch to be, Mathewson replied, "Anybody's best pitch is the one the batters aren't hitting that day."

Mathewson also possessed an advanced memory of hitter weaknesses, stating on one occasion, "I always tried to learn about the hitters. Anytime someone got a hit off me, I made a mental note of the pitch. He'd never see that one again."

Mathewson became equally known for his gentlemanly manner, which brought a greater sense of propriety to the national pastime. With major-league rosters littered with the loud and raucous sons of farmers, coal miners, and factory workers prior to Mathewson's arrival in New York, society as a whole looked down upon the sport of baseball. Connie Mack recalled that, when he began his professional career as a player during the 1880s, "the game was thought, by solid, respectable people, to be only one degree above grand larceny, arson, and mayhem, and those who engaged in it were beneath the notice of decent society."

However, with the emergence of the college-educated Mathewson as baseball's greatest pitcher, outsiders developed a newfound respect for the game. A pious Christian who abstained from pitching on Sundays, the tall, good-looking, blonde-haired and blue-eyed Mathewson came to represent everything that was good about the game. Intelligent, soft-spoken, and dedicated to his craft, Mathewson became the idol of millions, as writer Grantland Rice noted when he referred to the pitcher as "the knightliest of all the game's paladins," and suggested, "Christy Mathewson brought something to baseball no one else had ever given the game. He handed the game a certain touch of class, an indefinable lift in culture, brains, and personality."

While Mathewson tended to reject such notions, he begrudgingly accepted the responsibility thrust upon him of being a role model, stating on one occasion:

First of all, no one can live up to everything that's been written or said about me. And I keep to myself. I'm a private man. Yet, because I pitch for the New York Giants, I realize that I'm able to reach more young men than the President of the United States. That's not due to the fact that I'm more popular than Mr. Taft—I don't believe—but, it's a fact boys would rather read about yesterday afternoon's event at the Polo Grounds. Because of that, I feel very strongly that it is my duty to show those youth the good, clean, honest values that I was taught by my Mother when I was a youngster. That, really, is all I can do.

Mathewson surpassed 20 victories for the final time in 1914, finishing the season with a record of 24–13, an ERA of 3.00, 29 complete games, and 312 innings pitched, before *Father Time* finally caught up with him the following year. After Mathewson compiled a record of just 8–14 in 1915, the Giants included him in a five-player trade they completed with Cincinnati on July 20, 1916, that brought to an end his extraordinarily successful run in New York. Mathewson subsequently started just one game for the Reds before announcing his retirement at season's end. He concluded his playing career with a record of 373–188, giving him an exceptional .665 winning percentage. Mathewson also compiled a brilliant 2.13 ERA, struck out 2,507 batters and walked only 848 in 4,788 ⅔ innings of work, completed 435 of his 552 starts, and tossed 79 shutouts—the third-highest total in baseball history. Meanwhile, his WHIP of 1.058 ranks as the sixth best in major-league history. An outstanding fielder as well, Mathewson amassed the second-most assists of any pitcher, recording a total of 1,503 over the course of his career. Some 100 years after he threw his last pitch for the Giants, Mathewson continues to hold franchise records for most wins, strikeouts, shutouts, complete games, innings pitched, and games started. He also compiled the lowest ERA and WHIP in team history.

Longtime manager Connie Mack, whose Athletics Mathewson victimized in the 1905 World Series, had this to say about his former adversary: "Mathewson was the greatest pitcher who ever lived. He had knowledge, judgment, perfect control and form. It was wonderful to watch him pitch when he wasn't pitching against you."

Sportswriter Damon Runyon once expressed the admiration and respect everyone in baseball had for Mathewson when he wrote, "Mathewson pitched against Cincinnati yesterday. Another way of putting it is that Cincinnati lost a game of baseball. The first statement means the same as the second."

Unfortunately, Mathewson's life after baseball didn't prove to be nearly as fruitful. After managing the Reds for all of 1917, and for much of the ensuing campaign as well, he enlisted in the United States Army. While serving overseas during World War I, Mathewson inhaled poisonous gas during a training exercise in France. He subsequently developed tuberculosis, an illness that plagued him the remainder of his life. Mathewson finally lost his battle with the disease on October 7, 1925, passing away at only 45 years of age. Speaking at the memorial service held for Mathewson, Baseball Commissioner Kenesaw Mountain Landis said, "He was an inspiration to everybody, and may we have more of his kind. His sense of justice, his integrity, and sportsmanship made him far greater than Christy Mathewson the pitcher."

Giant Career Highlights:

Best Season: Although Mathewson surpassed 30 victories on four separate occasions, it could be argued that he pitched his best ball for the Giants in 1909, when he finished 25–6 and led the league with an .806 winning percentage, a 0.828 WHIP, and a career-best 1.14 ERA. Mathewson also performed brilliantly in 1905 when, in addition to winning his first pitcher's Triple Crown by leading the league with a record of 31–9, an ERA of 1.28, and 206 strikeouts, he topped the circuit with 8 shutouts and a WHIP of 0.933. Still, it would be hard to disagree with anyone who presented the notion that Mathewson had his greatest season in 1908 when, en route to capturing his second Triple Crown, he led N.L. hurlers in virtually every major statistical category, concluding the campaign with a record of 37–11, a 1.43 ERA, 259 strikeouts, 11 shutouts, 34 complete games, 390 ⅔ innings pitched, 5 saves, and a WHIP of 0.827. In the process, Mathewson established career-best marks in wins, shutouts, innings pitched, saves, and WHIP.

Memorable Moments/Greatest Performances: Mathewson compiled a pair of extremely impressive winning streaks over the course of his career, posting 11 straight victories in 1905 and winning 13 consecutive games in 1909.

Mathewson threw the first shutout of his career on May 6, 1901, blanking the Phillies, 4–0, on just 5 hits. He topped that performance five days later, tossing a 2-hit shutout during a 7–0 victory over Brooklyn at Washington Park. The rookie from Bucknell University continued to impress on May 24, winning his eighth straight game by surrendering just 3 hits during a 1–0 win over Cincinnati at the Polo Grounds. However, Mathewson saved his finest performance of the year for July 15, 1901, when he tossed a no-hitter against the Cardinals in St. Louis, defeating the Redbirds by a score of 5–0.

Mathewson turned in another brilliant effort on June 10, 1904, surrendering just a 4th-inning single to Johnny Kling during a 5–0, one-hit shutout of the Chicago Cubs.

Mathewson established a new major-league record on October 3, 1904, when he recorded 16 strikeouts during a 3–1 victory over the St. Louis Cardinals. "Big Six" needed only one hour and 15 minutes to dispose of the Redbirds.

Mathewson threw the second no-hitter of his career on June 13, 1905, outdueling Chicago's Mordecai "Three-Finger" Brown, in pitching the Giants to a 1–0 victory over the Cubs. Mathewson outpitched another Chicago hurler on August 10, 1905, allowing just three hits during a 1–0 win over Ed Reulbach and the Cubs.

On May 17, 1907, Mathewson surrendered just 3 hits, struck out 11, and singled in the game-winning run in the bottom of the 12th inning, in leading the Giants to a 2–1 victory over the Cardinals. He again allowed only 3 hits to the Cardinals a little over three months later, defeating them by a score of 1–0 on August 27, and driving in the game's only run with a double.

Mathewson nearly threw his third no-hitter on May 2, 1910, allowing just a disputed infield single that could easily have been ruled an error during a 6–0 whitewashing of Brooklyn.

Mathewson tossed another gem against Brooklyn on April 29, 1913, working 13 scoreless innings en route to recording a 6–0 win at Ebbets Field.

Nevertheless, Mathewson's performance against the Philadelphia Athletics in the 1905 World Series, which ESPN later selected as the greatest play-off performance of all time, would have to be considered the highlight of his career. After allowing just 4 hits during a 3–0 victory in Game 1, Mathewson tossed another 4-hit shutout just 3 days later in Game 3, giving the Giants a 2–1 lead in the Fall Classic by defeating the A's, 9–0. He then returned to the mound to pitch Game 5 on just one day of rest, clinching the Series for the Giants with a 2–0, 5-hit shutout. Over the span of six days, Mathewson threw three complete-game shutouts, surrendering just 13 hits and striking out 18 in the process.

Notable Achievements:

Won at least 20 games 13 times, surpassing 30 victories on four occasions.

Posted winning percentage in excess of .700 five times.

Compiled ERA below 2.25 10 times, posting mark under 2.00 on five occasions.

Struck out more than 200 batters five times.

Finished in double-digits in shutouts once (11 in 1908).

Threw more than 300 innings 11 times.

Threw more than 20 complete games 14 times, completing at least 30 of his starts seven times.

Compiled WHIP under 1.000 four times.

Led N.L. pitchers in: wins four times; winning percentage once; ERA five times; strikeouts five times; shutouts four times; WHIP four times; complete games twice; innings pitched once; saves once; games started twice; assists five times; putouts once; and fielding percentage twice.

Holds Giants career records for: wins (372); ERA (2.12); strikeouts (2,504); shutouts (79); WHIP (1.057); complete games (434); innings pitched (4,779.2); and games started (551).

Ranks among Giants career leaders in winning percentage (5th) and pitching appearances (2nd).

Holds Giants single-season records for most shutouts (11 in 1908) and lowest WHIP (0.827 in 1908).

Holds modern N.L. records for most: wins in a season (37); wins in a career (373); and consecutive 20-win seasons (12).

Ranks among MLB all-time leaders in: wins (tied-3rd); ERA (9th); shutouts (3rd); WHIP (6th); and assists by a pitcher (2nd).

Threw two no-hitters.

Two-time Triple Crown winner for pitchers (1905 & 1908).

Finished second in 1911 N.L. MVP voting.

Finished fourth in 1913 N.L. MVP voting.

Member of Major League Baseball's All-Century Team.

Number 7 on *The Sporting News'* 1999 list of Baseball's 100 Greatest Players.

Five-time N.L. champion (1904, 1905, 1911, 1912 & 1913).

1905 world champion.

Elected to Baseball Hall of Fame by members of BBWAA in 1936.

4 JUAN MARICHAL

Juan Marichal served as the ace of the Giants' pitching staff for most of the 1960s. *(Courtesy of Richard Albersheim of Albersheimsstore.com)*

Perhaps the most underrated and overlooked great pitcher in baseball history, Juan Marichal spent much of his career being overshadowed by the incomparable Sandy Koufax and legendary St. Louis Cardinals right-hander Bob Gibson. In the end, though, Marichal took a backseat to no one in terms of overall pitching efficiency during the 1960s. The high-kicking Giants right-hander surpassed 20 victories six times between 1963 and 1969, en route to winning more games (191) during the decade than any other hurler. Marichal also joined Koufax as the only pitchers of the post-war era (1946–date) to record as many as three 25-win seasons. While Marichal finished second to Koufax during the 1960s in ERA (2.36 to 2.57) and strikeouts-to-walks ratio (3.73 to 3.66), he tossed more shutouts (45) than any other hurler during that 10-year period. The man known as "The Dominican Dandy" also finished behind only Don Drysdale and Jim Bunning in total innings pitched (2,542 ⅔). It is likely that the lack of appreciation accorded Marichal through the years stems largely from the fact that he never won the Cy Young Award, and, also, that he never had much of an opportunity to display his consummate pitching skills in the World Series. Nevertheless, Marichal has to be considered one of the finest pitchers of his era and, with the exception of Christy Mathewson, the greatest hurler in Giants history.

Born in the small farming village of Laguna Verde, Dominican Republic, on October 20, 1937, Juan Antonio Marichal Sanchez nearly lost his life at the age of 10 when he lapsed into a coma for nine days due to poor digestion, before slowly regaining consciousness after his family treated him by giving him steam baths. Marichal acquired a love of the game of baseball at a very young age from his older brother, Gonzalo, who taught him the fundamentals of pitching, fielding, and batting using a homemade baseball. The younger Marichal received his big break as a teenager when Ramfis Trujillo, the son of the late Dominican dictator Rafael Leonidas Trujillo, discovered him and subsequently ordered that he be enlisted to the Dominican Air Force after watching him pitch its baseball team to a 2–1 victory in a game played in Marichal's home town of Monte Cristi.

Ultimately signed by the Giants as an amateur free agent in 1957, Marichal advanced rapidly through the team's farm system, compiling a total of 39 victories over the course of the next two seasons. After throwing sidearm exclusively during the early stages of his minor-league career, Marichal began employing an overhand motion while pitching for Springfield in the Class A Eastern League in 1959, allowing him to throw a wider variety of pitches with greater velocity, and leading to his easily identifiable high leg kick delivery. Promoted to Tacoma in the Triple-A Pacific Coast League at the start of the 1960 campaign, Marichal won 11 of his first 16 decisions, prompting the Giants to summon him to the parent club in mid-July. Excelling immediately upon his arrival in San Francisco, the 22-year-old right-hander shut out the Philadelphia Phillies on just one hit in his major-league debut. He followed that up four days later by throwing a four-hitter at the eventual world champion Pittsburgh Pirates. Marichal ended the year with a record of 6–2 and an ERA of 2.66.

Beginning the 1961 campaign as a regular member of the Giants' starting rotation, Marichal posted 13 victories while compiling a somewhat mediocre 3.89 earned run average. He proved to be an excellent complement to staff ace Jack Sanford the following year, when he went 18–11 with a 3.36 ERA, threw 262 ⅔ innings, and tossed 18 complete games, in helping the Giants capture the National League pennant. Marichal likely would have reached the 20-win plateau for the first time in his career had he not injured his foot in early September, causing him to miss his next few starts. He subsequently got his only taste of World Series play one month later, when the Giants faced the Yankees in the Fall Classic. Marichal started Game Four for San Francisco but had to be removed from the contest after tossing four shutout innings when he injured his finger trying to bunt.

Marichal took his game to the next level in 1963 when he surpassed 20 victories for the first of four straight times. Employing an exceptionally high leg kick and a wide variety of motions that enabled him to deliver his curveball, screwball, changeup, slider, and fastball from any number of angles, Marichal completely baffled National League hitters, tying Sandy Koufax for the league lead in wins by compiling a record of 25–8. Marichal also topped the circuit with 321 ⅓ innings pitched and placed among the leaders with a 2.41 ERA, 248 strikeouts, 5 shutouts, and 18 complete games.

Marichal continued his exceptional pitching in each of the next two seasons, leading all N.L. hurlers with 22 complete games in 1964, while also placing near the top of the league rankings with a record of 21–8, a 2.48 ERA, and 269 innings pitched. He followed that up by going 22–13 in 1965, with an ERA of 2.13, 24 complete games, 240 strikeouts, 295 innings pitched, and a league-leading 10 shutouts. Nevertheless, Marichal ended up having his outstanding year marred by an ugly incident that occurred on August 22 at Candlestick Park.

With the Giants and Dodgers involved in a hotly contested pennant race, tempers boiled over during a matchup between baseball's two finest hurlers, Marichal and Los Angeles pitching ace Sandy Koufax. After knocking down two Dodger batters with inside pitches earlier in the game, Marichal stepped to the plate for the Giants. Los Angeles catcher John Roseboro, the victim of one of Marichal's brush-back pitches, called for Koufax to retaliate in kind. However, Koufax refused since he did not believe in intentionally throwing at hitters. Roseboro subsequently decided to take matters into his own hands by returning one of Koufax's offerings to his pitcher by whistling the ball past Marichal's ear. Marichal directed a few choice words towards Roseboro, who stood up and ripped off his catcher's mask. Marichal responded by twice hitting Roseboro's unprotected head with his bat, sparking one of the most famous brawls in baseball history. A bloodied Roseboro left the field, accompanied by Willie Mays, while several other Giants and Dodgers players exchanged threatening gestures and verbal taunts. Marichal's actions resulted in a $1,750 fine and a week's suspension, causing him to miss his next two starts, as the Giants finished two games behind the Dodgers.

The unfortunate incident created a false impression in the minds of many as to the quality of Marichal's character. A quiet and gentle man who generally impressed others with his grace and elegance, Marichal acted completely out of character in his attack on Roseboro, with whom he eventually formed a close bond. In fact, Roseboro ended up campaigning for Marichal's election to the Hall of Fame when the right-hander's imprudent actions prevented him from being inducted in either of his first two years of eligibility.

Although Marichal's reputation suffered as a result of his 1965 altercation with Roseboro, his pitching did not. Picking up right where he left off the following year, Marichal concluded the 1966 campaign with a record of 25–6 that gave him a league-leading .806 winning percentage. He also finished among the leaders with a 2.23 ERA, 222 strikeouts, 25 complete games, and 307 innings pitched, while amazingly walking only 36 batters. Marichal's exceptional performance earned him a sixth-place finish in the N.L. MVP voting.

Marichal's extraordinary pitching prompted many notable baseball people to sing his praises. Onetime Giants' pitching ace Carl Hubbell proclaimed, "This guy is a natural. He's got ideas about what he wants to do, and he does it. He amazes me." Legendary general manager Branch Rickey stated, "No pitcher has made such magnificent use of his God-given equipment." And Alvin Dark, who served as Giants manager Marichal's first four years with the team, said, "Put your club a run ahead in the later innings, and Marichal is the greatest pitcher I ever saw."

Although Marichal pitched well in 1967, compiling a 2.76 ERA and tossing 18 complete games, a pulled hamstring forced him to miss most of the final two months of the season, limiting him to only 14 victories. Fully healthy by the start of the ensuing campaign, Marichal bounced back to have one of the finest seasons of his career, concluding "The Year of the Pitcher" with a 2.43 ERA, 218 strikeouts, a record of 26–9 that gave him the most wins of any N. L. hurler, and a league-leading 30 complete games and 325 ⅔ innings pitched, en route to earning a fifth-place finish in the MVP balloting. Marichal had another outstanding year in 1969, compiling a record of 21–11, leading the league with a 2.10 ERA and 8 shutouts, and finishing among the leaders with 27 complete games, 299 ⅔ innings pitched, and 205 strikeouts.

The 1969 campaign ended up being Marichal's last truly dominant season. After suffering a severe reaction to penicillin early in 1970 that led to chronic arthritis, he finished the year with a record of just 12–10 and an uncharacteristically high ERA of 4.12. Having lost much of the velocity on his fastball and slider, the 33-year-old Marichal used his guile and deceptive delivery to post 18 victories, compile a 2.94 ERA, and toss 18 complete games and 279 innings in 1971. He then went a combined 17–31 over the course of the next two seasons, prompting the Giants to sell him to the Boston Red Sox prior to the start of the 1974 campaign. Marichal left San Francisco with a career record of 238–140, a 2.84 ERA, 2,281 strikeouts in 3,443 ⅔ innings of work, 52 shutouts, 244 complete games, and a WHIP of 1.095. He continues to rank among the franchise's all-time leaders in virtually every major statistical category for pitchers, including wins (tied-3rd), strikeouts (2nd), shutouts (2nd), complete games (6th), innings pitched (5th), and WHIP (3rd).

Pitching sporadically for Boston, Marichal won five of his nine starts before being released by the team at the end of 1974. He appeared briefly with, of all teams, the Dodgers the following year, pitching ineffectively in his two starts before announcing his retirement. After making his decision to leave the game, Marichal told Dodgers owner Walter O'Malley, "If I can't pitch as well as I want to, I can't take your money."

Marichal ended his career with an overall record of 243–142, giving him an exceptional winning percentage of .631. He also compiled an outstanding ERA of 2.89, struck out 2,303 batters in 3,507 innings of work, tossed 52 shutouts and 244 complete games, and posted a WHIP of 1.101. In addition to winning more than 20 games six times, Marichal compiled an ERA below 2.50 and struck out more than 200 batters six times each, completed more than 20 of his starts five times, and threw more than 300 innings on three separate occasions. He led the N.L. in ERA once, and in wins, complete games, shutouts, and innings pitched twice each. Marichal appeared in 10 All-Star Games and earned four *Sporting News* All-Star selections.

Although Marichal never won the Cy Young Award, he gained widespread acclaim as one of the finest pitchers of his era, with only the greatness of Sandy Koufax and the brilliant 1968 campaign turned in by Bob Gibson preventing him from ever being recognized as baseball's premier pitcher. Pete Rose is among the many batters who have identified Marichal as the toughest pitcher they ever faced. And no one ever comported himself with more grace and elegance on the mound.

Sportswriter Bob Stevens once wrote, "If you placed all the pitchers in the history of the game behind a transparent curtain, where only a silhouette was visible, Juan's motion would be the easiest to identify. He brought to the mound beauty, individuality, and class."

Fellow sportswriter Ron Bellamy described Marichal's distinctive, high leg kick when he wrote, "The symbol of his artistry . . . was the wind-up, with the high, graceful kick that left the San Francisco Giant hurler poised precariously on one leg like a bronzed Nureyev before he swept smoothly forward and propelled the baseball toward the plate."

Meanwhile, former Pittsburgh Pirates pitcher Steve Blass stated, "To me, before Greg Maddux, Juan Marichal was the surgeon general of pitching."

Long after he retired from the game, Marichal spent four years serving in the cabinet of Dominican Republic President Leonel Fernández as his country's Minister of Sports and Physical Education. Marichal later discussed his ultimate goal in his autobiography, writing, "Before I die, I will be happy if people say of me that I did something good for other people. . . . I want to be remembered more for helping people than for what I did in baseball."

Giant Career Highlights:

Best Season: Marichal had a number of great seasons for the Giants, any of which could easily be classified as the finest of his career. Performing brilliantly in 1963, 1965, 1968, and 1969, Marichal ranked among the N.L. leaders in most statistical categories each year, topping the Senior Circuit in wins, innings pitched, and shutouts twice each, while also finishing first in ERA and complete games once. Nevertheless, the feeling here is that Marichal pitched his best ball for the Giants in 1966, when he earned a 6th-place finish in the N.L. MVP voting by finishing among the league leaders with 25 wins, a 2.23 ERA, 222 strikeouts, 4 shutouts, 25 complete games, and 307 ⅓ innings pitched, while topping the Senior Circuit with career-best marks in winning percentage (.806), WHIP (0.859), strikeouts-to-walks ratio (6.167), bases on balls per 9 innings pitched (1.054), and hits per 9 innings pitched (6.677). Particularly effective during the month of May, Marichal earned N.L. Player of the Month honors by going a perfect 6–0, with a 0.97 ERA, 3 shutouts, and 42 strikeouts.

Memorable Moments/Greatest Performances: As noted earlier, Marichal performed magnificently in his major-league debut, allowing just one hit and striking out 12, in defeating the Phillies by a score of 2–0 on July 19, 1960.

Marichal threw two other one-hitters over the course of his career, accomplishing the feat again on August 2, 1961, when he allowed only a single to Tommy Davis and struck out 11, in defeating the Dodgers by a score of 6–0. Marichal tossed his third one-hitter on September 12, 1969 when, in what he later called "my best game ever," he surrendered just a third-inning single to Tommy Helms during a 1–0 victory over the hard-hitting Cincinnati Reds.

"The Dominican Dandy" also tossed six two-hitters during his career, accomplishing the feat on June 16, 1962, when he defeated the Cardinals by a score of 5–0; July 10, 1965, when he shut out the Phillies, 7–0; August 13, 1968, when he defeated the Pirates by a score of 3–0; April 30, 1969, when he allowed just 2 singles during a 3–0 victory over the Dodgers; April 16, 1971, when he shut out the Cubs, 9–0; and August 10, 1971, when he won a 1–0 pitcher's duel against Montreal's Bill Stoneman.

However, Marichal's shining moment came on June 15, 1963, when he won a 1–0 decision over Houston, becoming in the process the first Giants pitcher to throw a no-hitter since Carl Hubbell accomplished the feat 34 years earlier.

Marichal turned in two other magnificent pitching performances during that 1963 campaign, with one of those efforts coming on September 12, when he shut out the Mets by a score of 6–0, allowing just 4 hits and striking out 13 batters in the process. He pitched arguably the most memorable game of his career earlier in the year, though, on July 2, when he squared off against Milwaukee's Warren Spahn in one of the greatest pitching duels ever. With the two hurlers locked up in a marathon that remained scoreless heading into the 16th inning, Giants manager Alvin Dark approached Marichal on the mound at one point during the latter stages of the contest with the thought in mind of removing the 25-year-old right-hander from the fray. An upset Marichal reproached his manager by saying, "I'm not coming out until that old man over there leaves the game." (Spahn was 42 at the time.) Marichal ended up working all 16 innings, surrendering just 8 hits and striking out 10, and winning the game when Willie Mays homered off Spahn in the final frame.

Marichal turned in a similarly heroic effort nearly three years later, on May 26, 1966, when he won a 1–0 decision over the Phillies in 14 innings, allowing just 6 hits and striking out 10.

Although Marichal didn't pitch nearly as well against the Pirates on September 21, 1966, surrendering 7 hits and 5 runs in his 9 innings of work, he experienced one of the greatest thrills of his career when his solo homer off Pittsburgh reliever Roy Face with one man out in the bottom of the 9th inning culminated a three-run Giants rally that gave them a 6–5 victory in walk-off fashion.

Notable Achievements:

Won more than 20 games six times, surpassing 25 victories on three occasions.

Won 18 games two other times.

Posted winning percentage in excess of .700 five times, topping the .800-mark once.

Compiled ERA below 3.00 nine times, posting mark under 2.50 six times.

Posted WHIP under 1.000 four times.

Struck out more than 200 batters six times.

Threw more than 300 innings three times, tossing more than 250 innings five other times.

Threw more than 20 complete games five times, reaching the 30-mark once (30 in 1968).

Tossed 10 shutouts in 1965.

Led N.L. pitchers in: wins twice; winning percentage once; ERA once; WHIP twice; complete games twice; innings pitched twice; shutouts twice; strikeouts-to-walks ratio three times; assists once; and putouts twice.

Ranks among Giants career leaders in: wins (tied-3rd); strikeouts (2nd); shutouts (2nd); complete games (6th); innings pitched (5th); WHIP (3rd); games started (2nd); and pitching appearances (6th).

Threw no-hitter vs. Houston on June 15, 1963.

1965 All-Star Game MVP.

May 1966 N.L. Player of the Month.

Four-time *Sporting News* All-Star selection (1963, 1965, 1966 & 1968).

Ten-time N.L. All-Star (1962 (2x), 1963, 1964, 1965, 1966, 1967, 1968, 1969 & 1971).

Number 71 on *The Sporting News'* 1999 list of Baseball's 100 Greatest Players.

1962 N.L. champion.

Elected to Baseball Hall of Fame by members of BBWAA in 1983.

5 MEL OTT

Mel Ott retired with more home runs, RBIs, runs scored, and walks than any other player in National League history. *(Courtesy of Boston Public Library, Leslie Jones Collection)*

The holder of numerous National League records upon his retirement in 1947, including most home runs, runs batted in, runs scored, and bases on balls, Mel Ott proved to be the Senior Circuit's premier slugger during the first half of the 20th century. Despite standing just 5'9" tall and weighing only 170 pounds, the diminutive outfielder hit 511 home runs and knocked in 1,860 runs over the course of his career, which he spent entirely with the Giants. Surpassing 30 homers eight times, 100 RBIs nine times, 100 runs scored nine times, and 100 bases on balls 10 times, Ott annually placed among the league leaders in all four categories, topping the Senior Circuit in home runs six times, RBIs once, runs scored twice, and walks six times. An 11-time N.L. All-Star, Ott also earned six top-10 finishes in the league MVP voting, placing in the top five of the balloting on three separate occasions. An outstanding defensive player as well, Ott possessed one of baseball's strongest throwing arms, accumulating more than 20 assists five times, en route to leading all N.L. right-fielders in that category twice. He also topped all players at his position in putouts once, double plays three times, and fielding percentage five times. Ott's stellar all-around play helped lead the Giants to three pennants and one world championship, with his contributions to the ball club and pleasant demeanor making him one of the most beloved players in franchise history.

Born in the New Orleans suburb of Gretna, Louisiana, on March 2, 1909, Melvin Thomas Ott attended Gretna High School, where he starred at catcher while simultaneously playing semipro ball. Recommended to Giants manager John McGraw by the owner of the semipro team for which he played, Ott reported to New York for a tryout at only 16 years of age in early September 1925. In describing the events that subsequently transpired, Giants' second baseman Frankie Frisch recalled: "Mel stepped into the first few pitches and smashed them solidly through the infield. Then he hit several deep into the outfield, and, finally, he parked a number of fastballs and curves high against the advertising signs on the right field wall."

Sufficiently impressed by the still-growing 5'7", 150-pounder, an enthusiastic McGraw told a writer, "That kid is remarkable. He's like a golfer; his body moves, but he keeps his head still with his eyes fixed on the ball. He's got the most natural swing I've seen in years . . . . This lad is going to be one of the greatest left-handed hitters the National League has seen."

After signing Ott to a contract and giving him a $400 bonus, McGraw elected to keep the youngster with him in New York rather than send him to the minor leagues for more seasoning, since he did not want anyone else to tinker with his unorthodox batting style, which included an unusually high leg kick just prior to the pitcher's release of the ball. Making the 17-year-old Ott his pet project in the spring of 1926, McGraw continued to work with him on his hitting, while also assigning veteran outfielders Ross Youngs and Emil "Irish" Meusel the task of teaching him the finer points of outfield play.

Used sparingly by McGraw his first two seasons in New York, Ott appeared in a total of only 117 games in 1926 and 1927, hitting just one home run in his first 223 official major-league at-bats. However, after earning the starting right-field job early in 1928, Ott rapidly developed into the team's foremost slugger, concluding the campaign with a .322 batting average, 77 RBIs, and a team-leading 18 home runs and .524 slugging percentage. Quickly learning how to take full advantage of the Polo Grounds' short right-field porch by pulling the ball into the stands over the 257-foot sign, Ott blossomed into a full-fledged star the following year, batting .328, leading the N.L. with 113 walks, and placing among the leaders with 42 home runs, 151 runs batted in, 138 runs scored, a .449 on-base percentage, and a .635 slugging percentage.

Still only 21 years old heading into the 1930 campaign, Ott continued to compile impressive numbers over the course of the next three seasons, placing among the league leaders in home runs, RBIs, runs scored, on-base percentage, and slugging percentage each year. Particularly outstanding in 1930 and 1932, Ott hit 25 homers, knocked in 119 runs, scored 122 times, batted a career-high .349, and led the league with a .458 on-base percentage in the first of those campaigns, before driving in 123 runs, scoring 119 times, batting .318, and topping the Senior Circuit with 38 home runs, 100 walks, and a .424 on-base percentage two years later.

Ott's 5'9", 170-pound frame hardly made him an imposing figure to opposing pitchers when he first stepped into the batter's box. However, they soon learned to fear the power he generated with his high leg kick and quick wrists. When asked by Al Stump to explain the source of his power in *Sport Magazine's All-Time All-Stars*, Ott responded, "Timing, I guess you'd call it. Mostly, it was a matter of connecting at exactly the right place in the swinging arc. That way, I was able to get every pound behind the bat."

As Ott established himself as one of the N.L.'s most feared batsmen, he also developed into one of the Senior Circuit's better defensive outfielders. In addition to his powerful throwing arm, Ott had good speed and did an exceptional job of playing caroms off the tricky right-field wall at the Polo Grounds. After recording 26 outfield assists in 1929, 23 the following year, and another 20 in 1931, he typically posted significantly lower numbers throughout the remainder of his career since opposing runners generally chose not to challenge his rifle arm.

Although Ott finished among the N.L. leaders in home runs (23), RBIs (103), and runs scored (98) in 1933, he failed to earn a spot on the league's inaugural All-Star team. However, the following year, he began a string of 11 consecutive All-Star appearances, establishing himself during that time as the

N.L.'s preeminent home-run hitter. Posting some of the best numbers of his career from 1934 to 1938, Ott averaged 32 homers over that five-year stretch, leading the league in that category four times. He also averaged 119 RBIs and 113 runs scored, while batting well in excess of .300 four times. Ott had one of his finest seasons in 1934, earning a fifth-place finish in the N.L. MVP voting by batting .326, scoring 119 runs, and leading the league with 35 home runs and 135 RBIs. He also performed particularly well in 1936 and 1938, helping the Giants capture the pennant in the first of those campaigns by knocking in 135 runs, scoring 120 times, batting .328, and leading the league with 33 homers and a 1.036 OPS, before earning a fourth-place finish in the MVP balloting two years later by batting .311, driving in 116 runs, and topping the circuit with 36 homers, 116 runs scored, and a .442 on-base percentage.

Ott never again posted such gaudy offensive numbers, although he had a big year in 1942, the same season he replaced Bill Terry as manager. In addition to guiding the Giants to a record of 85–67 that represented their best mark in five years, Ott led the league with 30 homers, 118 runs scored, 109 walks, and an OPS of .912, earning in the process a third-place finish in the N.L. MVP voting. He continued to manage the Giants until midway through the 1948 season, serving as the team's player-manager for all but the final campaign. In addition to retiring with 511 home runs and 1,860 runs batted in, Ott scored 1,859 runs, amassed 2,876 hits, collected 72 triples and 488 doubles, and compiled a lifetime batting average of .304, a career on-base percentage of .414, and a slugging percentage of .533. He continues to rank among the Giants all-time leaders in virtually every major offensive category. The first National League player to surpass 500 home runs, Ott remained the Senior Circuit's all-time home-run leader until Willie Mays finally surpassed him in 1966.

Still, Ott's status as a truly great home-run hitter has been questioned by many baseball historians, since the friendly right-field porch at New York's Polo Grounds enabled him to hit 324 of his 511 career homers (or 63 percent) at home. However, Ted Williams chose to view the success Ott experienced at the Polo Grounds from a different perspective, writing in his book *Ted Williams' Hit List*: "He (Ott) was a real slugger, and I think that, of all the hitters in baseball, Ott probably best adapted himself and his style to conform to his abilities. He could pull the ball, but his greatest skill was being able to conform to the greatest advantage to the park he hit in." Williams added, "He got the maximum return from his physical and mental abilities. You've got to give him a hell of a lot of credit for that, regardless of where he played."

The members of the BBWAA elected Ott to the Baseball Hall of Fame in 1951, just four years after he retired from the game. He spent his final few years as a radio and television commentator for Detroit Tigers broadcasts, before being seriously injured in an automobile accident in New Orleans on November 14, 1958. Ott died one week later, on November 21, at only 49 years of age.

Remembered for more than just his playing ability, Ott left behind him a legacy that made him one of the most popular men ever to play the game, being selected ahead of such icons as Babe Ruth, Lou Gehrig, Joe Louis, and Jack Dempsey in a 1944 nationwide vote by war bond buyers as the most popular sports hero of all time. Leo Durocher, who replaced Ott as Giants manager midway through the 1948 campaign, once famously critiqued his predecessor by saying, "Nice guys finish last." However, he praised Ott on another occasion when he stated, "I never knew a baseball player who was so universally loved. Why, even when he was playing against us he would be cheered, and there are no more rabid fans than in Brooklyn."

Meanwhile, sportswriter Arnold Hano expressed his admiration for Ott when he suggested, "When he died, he held 14 baseball records; a little man with a bashful smile and a silken swing—baseball's legendary nice guy. His death was the worst that could have happened to baseball, but his playing career had been the best."

Career Highlights:

Best Season: Ott posted the most impressive stat-line of his career in 1929, when he batted .328 and established career-high marks in homers (42), RBIs (151), runs scored (138), doubles (37), and OPS (1.084). He also led all players at his position in putouts, assists, and double plays. However, with the N.L. using a livelier ball in both 1929 and 1930, offensive numbers soared throughout the league, with no fewer than 10 players compiling a batting average in excess of .350 in the first of those campaigns. As a result, Ott topped the circuit in only one offensive category, finishing second in two others and third in another three.

On the other hand, Ott led the National League in multiple offensive categories in 1932, 1934, 1936, and 1938, posting extremely similar numbers in each of those years. The 1936 and 1938 campaigns stand out in particular, since Ott made his greatest overall impact those two seasons. In addition to batting .311 in 1938, Ott led the league with 36 home runs, 116 runs scored, and a .442 on-base percentage, while also finishing second with 116 RBIs, 118 walks, a .583 slugging percentage, and a 1.024 OPS. Furthermore, he displayed his unselfishness by playing the vast majority of his games at third base, earning in the process a fourth-place finish in the N.L. MVP voting. Nevertheless, I ultimately decided to go with 1936, since Ott helped lead the Giants to the pennant by batting .328, topping the circuit with 33 homers, a .588 slugging percentage, and a 1.036 OPS, and finishing either second or third in the league in RBIs (135), runs scored (120), walks (111) and on-base percentage (.448).

Memorable Moments/Greatest Performances: Although the Giants dropped both ends of a doubleheader to the Boston Braves on May 16, 1929, Ott had a big game in the nightcap, going 4-for-5 and hitting for the cycle.

A little over one month later, on June 19, 1929, Ott continued his string of 11 consecutive games with at least one RBI when he led the Giants to a doubleheader sweep of Philadelphia by driving in 7 runs on the day. After collecting 4 hits, 2 homers, a pair of doubles, and 6 RBIs in the opener, Ott had another 3 hits, 2 doubles, and 1 RBI in Game 2. He finished the day 7-for-11, with 2 home runs, 4 doubles, 7 RBIs, and 5 runs scored.

Ott had another big day on June 7, 1930, when he led the Giants to a 9–7 victory over the Cardinals by hitting a pair of homers and driving in 6 runs.

Ott led the Giants to a lopsided 13–3 victory over the Boston Braves on September 20, 1932 by going 4-for-5, with 2 homers, a double, and 6 RBIs. He had a similarly productive afternoon against Chicago on June 20, 1934, going 3-for-4, with a pair of homers, 6 RBIs, and 3 runs scored, during a 12–7 win over the Cubs. Ott again homered twice and knocked in 6 runs on July 28, 1936, doing so during an 11–3 win over the Reds.

On August 4, 1934, Ott became the first 20th-century player to score 6 runs in one game during a 21–4 victory over the Phillies. He also finished the day with 4 hits, 2 homers, and 4 RBIs.

The 24-year-old Ott handled himself extremely well in his first World Series appearance, batting .389 with 2 home runs and 4 RBIs against Washington in the 1933 Fall Classic. After going 4-for-4 with a homer and 3 RBIs during a 4–2 Giants win in Game 1, Ott hit a game-winning and Series-clinching home run with two men out in the top of the 10th inning of Game 5 that gave the Giants a 4–3 victory and their first world championship in 11 years.

Although the Giants dropped a 14–10 decision to the Braves on August 31, 1930, Ott had a huge day, going 4-for-5, with 3 home runs, a double, and 6 RBIs. He turned in another virtuoso performance on May 11, 1936, when he led the Giants to a 13–12 win over the Phillies by going 3-for-5, with a homer, double, 3 runs scored, and career-high 8 RBIs. Ott punctuated his memorable afternoon by hitting a game-winning, three-run homer in the top of the ninth inning.

Ott also hit a pair of dramatic game-winning home runs against the Reds, with the first of those coming on May 27, 1937, when his solo blast in the top of the ninth inning gave the Giants a 3–2 victory that made a winner out of Carl Hubbell for the 24th straight time. Ott provided further heroics on May 2, 1939, when his three-run homer with two out in the bottom of the ninth inning gave the Giants an 8–7 win over Cincinnati.

Ott hit another memorable home run during a 9–2 victory over the Braves on August 1, 1945, when his third-inning solo shot enabled him to join Babe Ruth and Jimmie Foxx as the only players in major-league history to reach the 500-homer plateau.

Notable Achievements:

Surpassed 30 home runs eight times, topping 40 homers once (42 in 1929).

Knocked in more than 100 runs nine times, topping 120 RBIs four times and 150 RBIs once (151 in 1929).

Scored more than 100 runs nine times, surpassing 120 runs scored on three occasions.

Batted over .300 11 times, surpassing the .320-mark on seven occasions.

Drew at least 100 bases on balls 10 times.

Finished in double-digits in triples once (10 in 1934).

Surpassed 30 doubles five times.

Compiled on-base percentage in excess of .400 14 times, surpassing the .440-mark five times.

Posted slugging percentage in excess of .500 12 times, topping the .600-mark twice.

Compiled OPS in excess of 1.000 seven times.

Led N.L. in: home runs six times; RBIs once; runs scored twice; walks six times; on-base percentage four times; slugging percentage once; and OPS twice.

Led N.L. outfielders in: assists twice; double plays twice; and fielding percentage once.

Led N.L. right-fielders in: fielding percentage five times; assists twice; put-outs once; and double plays three times.

First N.L. player to hit 500 home runs.

Holds MLB record for most home runs in one ballpark (323 at Polo Grounds).

Holds MLB record for most consecutive seasons leading his team in home runs (18).

Shares MLB record for most consecutive walks (7, from June 16 to June 18, 1943).

Ranks among MLB all-time leaders in: RBIs (12th); bases on balls (9th); and runs scored (14th).

Holds MLB record for most career double plays by a right-fielder (59).

Ranks among MLB all-time leaders in assists (2nd) and putouts (4th) by a right-fielder.

Holds Giants single-season record for most runs batted in (151 in 1929).

Holds Giants career record for most runs batted in (1,860).

Ranks among Giants career leaders in: home runs (3rd); runs scored (2nd); hits (2nd); extra-base hits (2nd); doubles (2nd); total bases (2nd); walks (2nd); on-base percentage (2nd); slugging percentage (7th); OPS (3rd); games played (2nd); plate appearances (2nd); and at-bats (2nd).

Hit for cycle vs. Boston on May 16, 1929.

Hit three home runs in one game vs. Boston on August 31, 1930.

Finished in top five of N.L. MVP voting three times.

Four-time *Sporting News* All-Star selection (1934, 1935, 1936 & 1938).

11-time N.L. All-Star (1934, 1935, 1936, 1937, 1938, 1939, 1940, 1941, 1942, 1943 & 1944).

Number 42 on *The Sporting News'* 1999 list of Baseball's 100 Greatest Players.

Three-time N.L. champion (1933, 1936 & 1937).

1933 world champion.

Elected to Baseball Hall of Fame by members of BBWAA in 1951.

6 WILLIE MCCOVEY

Willie McCovey was the most feared hitter in baseball for much of his career. *(Courtesy of LegendaryAuctions. com)*

Once called "the scariest hitter in baseball" by Bob Gibson, who rarely gave opposing hitters much credit, Willie McCovey not only intimidated National League pitchers, but he also weakened the knees of opposing managers throughout his Hall of Fame career. Gene Mauch, who managed the Philadelphia Phillies during the mid-1960s, said of McCovey, "He's the most awesome hitter I've ever seen."

Longtime Dodger manager Walter Alston expressed his admiration for McCovey's prodigious power when he stated, "McCovey didn't hit any cheap ones. When he belts a home run, he does it with such authority it seems like an act of God. You can't cry about it."

Cincinnati Reds manager Sparky Anderson commented, "If you pitch to him, he'll ruin baseball. He'd hit 80 home runs. There's no comparison between McCovey and anybody else in the league."

The 6'4", 230-pound McCovey teamed up with Willie Mays during the 1960s to give the Giants one of the most lethal combinations in baseball history, with the two men combining for six National League home-run titles between 1962 and 1969. For his part, McCovey topped the Senior Circuit in homers three times, surpassing 40 round-trippers twice and 30 long balls five other times. The massive slugger also led the league in RBIs twice, walks and on-base percentage once, and slugging percentage and OPS three times each, en route to earning six All-Star nominations, four top-10 finishes in the N.L. MVP voting, and one MVP trophy. By the time he announced his retirement in 1980, McCovey had compiled a total of 521 home runs, placing him third among National League players, and tying him with Ted Williams for 10th-place on the all-time home-run list. McCovey's prolific slugging gained him admittance to Cooperstown in his very first year of eligibility.

Born in Mobile, Alabama, on January 10, 1938, Willie Lee McCovey excelled in baseball to such a degree during his formative years that he played on men's teams in his hometown as a teenager. After dropping out of Mobile's Central High School a year early to help improve his family's financial situation, McCovey signed with the New York Giants as an amateur free agent in 1955. He spent the next three years advancing through their farm system, finally making it to the Pacific Coast League in 1958, the same year the Giants relocated to the West Coast. Although the big first baseman hit .319 and knocked in 89 runs for the team's Triple-A affiliate that year, he found himself back in the minors the following season since the Giants already had 1958 N.L. Rookie of the Year Orlando Cepeda playing first base for them. Yet, in spite of Cepeda's presence, the Giants found it necessary to promote McCovey to the majors after he batted .372, hit 29 home runs, and drove in 92 runs in the first 95 games of the 1959 campaign. Continuing his hot-hitting after he arrived in San Francisco, McCovey ended up earning N.L. Rookie of the Year honors by hitting 13 homers, driving in 38 runs, and batting .354 in his 52 games with the Giants over the season's final two months.

McCovey slumped badly the following year, prompting the Giants to demote him to the minor leagues for a brief period of time. Although the left-handed-hitting slugger eventually righted himself after he returned to the team later in the year, he concluded the campaign with only 13 homers, 51 RBIs, and a .238 batting average. Used primarily as a platoon player in each of the next two seasons, McCovey generally gave way to right-handed hitters Cepeda, Felipe Alou, and Harvey Kuenn whenever the Giants faced left-handed pitching. Nevertheless, whether playing first base or the outfield, McCovey proved to be a productive hitter whenever he found his name written on the lineup card, posting batting averages of .271 and .293, while totaling 38 home runs and 104 RBIs in only 557 official at-bats between 1961 and 1962.

Although McCovey continued to split his time between first base and the outfield in 1963, he finally became a full-time starter, earning his first All-Star selection by hitting a league-leading 44 homers, driving in 102 runs, scoring 103 times, and batting .280. Burdened by the loss of his father, and hampered by a painful and mysterious ailment to the sole of his left foot, McCovey subsequently suffered through a horrendous 1964 campaign that saw him hit just 18 home runs, knock in only 54 runs, and compile a batting average of just .220. However, after being inserted at first base full time the following year, he rebounded to hit 39 homers, drive in 92 runs, score 93 times, and bat .276, earning in the process a 10th-place finish in the N.L. MVP balloting. McCovey followed that up with another extremely productive year in 1966, earning his second All-Star selection by batting .295 and placing among the league leaders with 36 homers, 96 RBIs, a .391 on-base percentage, and a .586 slugging percentage.

McCovey's powerful left-handed swing and imposing physical presence made him arguably baseball's most feared hitter by the mid-1960s. Known equally for his long home runs and vicious line drives, McCovey instilled fear in the hearts and minds of opposing pitchers, as Jim Bouton revealed in his classic book *Ball Four*, when he described a late September 1969 scene at Candlestick Park:

> A group of terrorized pitchers stood around the batting cage watching Willie McCovey belt some tremendous line drives over the right-field fence. Every time a ball bounced into the seats we'd make little whimpering animal sounds. 'Hey, Willie,' I said. 'Can you do that whenever

you want to?' He didn't crack a smile. 'Just about,' he said, and he hit another one; more animal sounds.

Before long, McCovey became a favorite of Giant fans, who admired him as much for his gentle nature as for his prodigious power. While the San Francisco faithful never fully accepted Willie Mays as one of their own since the team's greatest player had his baseball roots in New York, they totally embraced McCovey, who later noted, "When I first came here, Major League Baseball was still fairly new . . . Fans adopted players, and I was one of those adopted, partly because I made San Francisco my home. Most players didn't live here, but I was here year-round and did a lot of offseason promotions for the club, so they got to know me."

McCovey's powerful left-handed bat added to his popularity with Giant fans. Capable of hitting a ball as far as anyone in the game, McCovey registered a home run in 1966 that traveled an estimated 500 feet, making it the longest home run in the history of Candlestick Park. The swirling winds at the Giants' home ballpark seemed to have little effect on McCovey's powerful blows, which provided numerous souvenirs over the years to fans adventurous enough to pursue them as they traveled well beyond the right-field fence.

McCovey's tendency to pull almost everything to the right side of the diamond caused opposing teams to adopt what became known as "the McCovey Shift"—an alignment in which they typically placed three infielders between first and second base. Some teams even shifted one of their infielders to the outfield, presenting a defense to the slugger that featured a four-man outfield.

Commenting on the strategy opposing managers often employed against him, McCovey later suggested, "Even with the cold and the wind, I never changed my game. They pulled more crazy shifts on me than anyone in baseball, including Ted Williams. They did a lot of things to try to make me change, but I never altered my approach at the plate. I tried to do the same thing, whether I was at Candlestick Park, Dodger Stadium, or Wrigley Field."

After spending his first several years playing in the shadow of the great Willie Mays, McCovey began to establish himself as the Giants' primary power threat in 1967, finishing first on the team with 31 homers, while also driving in 91 runs. He followed that up by leading the National League in home runs, RBIs, slugging percentage, and OPS in each of the next two seasons, concluding the 1968 campaign with 36 homers, 105 RBIs, a .293 batting average, a .545 slugging percentage, and an OPS of .923, before having his finest statistical season in 1969, when he scored 101 runs, batted .320, and established career highs with 45 homers, 126 RBIs, a .453 on-base percentage, and a .656 slugging percentage. McCovey's dominating performance in the second of those years earned him league MVP honors. He had another big year in 1970, batting .289, scoring 98 runs, placing among the league leaders with 39 home runs, 126 runs batted in, and a .444 on-base percentage, and topping the circuit with 137 bases on balls, a .612 slugging percentage, and an OPS of 1.056.

Unfortunately, the 1970 campaign turned out to be McCovey's last year as an elite player. Although McCovey remained a productive hitter the next few years, he found himself being constantly plagued by knee and hip problems that severely limited his playing time the rest of his career, reducing him to just a shell of his former self. After tearing cartilage in his knee in the final exhibition game in the spring of 1971, McCovey ended up appearing in only 105 games, later describing the effort he had to put forth merely to take the field: "Every town we went to, I had to have it drained because it would swell up as big as my head. I was on medication throughout the year to try to keep the soreness and inflammation to a minimum."

Finding his playing time further reduced in 1972 by a broken arm he suffered in an early-season collision at first base, McCovey appeared in only 81 games, concluding the campaign with just 14 homers, 35 RBIs, and a .213 batting average. Even though he rebounded somewhat the following year to hit 29 home runs and drive in 75 runs, the Giants traded him to the San Diego Padres for pitcher Mike Caldwell at season's end. McCovey spent most of the next three years in San Diego, serving mostly as a part-time player, before making a brief stop in Oakland towards the tail end of the 1976 campaign.

Reacquired by the Giants early in 1977, McCovey found himself reduced to tears when the hometown fans greeted him with a lengthy standing ovation prior to the start of the Giants home opener. Reflecting back on his feelings at the time, McCovey revealed, "I knew then what it felt like to be a Giant. I knew then that there is still some loyalty around." He added, "I'd like to think that, when people think of San Francisco, they also think of Willie McCovey. It's where I want to be, where I belong. I hope the people there love me a little in return."

Playing in pain throughout that 1977 campaign, McCovey still managed to hit 28 home runs, knock in 86 runs, and bat .280 for the team that originally signed him to a major-league contract. He spent another three years in San Francisco, finally retiring midway through the 1980 campaign with 521 career home runs, 1,555 runs batted in, 1,229 runs scored, 2,211 hits, 46 triples, 353 doubles, a .270 batting average, a .374 on-base percentage, and a .515 slugging percentage. In his 19 seasons with the Giants, McCovey hit 469 homers, knocked in 1,388 runs, scored 1,113 times, amassed 1,974 hits, 45 triples, and 308 doubles, batted .274, compiled a .377 on-base percentage, and posted a .524 slugging percentage. He continues to rank among the franchise's all-time leaders in most offensive categories. McCovey also holds the National League record for most career grand slams, with a total of 18 to his credit.

Following his retirement, McCovey initially stayed away from the game, although he returned briefly to the limelight when the members of the BBWAA elected him to the Hall of Fame in 1986, in his first year of eligibility. He has since returned to the Giants as an advisor. The team honored the former slugger by erecting a statue of him across from AT&T Park, and by naming the land on which it stands McCovey Point. The inlet of San Francisco Bay beyond the right-field fence at the Giants' new ballpark, historically known as China Basin, has been redubbed McCovey Cove in his honor.

Unfortunately, the knee and hip problems that plagued McCovey throughout the second half of his career have gotten progressively worse since he left the game. Several ill-advised surgeries did more harm than good, and the former Giants great now finds himself unable to walk without assistance. Once the epitome of youth and power, Willie McCovey now says, "I can only get around on crutches and walkers."

Giant Career Highlights:

Best Season: McCovey had a monster year in 1970, batting .289, scoring 98 runs, placing among the league leaders with 39 homers, 126 RBIs, 39 doubles, and a .444 on-base percentage, and topping the circuit with 137 bases on balls, a .612 slugging percentage, and an OPS of 1.056. However, he had the greatest season of his career one year earlier, concluding the 1969 campaign with a .320 batting average, 101 runs scored, 121 bases on balls, and a league-leading 45 home runs, 126 runs batted in, .453 on-base percentage, and .656 slugging percentage, earning in the process N.L. MVP honors.

Memorable Moments/Greatest Performances: McCovey made his major-league debut a memorable one, going 4-for-4, with 2 triples, 2 RBIs, and 3 runs scored, during a 7–2 Giants win over Robin Roberts and the Phillies on July 30, 1959.

McCovey had a huge game against the New York Mets on July 4, 1962, leading the Giants to an 11–4 victory by going 3-for-3, with a pair of homers and a career-high 7 RBIs.

McCovey had another big day on July 9, 1966, going 4-for-5, with 2 homers and 6 RBIs, during an 8–7 win over the Reds in 12 innings. McCovey delivered his second round-tripper of the contest with one man on base in the bottom of the ninth inning, tying the score at 6 runs apiece.

McCovey again knocked in 6 runs against the Reds on June 28, 1969, leading the Giants to a 12–5 victory over Cincinnati by hitting a pair of homers, including a first-inning grand slam. He also drove in 6 runs with a pair of homers against the Mets on May 10, 1970, hitting a grand slam and a two-run shot during an 11–7 Giants win.

During his time in San Francisco, McCovey established himself as the only player ever to hit two home runs in the same inning on two separate occasions, doing so for the first time in the 4th inning of a 9–3 win over the Houston Astros on April 12, 1973. He accomplished the feat again on June 27, 1977, reaching the seats twice in the 6th inning of a 14–9 victory over the defending world champion Cincinnati Reds.

McCovey also hit three home runs in one game on three separate occasions, accomplishing the feat for the first time on September 22, 1963, when he led the Giants to a 13–4 mauling of the Mets by going 3-for-4, with 5 RBIs and 4 runs scored. McCovey again went deep three times in one game on April 22, 1964, leading the Giants to an 8–6 win over the Braves in the process. He accomplished the feat for the last time on September 17, 1966, doing so during a 6–4 victory over the Mets in 10 innings. McCovey delivered his last blow with one man on base in the bottom of the 10th inning, winning the game for the Giants in walk-off fashion. McCovey became the 12th member of the 500-home run club on June 30, 1978, when he connected in the second inning against Atlanta's Jamie Easterly during a 10–9 loss to the Braves.

Although the Giants ended up losing the 1971 NLCS to Pittsburgh in four games, McCovey came up big in the series, batting .429, with 2 homers and 6 RBIs.

Still, McCovey will perhaps always be remembered more than anything else for a ball he hit that resulted in a devastating Giants loss. With the Giants trailing the Yankees 1–0 in the bottom of the 9th inning of Game 7 of the 1962 World Series, McCovey stepped into the batter's box with two men out and runners on second and third. After driving New York pitcher Ralph Terry's first offering just foul beyond the outfield fence in right field, McCovey hit a screaming line drive right at Yankee second baseman Bobby Richardson that he snared to bring the Fall Classic to an abrupt ending. McCovey later called the drive "the hardest ball I ever hit."

Notable Achievements:

Surpassed 30 home runs seven times, topping 40 homers twice.

Knocked in more than 100 runs four times, topping 120 RBIs twice.

Scored more than 100 runs twice.

Batted over .300 twice.

Drew more than 100 bases on balls three times.

Surpassed 30 doubles once (39 in 1970).

Compiled on-base percentage in excess of .400 four times, surpassing the .440-mark twice.

Posted slugging percentage in excess of .500 11 times, topping the .600-mark three times.

Compiled OPS in excess of 1.000 three times.

Led N.L. in: home runs three times; RBIs twice; walks once; on-base percentage once; slugging percentage three times; and OPS three times.

Led N.L. first basemen in assists once.

Holds N.L. record for most career grand slams (18).

Ranks among Giants career leaders in: home runs (4th); RBIs (4th); runs scored (6th); hits (4th); extra-base hits (4th); doubles (5th); total bases (4th); walks (4th); slugging percentage (8th); OPS (6th); games played (3rd); plate appearances (3rd); and at-bats (3rd).

Hit three home runs in one game three times.

1959 N.L. Rookie of the Year.

1969 N.L. MVP.

1969 Major League Player of the Year.

1969 All-Star Game MVP.

1977 Hutch Award winner.

Four-time *Sporting News* All-Star selection (1965, 1968, 1969 & 1970).

Six-time N.L. All-Star (1963, 1966, 1968, 1969, 1970 & 1971).

Number 56 on *The Sporting News'* 1999 list of Baseball's 100 Greatest Players.

1962 N.L. champion.

Elected to Baseball Hall of Fame by members of BBWAA in 1986.

7 CARL HUBBELL

Carl Hubbell won two Most Valuable Player Awards during the 1930s. *(Courtesy of Boston Public Library, Leslie Jones Collection)*

Nicknamed "King Carl" due to the dominance he displayed on the mound, Carl Hubbell established himself as one of the greatest left-handed pitchers in baseball history in his 16 seasons with the Giants. The National League's finest hurler for much of the 1930s, Hubbell posted 188 of his 253 victories during that decade, proving to be particularly dominant from 1933 to 1937, when he compiled an overall mark of 115–50. Rivaling Dizzy Dean as the Senior Circuit's greatest pitcher during that five-year period, "The Meal Ticket," as Hubbell also came to be known, led the league in numerous statistical categories, including wins and ERA three times each. Along the way, Hubbell accomplished some truly remarkable things, including winning a major-league record 24 consecutive games, throwing an 18-inning shutout, and turning in arguably the most memorable performance in All-Star Game history. A nine-time N.L. All-Star and two-time league MVP, Hubbell remains the only pitcher in the history of the Senior Circuit to capture MVP honors on two separate occasions. In the process, he helped lead the Giants to three pennants and one world championship, proving to be the central figure in their World Series triumph of 1933. Hubbell's brilliant pitching eventually earned him a place in Cooperstown and a spot on *The Sporting News'* 100 Greatest Players List.

Born in Carthage, Missouri, on June 22, 1903, Carl Owen Hubbell grew up on a pecan farm near the small community of Meeker, Oklahoma. After graduating from Meeker High School, Hubbell went to work for an oil company, for whose baseball team he also pitched. Subsequently signed to his first pro contract by Cushing of the Oklahoma State League in 1923, Hubbell spent two years at Cushing, before advancing to Oklahoma City of the Western League in 1925. While at Oklahoma City, Hubbell added to his pitching repertoire a screwball, which eventually became his signature pitch. The offering, which the lanky left-hander discovered while attempting to turn the ball over in order to make it sink, made him a far more effective pitcher, enabling him to post 17 victories in his lone season at Oklahoma City.

Sold to the Detroit Tigers following the conclusion of the 1925 campaign, Hubbell experienced a major setback when Tigers player-manager Ty Cobb told him to discard the screwball since the unnatural arm motion associated with throwing it previously caused several other hurlers to develop arm ailments. Forbidden from throwing his best pitch, Hubbell struggled during spring training, prompting the Tigers to send him to the minor leagues, where he spent the next two years wallowing in mediocrity.

Hubbell finally received a reprieve early in 1928, when the Tigers sold him to Beaumont of the Texas League. Permitted to use the screwball by Beaumont manager Claude Robertson, Hubbell posted 12 victories by midseason, causing Giants scout Dick Kinsella to purchase his contract for $30,000.

After reporting to the Giants in late July, Hubbell spent the remainder of the 1928 campaign in New York, compiling a record of 10–6 and an ERA of 2.83 in his first big-league season. Establishing himself as the anchor of the Giants' starting rotation the following year, Hubbell finished 18–11, with a

3.69 ERA, 19 complete games, and 268 innings pitched. He pitched effectively in each of the next two seasons as well, going a combined 31–24 in 1930 and 1931, while placing among the league leaders in ERA, strikeouts, shutouts, innings pitched, and complete games each year.

Although the Giants finished well out of contention in 1932, placing sixth in the league with a record of 72–82 that represented their worst mark in 17 years, Hubbell emerged as an elite pitcher, compiling a record of 18–11, finishing second in the league with a 2.50 ERA, 137 strikeouts, and 284 innings pitched, placing third with 22 complete games, and leading all N.L. hurlers in WHIP for the second of six times, with a mark of 1.056. The following year, Hubbell began an extraordinarily successful five-year run during which he won at least 21 games each season. In addition to leading all N.L. pitchers in wins and ERA three times each during the period, he topped the circuit in winning percentage twice, WHIP four times, and shutouts, strikeouts, saves, complete games, and innings pitched one time each.

Hubbell won the first of his two MVP Awards in 1933, when he finished 23–12, with 156 strikeouts, 22 complete games, and a league-leading 1.66 ERA, 10 shutouts, 308 ⅔ innings pitched, and 0.982 WHIP. He then led the Giants to their first World Series triumph in 11 years by defeating Washington twice in the Fall Classic, allowing in the process no earned runs over 20 innings. Hubbell followed that up by going 21–12 in 1934, with a league-leading 2.30 ERA, 25 complete games, 8 saves, and 1.032 WHIP. He also created a permanent place for himself in baseball lore in that year's All-Star Game by striking out five future Hall of Famers (Babe Ruth, Lou Gehrig, Jimmie Foxx, Al Simmons, and Joe Cronin) in succession. Hubbell pitched brilliantly again in 1935, placing among the N.L. leaders with 23 wins, a 3.27 ERA, 150 strikeouts, 24 complete games, 302 ⅔ innings pitched, and a WHIP of 1.199.

Hubbell's dominance on the mound, and the heavy reliance the Giants placed on his left arm, prompted the media to nickname him "King Carl" and "The Meal Ticket." Yet, writer Bob Broeg discussed the physical traits that made the 6-foot, 170-pound Hubbell the unlikeliest of heroes, describing him as "awkwardly angular, gaunt, lean-visaged, and almost Lincolnesque in appearance, with no hips, less derriere, and the longest shinbones in captivity."

Although Hubbell also possessed a good fastball and curve, he depended primarily on his screwball to mesmerize opposing batters. In discussing the deceptiveness of his signature pitch years later, Hubbell explained, "What made the screwball so successful was throwing it over the top with exactly the same motion as a fastball. If a hitter is ready for a fastball, he can adjust to the breaking ball. But with a screwball, it isn't the break that fools the hitter—it's the change of speed. They couldn't time it and were out in front of it."

Hubbell's screwball certainly contributed tremendously to the success he experienced on the mound. But Hall of Fame pitcher Waite Hoyt believed that the left-hander had several other qualities that made him a truly great pitcher, suggesting, "Hubbell is one of the great pitchers, yet he presents no mystery to the onlooker. The source of his skill is his matchless control in using his curveball to set up his screwball. Emotions, if he has any, never affect him. His timing, his conservation of energy, and influence on the ball club are other factors in rating him among the great pitchers of all time."

A knowledgeable Giants fan, who spent much of his life watching the team from a Polo Grounds bleacher seat, described Hubbell in Fred Stein's *Under Coogan's Bluff*:

> When most people talk about Hubbell they usually have in mind his screwball, his 18-inning masterpiece . . . in 1933, his 1934 All-Star Game strikeout feat. . . . I don't think of his individual games. I think of an artist painting a portrait, every stroke of the brush with a purpose. . . . Hub would start a batter off with a curve, and it was usually a beaut, always low and on the corner of the plate. Then, with that uncanny control and that good speed of his, he'd bust one in, either on the fists or high and outside; then, maybe a changeup; next, the screwball. Jeez, what a pitch! It gave those right-hand hitters fits, especially after Hub set them up with the curve and the fastball. . . .
>
> Hubbell had the perfect temperament. He never got excited or lost his concentration when we blew an easy chance behind him. And I used to get a kick just watching him in the dugout on days he wasn't pitching. Even at the end of his career when he'd seen it all, he would sit there quietly and never take his eyes off the batter or the pitcher. I think he knew their strengths and weaknesses better than they did themselves. All in all, Hub was the greatest left-hander I've ever seen, and most of the players I know feel the same.

Hubbell captured N.L. MVP honors for the second time in 1936, when he led the Giants to the pennant by finishing 26–6, with a 2.31 ERA, 25 complete games, and 304 innings pitched. Unbeatable during the season's second half, he won his final 16 decisions, before posting another 8 straight wins at the start of the ensuing campaign. Hubbell's 24 consecutive victories remain a major-league record. He had another great year in 1937, helping the Giants capture their second straight pennant by going 22–8, with a 3.20 ERA, 18 complete games, 261 ⅔ innings pitched, and a league-leading 159 strikeouts. However, even with Hubbell, the Giants could not defeat the Yankees in either the 1936 or 1937 World Series, losing to their crosstown rivals in six and five games, respectively.

Unfortunately, Hubbell's constant use of the screwball for nearly a decade finally began to take its toll on him by the mid-1930s. Feeling discomfort in his left elbow as early as 1934, Hubbell found himself unable to cope with the pain any longer by the latter stages of the 1938 campaign, limiting him to only 22 starts and 13 victories—his lowest totals since his rookie year of 1928. Forced to undergo elbow surgery in late August, Hubbell assumed a less prominent role on the Giants pitching staff the remainder of his career, never again making more than 28 starts, and posting 11 victories in each of the next four seasons. After Hubbell finished just 4–4 with an uncharacteristically high 4.91 ERA in 1943, the Giants released him on December 2, prompting the 40-year-old southpaw to announce his retirement. He ended his career with a record of 253–154, an ERA of 2.98, 1,677 strikeouts in 3,590 ⅓ innings of work, 260 complete games, 36 shutouts, 33 saves, and a WHIP of 1.166. In addition to ranking second all-time to Christy Mathewson among Giants pitchers in wins, Hubbell ranks second in franchise history in innings pitched, third in shutouts and games started, fourth in complete games and pitching appearances, and fifth in strikeouts. The members of the BBWAA elected Hubbell to the Hall of Fame in 1947, in just his third year of eligibility.

Named Giants director of player development following his retirement, Hubbell remained in that position for the next 34 years, until a stroke he suffered in 1977 relegated him to part-time scouting duties. Hubbell continued to serve the team in that capacity until he tragically lost his life due to injuries suffered in an automobile accident in Scottsdale, Arizona, in November 1988. Hubbell passed away at 85 years of age, on November 21, 1988, 30 years to the day that his former teammate and close friend Mel Ott died of the same cause.

Career Highlights:

Best Season: Although Hubbell pitched exceptionally well for the Giants from 1933 to 1937, he clearly had his two best seasons in 1933 and 1936.

Hubbell's 22 complete games, 156 strikeouts, and league-leading 23 wins, 1.66 ERA, 10 shutouts, 308 ⅔ innings pitched, and 0.982 WHIP earned him N.L. MVP and *Associated Press* Male Athlete of the Year honors in 1933. He won his second MVP trophy and earned *Sporting News* MLB Player of the Year honors in 1936, when he placed near the top of the league rankings with 25 complete games, 304 innings pitched, 3 shutouts, and 123 strikeouts, while also leading all N.L. hurlers with 26 victories, an .813 winning percentage, a 2.31 ERA, and a WHIP of 1.059. The numbers would seem to suggest that Hubbell pitched slightly better in 1933. However, it must be considered that, after watching offensive numbers soar throughout the league in 1929 and 1930, the N.L. used a deadened ball the next few seasons, contributing, at least to some degree, to the magnificent figures Hubbell compiled in 1933. On the other hand, after the Senior Circuit began using a somewhat livelier ball the following year, offensive numbers rose dramatically, making Hubbell's 1936 statistics all that much more impressive. Furthermore, Hubbell's 16 consecutive wins during the second half of the 1936 campaign proved to be absolutely critical to the success of the pennant-winning Giants, whose record stood at only 41–41 as late as July 15. All things considered, Hubbell had his finest season in 1936.

Memorable Moments/Greatest Performances: In addition to his major-league record 24-game winning streak that lasted from 1936 into 1937, Hubbell compiled a pair of impressive scoreless inning streaks in his first MVP season of 1933, not allowing the opposition to cross home plate for 45 ⅓ and 27 ⅔ innings at different points during the campaign.

Hubbell pitched a number of memorable games for the Giants, with the first of those coming on May 8, 1929, when he tossed an 11–0 no-hitter against the Pirates. After surrendering just one walk over the first 8 innings, Hubbell ran into his only problem in the top of the 9th, when a pair of Giant errors allowed the first two Pirate batters to reach base. However, Hubbell subsequently struck out Lloyd Waner and induced Paul Waner to hit into a game-ending double play.

Hubbell threw three one-hitters as well, striking out 9 and allowing just one hit and one walk during an 11–0 win over the Phillies on May 28, 1938; surrendering just a single and pitching to the minimum 27 batters during a 7–0 victory over the Dodgers on May 30, 1940; and defeating the Pirates 5–1 on a one-hitter on June 5, 1943.

Although Hubbell lost to the Dodgers in 12 innings by a score of 3–2 on May 26, 1932, he recorded a career-high 15 strikeouts during the contest. He nearly matched that total on April 20, 1933, when he struck out 13 batters and allowed just 4 hits during a 1–0 victory over the Braves. Hubbell, though, pitched arguably the greatest game of his career on July 2, 1933, when he defeated the Cardinals by a score of 1–0 in 18 innings. Retiring the side in order in 12 of the 18 frames, Hubbell finished the game with 12 strikeouts, allowing just 6 hits and no walks.

Hubbell also performed brilliantly in the 1933 World Series, throwing two complete-game victories against the Washington Senators, one of them an 11-inning, 2–1 win. Allowing no earned runs in his 20 innings of work, Hubbell finished the Series with a record of 2–0, an ERA of 0.00, and 15 strikeouts.

Nevertheless, Hubbell experienced the seminal moment of his career when he struck out five future Hall of Famers in a row in the second annual MLB All-Star Game, played at the Polo Grounds on July 10, 1934. After using his screwball to whiff Babe Ruth, Lou Gehrig, and Jimmie Foxx in the first inning, Hubbell began the ensuing frame by fanning Al Simmons and Joe Cronin. In discussing Hubbell's extraordinary feat in an article that appeared in the *Boston Globe* in 2002, sportswriter Bob Ryan wrote:

> In terms of All-Star Game pitching feats, there is one standing far, far apart from all others. On July 10, 1934, in the Polo Grounds, the National League's Carl Hubbell wrote himself some baseball history by striking out the final three men of the first inning and the first two of the second. Any self-respecting baseball historian knows the names by heart, and almost invariably rattles them off so quickly it's as if the five men had one name: Ruthgehrigfoxxsimmonscronin.

Notable Achievements:

Won more than 20 games five times, surpassing 17 victories on three other occasions.

Posted winning percentage in excess of .700 twice.

Compiled ERA below 3.00 seven times, posting mark under 2.00 once (1.66 in 1933).

Posted WHIP under 1.000 once (0.982 in 1933).

Threw more than 300 innings four times.

Threw more than 20 complete games six times.

Tossed 10 shutouts in 1933.

Led N.L. pitchers in: wins three times; winning percentage twice; ERA three times; WHIP six times; strikeouts once; complete games once; innings pitched once; shutouts once; saves once; assists three times; putouts twice; and fielding percentage twice.

Ranks among Giants career leaders in: wins (2nd); strikeouts (5th); shutouts (3rd); complete games (4th); innings pitched (2nd); games started (3rd); and pitching appearances (4th).

Holds Major League record for most consecutive wins by a pitcher (24).

Threw no-hitter vs. Pittsburgh on May 8, 1929.

Threw 45 ⅓ consecutive scoreless innings in 1933.

Holds share of MLB record for longest 1–0 victory (18 innings vs. St. Louis on July 2, 1933).

Two-time N.L. MVP (1933 & 1936).

1933 *Associated Press* Male Athlete of the Year.

1936 *Sporting News* Major League Player of the Year.

Four-time *Sporting News* All-Star selection (1933, 1935, 1936 & 1937).

Nine-time N.L. All-Star (1933, 1934, 1935, 1936, 1937, 1938, 1940, 1941 & 1942).

Number 45 on *The Sporting News'* 1999 list of Baseball's 100 Greatest Players.

Three-time N.L. champion (1933, 1936 & 1937).

1933 world champion.

Elected to Baseball Hall of Fame by members of BBWAA in 1947.

8 BILL TERRY

The last N.L. hitter to top the .400-mark, Bill Terry batted .401 for the Giants in 1930. *(Courtesy of Boston Public Library, Leslie Jones Collection)*

Playing first base in the city of New York during the 1920s and 1930s caused Bill Terry to spend his entire career being overshadowed by the immortal Lou Gehrig, who manned the same position for the crosstown rival New York Yankees during that period. Nevertheless, Terry established himself as the National League's finest first baseman during his playing days, teaming up with Mel Ott to give the Giants the Senior Circuit's most formidable one-two punch. The last N.L. player to hit .400, Terry posted a major-league best .352

batting average during the 1930s, en route to compiling a lifetime mark of .341 that ranks as the 15th best in the history of the game. Terry also surpassed 20 home runs three times, knocked in more than 100 runs six times, scored more than 100 runs seven times, and topped 200 hits on six occasions, amassing a total of 254 safeties in 1930 that remains a National League record. An outstanding fielder as well, Terry gained general recognition over the course of his career as the Senior Circuit's top glove man at his position, leading all N.L. first sackers in putouts five times, assists five times, double plays three times, and fielding percentage twice. Terry's exceptional all-around play helped the Giants capture three pennants and one world championship, before he managed them to another pennant one year after his playing career ended.

Born in Atlanta, Georgia, on October 30, 1898, William Harold Terry didn't make his major-league debut with the New York Giants until shortly before he turned 26 years of age. Terry got his start in organized ball pitching for a local team in the Georgia-Alabama League in 1915. After being sold to Shreveport of the Texas League at the end of the season, he spent the next two years laboring in mediocrity, compiling a record of 14–11 with a 3.00 ERA in 1917, while batting just .231. Not offered a contract at the conclusion of the 1917 campaign, Terry moved to Memphis, where he worked for Standard Oil and played first base for the company's semipro baseball team. Discovered almost five years later by New York Giants manager John McGraw on one of the latter's annual trips to Memphis, Terry signed with the Giants for $5,000, after which he acquired the nickname "Memphis Bill."

Terry spent most of the next two seasons tearing up the American Association. But, with future Hall of Famer George Kelly firmly entrenched at first base for the Giants, Terry's road to the big leagues proved to be a slow and arduous one. Finally called up to New York during the latter stages of the 1923 campaign, Terry hit safely in just one of his seven official trips to the plate before assuming a backup role with the team the following year, when he compiled a batting average of just .239 in his 163 official plate appearances.

Terry garnered significantly more playing time in 1925, appearing in a total of 133 games, 124 of which he started at first base. Amassing nearly 500 official at-bats, Terry finished his first full season with 11 home runs, 70 RBIs, 75 runs scored, and a .319 batting average. Yet, in spite of his solid performance, Terry again found himself relegated to a part-time role the following year, when he compiled a batting average of .289 and knocked in 43 runs in only 225 official plate appearances.

With the Giants trading George Kelly to the Cincinnati Reds prior to the start of the 1927 season, Terry finally established himself as the team's starting first baseman—a position he maintained for the next nine years. Starting virtually every game for the Giants for the first of six straight times, Terry had his breakout season in 1927, finishing among the league leaders in 10 different offensive categories, including home runs (20), RBIs (121), runs scored (101), triples (13), batting average (.326), and OPS (.907). He followed that up with a similarly productive 1928 campaign in which he hit 17 homers, knocked in 101 runs, scored 100 times, again batted .326, and compiled an OPS of .912.

The left-handed-hitting Terry, who stood close to 6'2" and weighed well in excess of 200 pounds, subsequently began an exceptional four-year run during which he consistently ranked among the National League leaders in numerous statistical categories. After earning a third-place finish in the 1929 N.L. MVP voting by hitting 14 home runs, scoring 103 runs, and placing near the top of the league rankings with 117 RBIs, 226 hits, and a .372 batting average, Terry turned in a historic performance the following year when he became the last N.L. player to hit over .400. In addition to batting .401, Terry hit 23 home runs, amassed 15 triples and 39 doubles, and established career highs with 129 runs batted in, 139 runs scored, an OPS of 1.071, and a National League record 254 hits. Although the Senior Circuit did not present an official MVP Award at the conclusion of the campaign, *The Sporting News* named Terry its "unofficial" winner, despite the fact that Hack Wilson knocked in a major-league record 191 runs for the Chicago Cubs. Reflecting back on his memorable season, Terry later said, "To hit .400 you need a great start and you can't have a slump. The year I did it, I was around .410, .412 all season and I was really hitting the ball on the nose."

When asked to discuss his formula for hitting, Terry responded, "Confidence, my boy, confidence. I don't mean a fellow can start right out knocking a ball lopsided by simply saying to himself he can do it. What I do mean is that, if you want to accomplish something, you must have confidence in your method of doing it."

In spite of his good size and ability to hit the long ball, Terry became known primarily as a gap-hitter who accumulated the vast majority of his hits by driving the ball back up the middle and towards the outfield gaps. Standing in the batter's box with his feet close together and his arms held close to his body, Terry preferred to use the entire field, unlike his teammate Mel Ott, who constantly looked to pull the ball into the short right-field stands at the

Polo Grounds. For that reason, some observers felt that Terry should have hit more than the 154 home runs he ended up compiling over the course of his career. In his defense, though, Terry later claimed that he began his career as a pull hitter, before John McGraw inexplicably advised him to hit the ball to the opposite field.

Terry also did an outstanding job in the field, using his soft hands, excellent quickness, and silky moves around the bag to establish himself as the Senior Circuit's top defensive first baseman. Possessing exceptional range, Terry led all N.L. first sackers in assists five times and total chances per-game nine times. Burgess Whitehead, who spent one season playing alongside Terry on the right side of the Giants infield, said, "Bill Terry was the finest playing manager I ever saw. He was always thinking ahead. He was a great fielder and, when he was on first, I did not have to worry about my left."

Following his extraordinary performance in 1930, Terry continued to excel in each of the next two seasons, finishing a close second in the N.L. batting race each year, with marks of .349 and .350, respectively. En route to earning a third-place finish in the league MVP voting in the first of those campaigns, Terry also drove in 112 runs, collected 213 hits and 43 doubles, and topped the circuit with 20 triples and 121 runs scored. He followed that up in 1932 by placing among the league leaders with 117 RBIs, 124 runs scored, and a career-high 28 home runs.

Terry's offensive production fell off somewhat after he assumed the managerial reins from an ailing John McGraw midway through the 1932 campaign. Yet, he remained a solid offensive performer until he elected to concentrate solely on managing at the end of the 1936 season. After hitting 28 home runs in 1932, Terry never again finished in double-digits in that category. Nor did he ever again drive in as many as 100 runs. But Terry batted well over .300 in each of his four remaining years, compiling averages of .354 in 1934 and .341 in 1935. In the first of those campaigns, he also knocked in 83 runs, scored 109 times, collected 213 hits, and compiled a .414 on-base percentage, en route to earning the fifth of his six top-10 finishes in the league MVP voting.

After batting .310 in just 79 games in 1936 while battling through severe knee problems, Terry chose to announce his retirement, ending his playing career with a lifetime batting average of .341 that represents the highest mark ever compiled by a left-handed hitter in the National League. He also hit 154 home runs, knocked in 1,078 runs, scored 1,120 times, amassed 2,193 hits, 112 triples, and 373 doubles, compiled a .393 on-base percentage, and posted a .506 slugging percentage. Terry represented the National League at first base in each of the first three All-Star Games.

Following his retirement as an active player, Terry continued to manage the Giants until 1941, posting an overall record of 823–661 over the course of his managerial career, which saw him lead the Giants to the National League pennant in 1933, 1936, and 1937, and to the world championship in 1933. After retiring from managing, Terry settled in Jacksonville, Florida, where he purchased an automobile dealership and amassed a fortune in oil and cotton speculation. He also served as a member of the Hall of Fame Veteran's Committee for several years, after being inducted to Cooperstown himself in 1954. Terry passed away on January 9, 1989, at age 90.

Terry's bluntness and unwillingness to cater to the media as both a player and as a manager may have been at least partly responsible for the lengthy wait he endured before finally being voted into the Hall of Fame. Baseball historian Lee Allen attempted to defend Terry's actions by stating, "He has often been misunderstood, and what passed for coldness has merely been an impatience with stupid questions."

Another contributing factor to Terry's lengthy wait might well have been his somewhat rebellious nature. A staunch critic of the baseball establishment, Terry incurred the wrath of owners at different times by speaking out against the way they governed the game. Among his more memorable quotes, Terry proclaimed, "Baseball must be a great game to survive the fools who run it." He also stated, "No business in the world has ever made more money with poorer management."

During his Hall of Fame induction speech, Terry quipped, "I don't know what kept me out (of the Hall of Fame)—newspapermen, or just that you don't want me up here."

Career Highlights:

Best Season: Even though Terry batted over .400 two years earlier, it could be argued that he had his finest all-around season in 1932, especially when it is considered that the livelier ball the National League used in 1930 resulted in an offensive explosion throughout the league. Not only did Hack Wilson drive in a major-league record 191 runs that year, but four different N.L. players batted over .380, with another five posting a mark in excess of .360. That being the case, Terry's 1932 campaign must be seriously considered for the top spot here. Placing among the league leaders in virtually every major offensive category, Terry finished second in batting average (.350), hits (225), runs scored (124), and total bases (373), third in home runs (28) and slugging percentage (.580), fourth in triples (11) and OPS (.962), fifth in doubles (42), sixth in runs batted in (117), and 10th in on-base percentage (.382). Nevertheless, 1930 is generally considered to be Terry's signature season, and with good reason. In addition to leading the league with a .401 batting average and 254 hits, he hit 23 home runs, amassed 15 triples and 39 doubles, and established career highs with 129 RBIs, 139 runs scored, 392 total bases, a .452 on-base percentage, and a .619 slugging percentage, placing near the top of the league rankings in each category. Terry's .401 batting average and 254 hits remain franchise records, while his 139 runs scored continue to represent the highest total compiled by any Giants player since 1900.

Memorable Moments/Greatest Performances: Although just a raw rookie at the time, Terry gave an extremely good account of himself in the 1924 World Series, accumulating 6 hits in 14 at-bats, for a .429 batting average.

After laying claim to the starting first-base job in 1927, Terry got the Giants off to a good start by hitting the first-ever grand slam on Opening Day, in leading them to a 15–7 victory over the Phillies. He finished the game 3-for-5, with 6 RBIs and 3 runs scored.

Terry had another huge afternoon on May 29, 1928, hitting for the cycle and driving in 6 runs during a 12–5 win over Brooklyn.

Terry turned in one of his finest performances in a losing cause, collecting 9 hits during a doubleheader loss to Brooklyn on June 18, 1929. He finished the day 9-for-10, with a homer and 5 RBIs.

Terry had a big day at the plate on July 28, 1930, when he led the Giants to a 5–4 win over the Phillies by going 4-for-4, with a pair of homers, 3 RBIs, and 3 runs scored.

Terry again feasted off Philadelphia pitching a few weeks later, when he went 4-for-5, with a homer, double, 7 RBIs, and 3 runs scored during an 18–5 mauling of the Phillies on Sept. 2, 1930.

Terry had a number of memorable days in 1932, with the first of those coming on April 17, when he tied a National League record by recording 21 putouts during a 5–0 win over Boston. Although the Giants lost their matchup with the Braves two days later by a score of 8–7 in 13 innings, Terry had a huge game, driving in six of his team's seven runs with a triple and a pair of homers. Terry continued to flex his muscles against Philadelphia the following day, hitting another 2 homers and knocking in 5 runs during a 14–5 victory over the Phillies. Concluding the greatest power surge of his career against Philadelphia the very next day, Terry hit his sixth home run in four games during a 5–4 win over the Phillies. Yet, Terry turned in arguably his most memorable performance of the year in a losing effort, going 4-for-5 and hitting 3 home runs during an 18–9 loss to Brooklyn on August 13.

Notable Achievements:

Batted over .300 11 times, surpassing the .350-mark four times and topping .400 once (.401 in 1930).

Knocked in more than 100 runs six times, surpassing 120 RBIs twice.

Scored more than 100 runs seven times, topping 120 runs scored on three occasions.

Surpassed 20 home runs three times.

Topped 200 hits six times.

Finished in double-digits in triples five times, amassing 20 three-baggers in 1931.

Surpassed 30 doubles nine times, topping the 40-mark twice.

Compiled on-base percentage in excess of .400 three times.

Posted slugging percentage in excess of .500 six times, topping the .600-mark once (.619 in 1930).

Compiled OPS in excess of 1.000 once (1.071 in 1930).

Led N.L. in: batting average once; runs scored once; hits once; and triples once.

Led N.L. first basemen in: putouts five times; assists five times; fielding percentage twice; and double plays three times.

Last N.L. player to hit .400 (.401 in 1930).

Owns highest lifetime batting average (.341) in N.L. history by a left-handed batter.

Holds N.L. record for most hits in a season (254 in 1930).

Holds Giants single-season records for highest batting average (.401) and most hits (254), both in 1930.

Holds Giants career record for highest batting average (.341).

Ranks among Giants career leaders in: runs batted in (5th); runs scored (5th); hits (3rd); extra-base hits (5th); doubles (4th); triples (5th); total bases (5th); on-base percentage (tied-6th); slugging percentage (9th); OPS (7th); games played (5th); plate appearances (5th); and at-bats (4th).

Hit for cycle vs. Brooklyn on May 29, 1928.

Hit three home runs in one game vs. Brooklyn on August 13, 1932.

1930 *Sporting News* N.L. MVP.

Finished in top five of official N.L. MVP voting three times.

1930 *Sporting News* All-Star selection.

Three-time N.L. All-Star (1933, 1934 & 1935).

Number 59 on *The Sporting News'* 1999 list of Baseball's 100 Greatest Players.

Three-time N.L. champion (1924, 1933 & 1936).

1933 world champion.

Elected to Baseball Hall of Fame by members of BBWAA in 1954.

9 ORLANDO CEPEDA

Orlando Cepeda led the National League with 46 home runs and 141 RBIs in 1961. *(Courtesy of LegendaryAuctions.com)*

The first in a long line of outstanding Latin-American players to come through the Giants' expansive farm system during the latter half of the 1950s, Orlando Cepeda ended up establishing himself as one of the elite hitters of his generation. A slugger in the truest sense of the word, the 6'2", 220-pound Cepeda possessed tremendous physical strength that enabled him to drive a ball out of any part of the park. Nicknamed "The Baby Bull," Cepeda hit more than 30 home runs four times and knocked in more than 100 runs three times in his seven full seasons with the Giants, en route to amassing 379 homers and 1,365 RBIs over the course of his Hall of Fame career. Yet, Cepeda proved to be more than just a home-run hitter, posting a batting average in excess of .300 six times for the Giants, while also finishing in double-digits in stolen bases in each of his first five campaigns, before knee problems severely limited his effectiveness on the base paths. Cepeda's exceptional play earned him six consecutive All-Star selections and two top-10 finishes in the N.L. MVP voting during his time in San Francisco. He also earned league MVP honors and one more All-Star nomination as a member of the Cardinals, who he led to the 1967 National League pennant after leaving the Giants.

Born in the southern seaport city of Ponce, Puerto Rico, on September 17, 1937, Orlando Manuel (Pennes) Cepeda grew up idolizing his father, Perucho, who became more commonly known as "The Bull" or "The Babe Ruth of the Caribbean" while reaching legendary status in the Caribbean as a big, power-hitting shortstop. Developing a strong desire to follow in his father's footsteps after traveling with him throughout Latin America during his playing days, young Orlando briefly lost interest in baseball after he failed to make a local team. However, he refocused his attention on the sport he grew up playing after injuring his right knee playing basketball around the age of 13. Cepeda's injury eventually required corrective surgery that included the removal of knee cartilage. Although the healing process proved to be a lengthy one that kept Cepeda in bed for two months and on crutches for almost half a year, it ended up benefiting him since he added some 40 pounds of bulk during his period of convalescence that he eventually converted into muscle. The added weight transformed the teenager from a skinny singles hitter into a powerful slugger.

After watching Cepeda compete as an amateur, Pedro Zorilla, owner of the Santurce Crabbers, convinced the 17-year-old's family to allow the youngster to travel to Florida to participate in a tryout for the New York Giants. Cepeda's combination of power and speed very much impressed the Giants, prompting them to offer him a contract. However, after being assigned to the Salem Rebels, a Class D team in the southern Appalachian League, Cepeda seriously considered quitting baseball and returning to his homeland when he had a difficult time adapting to his new environment because of his inability to speak the English language and the racial discrimination he encountered. Cepeda became even more despondent when he learned that his father had succumbed to a stomach disorder.

Choosing in the end to remain in the United States, Cepeda soon found himself playing third base for the Kokomo Giants, a team in the Mississippi-Ohio Valley League. Although Cepeda did not possess the surest of hands, he impressed the team's coaching staff with his exuberance and willingness to learn. He made a much stronger impression, though, with his bat, displaying an ability to drive the ball with power to all fields from his closed batting stance. Despite being a bit flat-footed, Cepeda also ran well for a big man.

After gradually transitioning to first base while advancing through the Giants' farm system the next three years, Cepeda earned the team's starting job at that position in spring training of 1958, which marked the year the ball club moved to San Francisco. Excelling in his first major-league season, Cepeda became just the second player to earn unanimous N.L. Rookie of the Year honors by hitting 25 homers, driving in 96 runs, scoring 88 times, collecting 188 hits, batting .312, and topping the circuit with 38 doubles. He also placed ninth in the league MVP voting and was selected the "Most Valuable Giant" in a poll conducted by the *San Francisco Examiner*. The 21-year-old first baseman so impressed Giants manager Bill Rigney that the latter later called him "the best young right-handed power hitter I'd seen." Meanwhile, Willie Mays praised his young teammate by stating, "He is annoying every pitcher in the league. He is strong, he hits to all fields, and he makes all the plays. He's the most relaxed first-year man I ever saw."

Cepeda followed his exceptional rookie season with an outstanding sophomore campaign, earning his first All-Star nomination by finishing among the league leaders with 27 home runs, 105 RBIs, 192 hits, 35 doubles, a .317 batting average, a .522 slugging percentage, and a career-high 23 stolen bases, which placed him second in the N.L. rankings. Cepeda continued his success in 1960, even though the Giants moved from Seals Stadium to windy Candlestick Park that year. The swirling winds at the Giants' new home ballpark made it extremely difficult for right-handed hitters to drive the ball over the left-field fence. Therefore, Cepeda, who previously pulled almost everything from a closed batting stance, changed his style of hitting. Adopting a more open stance in the batter's box, Cepeda began driving the ball more to right and right-center, hitting many of his home runs to the opposite field. Showing just a slight decrease in offensive production in his first year at Candlestick, Cepeda finished the season with 24 homers, 96 runs batted in, 81 runs scored, 36 doubles, and a .297 batting average.

Cepeda's excellent play and effervescent personality made him wildly popular with San Francisco fans, who adopted him as one of their own, unlike Willie Mays, who they treated more like a transplanted New Yorker. Cepeda further endeared himself to Giants fans in 1961, when he compiled the most prolific offensive numbers of his career. In addition to placing among the league leaders with 105 runs scored, a .311 batting average, and a .609 slugging percentage, Cepeda topped the Senior Circuit with 46 home runs and 142 RBIs, earning in the process a second-place finish to Cincinnati's Frank Robinson in the N.L. MVP balloting.

Yet, in spite of the tremendous amount of success Cepeda experienced on the playing field in 1961, the campaign did not prove to be a particularly enjoyable one for him. Frequently butting heads with new Giants manager Alvin Dark, who ordered the team's Latin American players to stop speaking Spanish in the clubhouse, Cepeda nearly elected to sit out a few games as a form of protest. The relationship between the two men only worsened after Cepeda reinjured his right knee in a home-plate collision with Dodgers catcher John Roseboro. Although Cepeda subsequently missed only a handful of games, Dark accused him of putting forth less than a 100 percent effort when he returned to the Giants lineup. Enraged by his manager's accusation, Cepeda held a grudge against Dark, who he felt never respected him nor his Spanish-speaking teammates, until the latter apologized to him years later for not taking his injury more seriously.

Unfortunately, the 1961 campaign marked the final season in which Cepeda played entirely pain-free. Aggravating the knee again while working out with weights during the subsequent offseason, Cepeda spent the next three years playing in mild to severe discomfort. Nevertheless, he continued to compile outstanding numbers, averaging 33 home runs and 103 RBIs from 1962 to 1964, while posting batting averages of .306, .316, and .304. Performing particularly well for a Giants team that captured the National League pennant in 1962, Cepeda concluded the campaign with 35 home runs, 114 RBIs, 105 runs scored, 191 hits, and a .306 batting average. However, after playing first base almost exclusively in each of those seasons, Cepeda moved to left field at the start of the 1965 campaign to create a full-time spot at first for Willie McCovey.

The switch in positions proved to be disastrous for Cepeda, whose season ended prematurely when he injured his right knee again early in the year while diving for a ball in the outfield. After appearing in a total of only 33 games over the course of the campaign, Cepeda had to undergo surgery during the offseason to repair his injured knee, which severely limited his mobility the remainder of his career.

After subsequently performing various types of manual labor to strengthen the joint and stay in shape, Cepeda returned to the Giants in the spring asking to play first base. However, San Francisco manager Herman Franks informed him that he intended to use McCovey at first instead. Despite asking to be traded, Cepeda began the 1966 campaign in left field for the Giants, until the team finally dealt him to the Cardinals in early May for veteran left-handed starter Ray Sadecki. Cepeda left the Giants having hit 226 home runs, driven in 767 runs, scored 652 times, collected 1,286 hits, 22 triples, and 226 doubles, batted .308, compiled a .352 on-base percentage, and posted a .535 slugging percentage as a member of the team. He continues to rank among the franchise's all-time leaders in numerous statistical categories, including homers, RBIs, and slugging percentage.

Moving back to his more familiar position of first base after joining the Cardinals, Cepeda re-established himself as one of the Senior Circuit's elite players, earning N.L. Comeback Player of the Year honors by leading the Redbirds with 17 home runs, 24 doubles, a .303 batting average, and a .469 slugging percentage, despite appearing in only 123 games with them. Serving as the team's primary power threat and inspirational leader in the clubhouse the following year, Cepeda led the Cardinals to the pennant and earned league MVP honors by hitting 25 home runs, batting .325, scoring 91 runs, and topping the circuit with 111 RBIs.

Cepeda spent one more year in St. Louis, posting far less impressive numbers in 1968, before spending most of the next four seasons with the Atlanta Braves. Cepeda had his best year for the Braves in 1970, when he hit 34 homers, knocked in 111 runs, and batted .305. However, his days as a full-time player all but ended the following season when he freakishly injured his left knee in early May while rising from a chair in his living room to answer the telephone. After feeling his knee give out, Cepeda attempted to play through pain the next few weeks, before finally electing to have season-ending surgery.

Finding it increasingly difficult to play on his aching knees, Cepeda split the 1972 campaign between Atlanta and Oakland, appearing in a total of only 31 games. After being released by Oakland at the end of the year, Cepeda signed with the Boston Red Sox as a free agent when the American League announced its intention to begin using a designated hitter in its games beginning in 1973. Despite limping noticeably whenever he stepped onto the field, Cepeda hit 20 home runs, drove in 86 runs, and batted .289 for the Red Sox in 142 games, en route to earning DH of the Year honors.

A subsequent youth movement in Boston marked the end of the 36-year-old Cepeda's days in a Red Sox uniform. Signing with Kansas City after being released by Boston at season's end, Cepeda appeared in only 33 games with the Royals over the course of the 1974 campaign before announcing his retirement at the end of the year. In addition to concluding his career with 379 home runs and 1,365 runs batted in, Cepeda scored 1,131 runs, amassed 2,351 hits, 27 triples, and 417 doubles, stole 142 bases, batted .297, compiled a .350 on-base percentage, and posted a .499 slugging percentage.

Following his playing career, Cepeda ran afoul of the law, serving time in prison for attempting to smuggle marijuana into his native Puerto Rico. However, after eventually returning to the United States, he received an offer to work for the Chicago White Sox, first as a hitting instructor, and later as a scout. He also opened a baseball school in San Juan. Shortly after Cepeda moved back to Northern California in 1986, the Giants hired him for a Community Relations position. He moved into scouting and player development for the club and eventually became a sort of goodwill ambassador for the organization.

Giant Career Highlights:

Best Season: Cepeda had a big year for the pennant-winning Giants in 1962, finishing in the league's top 10 in homers (35), RBIs (114), runs scored (105), hits (191), and batting average (.306). He also performed extremely well the following year, hitting 34 home runs, driving in 97 runs, scoring 100 times, batting .316, and compiling an OPS of .929 that placed him third in the N.L. rankings. However, Cepeda had his finest season for the Giants in 1961, when he earned a second-place finish in the league MVP voting by batting .311, scoring 105 runs, posting a career-high OPS of .970, and topping the Senior Circuit with 46 home runs and 141 RBIs.

Memorable Moments/Greatest Performances: Cepeda gave an early indication of his tremendous power by hitting an opposite-field home run against Dodger reliever Don Bessent in just his third major-league at-bat, in helping the Giants post an 8–0 victory over Los Angeles in the 1958 regular-season opener.

Cepeda had a huge day against Milwaukee on June 4, 1959, leading the Giants to an 11–5 victory over the Braves by going 4-for-5, with a pair of homers and 7 RBIs. One of Cepeda's blasts carried over the left-field bleachers at County Stadium, making him the first player to hit a ball completely out of that ballpark.

Cepeda hit another tape-measure home run during a 7–0 win over the Phillies on May 7, 1961, hitting a three-run shot against Hall of Fame right-hander Robin Roberts that cleared the roof at Philadelphia's Connie Mack Stadium.

Though not known for his thievery on the base paths, Cepeda went 3-for-3 and swiped 3 bases during a 9–5 victory over the Pirates on August 1, 1959.

Cepeda led the Giants to a 14–1 mauling of the Cubs on May 15, 1961, by going 3-for-4, with a pair of homers, 5 RBIs, and 3 runs scored. He again torched Chicago's pitching staff later in the year, leading the Giants to a lop-sided 19–3 victory over the Cubs on July 4 by going 5-for-5, with a homer, 2 doubles, and a career-high 8 runs batted in.

Cepeda continued to torment Cubs pitchers the following year, having another huge game against them on May 4, 1962, when he went 3-for-4, with a homer and 5 RBIs, during an 11–6 Giants win.

Cepeda led the Giants to a 6–0 victory over Philadelphia on August 24, 1962, by going 5-for-5, with 2 homers and 4 RBIs. He also stole a base during the contest.

Cepeda had his last big game for the Giants on September 12, 1964, homering twice and knocking in 6 runs during a 9–1 win over the Phillies.

Notable Achievements:

Surpassed 30 home runs four times, topping 40 homers once (46 in 1961).

Knocked in more than 100 runs three times, topping 140 RBIs once (142 in 1961).

Scored more than 100 runs three times.

Batted over .300 six times.

Surpassed 30 doubles four times.

Stole more than 20 bases once (23 in 1959).

Posted slugging percentage in excess of .500 six times, topping the .600-mark once (.609 in 1961).

Led N.L. in: home runs once; RBIs once; and doubles once.

Led N.L. first basemen in putouts once.

Ranks among Giants career leaders in: home runs (6th); RBIs (10th); extra-base hits (8th); total bases (9th); slugging percentage (tied-5th); and OPS (10th).

1958 N.L. Rookie of the Year.

Finished second in 1961 N.L. MVP voting.

Three-time *Sporting News* All-Star selection (1959, 1961 & 1962).

Six-time N.L. All-Star (1959, 1960, 1961, 1962, 1963 & 1964).

1962 N.L. champion.

Elected to Baseball Hall of Fame by members of Veteran's Committee in 1999.

10 FRANKIE FRISCH

Frankie Frisch starred for the Giants during the 1920s before serving as player/manager of the St. Louis Cardinals' "Gas House Gang" the ensuing decade. *(Courtesy of Library of Congress)*

Although Frankie Frisch is perhaps best remembered for being the unquestioned leader of the St. Louis Cardinals' famed "Gas House Gang," he previously spent eight years in New York, during which time he established himself as arguably the best all-around player on Giant teams that won four straight pennants and two World Series. A versatile athlete who played both second and third base during his time in New York, Frisch proved to be an extension of John McGraw on the playing field, bringing to the team a "win-at-all-cost" mentality that prompted the Giants manager to name him team captain in just his second season. The hard-nosed Frisch, who became known for his aggressive style of play, also gave the Giants solid defense, excellent offense, and outstanding speed on the base paths. In addition to batting well over .300 in each of his final six seasons in New York, Frisch knocked in more than 100 runs twice, scored more than 100 runs four times, amassed more than 200 hits twice, and stole more than 30 bases three times, consistently placing among the National League leaders in the last category. Frisch also led all N.L. second basemen in putouts once and fielding percentage once, with his outstanding all-around play earning him two top-10 finishes in the league MVP voting.

Born to German immigrants in the Bronx, New York, on September 9, 1897, Frank Francis Frisch attended Fordham University, where he starred in baseball, football, basketball, and track, acquiring in the process the nickname "The Fordham Flash." After earning College Football All-American honors as a halfback in 1918, Frisch joined the Giants following his graduation one year later without ever having played a single game of minor-league ball. The switch-hitting infielder spent the final three months of the 1919 season filling in at both second and third base, failing to distinguish himself as a hitter by batting just .226, but leaving a lasting impression on Giants manager John McGraw with his speed (he stole 15 bases in only 54 games) and mental toughness. The 5'11", 165-pound rookie made a particularly strong impression on McGraw in his first start at second base when, in a crucial game, he knocked down a hard-hit drive that bounced off his chest, pursued the ball, and threw out the runner at first base. Taking note of Frisch's composure on the play, McGraw later said, "That was all I had to see. The average youngster, nervous anyway at starting his first game in a pennant situation like that, would have lost the ball. Frisch proved to me right there that he is going to be a great ball player."

Frisch soon became a favorite of his new manager, who admired the young infielder's speed, athleticism, versatility, and aggressiveness. McGraw installed Frisch as the team's starting third baseman early the following year, before naming him team captain shortly thereafter. Frisch responded by batting .280, driving in 77 runs, and finishing third in the league with 34 stolen bases.

McGraw used Frisch extensively at both second and third base in each of the next two seasons, during which time the latter established himself as one of the Senior Circuit's most dynamic players. Frisch had his breakout season in 1921, when he hit 8 home runs, led the league with 49 stolen bases, and finished among the leaders with 100 RBIs, 121 runs scored, 211 hits, 17 triples, 31 doubles, 300 total bases, a .341 batting average, and a .485 slugging percentage. He followed that up by batting .327, scoring 101 runs, and stealing 31 bases in 1922, en route to helping the Giants capture the second of their four consecutive league championships.

Although the switch-hitting Frisch lacked home-run power from both sides of the plate, he tended to drive the ball a bit more when batting right-handed. However, he proved to be somewhat more consistent through the years as a left-handed hitter, often punching outside pitches to left field and dragging bunts to the right side of the diamond for base hits. Meanwhile, no one else in the league played the game with more abandon, as sportswriter Bob Broeg noted when he wrote, "Frisch was tremendous; a whirling dervish on the diamond, knocking down hot smashes with his chest, diving for others that seemed out of reach, ranging far and wide for pop flies, pawing at the dirt to get a long lead, and then stealing bases."

Sportswriter Damon Runyon also praised Frisch for his fielding ability, saying, "His range was such that he played second base, some of center field, and a slice of right field too."

Frisch's spirited play helped lead the Giants to their third straight pennant in 1923 when, after being inserted at second base full-time, he topped the circuit with 223 hits and 311 total bases, and also finished among the leaders with 111 runs batted in, 116 runs scored, a .348 batting average, 29 stolen bases, and a career-high 12 home runs. Frisch had another big year in 1924, when he earned a third-place finish in the N.L. MVP voting by batting .328, amassing 15 triples, stealing 22 bases, and leading the league with 121 runs scored.

Although Frisch continued to play well in each of the next two seasons, posting batting averages of .331 and .314, his relationship with McGraw gradually deteriorated as the team's failures caused the Giants manager to take out many of his frustrations on his captain. Becoming more and more irritable, McGraw singled out Frisch on numerous occasions and verbally abused him in the clubhouse after difficult losses, with words meant not so much for him as for other members of the team. After accepting McGraw's harsh treatment for the good of the ball club, Frisch finally reached his boiling point when his manager berated him in front of the entire team for missing a sign during an

August 1926 loss. Frisch subsequently left the team, bringing to an end his previously close relationship with McGraw. Frisch finished out the year in New York but departed for St. Louis at season's end when the Giants traded him and pitcher Jimmy Ring to the Cardinals for the equally unhappy Rogers Hornsby, whose relationship with St. Louis management had soured as well. In his eight years with the Giants, Frisch hit 54 home runs, knocked in 524 runs, scored 701 times, collected 1,303 hits, including 77 triples and 180 doubles, stole 224 bases, batted .321, compiled a .367 on-base percentage, and posted a .444 slugging percentage. He continues to rank among the franchise's all-time leaders in batting average.

Upon his arrival in St. Louis in 1927, Frisch received a cool reception from Cardinals fans, who voiced their displeasure over having lost Hornsby—the league's dominant player the previous several seasons. However, employing the same aggressive style of play on which he built his reputation in New York, Frisch eventually won them over with his outstanding hitting, excellent defense, and superb base running. In one of his finest all-around seasons, Frisch began his tenure in St. Louis by stealing a league-leading 48 bases, placing among the leaders with a .337 batting average, 112 runs scored, and 208 hits, and topping all N.L. second sackers in assists, double plays, and fielding percentage, en route to earning a second-place finish in the league MVP voting.

Frisch continued to ingratiate himself to Cardinals fans in the years that followed, leading St. Louis to four pennants and two world championships between 1928 and 1934. He performed particularly well in 1930, when he batted .346, scored 121 runs, and reached career highs in RBIs (114), doubles (46), and OPS (.927). Frisch captured N.L. MVP honors the following year, when he helped lead the Cardinals to the pennant by batting .311, driving in 82 runs, scoring 96 times, and leading the league with 28 stolen bases.

Although Frisch's offensive numbers fell off somewhat in subsequent seasons, he remained the leader and driving force behind the St. Louis "Gas House Gang" squad that won the World Series in 1934. Named player-manager of the Cardinals in 1933, Frisch continued to manage the team until 1938, one year after he retired as an active player. He ended his career with 105 home runs, 1,244 runs batted in, 1,532 runs scored, 2,880 hits, 138 triples, 466 doubles, 419 stolen bases, a .316 batting average, a .369 on-base percentage, and a .432 slugging percentage. One of the most difficult men in baseball to strike out,

Frisch fanned more than 20 times in a season just twice in his career, whiffing a total of only 272 times in more than 10,000 total plate appearances.

After surrendering his managerial position with the Cardinals, Frisch did radio play-by-play for the Boston Braves in 1939, before managing the Pittsburgh Pirates from 1940 to 1946. He rejoined the Giants in 1947, the same year that the members of the BBWAA elected him to the Hall of Fame. Frisch served one year as a radio announcer for the Giants, and another as a coach, before managing the Chicago Cubs for three seasons. He resumed his announcing career with the Giants in 1952, although he entered the broadcast booth less frequently after suffering a heart attack in September of 1956. Frisch later served as chairman of the Hall of Fame Veteran's Committee, where he used his influence to get many of his former Giants and Cardinals teammates elected to Cooperstown. Among those players who Frisch argued for extensively were George Kelly, Fred Lindstrom, Jesse Haines, Dave Bancroft, Chick Hafey, Ross Youngs, and Rube Marquard—whose selections have since been questioned by many.

Frisch died in Wilmington, Delaware, on March 12, 1973, from injuries he suffered during a car accident he was involved in near Elkton, Maryland, one month earlier. The 74-year-old Frisch had been returning to his home in Rhode Island from a Veteran's Committee meeting in Florida when he lost control of his car.

Giant Career Highlights:

Best Season: Frisch had his two best seasons for the Giants in 1921 and 1923, placing among the N.L. leaders in numerous statistical categories both years. In addition to topping the Senior Circuit with a career-high 49 stolen bases in the first of those campaigns, Frisch ranked among the leaders with 100 RBIs, 121 runs scored, 211 hits, 17 triples, 31 doubles, 300 total bases, a .341 batting average, and an OPS of .870. Frisch posted extremely similar numbers in 1923, finishing the year with 12 homers, 111 RBIs, 116 runs scored, 10 triples, 32 doubles, 29 stolen bases, a .348 batting average, an OPS of .880, and a league-leading 223 hits and 311 total bases. It's an extremely close call, but we'll opt for 1923 since Frisch established career-high marks in four different offensive categories (home runs, hits, total bases, and batting average) that year. Furthermore, he performed better in the field than he did two years earlier, compiling many more assists (493 to 418) and committing far fewer errors (22 to 33).

Memorable Moments/Greatest Performances: Frisch recorded his first major-league home run against one of baseball's greatest pitchers, connecting for a three-run blast against Chicago's Grover Cleveland Alexander during a 7–3 Giants victory over the Cubs on September 11, 1919.

Frisch turned in a tremendous offensive performance against Philadelphia in the second game of the Giants' doubleheader sweep of the Phillies on June 25, 1921, leading his team to a 17–4 win by homering, collecting 4 hits, driving in 2 runs, scoring 4 times, and stealing 3 bases.

Frisch had another big day at the plate on September 10, 1924, when he led the Giants to a 22–1 mauling of the Braves in the first game of their doubleheader sweep of Boston by going 6-for-7, with a homer, 4 RBIs, 3 runs scored, and a stolen base.

Frisch had his only 5-for-5 day as a member of the Giants on June 24, 1926, leading his team to a 12–7 victory over Philadelphia by collecting 5 hits, driving in a run, and scoring 4 times.

Frisch delivered one of his most memorable hits for the Giants on September 17, 1926, when he gave them a 5–4 victory over the Reds with a walk-off homer in the bottom of the 10th inning.

An outstanding World Series performer during his time in New York, Frisch never hit below .300 in any of the four Fall Classics in which he competed as a member of the Giants.

Particularly effective in the 1922 and 1923 Series, Frisch helped lead the Giants to victory over the Yankees in the first of those Fall Classics by collecting 8 hits in 17 official trips to the plate, for a batting average of .471. Although the Giants lost to the Yankees in the World Series the following year, Frisch again performed exceptionally well, collecting 10 hits in 25 at-bats, for a batting average of .400.

Notable Achievements:

Batted over .300 six times, surpassing the .330-mark on three occasions.

Scored more than 100 runs four times, topping 120 runs scored twice.

Knocked in more than 100 runs twice.

Surpassed 200 hits twice.

Finished in double-digits in triples five times.

Topped 30 doubles three times.

Stole more than 20 bases seven times, surpassing 30 steals three times and 40 thefts once (49 in 1921).

Led N.L. in: hits once; runs scored once; stolen bases once; and total bases once.

Led N.L. second basemen in putouts once and fielding percentage once.

Ranks among Giants career leaders in batting average (tied-5th).

Finished third in 1924 N.L. MVP voting.

Number 88 on *The Sporting News'* 1999 list of Baseball's 100 Greatest Players.

Four-time N.L. champion (1921, 1922, 1923 & 1924).

Two-time world champion (1921 & 1922).

Elected to Baseball Hall of Fame by members of BBWAA in 1947.

11 JEFF KENT

Jeff Kent knocked in more than 100 runs six straight times for the Giants. *(Courtesy of Jude Seymour)*

One of the greatest hitting second basemen in National League history, Jeff Kent spent virtually his entire career playing in the Senior Circuit, with most of his finest seasons coming as a member of the San Francisco Giants. En route to amassing more home runs than any other second sacker in MLB history, Kent hit 175 round-trippers in his six years with the Giants. He also averaged 115 RBIs per season and batted over .300 twice during his time in San Francisco, earning in the process three Silver Sluggers, three All-Star selections, four top-10 finishes in the N.L. MVP voting, and one MVP trophy. Meanwhile, although initially considered to be something of a liability in the field, Kent gradually developed into a solid defensive player, leading all players at his position in assists and double plays once each. Unfortunately, Kent acquired a reputation over the course of his career for having a bad attitude—something that has detracted somewhat from his overall accomplishments. However, it could be argued that, as a fierce competitor with a burning desire to win, Kent has been misrepresented and misunderstood through the years, as he himself suggested when he said, "If you want to get to know me, you have to get off the baseball field. Because when I'm on the field, and in the clubhouse, I'm doing what I'm paid to do, what I love to do, and man, I hate it when I fail."

Born in Bellflower, California, on March 7, 1968, Jeffrey Franklin Kent grew up in Huntington Beach, a laid-back suburb of Los Angeles, where he attended Edison High School. Starring in baseball at the University of California, Berkeley, following his graduation from Edison High, Kent began his professional career in the Toronto organization after the Blue Jays selected him in the 20th round of the 1989 amateur draft. He spent the next three years in the minor leagues, gradually transitioning from shortstop to second base during that time, before earning a spot on the Blue Jays roster at the start of the 1992 campaign. Spending most of his time in Toronto filling in for injured third baseman Kelly Gruber, Kent appeared in a total of 65 games for the Blue Jays, hitting 8 homers, driving in 35 runs, and batting .240, before being traded to the New York Mets for pitcher David Cone on August 27, 1992.

Kent spent the next three-plus years serving as the Mets' regular second baseman, establishing himself during that time as one of the National League's better hitters at the position. He played his best ball for New York in 1994, concluding the strike-shortened campaign with 14 homers, 68 RBIs, and a .292 batting average. However, while with the Mets, Kent also developed a reputation as a below-average fielder, leading all N.L. second sackers in errors twice, while failing to display anything more than average range. Furthermore, he became known in the clubhouse for his quick temper and sour disposition, which he defended years later by saying, "Winning is the only thing that makes me happy. Ask my wife. I don't get happy about anniversaries or birthdays. I don't care about that . . . just winning."

Seeking to improve themselves on the field and in the clubhouse, the Mets dealt Kent and fellow infielder José Vizcaíno to the Cleveland Indians for shortstop Álvaro Espinoza and second baseman Carlos Baerga just prior to the July 1996 trade deadline. Kent's stay in Cleveland proved to be short-lived, though, since the Indians included him in a seven-player trade they completed with the Giants at season's end that netted them, among others, slugging third baseman Matt Williams.

Although the local newspapers initially criticized new Giants general manager Brian Sabean for dealing away the popular Williams, the success that Kent subsequently experienced in San Francisco ended up justifying the trade. Inserted into the cleanup spot in the Giants batting order, immediately behind Barry Bonds, Kent soon developed into one of the National League's most productive hitters, concluding the 1997 campaign with 29 home runs, 121 RBIs, 90 runs scored, and a .250 batting average. He followed that up with an even stronger 1998 season in which he hit 31 homers, knocked in 128 runs, scored 94 times, and batted .297. Kent then earned the first of his three straight All-Star selections by hitting 23 home runs, driving in 101 runs, scoring 86 times, and batting .290 in 1999.

As Kent continued his ascension into stardom, he slowly developed into one of the Giants' team leaders, even winning the 1998 Willie Mac Award for his spirit and leadership. In fact, many members of the media came to feel that his voice was the most important in the Giants clubhouse. An extremely intense and driven individual, Kent revealed his inner thinking on one occasion when he stated, "On the diamond, I'm driven by the fear and embarrassment of failure. I'm terrified I'll let my teammates down."

Kent added, "Some guys play not to get hurt, and they're never really as good as they can be. That's not the way I play."

Although Kent lacked outstanding foot speed and possessed somewhat limited range in the field, he also began to gradually shed his reputation as a below-average defender, committing a total of only 33 errors from 1999 to 2001, after leading all N.L. second basemen with 20 miscues in 1998. He also did an excellent job of turning two, leading all players at his position with 113 double plays in 2002, one year after he topped all N.L. second sackers with 390 assists.

After spending his first three years in San Francisco playing second fiddle to Barry Bonds, Kent raised himself to the same lofty level as his teammate in 2000, capturing N.L. MVP honors by hitting 33 homers, driving in 125 runs, scoring 114 times, batting .334, compiling a .424 on-base percentage, and posting a .596 slugging percentage. He followed that up with two more exceptional years, hitting 22 home runs, knocking in 106 runs, batting .298, and amassing a franchise-record 49 doubles in 2001, before hitting 37 homers, driving in 108 runs, scoring 102 times, collecting 195 hits, and batting .313 in 2002.

Yet, in spite of the outstanding offensive numbers Kent compiled for the Giants year after year, his relationship with the team deteriorated over time, reaching its nadir during spring training of 2002, when he proved to be less than honest about how he broke his left wrist. After Kent initially claimed that he injured himself during a fall while washing his pickup truck, it later surfaced that he crashed his motorcycle while performing wheelies and other stunts, in direct violation of his contract. Although Kent healed in time for the start of the regular season, the episode lent more credence to his image around baseball as a selfish player.

Kent also periodically feuded with Barry Bonds, with the most notable incident taking place in the Giants dugout during a 2002 game, when the two stars engaged in a shoving match. In describing the relationship he shared with his enigmatic teammate, Kent told *Sports Illustrated* in 2002, "On the field, we're fine, but, off the field, I don't care about Barry, and Barry doesn't care about me—or anybody."

Weary of the inner turmoil and constant bickering, Kent elected to sign a two-year, $19.9 million contract with the Houston Astros when he became a free agent at the conclusion of the 2002 campaign. Although Kent cited at the time his desire to be closer to his family's ranch in Texas, he later shed more light on his decision to leave San Francisco when he explained, "During the (2002) World Series, we were hugging . . . it was great. Then Dusty (Baker) was the first to leave, and it just wasn't the same. He was the ringleader of how we performed on the field, and, when he left, it opened up a wound or gap and it probably was the biggest determining factor why I didn't come back."

Still, Kent looks back fondly at the time he spent with the Giants, stating, "I've had my best years in San Francisco. I've had the most fun throughout my career in San Francisco. There's no doubt all my accomplishments, my passion, and my heart were left in San Francisco."

Kent continued his outstanding offensive production in Houston, totaling 49 home runs and 200 RBIs over the course of the next two seasons, while posting batting averages of .297 and .289. While playing for the Astros, Kent hit his 288th home-run as a second baseman, surpassing Ryne Sandberg as the all-time home-run leader at that position.

After becoming a free agent again at the end of 2004, Kent signed a four-year deal with the Los Angeles Dodgers, with whom he spent the remainder of his career. Kent had his best season for the Dodgers in 2005, when he hit 29 homers, drove in 105 runs, scored 100 times, and batted .289. His production gradually fell off to 12 homers, 59 RBIs, and 42 runs scored in the final year of the contract, though, prompting him to announce his retirement at the conclusion of the 2008 campaign. Kent ended his career with 377 home runs, 1,518 RBIs, 1,320 runs scored, 2,461 hits, 47 triples, 560 doubles, a .290 batting average, a .356 on-base percentage, and a .500 slugging percentage. In addition to hitting 175 home runs in his six years with the Giants, Kent drove in 689 runs, scored 570 times, amassed 1,021 hits, 22 triples, and 247 doubles, batted .297, compiled a .368 on-base percentage, and posted a .535 slugging percentage. He continues to rank among the franchise's all-time leaders in home runs, slugging percentage, and OPS (.903).

After leaving the game, Kent retired to his home near Austin, Texas, and continued to manage his 4,000-acre "Diamond K" cattle ranch near Tilden, Texas. He also owns Kent Powersports, a chain of motorcycle and ATV dealerships. Kent later had a reconciliation of sorts with the Giants front office, serving the team since 2011 as a spring training instructor.

Giant Career Highlights:

Best Season: Although Kent also posted big numbers for the Giants in 1998 and 2002, he had his finest all-around season in 2000. Finishing among the N.L. leaders in 10 different offensive categories, Kent earned league MVP honors by hitting 33 homers, knocking in 125 runs, collecting 7 triples and 41 doubles, and establishing career highs with 114 runs scored, 196 hits, 350 total bases, a .334 batting average, a .424 on-base percentage, a .596 slugging percentage, and an OPS of 1.021.

Memorable Moments/Greatest Performances: Kent got off to a great start with the Giants, collecting 5 hits, including a homer and double, driving in 4 runs, and scoring twice during a 9–4, 13-inning win over the Astros on Opening Day of 1998.

Later that same year, on July 24, 1998, Kent drove in a career-high 7 runs with a pair of homers, in leading the Giants to a lopsided 12–2 victory over the Cincinnati Reds.

Although the Giants lost their May 3, 1999, matchup with Pittsburgh by a score of 9–8, Kent had a tremendous day at the plate, going 5-for-5, hitting for the cycle, and knocking in 5 runs. He had the only other 5-for-5 day of his career a few weeks later, leading the Giants to a 15–11 win over Seattle on June 12 by homering once, collecting 2 doubles and 2 singles, driving in 4 runs, and scoring 3 times.

Kent had another huge game four days later, getting 3 hits, including a pair of homers, knocking in 6 runs, and scoring 4 times during a 15–2 pounding of Colorado.

Kent helped pace the Giants to a lopsided 18–2 victory over Oakland on June 4, 2000, by hitting 2 homers and 2 doubles, driving in 5 runs, and scoring 3 times.

Some two months later, on August 3, he homered once, doubled twice, and knocked in 6 runs during a 10–2 win over the Pirates.

Kent drove in 5 runs with a pair of homers, in leading the Giants to an 11–6 win over San Diego on April 10, 2001. He led the Giants to another 11–6 victory over the Padres on June 27, 2002, by going 3-for-5, with 6 RBIs. Kent equaled his career high of 7 RBIs on May 1, 2001, homering once and doubling twice during another 11–6 win, this time over the Pirates.

In one of his final games as a member of the team, Kent helped the Giants rout the Angels by a score of 16–4 in Game 5 of the 2002 World Series by going 3-for-5, with 2 home runs, a double, 4 RBIs, and 4 runs scored.

Notable Achievements:

Hit more than 20 home runs six times, surpassing 30 homers on three occasions.

Knocked in more than 100 runs six times, topping 120 RBIs on three occasions.

Scored more than 100 runs twice.

Batted over .300 twice.

Surpassed 30 doubles six times, topping 40 two-baggers on four occasions.

Compiled on-base percentage in excess of .400 once (.424 in 2000).

Posted slugging percentage in excess of .500 five times.

Compiled OPS in excess of 1.000 once (1.021 in 2000).

Led N.L. in sacrifice flies twice.

Led N.L. second basemen in assists once and double plays turned once.

Ranks among Giants career leaders in: home runs (10th); slugging percentage (tied-5th); and OPS (5th).

Holds Giants single-season record for most doubles (49 in 2001).

Holds MLB record for most home runs by a second baseman (351).

Only second baseman in major-league history to knock in more than 100 runs six straight seasons (1997–2002).

2000 N.L. MVP.

Three-time N.L. Player of the Month.

Three-time Silver Slugger winner (2000, 2001 & 2002).

Two-time *Sporting News* All-Star selection (2000 & 2002).

Three-time N.L. All-Star (1999, 2000 & 2001).

2002 N.L. champion.

12 JOE MCGINNITY

"Iron Man" Joe McGinnity set 20th-century single-season N.L. records in 1903 when he threw 48 complete games and 434 innings for the Giants. *(Courtesy of George Eastman House Collection)*

Although Joe McGinnity didn't make his first start in the major leagues until after he celebrated his 28th birthday, he eventually earned a place in the Baseball Hall of Fame by posting a total of 246 victories over the course of his big-league career, which lasted only 10 seasons. Leading all National League pitchers in wins five times between 1899 and 1908, McGinnity won more than 20 games in each of his first eight seasons, surpassing 30 victories on two separate occasions. In his seven years with the Giants alone, McGinnity won a total of 151 games, topping the Senior Circuit in wins three times, while also leading the league in innings pitched twice, saves three times, and winning percentage, ERA, complete games, shutouts, and WHIP one time each. Living up to his "Iron Man" nickname that he acquired due to his offseason work in his wife's family business, an iron foundry in McAlester, Oklahoma, McGinnity proved to be one of baseball's most durable pitchers, averaging 344 ⅓ innings a season over the course of his career, including a 20th-century National League record 434 innings and 44 complete games for the Giants in 1903. And, even after his career in the major leagues ended, McGinnity went on to pitch another 17 years of minor-league ball, amassing in the process another 199 victories that gave him a total of 486 victories as a professional that places him second only to the legendary Cy Young in baseball annals.

Born to Irish immigrants in Cornwall, Illinois, on March 20, 1871, Joseph Jerome McGinnity received little in the way of a formal education, spending most of his youth working in the coal mines of Illinois with his older brothers to help support his family following the death of his father in 1879. McGinnity began playing baseball with other local miners after his family moved to Decatur, Illinois, eventually performing for several local semipro teams, before beginning his professional career with the Montgomery Colts of the Class-B Southern League in 1893 after traveling west with his family to Oklahoma.

Experiencing very little success over the course of his first two minor-league seasons, McGinnity returned to Illinois, where he opened a saloon and developed a reputation as a tough character, serving as his own bouncer when the need arose. At the same time, though, McGinnity continued to pursue his dream of playing in the major leagues, spending the next three years pitching semipro ball, where he discovered "Old Sal," a sharp-breaking underhand curve that changed his career.

Armed with his new weapon, which he added to his repertoire of other pitches, McGinnity returned to professional baseball, spending 1898 with Peoria of the Western Association, before making his National League debut with the Baltimore Orioles the following year. The 28-year-old right-hander had an exceptional rookie season for the Orioles, compiling a record of 28–16, en route to leading all N.L. hurlers in wins for the first of five times. He also placed among the league leaders with a 2.68 ERA, 4 shutouts, 38 complete games, and 366 ⅓ innings pitched.

With the National League consolidating from 12 teams to eight in 1900, McGinnity joined several of his former Oriole teammates in moving to Brooklyn, where he continued his winning ways as a member of the Superbas. In addition to posting a record of 28–8 that made him the league's top winner for the second consecutive season, McGinnity led the N.L. with a .778 winning percentage and 343 innings pitched, while also placing among the leaders with a 2.94 ERA and 32 complete games.

Despite being offered nearly twice as much to remain in Brooklyn at season's end, McGinnity elected to jump to the rival American League, where he rejoined former Baltimore manager and teammate John McGaw on a newly formed version of the Orioles. Pitching for a mediocre Baltimore ball club in 1901, McGinnity compiled a record of 26–20, along with a league-leading 39 complete games and 382 innings pitched.

The 1901 campaign proved to be McGinnity's only full season in the American League. After posting a record of 13–10 over the first 3 ½ months of the ensuing campaign, McGinnity followed McGraw to New York when the latter accepted the position of player-manager for the Giants in mid-July. McGinnity went 8–8 for the Giants the rest of the way, giving him a composite record of 21–18 for the year.

McGinnity ended up having some of his finest seasons for the Giants, concluding his first full season in New York with an ERA of 2.43 and a league-leading 31 wins. He also topped the circuit with 44 complete games and 434 innings pitched, amassing in the process the highest single-season total compiled in each category by any National League pitcher since the beginning of the 20th century. McGinnity followed that up in 1904 by leading all N.L. hurlers with a record of 35–8, an ERA of 1.61, 408 innings pitched, 9 shutouts, and 5 saves, in helping the Giants win the pennant for the first of two straight times. After a slightly subpar 1905 season in which he won "only" 21 games, posted an ERA of 2.87, and threw "just" 320 ⅓ innings, the 35-year-old McGinnity returned to top form the following year, going 27–12, with a 2.25 ERA, 32 complete games, and 339 ⅔ innings pitched.

Although he spent much of his time in New York being overshadowed by the great Christy Mathewson, McGinnity proved to be equally durable during their time together, throwing more complete games and tossing more innings in three of their six full seasons as teammates. Called by John McGraw "the hardest working pitcher I ever had on my ball club," the stocky 5'11" McGinnity, who typically tipped the scales at far more than the 206 pounds he is listed at in the record books, frequently started both ends of doubleheaders. Crediting his amazing durability to a delivery that saw him alternate between overhand, sidearm, and his mesmerizing underhand curve he called "Old Sal," McGinnity revealed during the latter stages of his career, "I've pitched for 30 years and I believe I've averaged over 30 games a season, and, in all my experiences, I've never had what I could truthfully call a sore arm."

In discussing the craftiness McGinnity displayed on the mound, legendary Philadelphia Athletics manager Connie Mack stated, "It was difficult for a batter to get his measure. Sometimes his fingers would almost scrape the ground as he hurled the ball. He knew all the tricks for putting a batter on the spot."

Meanwhile, Hall of Fame shortstop Hughie Jennings discussed the manner in which McGinnity revolutionized the art of fielding the pitcher's position by attempting to make force outs at any base, rather than just throwing the ball to first: "I have never seen a pitcher with more confidence in himself than McGinnity had. He was so cocksure of his fielding ability that he would take any sort of chance, throwing to any base under any circumstance, and this fielding ability lifted him out of many tight spots."

A hard-nosed player as well, McGinnity brought his "bouncer's" mentality with him to the playing field, hitting a then major-league record 179 batters over the course of his career. Confrontational and quick to anger, McGinnity allowed his temper to get the better of him more than once, with the most notable instance taking place during a 1906 contest against the Pittsburgh Pirates.

After exchanging verbal insults with Pittsburgh catcher Heinie Peitz throughout much of the game, McGinnity reached his breaking point, giving chase to Peitz, throwing him to the ground, and belaboring him with a series of punches. National League president Harry Pulliam subsequently fined McGinnity and suspended him for 10 days, for what he called "attempting to make the ball park a slaughterhouse."

The 1906 campaign proved to be McGinnity's last big year. After going just 18–18 with a 3.16 ERA in 1907, McGinnity spent the first several weeks of the ensuing campaign suffering from a severe fever that prevented him from taking his regular turn in the rotation. Although McGinnity pitched relatively well upon his return to the team, finishing the year with a record of 11–7, an ERA of 2.27, 5 shutouts, and a league-leading 5 saves, Giants owner John Brush spent most of the season trying to rid himself of his contract. Having failed in his attempts to trade McGinnity to another team, Brush released the 38-year-old right-hander on February 27, 1909, bringing to an end his major-league career. Over the course of 10 big-league seasons, McGinnity compiled a record of 246–142, for an outstanding .634 winning percentage. He also posted an ERA of 2.66, tossed 32 shutouts, struck out 1,068 batters in 3,441 ⅓ innings of work, completed 314 of his 381 starts, and compiled a WHIP of 1.188. In his 6 ½ years with the Giants, McGinnity went 151–88, with a 2.38 ERA, 26 shutouts, 787 strikeouts in 2,151 ⅓ innings, 186 complete games, and a WHIP of 1.116.

Following his release by the Giants, McGinnity entered a whole new phase of his career, spending the next 17 seasons serving as part-owner and player-manager of minor-league teams situated in Newark, Tacoma, Butte, and Dubuque. During that time, the ageless right-hander posted another 199 victories, bringing his total number of wins as a professional to 486. McGinnity pitched his last game in organized ball in 1925, at the ripe old age of 54, before joining old friend and teammate Wilbert Robinson as a coach with the Brooklyn Dodgers the following year. While working with the Williams College baseball team some three years later, McGinnity became ill, forcing him to return to Brooklyn where his daughter lived. After subsequently having surgery to remove tumors from his bladder, McGinnity was quoted as saying, "It's the ninth inning, and I guess they're going to get me out." He died at the home of his daughter shortly thereafter, on November 14, 1929, at the age of 58. The members of the Old Timers Committee elected him to the Baseball Hall of Fame 17 years later, in 1946.

Giant Career Highlights:

Best Season: McGinnity had a tremendous year for the Giants in 1903, compiling a record of 31–20, along with a 2.43 ERA and a 20th-century N.L. record 44 complete games and 434 innings pitched. Amazingly, McGinnity tossed over 100 innings in the month of August alone. However, he pitched even better the following year, when he led N.L. hurlers in seven different categories. In addition to topping the circuit with 35 victories, McGinnity finished first in winning percentage (.814), ERA (1.61), innings pitched (408), shutouts (9), saves (5), and WHIP (0.963), establishing career-best marks in each category, with the exception of innings pitched. He also completed 38 of his 44 starts.

Memorable Moments/Greatest Performances: McGinnity made his first win of the 1903 season a memorable one, allowing just one hit during a 6–1 victory over Brooklyn on April 19. Later that year, McGinnity had a remarkable month of August, starting and winning both games of a doubleheader on three separate occasions. After recording 4–1 and 5–2 victories over Boston on August 1, allowing just 6 hits in each game in the process, McGinnity posted another pair of wins seven days later, defeating Brooklyn by scores of 6–1 and 4–3. He closed out the month by beating Philadelphia twice on August 31, needing only 3 hours and 3 minutes to defeat the Phillies by scores of 4–1 and 9–2. Following the conclusion of Game 2, *The New York Times* reported, "He seemed fresh enough to tackle the visitors for a third contest if that were necessary."

McGinnity experienced the finest stretch of his career in 1904, winning 14 consecutive games before finally losing to the Chicago Cubs on June 11. His streak ended when he surrendered a run-scoring single to Chicago's Johnny Evers with two men out in the top of the 12th inning, giving the Cubs a 1–0 win over the Giants.

McGinnity also pitched extremely well against Philadelphia in the 1905 World Series, allowing just 3 unearned runs and 6 hits during a 3–0 loss to Chief Bender in Game 2, before returning to the mound three days later to record a 1–0, 5-hit victory over the A's and their Hall of Fame left-hander Eddie Plank.

Notable Achievements:

Won more than 20 games four times, surpassing 30 victories on two occasions.

Compiled ERA below 2.50 five times, finishing with mark under 2.00 once (1.61 in 1904).

Posted winning percentage in excess of .800 once (.814 in 1904).

Threw more than 300 innings five times, tossing more than 400 innings twice.

Completed more than 20 games five times, completing more than 30 of his starts three times, and tossing more than 40 complete games once (44 in 1903).

Compiled WHIP under 1.000 once (0.963 in 1904).

Led N.L. pitchers in: wins three times; winning percentage once; ERA once; complete games once; innings pitched twice; shutouts once; WHIP once; saves three times; games started once; assists once; and putouts once.

Ranks among Giants career leaders in: wins (9th); ERA (3rd); shutouts (tied-8th); complete games (7th); innings pitched (10th); and WHIP (6th).

Holds 20th-century single-season N.L. records for most complete games (48) and most innings pitched (434)—both set in 1903.

Two-time N.L. champion (1904 & 1905).

1905 world champion.

Elected to Baseball Hall of Fame by members of Old Timers Committee in 1946.

13 WILL CLARK

Will Clark earned four top-five finishes in the N.L. MVP voting while playing for the Giants. *(Courtesy of George A. Kitrinos)*

An extremely intense player who excelled both at the bat and in the field, Will Clark established himself as the National League's premier first baseman during his time in San Francisco. Nicknamed "The Natural" due to his abundance of God-given talent, Clark spent less than one full season in the minor leagues before becoming the Giants' starting first sacker in 1986. The former first-round draft pick subsequently went on to earn five All-Star selections, four top-five finishes in the league MVP voting, two Silver Sluggers, and one

Gold Glove over the course of the next eight seasons, in helping the Giants capture two division titles and one league championship. Along the way, the lefty-swinging Clark batted over .300 four times and surpassed 20 homers four times, 100 RBIs three times, and 100 runs scored twice, displacing Keith Hernandez as the Senior Circuit's top player at his position in the process. Teaming up with slugging outfielder Kevin Mitchell to lead the Giants to their first pennant in 27 years in 1989, Clark proved to be the dominant figure in that year's NLCS, earning Series MVP honors by homering twice, driving in 8 runs, and batting .650 during the Giants' five-game triumph over the Chicago Cubs.

Born in New Orleans, Louisiana, on March 13, 1964, William Nuschler Clark starred in baseball at local Jesuit High School, before enrolling at Mississippi State University, where he became noted for his "sweet swing." After being selected to play in the 1984 Summer Olympics, Clark earned *Sporting News* All-America honors the following year, as well as the distinction of being named the winner of the Golden Spikes Award, presented annually to the nation's top collegiate player. Subsequently selected by the Giants with the second overall pick of the 1985 amateur draft, Clark appeared in only 65 games at Single-A Fresno, homering in his first minor-league at-bat, before joining the big club at the start of the ensuing campaign.

Opening the 1986 season as the Giants' starting first baseman, the 22-year-old Clark continued to show remarkable poise for such a young man, homering against future Hall of Fame pitcher Nolan Ryan in his first major-league at-bat. Although Clark ended up missing 47 games with an elbow injury he sustained while running the bases, he had a solid rookie year, hitting 11 home runs, driving in 41 runs, scoring 66 times, and batting .287. The 6'2", 200-pound Clark developed into a star the following season, helping the Giants capture the N.L. West title by hitting a career-high 35 homers, knocking in 91 runs, scoring 89 times, batting .308, and finishing among the league leaders with a .580 slugging percentage and a .951 OPS. His outstanding performance earned him a fifth-place finish in the league MVP voting.

Although the Giants failed to repeat as division champions in 1988, Clark again finished fifth in the MVP balloting and earned the first of five straight All-Star selections by batting .282, placing near the top of the league rankings with 29 home runs, 102 runs scored, a .386 on-base percentage, and a .508 slugging percentage, and topping the circuit with 109 RBIs and 100 bases on balls. Clark followed that up by posting even better numbers in 1989, helping the Giants advance to the postseason and earning a second-place finish in the MVP voting by hitting 23 homers, driving in 111 runs, compiling an OPS of .953, leading the league with 104 runs scored, and finishing second in the batting race to Tony Gwynn, with a mark of .333. Even though the Giants ended up losing the World Series to the Oakland A's in four straight games, Clark's performance against Chicago in the NLCS remains one of the most memorable in Giants playoff history.

Subsequently ranked as the best clutch performer in all of baseball by a 1990 poll of 65 major league players, Clark earned that honor even though he rubbed many of his peers the wrong way with his cocky and arrogant demeanor. Nicknaming himself "Will the Thrill," Clark possessed a tremendous amount of self-confidence, which many others construed as conceit. Clark also developed a reputation as one of the game's fiercest competitors, gaining particular notoriety for his practice of glaring fiercely at the pitcher as he stood in the batter's box. In attempting to explain his angry expression, Clark stated on one occasion, "The big thing people say to me is, 'Why don't you ever smile!' Well, I'm too interested in trying to beat somebody right now to smile."

Meanwhile, in discussing his approach to hitting, Clark revealed, "I never go up to the plate without a plan. The plan, however, depends on what you've seen from the pitcher, what his tendencies are, how you're feeling that day, what the game situation is, and what he's most likely to throw at that point in time."

Clark continued his string of five consecutive All-Star selections in 1990 and 1991, hitting 19 homers, driving in 95 runs, scoring 91 times, and batting .295 in the first of those campaigns, before hitting 29 home runs, knocking in a career-high 116 runs, batting .301, and leading the league with 303 total bases and a .536 slugging percentage the following year. Despite missing almost 20 games due to injury in 1992, Clark earned his final All-Star nomination as a member of the Giants by hitting 16 homers, driving in 73 runs, batting .300, and finishing second in the league with 40 doubles.

After injuries again forced Clark to miss a significant amount of playing time in 1993, the Giants refused to offer him a long-term contract when he became a free agent at season's end, enabling the Texas Rangers to swoop in and sign him to a five-year, $30 million deal. Clark left San Francisco with career totals of 176 home runs, 709 RBIs, 687 runs scored, 1,278 hits, 37 triples, and 249 doubles, a .299 batting average, a .373 on-base percentage, and a .499 slugging percentage. He continues to rank among the franchise's all-time leaders in home runs (9th) and slugging percentage (10th).

Replacing former Mississippi State teammate Rafael Palmeiro as the starting first baseman in Texas, Clark went on to have five very productive, albeit injury-plagued, seasons for the Rangers, batting over .300 four times, compiling an on-base percentage in excess of .400 twice, posting a slugging percentage in excess of .500 twice, and earning the last of his six All-Star selections. Performing particularly well in 1998, Clark hit 23 homers, drove in 102 runs, scored 98 times, amassed a career-high 41 doubles, and batted .305. Impressed with Clark's intensity and on-field leadership, Texas manager Kevin Kennedy stated, "He's got the will to win, and knows what is involved in getting it done; not just some days—every day. It's the kind of intensity that this organization needed."

Nevertheless, the Rangers elected to re-sign Palmeiro prior to the start of the 1999 campaign, prompting Clark to ink a two-year deal with the Baltimore Orioles. After spending the better part of two injury-marred seasons in Baltimore, Clark returned to the National League when St. Louis acquired him just prior to the 2000 trade deadline. The 36-year-old first baseman played well for the Cardinals down the stretch, hitting 12 homers, driving in 42 runs, and batting .345 over the season's final two months, in helping them capture the N.L. Central title. However, he ultimately decided to retire less than a month after St. Louis dropped the NLCS to the New York Mets in five games. Clark ended his career with 284 home runs, 1,205 runs batted in, 1,186 runs scored, 2,176 hits, 47 triples, 440 doubles, a .303 batting average, a .384 on-base percentage, and a .497 slugging percentage.

Following his playing career, Clark spent five seasons serving as an advisor for the Arizona Diamondbacks, before returning to San Francisco, where he currently works in the Giants front office.

Giant Career Highlights:

Best Season: Clark had his first big year for the Giants in 1987, when he batted .308, knocked in 91 runs, and hit a career-high 35 homers. He also performed extremely well in 1988 and 1991, hitting 29 home runs, scoring 102 times, batting .282, and leading the league with 109 RBIs and 100 bases on balls in the first of those campaigns, before hitting another 29 homers, driving in a career-high 116 runs, batting .301, and topping the circuit with 303 total bases and a .536 slugging percentage in 1991. However, Clark had his finest all-around season in 1989, when, in addition to hitting 23 home runs, he placed in the league's top five in 10 different offensive categories, including RBIs (111), runs scored (104), hits (196), batting average (.333), and OPS (.953), establishing career-high marks in each of the last four categories. Clark's exceptional performance earned him his first Silver Slugger and a runner-up finish to teammate Kevin Mitchell in the N.L. MVP balloting.

Memorable Moments/Greatest Performances: Clark began his major-league career in grand fashion, hitting a home run off Nolan Ryan in his first big-league at-bat during an 8–3 Giants win over Houston on April 8, 1986.

Although the Giants lost their home opener to the Astros by the same score one week later, Clark quickly ingratiated himself to the fans at Candlestick Park by once again homering in his first at-bat, en route to collecting 3 hits and driving in 2 runs.

Clark had the only 5-for-5 day of his career on April 23, 1989, when he homered, doubled, collected 3 singles, knocked in 3 runs, and scored 3 times during a 7–6 loss to the Dodgers.

On June 8, 1990, Clark helped lead the Giants to a 23–8 pasting of the Atlanta Braves by driving in 6 runs, with a double and 2 homers.

Clark proved to be a one-man wrecking crew on June 22, 1988, knocking in 7 of the Giants' 8 runs during an 8–7 victory over the San Diego Padres. Clark finished the day with 4 hits, including a homer and 2 doubles, with his bases-loaded two-bagger in the bottom of the 9th inning driving in the game's final 3 runs.

Clark had a similarly productive afternoon against Philadelphia on July 14, 1991, when he went 5-for-6, with a homer, double, 7 RBIs, and 3 runs scored, in leading the Giants to a lopsided 17–5 victory over the Phillies.

Clark had another big day at the plate on April 9, 1992, when he went 4-for-4, with a homer, double, 4 RBIs, and 3 runs scored, during an 11–4 win over the Braves in Atlanta.

Still, Clark will always be remembered most fondly by Giants fans for his performance in the 1989 NLCS. En route to leading the Giants to a four-games-to-one victory over the Cubs, Clark went 4-for-4 in Game 1, with 2 home runs, a double, 6 RBIs, and 4 runs scored. He again came up big in Game 5, collecting 3 hits and delivering a 2-out, bases-loaded single off hard-throwing southpaw Mitch Williams in the bottom of the 8th inning that broke a 1–1 tie in a contest the Giants ended up winning by a score of 3–2. Clark earned Series MVP honors by batting .650, with 2 homers, 8 RBIs, and 8 runs scored.

Notable Achievements:

Hit more than 20 home runs four times, topping 30 homers once (35 in 1987).

Knocked in more than 100 runs three times.

Scored more than 100 runs twice.

Batted over .300 four times.

Surpassed 30 doubles four times, topping 40 two-baggers once (40 in 1992).

Walked 100 times in 1988.

Compiled on-base percentage in excess of .400 once (.407 in 1989).

Posted slugging percentage in excess of .500 four times.

Led N.L. in: RBIs once; runs scored once; bases on balls once; total bases once; and slugging percentage once.

Led N.L. first basemen in: putouts three times; double plays five times; and fielding percentage once.

Ranks among Giants career leaders in: home runs (9th); extra-base hits (9th); and slugging percentage (10th).

Finished in top five of N.L. MVP voting four times, placing second in 1989.

1989 NLCS MVP.

Four-time N.L. Player of the Month.

Two-time Silver Slugger winner (1989 & 1991).

1991 Gold Glove winner.

Three-time *Sporting News* All-Star selection (1988, 1989 & 1991).

Five-time N.L. All-Star (1988, 1989, 1990, 1991 & 1992).

1989 N.L. champion.

14 ROSS YOUNGS

Ross Youngs ranks fourth in Giants history with a lifetime batting average of .322. *(Courtesy of Library of Congress)*

His career tragically cut short by an illness that ended up taking his life, Ross Youngs nevertheless accomplished enough in his 10 years with the Giants to eventually gain induction into the Baseball Hall of Fame. A hustling, hard-nosed player who epitomized manager John McGraw's aggressive style of play, Youngs compiled a lifetime batting average of .322 for the Giants, surpassing the .300-mark in nine of his 10 seasons with the club. Youngs also knocked in more than 100 runs once, scored more than 100 runs three times, amassed more than 200 hits twice, stole more than 20 bases three times, and finished in double-digits in triples on five separate occasions. Equally known for his outstanding defense, Youngs drew praise from McGraw, who called him "the greatest outfielder I ever saw." In addition to leading all N.L. right-fielders in assists five times, he finished first among players at his position in putouts twice and double plays three times. Youngs' exceptional all-around play helped lead the Giants to four straight pennants and two world championships, from 1921 to 1924.

Born in Shiner, Texas, on April 10, 1897, Royce Middlebrook Youngs generally went by the name "Ross," although he eventually acquired the nickname "Pep" as well. After moving with his family to San Antonio as a youngster, Youngs developed a reputation as an outstanding athlete, starring in both football and baseball while attending West Texas Military Academy. Having spurned numerous scholarship offers to play football in college, Youngs instead elected to sign with the Austin Senators of the Texas League in 1914. Released by the Senators after appearing in only 17 games, Youngs spent the ensuing campaign playing in two different leagues, both of which disbanded during the season. Finally finding a semblance of stability after joining the Sherman Lions of the Class-D Western Association in 1916, Youngs posted a batting average of .362, drawing the attention of the New York Giants, who purchased his contract in August for $2,000. The Giants subsequently assigned Youngs to the Rochester Hustlers of the International League, whose manager, Mickey Doolan, received the following stern warning from John McGraw: "I'm giving you one of the greatest players I've ever seen. Play him in the outfield. If anything happens to him, I'm holding you responsible."

The stocky 5'8", 170-pound Youngs, who batted left-handed and threw right-handed, lived up to McGraw's expectations, earning a late-season call-up to the Giants by batting .356 in his 140 games at Rochester. Making his major-league debut with the Giants on September 25, 1917, the 20-year-old outfielder batted .346 over the season's final week, collecting 9 hits in 26 official trips to the plate, scoring 5 runs, and earning the nickname "Pep" with his hustle.

Inserted into the Giants everyday lineup as the starting right-fielder the following year, Youngs had a solid rookie campaign. Although he hit just 1 home run and knocked in only 25 runs in 121 games, he batted .302, scored 70 runs, and collected 16 outfield assists. Youngs followed that up with a similarly productive 1919 season in which he hit 2 homers, drove in 43 runs, scored 73 times, batted .311, stole 24 bases, and led all N.L. right-fielders with 235 putouts, 23 assists, and 7 double plays.

Youngs developed into one of the league's top outfielders in 1920, hitting 6 homers, driving in 78 runs, scoring 92 times, amassing 14 triples, finishing second in the circuit with 204 hits, a .351 batting average, a .427 on-base percentage, and a .904 OPS, and once again leading all players at his position in assists (26) and double plays (7). He had another big year in 1921, scoring 90 runs and placing among the N.L. leaders with 102 RBIs, 16 triples, 21 stolen bases, a .327 batting average, and a .411 on-base percentage.

Generally hitting either fourth or fifth in John McGraw's lineup, Youngs lacked the power of a prototypical middle-of-the-order hitter. But the Giants manager typically built his team's offense around players who hit for a high batting average and ran the bases well—two areas in which Youngs excelled. In addition to consistently batting well over .300, Youngs possessed a keen batting eye, annually placing among the N.L. leaders in walks and on-base percentage. And, as for his base-running, longtime teammate Frankie Frisch commented, "He was the hardest-running, devil-may-care guy I ever saw; the best at throwing those savage cross-blocks to break up a double play."

Meanwhile, Young's defense made him one of the Senior Circuit's most respected outfielders. Blessed with a powerful throwing arm, he amassed more than 20 assists five times, leading all N.L. outfielders in that category on three separate occasions. Youngs also finished among the league's top three players at his position in putouts each year from 1918 to 1924, topping the circuit twice.

Youngs continued his ascension into stardom in 1922, batting .331, driving in 86 runs, amassing 185 hits, 10 triples, and a career-high 34 doubles, and scoring 105 runs. He batted well over .300 and scored well in excess of 100 runs in each of the next two seasons as well, concluding the 1923 campaign with a .336 batting average, 87 RBIs, 200 hits, and a league-leading 121 runs scored, before scoring 112 times, collecting 187 hits, knocking in 74 runs, and establishing career-high marks in batting average (.356) and home runs (10) the following year, en route to earning a fifth-place finish in the league MVP voting.

Beset by the early stages of a kidney disorder known at the time as Bright's disease, Youngs missed a significant amount of playing time in 1925, finishing the year with only 53 RBIs, 82 runs scored, and a career-low .264 batting average. After being diagnosed with the fatal illness the following spring, Youngs played through his discomfort while being treated by a full-time nurse the Giants hired to travel with the team. Despite missing nearly 60 games, Youngs posted respectable numbers, concluding the campaign with 43 RBIs, 62 runs scored, 21 stolen bases, and a .306 batting average. He also made significant contributions to the Giants by teaching 17-year-old rookie outfielder Mel Ott everything he knew about the game.

Too ill to play after August 10, 1926, Youngs returned home to San Antonio on McGraw's insistence. After receiving a blood transfusion in March 1927, Youngs lived another seven months, losing his battle with the disease on October 22, 1927, at only 30 years of age. Once a solid 170-pounder, Youngs weighed only 100 pounds at the time of his death.

Youngs ended his abbreviated playing career with 42 home runs, 592 runs batted in, 812 runs scored, 1,491 hits, 93 triples, 236 doubles, 153 stolen bases, a .322 batting average, a .399 on-base percentage, and a .441 slugging percentage—numbers good enough to get him elected to the Hall of Fame by the members of the Veteran's Committee in 1972.

Following Young's passing, the Giants honored him by installing a plaque at the Polo Grounds that read:

A BRAVE UNTRAMMELED SPIRIT OF THE DIAMOND, WHO BROUGHT GLORY TO HIMSELF AND HIS TEAM BY HIS STRONG, AGGRESSIVE, COURAGEOUS PLAY. HE WON THE ADMIRATION OF THE NATION'S FANS, THE LOVE AND ESTEEM OF HIS FRIENDS AND TEAMMATES, AND THE RESPECT OF HIS OPPONENTS. HE PLAYED THE GAME.

John McGraw, who kept only two framed photos in his office at the Polo Grounds, one of Christy Mathewson and one of Youngs, expressed his admiration for the latter at his funeral when he said, "He was the greatest outfielder I ever saw on a ball field. The game was never over with Youngs until the last man was out. He could do everything a ball player should do – and do it better than most players. As an outfielder he had no superiors, and he was the easiest man I ever knew to handle. In all his years with the Giants, he never caused one minute's trouble for myself or the club . . . On top of all this, a gamer ballplayer than Youngs never played ball."

Career Highlights:

Best Season: Although Youngs also played extremely well for the Giants in 1921 and 1923, he had the two best seasons of his career in 1920 and 1924. En route to earning a fifth-place finish in the N.L. MVP voting in the second of those campaigns, Youngs posted career-high marks in home runs (10), batting average (.356), and OPS (.962), while also driving in 74 runs and scoring 112 times. But 1920 proved to be his finest all-around season. In addition to finishing second in the N.L. in batting average (.351), on-base percentage (.427), OPS (.904), hits (204), and walks (75), Youngs placed in the league's top five in runs scored (92), slugging percentage (.477), and total bases (277). He also recorded a career-high 288 putouts in right field and led all N.L. outfielders with 26 assists and 7 double plays.

Memorable Moments/Greatest Performances: Youngs recorded the longest hitting streak of his career as a rookie in 1918, hitting safely in 23 straight games during the month of July.

Although the Giants lost their May 11, 1920, matchup with the Cincinnati Reds by a score of 9–4, Youngs tied a major-league record by hitting three triples during the contest.

On April 15, 1922, Youngs helped the Giants improve their early-season record to 3–1 by going 4-for-6, with 5 runs batted in, during a 17–10 rout of Brooklyn.

Exactly two weeks later, on April 29, 1922, Youngs hit for the cycle, in leading the Giants to a lopsided 15–4 victory over the Boston Braves. He finished the day 5-for-5, with 2 RBIs and 5 runs scored.

Youngs knocked in a career-high 7 runs during a 22–8 mauling of the Phillies on June 1, 1923, concluding the game with a triple, 5 hits in 6 official trips to the plate, and 3 runs scored. Youngs had another huge day on August 26, 1924, when he led the Giants to an 11–9 victory over the Cubs by going 5-for-5, with 3 RBIs and 2 runs scored.

A key contributor to the Giants' 1921 and 1922 World Series victories over the Yankees, Youngs batted .280, knocked in 4 runs, collected 7 hits, walked 7 times, and posted a .438 on-base percentage in the first of those Fall Classics. Particularly effective in the Giants' 13–5 win in Game 3, Youngs became the first player to get two hits in one inning of a Series game when he doubled, tripled, and drove in 4 runs during an 8-run outburst in the bottom of the seventh. He performed even better in the 1922 Fall Classic, driving in 2 runs, scoring twice, and collecting 6 hits in 16 official trips to the plate, for a .375 batting average.

Notable Achievements:

Batted over .300 nine times, topping the .350-mark twice.

Scored more than 100 runs three times, topping 120 runs scored once (121 in 1923).

Knocked in more than 100 runs once (102 in 1921).

Surpassed 200 hits twice.

Finished in double-digits in triples five times.

Topped 30 doubles four times.

Stole more than 20 bases three times.

Compiled on-base percentage in excess of .400 four times.

Posted slugging percentage in excess of .500 twice.

Led N.L. in runs scored once and doubles once.

Led N.L. outfielders in assists three times and double plays three times.

Led N.L. right-fielders in: assists five times; putouts twice; and double plays three times.

Ranks among Giants career leaders in: batting average (4th); on-base percentage (5th); and triples (8th).

Ranks sixth all-time among MLB right-fielders with 190 career assists.

Finished fifth in 1924 N.L. MVP voting.

Four-time N.L. champion (1921, 1922, 1923 & 1924).

Two-time world champion (1921 & 1922).

Elected to Baseball Hall of Fame by members of Veteran's Committee in 1972.

15 JOHNNY MIZE

Johnny Mize led the National League with 51 home runs, 138 RBIs, and 137 runs scored while playing for the Giants in 1947. *(Courtesy of LegendaryAuctions. com)*

Already an established star by the time he joined the Giants in 1942, Johnny Mize spent his first six years in the Major Leagues terrorizing National League pitchers as a member of the St. Louis Cardinals. Displaying a rare combination of power and discipline at the plate, Mize averaged 26 home runs, 109 RBIs, and only 47 strikeouts a year for the Cardinals, while also compiling a batting average of .336, an on-base percentage of .419, and a slugging percentage of .600, en route to earning four All-Star selections and four top-10 finishes in the N.L. MVP voting. Despite missing three peak seasons while serving in the military during World War II, the slugging first baseman continued his onslaught against N.L. hurlers in his five years with the Giants, batting over .300 three times, surpassing 40 home runs twice, 100 RBIs three times, and 100 runs scored twice, and earning five more All-Star nominations and a pair of top-five finishes in the MVP balloting. Along the way, Mize became the only player in major-league history to hit more than 50 home runs in a season while also striking out fewer than 50 times. The big first baseman's proficiency as a hitter eventually earned him a spot in Cooperstown in spite of the fact that he played regularly in the Major Leagues for only 11 full seasons.

Born in Demorest, Georgia, on January 7, 1913, John Robert Mize displayed an early affinity for tennis, later attributing his tremendous hand-eye coordination to the hours he spent as a youngster batting a tennis ball against the family barn with a broomstick. After developing a similar passion for baseball as a teenager, Mize began playing college ball while still in high school, admitting years later, "The fact is, when I was 15 and a sophomore at high school, I played on the varsity baseball team for the college. I could do this because Piedmont College didn't belong to any athletic conference and, therefore, there were no rules governing eligible players."

Although Mize signed with the St. Louis Cardinals as an amateur free agent after graduating from Piedmont Academy High School in 1930, he elected to attend Piedmont College before beginning his professional playing career. However, he first needed to have corrective surgery to repair an upper-leg bone spur that threatened to end his career before it began. Following his graduation from college, Mize spent a brief amount of time in the St. Louis farm system, before the Cardinals sold him to Cincinnati for $55,000 on December 13, 1934. The Reds later returned the 21-year-old first sacker to the Cardinals, though, due to concerns about the health of his leg.

Finally arriving in St. Louis in 1936, Mize quickly established himself as the Cardinals' starting first baseman, finishing his first big-league season with 19 home runs, 93 RBIs, and a batting average of .329. In the process, he made an extremely favorable impression on Cincinnati Reds manager Charlie Dressen, who referred to him as " . . . the greatest rookie I've ever seen." The left-handed-hitting Mize improved upon those numbers in his sophomore campaign of 1937, placing among the N.L. leaders in most statistical categories, including home runs (25), RBIs (113), runs scored (103), hits (204), and batting average (.364), en route to earning All-Star honors for the first time.

Standing 6'2" and weighing close to 220 pounds, Mize possessed little foot speed and only marginal range in the field. But he had sure hands and an extremely quick bat that soon earned him the nickname "The Big Cat." And, despite his burly appearance, Mize displayed a great deal of finesse at the plate, rarely swinging at bad pitches and hitting for a high batting average, especially early in his career.

Mize posted big numbers in each of the next three seasons as well, surpassing 25 homers and 100 RBIs each year, while also batting well over .300 and leading the league in total bases, slugging percentage, and OPS each season. After earning a second-place finish in the 1939 N.L. MVP voting by topping the circuit with 28 home runs and a .349 batting average, Mize placed second in the balloting again the following year after leading the league with 43 homers and 137 RBIs. Although Mize put up solid numbers again in 1941, concluding the campaign with 100 runs batted in and a league-leading 39 doubles, he showed decreased offensive production in virtually every statistical category, prompting Cardinals general manager Branch Rickey to trade him to the Giants for three prospects and $50,000 at season's end.

Mize had an outstanding first season in New York, earning a fifth-place finish in the N.L. MVP voting by leading the league with 110 RBIs and a .521 slugging percentage, while also placing among the leaders with 26 home runs, 97 runs scored, a .305 batting average, a .380 on-base percentage, and an OPS of .901. However, the Giants soon found themselves forced to do without his services when he entered the military following the conclusion of the 1942 campaign. Mize spent the next three years serving in the U.S. Navy, spending most of his time entertaining the troops by competing on the baseball diamond against other professional players.

Following his return to the Giants in 1946, Mize suffered a broken toe that limited him to just 101 games and 377 official plate appearances. Nevertheless, he managed to earn All-Star honors by batting .337 and finishing second in the league with 22 home runs. Mize subsequently posted his best numbers as a member of the Giants in 1947, when he batted .302 and topped the Senior Circuit with 51 home runs, 138 RBIs, and 137 runs scored. By also striking out just 42 times, he became the only player in MLB history to fan fewer than 50 times while also hitting 50 homers. Mize's historic performance earned him the seventh of his 10 All-Star selections and a third-place finish in the N.L. MVP voting. He followed that up with another big year in 1948, leading the league with 40 home runs, while also placing among the leaders with 125 RBIs, 110 runs scored, 316 total bases, a .395 on-base percentage, and a .564 slugging percentage.

Mize's proficiency as a hitter could be attributed largely to his keen batting eye and exceptional patience at the plate. Sportswriter Tom Meany once wrote, "Taking a pitch, Mize actually followed the ball with his eyes right into the catcher's mitt, and he maintains that he actually could see the ball hit the bat."

Stan Musial, who played briefly with Mize in St. Louis, discussed the poise and grace his former teammate exhibited in the batter's box: "Did you ever see a pitcher knock him down at the plate? Remember how he reacted when brushed back? He'd just lean back on his left foot, bend his body back and let the pitch go by. Then he'd lean back into the batter's box and resume his stance, as graceful as a big cat."

Don Gutteridge, another teammate of Mize in St. Louis, stated, "Nobody had a better, smoother, easier swing than John. It was picture perfect."

A true student of hitting, Mize relied as much on his knowledge of pitchers and his excellent mechanics at the plate as he did on his considerable strength. Known to use multiple bats over the course of a game, depending on the situation and the opposing pitcher, Mize took a scientific approach to hitting that forced the Giants to carry two trunks of bats whenever they went on the road in 1947, with teammate Buddy Blattner remarking, "One truck was for Johnny Mize. The other was for the rest of the team."

The 1948 campaign proved to be Mize's last full season with the Giants. Dissatisfied with his playing time under new Giants manager Leo Durocher the following year, Mize expressed a desire to go elsewhere. After Mize hit 18 home runs, knocked in 62 runs, and batted just .263 in 106 games over the first five months of the 1949 season, the Giants granted his request by selling him to the Yankees for $40,000 in late August. Mize left the Giants having hit 157 home runs, driven in 505 runs, scored 473 times, collected 733 hits, 16 triples, and 110 doubles, batted .299, compiled an on-base percentage of .389, and posted a slugging percentage of .549 as a member of the team.

Although Mize remained a part-time player during his time with the Yankees, he proved to be a key contributor to five consecutive world championship teams on the other side of town, providing a powerful left-handed bat against opposing right-handers and serving as a pinch-hitter deluxe. He also continued to impress all those who observed his hitting style, with Yankees manager Casey Stengel noting, "His bat doesn't travel as far as anybody else's. He just cocks it and slaps, and when you're as big as he is, you can slap a ball into the seats. That short swing is wonderful."

Mize announced his retirement from the game at the conclusion of the 1953 season, ending his career with 359 home runs, 1,337 runs batted in, 1,118 runs scored, 2,011 hits, 83 triples, 367 doubles, a .312 batting average, a .397 on-base percentage, and a .562 slugging percentage. He also drew 856 bases on balls and struck out only 524 times, in nearly 7,400 total plate appearances over the course of his career. Although Mize's relatively modest career numbers prevented him from gaining admittance to Cooperstown during his initial period of eligibility, the members of the Veteran's Committee ended up electing him to the Hall of Fame in 1981 knowing that he lost three peak seasons due to time spent serving in the military during World War II. They also voted for him on the strength of his major-league record six games with 3 home runs, six top-10 finishes in the league MVP voting, and outstanding walk-to-strikeout ratio of better than 1.5 to 1.

Following his playing career, Mize worked as a radio commentator and hitting coach for the Giants, before briefly serving as a coach with the Kansas City Athletics. He also later worked for a housing development in St. Augustine, Florida, during the 1970s. Mize eventually returned to Demorest, Georgia, where he spent the last few years of his life before dying in his sleep at 80 years of age on June 2, 1993.

Giant Career Highlights:

Best Season: Although Mize also performed extremely well for the Giants in 1948, driving in 125 runs, scoring 110 times, and leading the league with 40 home runs, he played his best ball for them one year earlier. In addition to topping the Senior Circuit with 51 home runs, 138 RBIs, and 137 runs scored in 1947, Mize batted .302, compiled an on-base percentage of .384, and finished second in the league in slugging percentage (.614), OPS (.998), and total bases (360).

Memorable Moments/Greatest Performances: During his fabulous 1947 campaign, Mize set a new N.L. record (since broken) by scoring at least one run in 16 straight games.

Mize delivered several game-winning hits during his time with the Giants, with one of the most notable coming on July 24, 1946, when his two-run homer in the bottom of the ninth inning gave the Giants a 3–1 win over the Cardinals. Mize came up big in the clutch again on May 5, 1949, when he homered in the bottom of the 10th inning to give the Giants a 3–2 victory over the Pirates.

Mize had one of his biggest days at the plate for the Giants on August 26, 1947, when he went 4-for-5, with 2 homers and 5 RBIs during a 7–6 victory over the Chicago Cubs. However, he had his greatest game as a member of the team earlier in the year, hitting 3 home runs and driving in 4 runs during a 14–5 loss to the Boston Braves on April 24. His three round-trippers made him the first major leaguer to reach the seats three times in one game as many as five times. He later accomplished the feat again while playing for the Yankees in 1950.

Notable Achievements:

Surpassed 40 home runs twice, topping 50 homers once (51 in 1947).

Knocked in more than 100 runs three times, surpassing 120 RBIs twice.

Scored more than 100 runs twice, topping 130 runs scored once (137 in 1947).

Batted over .300 three times.

Compiled on-base percentage in excess of .400 once (.437 in 1946).

Posted slugging percentage in excess of .500 four times, topping .600-mark once (.614 in 1947).

Compiled OPS in excess of 1.000 once (1.013 in 1946).

Led N.L. in: home runs twice; RBIs twice; runs scored once; and slugging percentage once.

Led N.L. first basemen in: putouts twice; assists twice; fielding percentage twice; and double plays once.

Ranks among Giants career-leaders in: slugging percentage (3rd); on-base percentage (tied-9th); and OPS (4th).

Hit three home runs in one game vs. Boston on April 24, 1947.

Only player in MLB history to hit more than 50 home runs and strike out fewer than 50 times in a season (1947).

Finished in top five of N.L. MVP voting twice (1942 & 1947).

Three-time *Sporting News* All-Star selection (1942, 1947 & 1948).

Five-time N.L. All-Star (1942, 1946, 1947, 1948 & 1949).

Elected to Baseball Hall of Fame by members of Veteran's Committee in 1981.

16 MATT WILLIAMS

Matt Williams finished second in the 1994 N.L. MVP voting, when he topped the Senior Circuit with 43 home runs. *(Courtesy of George A. Kitrinos)*

A hard-hitting third baseman with outstanding defensive skills, Matt Williams spent 10 seasons in San Francisco, serving as the Giants' starter at the hot corner in seven of those. Possessing excellent power to all fields, Williams hit more than 30 home runs four times as a member of the Giants, topping the Senior Circuit with 43 round-trippers in the strike-shortened 1994 campaign. The right-handed-hitting Williams also surpassed 100 RBIs twice and 100 runs scored once, en route to earning three Silver Sluggers during his time in

San Francisco. Meanwhile, Williams's soft hands, quick reflexes, and strong throwing arm enabled him to also win three Gold Gloves as a member of the team. Williams' solid all-around play helped the Giants top 90 victories three times and advance to the playoffs twice, earning him in the process four All-Star selections and three top-10 finishes in the N.L. MVP voting.

Born in Bishop, California, on November 28, 1965, Matthew Derrick Williams grew up in Carson City, Nevada, where he attended Carson City High School. Originally drafted by the New York Mets following his graduation from Carson City, Williams instead opted to accept a baseball scholarship from the University of Nevada, Las Vegas, where he spent the next few years excelling on the diamond to such an extent that the Giants selected him in the first round of the 1986 amateur draft, with the third overall pick.

A shortstop in college, Williams continued to man that position during his relatively brief stay in the minor leagues, before joining the Giants at the start of the 1987 campaign. He subsequently spent most of his rookie season assuming the role of a utility infielder, appearing in 84 games at shortstop and third, accumulating 245 official at-bats, hitting 8 homers, driving in 21 runs, and batting just .188. Williams continued to struggle at the plate in each of the next two seasons in a somewhat limited role, compiling batting averages of just .205 and .202, although he did manage to hit 18 homers and knock in 50 runs, in only 292 official at-bats in 1989.

The 24-year-old Williams finally developed into a consistent offensive threat in 1990 after he laid claim to the Giants' starting third-base job. Starting all but 5 games at the hot corner, Williams earned All-Star honors, his first Silver Slugger, and a sixth-place finish in the N.L. MVP voting by hitting 33 home runs, scoring 87 times, batting .277, topping the circuit with 122 RBIs, and leading all players at his position in putouts and double plays. He followed that up with another very solid year, concluding the 1991 campaign with 34 homers, 98 RBIs, and a .268 batting average, and winning his first Gold Glove.

Williams subsequently suffered through a subpar 1992 season in which he hit just 20 homers, knocked in only 66 runs, and batted just .227. However, he rebounded the following year after Dusty Baker replaced Roger Craig as manager of the Giants, compiling a batting average of .294, and placing among the league leaders with 38 home runs, 110 RBIs, and 105 runs scored. Williams also earned Gold Glove honors for the first of two straight times.

Williams ended up having most of his finest seasons under Baker, with whom he developed an extremely close relationship. He also developed a strong rapport with Giants fans and a fondness for Candlestick Park, even though he found his home-run totals being adversely affected by its swirling winds. Looking back years later at the time he spent playing in Candlestick, Williams told a reporter from the *San Francisco Chronicle*, "If there's one thing I learned here, it's never to take your eyes off the ball."

Williams continued his success under Baker in 1994, batting .267, finishing second in the National League with 96 RBIs, and topping the circuit with 43 home runs, even though a player's strike shortened the season to only 115 games. His exceptional performance earned him All-Star honors for the second time and a runner-up finish in the N.L. MVP balloting. Limited by injuries to a total of just 181 games the next two seasons, Williams nevertheless posted outstanding numbers each year. Appearing in just 76 games in 1995, Williams hit 23 homers, drove in 65 runs, and batted a career-high .336. He followed that up by batting .302, hitting 22 homers, and knocking in 85 runs, in only 105 games in 1996.

Ironically, the 1996 campaign turned out to be Williams's last in San Francisco. Having endured three consecutive losing seasons, the Giants named as their new general manager Brian Sabean, who, in his first major move, included Williams in a multi-player trade he completed with the Cleveland Indians that brought in return second baseman Jeff Kent, shortstop José Vizcaíno, and bullpen setup man Julián Tavárez. Although the deal ended up working out well for the Giants, Sabean initially found himself being lambasted in the press for dealing the popular Williams for what the hometown newspapers referred to as a "bunch of spare parts."

Williams had an extremely productive year for Cleveland in 1997, hitting 32 homers, driving in 105 runs, and winning his fourth Gold Glove. Nevertheless, the Indians elected to trade him to Arizona at season's end for fellow third baseman Travis Fryman and pitcher Tom Martin. Williams spent his six remaining big-league seasons with the Diamondbacks, having easily his best year for them in 1999, when he earned his final All-Star selection and a third-place finish in the N.L. MVP voting by hitting 35 homers, knocking in 142 runs, scoring 98 times, and batting .303. Plagued by a series of injuries that included a bad back, sore hamstrings, and hip flexor problems, Williams failed to appear in more than 106 games in any of his final four seasons, prompting him to announce his retirement after Arizona released him on June 29, 2003. He ended his career with 378 home runs, 1,218 RBIs, 997 runs scored, 1,878 hits, 35 triples, 338 doubles, a .268 batting average, a .317 on-base percentage, and a .489 slugging percentage. During his time in San Francisco, Williams hit 247 homers, drove in 732 runs, scored 594 times, collected 1,092 hits, 25 triples, and 179 doubles, batted .264, compiled an on-base percentage of .312, and posted a slugging percentage of .498.

Some four years after Williams retired his name appeared in the Mitchell Report, identifying him as one of the dozens of players that allegedly used steroids prior to 2007. He later spent two years coaching for the Diamond-backs, before being hired to manage in Washington, where he earned 2014 N.L. Manager of the Year honors in his first year at the helm. However, after failing to lead the Nationals into the playoffs the following year, Williams was relieved of his duties.

Giant Career Highlights:

Best Season: Williams posted his best overall numbers in San Francisco in 1993, when he hit 38 homers, knocked in 110 runs, scored a career-high 105 times, batted .294, accumulated 170 hits and 33 doubles, amassed 325 total bases, and compiled an OPS of .886. However, he actually played his best ball for the Giants the following year, concluding the strike-shortened 1994 campaign with 96 RBIs, 74 runs scored, 270 total bases, a .267 batting average, an OPS of .926, and a league-leading 43 home runs, en route to earning a second-place finish in the N.L. MVP balloting. Williams also led all league third basemen in assists, earning in the process the third Gold Glove of his career.

Memorable Moments/Greatest Performances: Williams had a big day at the plate on August 11, 1989, leading the Giants to a lopsided 10–2 victory over the Dodgers by driving in a career-high 6 runs with a pair of homers.

Williams equaled his single-game high in RBIs some four years later, on June 19, 1993, when he went 3-for-5, with a homer, double, and 6 runs batted in during a 10–3 win over the Astros.

Williams had an extremely productive afternoon against the Padres on September 26, 1990, leading the Giants to a 7–6 win over their N.L. West rivals by going 3-for-4, with 2 homers, a double, 5 RBIs, and 3 runs scored.

Williams delivered one of his most memorable hits as a member of the Giants on April 18, 1993, when he led off the bottom of the 11th inning with a home run off Steve Bedrosian that gave the Giants a 13–12 walk-off win over the Atlanta Braves. Williams's game-winning blast punctuated a 4-for-6, 2-homer performance during which he knocked in 3 runs and scored 4 times.

Williams had another big day on September 19, 1993, when he led the Giants to a 7–3 win over Cincinnati by hitting 2 homers and driving in 5 runs.

Williams helped the Giants start off the 1994 campaign on the right foot, homering twice and knocking in 5 runs during an 8–0 win over Pittsburgh on Opening Day. Williams had a similarly productive evening later in the year, on July 1, when he helped lead the Giants to a 14–7 win over Montreal by going 4-for-5, with a homer and 5 RBIs. He subsequently concluded the month of July in grand fashion, hitting a pair of homers and driving in 5 runs during a 9–4 win over Colorado on July 31.

Notable Achievements:

Hit more than 30 home runs four times, surpassing 40 homers once (43 in 1994).

Knocked in more than 100 runs twice, topping 120 RBIs once (122 in 1990).

Scored more than 100 runs once (105 in 1993).

Batted over .300 twice.

Surpassed 30 doubles once (33 in 1993).

Posted slugging percentage in excess of .500 four times, topping the .600-mark twice.

Compiled OPS in excess of 1.000 once (1.046 in 1995).

Led N.L. in home runs once and RBIs once.

Led N.L. third basemen in: putouts twice; assists once; and double plays three times.

Ranks among Giants career leaders in home runs (5th).

Finished second in 1994 N.L. MVP voting.

May 1995 N.L. Player of the Month.

Three-time Silver Slugger winner (1990, 1993 & 1994).

Three-time Gold Glove Award winner (1991, 1993 & 1994).

Three-time *Sporting News* All-Star selection (1990, 1993 & 1994).

Four-time N.L. All-Star (1990, 1994, 1995 & 1996).

1989 N.L. champion.

17 GEORGE "HIGH POCKETS" KELLY

George "High Pockets" Kelly helped the Giants win four straight pennants and two world championships during the 1920s. *(Courtesy of Library of Congress)*

An outstanding RBI-man who excelled both at the bat and in the field, George "High Pockets" Kelly served as one of the key members of Giants teams that won four consecutive pennants and two World Series during the early 1920s. Before being succeeded by Bill Terry as the Giants' regular first baseman, Kelly surpassed 20 home runs three times, knocked in more than 100 runs four times, and batted over .300 six times between 1920 and 1926, leading the National League in homers once and RBIs twice. An exceptional fielder as well, Kelly possessed soft hands, excellent range, and a powerful throwing arm that enabled him to lead all players at his position in assists three times. He also topped all N.L. first sackers in putouts three times, double plays twice, and fielding percentage once, with his positioning and footwork on extra-base hits serving as the blueprint for all future first basemen on relays.

Born in San Francisco, California, on September 10, 1895, George Lange Kelly got his start in organized baseball as a teenager when he dropped out of high school and began playing semipro ball around the city and across the Bay in the Oakland area. Blessed with grace and fluidity in spite of his gangly 6'4" frame, Kelly displayed an ability to pitch, hit, and field his position extremely well. After beginning his professional career at the age of 18 with the Victoria Bees of the Class-B Northwestern League, for whom he spent two years playing first base and the outfield, Kelly had his contract purchased by the Giants for $1,500 midway through the 1915 campaign. Reflecting back years later on his feelings at the time, Kelly revealed, "In 1915, I was sold to the Giants for $1,500. There was one thought in my mind: 'McGraw wants me.' You cannot imagine the thrill I had, as did every other player picked by McGraw. Hell, boy, I felt I was a giant—12 feet tall!"

After making his major-league debut with the Giants three weeks shy of his 20th birthday, on August 18, 1915, Kelly received very little playing time over the course of the next two seasons, appearing in a total of only 75 games before being placed on waivers by the team. He subsequently joined the Pittsburgh Pirates, for whom he appeared in just 8 games before the Giants reclaimed him off waivers on August 4, 1917. Optioned immediately to the Rochester Hustlers of the Class-AA International League, Kelly spent the remainder of 1917 in the minor leagues. He then missed the entire 1918 campaign while serving in the military, before rejoining the Giants in 1919, when he compiled a .290 batting average over 32 games.

Inserted at first base full time by Giants manager John McGraw at the start of the ensuing campaign, the 24-year-old Kelly had a solid year, hitting 11 home runs, batting .266, and driving in 94 runs, which tied him with Rogers Hornsby for the N.L. lead. He also led all players at his position in putouts, assists, and double plays for the first of two straight times, recording a league-record 1,759 putouts at first base. Kelly followed that up with a significantly more productive 1921 season in which he helped lead the Giants to the first of their four consecutive pennants by scoring 95 runs, batting .308, topping the circuit with 23 home runs, and finishing second in the league with 122 RBIs,

42 doubles, and 310 total bases. Kelly continued to post outstanding numbers in each of the next three seasons, batting well over .300 each year, while annually placing among the N.L. leaders in home runs and RBIs. Particularly effective in 1924, Kelly earned a sixth-place finish in the league MVP voting by hitting 21 homers, scoring 91 runs, batting .324, and leading the league with a career-high 136 RBIs.

The right-handed-hitting Kelly established himself as one of the N.L.'s most productive hitters even though he lacked patience at the plate and regularly finished among the league leaders in strikeouts. A notorious free-swinger, Kelly never drew more than 47 bases on balls in a season, striking out significantly more times than he walked in each of his 16 major-league seasons. Nevertheless, he developed a reputation as an outstanding clutch hitter, with John McGraw stating on numerous occasions that he preferred to have no one else at the plate in an important situation.

Kelly, though, perhaps became even more well-known for his defense. Using the same glove throughout his entire career, the right-handed-throwing Kelly set single-season marks for first basemen in putouts, assists, double plays, and total chances during his time in New York, with his 1,759 putouts in 1920 remaining a National League record. Meanwhile, his rifle arm often prevented opposing runners from advancing on infield plays. In fact, Kelly regularly went far into the outfield for cutoff throws, as former teammate Frankie Frisch told *The Reading Eagle* in January 1973 when he said, "His arm was so tremendous that he was directed to be the relay man on throws from the outfield. His arm was better, in fact, than any of today's players that I can think of."

Yet, in spite of his outstanding defensive work at first base, Kelly spent most of 1925 playing other positions in order to allow young first sacker Bill Terry to see more playing time. Starting 107 games at second base, 24 at first, and another 16 in the outfield, Kelly acquitted himself well wherever McGraw put him, committing a total of only 18 errors in the field, while placing second among N.L. second basemen in fielding percentage. He also had a solid year at the plate, earning a third-place finish in the league MVP balloting by hitting 20 home runs, driving in 99 runs, and batting .309. Returning to first base in 1926, Kelly knocked in 80 runs and batted .303, before the desire to insert Terry into the everyday lineup prompted the Giants to part ways with the veteran first sacker at season's end. Traded to the Cincinnati Reds for outfielder Edd Roush on February 9, 1927, Kelly left New York with career totals of 123 home runs, 762 RBIs, 608 runs scored, 1,270 hits, 52 triples, and 218 doubles, a batting average of .301, an on-base percentage of .348, and a slugging percentage of .465.

Kelly spent the next 3 ½ seasons with the Reds, having his best year for them in 1929, when he knocked in 103 runs, batted .293, and amassed a career-high 45 doubles. After being released by Cincinnati on July 10, 1930, he joined the American Association's Minneapolis Millers one week later. Kelly spent just one month in Minneapolis before the Millers traded him to the Chicago Cubs for a pair of players. After finishing out the year in Chicago, Kelly rejoined the Millers in 1931. He then returned to the majors for a brief tour of duty with the Brooklyn Dodgers in 1932 before concluding his playing career with the Pacific Coast League's Oakland Oaks the following year. Over parts of 16 major-league seasons, Kelly hit 148 home runs, knocked in 1,020 runs, scored 819 times, collected 1,778 hits, including 76 triples and 337 doubles, batted .297, compiled a .342 on-base percentage, and posted a .452 slugging percentage.

Following his retirement as an active player, Kelly began a lengthy career as a coach at both the major- and minor-league levels, serving on the coaching staffs of the Cincinnati Reds from 1935 to 1937, the Boston Braves from 1938 to 1943, the Reds again from 1947 to 1948, and the Oakland Oaks in 1949. After suffering a stroke eight days earlier, Kelly passed away at the age of 89 on October 13, 1984, 11 years after the members of the Veteran's Committee elected him to the Baseball Hall of Fame. Unquestionably, the influence exerted on the other members of the Committee by Kelly's former Giants teammates Frankie Frisch and Bill Terry had a great deal to do with his selection, since his admission to Cooperstown has since been criticized by many. Nevertheless, upon his induction, the AP wrote: "To Frankie Frisch, he was one of the finest first basemen who ever lived. To Waite Hoyt, he was a dangerous man in the clutch. And to the people who vote for such things, he is a perfect choice for the Baseball Hall of Fame."

Giant Career Highlights:

Best Season: Kelly played his best ball for the Giants from 1921 to 1924, averaging 19 home runs and 117 RBIs during that time, while batting over .300 in each of those four campaigns. He perhaps posted his best overall numbers in 1924, finishing the year with 21 homers, 91 runs scored, 185 hits, a .324 batting average, a career-high .902 OPS, and a league-leading and career-best

136 RBIs. However, Kelly compiled similar numbers in 1921, concluding the campaign with 122 runs batted in, 95 runs scored, 181 hits, a batting average of .308, an OPS of .884, and a league-leading 23 home runs. And, while Kelly finished higher than fourth in only two major offensive categories in 1924, he placed in the league's top three in five different categories three years earlier. Furthermore, Kelly led all N.L. first basemen in putouts, assists, and double plays in 1921, while he failed to finish higher than fifth in any of those categories in 1924. All things considered, Kelly had his best all-around season for the Giants in 1921.

Memorable Moments/Greatest Performances: Kelly had one of his most productive days at the plate on July 10, 1920, when he led the Giants to an 8–5 victory over the Cubs by driving in six runs with a homer, triple, and single.

Kelly got off to a fast start in 1921, setting a major-league record that stood for 89 years by opening the season with at least one hit and one RBI in eight consecutive games.

Later during that 1921 campaign, Kelly defeated the Phillies almost single-handedly when he knocked in all four Giant runs with a homer, double, and single during a 4–3 Giants victory on July 24.

On April 29, 1922, Kelly hit two of the four inside-the-park home runs the Giants recorded during a 15–4 win over the Braves at windswept Braves Field.

Kelly had the first 5-for-5 day of his career later in the year when he collected a triple, two doubles, and two singles during a 19–7 home win over the Cubs on August 5, 1922.

Kelly hit three home runs in one game for the first time in his career on September 17, 1923, when he led the Giants to a 13–6 victory over the Cubs by going 5-for-5, with 3 homers, 4 RBIs, and 4 runs scored. By reaching the seats in the 3rd, 4th, and 5th innings, he became the first player to homer in three successive innings.

Kelly again homered three times in one game during an 8–7 win over the Pirates on June 14, 1924, making him the first player to accomplish the feat more than once. He finished the day 4-for-4, with a career-high 8 RBIs, driving in all eight Giant runs in the process.

A little over one month later, on July 16, 1924, Kelly became the first National League player to hit 7 home runs over the course of six games when he reached the seats once during an 8–7 win over the Pirates. Kelly's blast also made him the first player to homer in six straight games.

Kelly also used his powerful throwing arm to create an enduring memory for Giants fans, helping to preserve a 1–0 Giants victory in the final game of the 1921 World Series by making a brilliant first-to-third throw to nip Aaron Ward for a game-ending, Series-winning double play.

Notable Achievements:

Surpassed 20 home runs three times.

Knocked in more than 100 runs four times, topping 120 RBIs twice.

Batted over .300 six times.

Finished in double-digits in triples once (11 in 1920).

Surpassed 30 doubles three times, topping 40 two-baggers once (42 in 1921).

Posted slugging percentage in excess of .500 twice.

Led N.L. in home runs once and RBIs twice.

Led N.L. first basemen in: putouts three times; assists three times; fielding percentage once; and double plays twice.

First MLB player to hit three home runs in one game twice.

First MLB player to homer in six straight games.

Finished third in 1925 N.L. MVP voting.

Four-time N.L. champion (1921, 1922, 1923 & 1924).

Two-time world champion (1921 & 1922).

Elected to Baseball Hall of Fame by members of Veteran's Committee in 1973.

18 TRAVIS JACKSON

Travis Jackson batted over .300 six times and led N.L. shortstops in assists four times in his 15 seasons with the Giants. *(Courtesy of LegendaryAuctions.com)*

The National League's premier shortstop for much of his career, Travis Jackson contributed significantly to four pennant-winning teams and one world championship ball club during his time in New York. The one constant in a Giants infield that underwent numerous changes during the 1920s, Jackson served as the team's starting shortstop from 1924 to 1936, battling several injuries along the way to eventually establish himself as arguably the best player ever to man the position for the Giants. A solid hitter, Jackson batted over .300 six times, en route to compiling a lifetime mark of .291. He also surpassed 20 homers once and 90 RBIs three times, driving in as many as 101 runs in 1934. Although something of a defensive liability early in his career, Jackson gradually developed into a strong defender as well, enabling him to earn *Sporting News* All-Star honors three straight times, from 1927 to 1929.

Born in Waldo, Arkansas, on November 2, 1903, and named after William B. Travis, a Lieutenant Colonel who died at the Battle of the Alamo, Travis Calvin Jackson acquired his love of baseball from his father, who spent many hours playing catch with his young son outside their home. After moving with his family to Memphis, Tennessee, Jackson played for his high school team, developing into such a talented player that he made a lasting impression on former major-league shortstop Kid Elberfield at only 14 years of age. Introduced to Elberfield by his uncle at a game of the Little Rock Travelers, who played minor-league ball in the Class-A Southern Association, Jackson received an impromptu tryout from the former major leaguer, who told him to contact him when he was ready to begin his professional career.

Jackson subsequently attended Ouachita Baptist University in Arkadelphia, Arkansas, where he starred in baseball before signing with Elberfield in 1921. He spent the next two years playing shortstop for Little Rock, committing a league-high 72 errors in 1922. Reflecting back on his early struggles in the field, Jackson said, "I guess I set a world record for errors. I had a pretty good arm, but I didn't have much control. A lot of those were double errors—two on the same play; a boot and then a wild throw. The people in the first base and right field bleachers knew me. When the ball was hit to me they scattered. 'Watch out! He's got it again.'"

In spite of Jackson's defensive deficiencies, Elberfield recommended him to John McGraw, who signed the young shortstop to a contract on June 30, effective at the end of the Southern Association's 1922 season. Jackson joined the Giants in late September, appearing in three games for them and failing to hit safely in his eight official trips to the plate. After beginning the ensuing campaign on the Giants bench, Jackson ended up seeing a significant amount of action at both shortstop and third base due to injuries suffered by starters Dave Bancroft and Heinie Groh. Making the most of his playing time, the 19-year-old rookie batted .275, with 4 home runs, 37 RBIs, and 45 runs scored, in 96 games and 327 official at-bats. He proved to be somewhat less impressive in the field, though, committing a total of 23 errors.

Convinced that Jackson had all the tools to replace Bancroft as the Giants' starting shortstop, McGraw dealt the future Hall of Famer to the Boston

Braves for a pair of players at season's end, creating in the process an opening for Jackson at short. Rewarding his manager for the confidence he placed in him, Jackson hit 11 home runs, knocked in 76 runs, scored 81 times, collected 180 hits, and batted .302 in his first year as a full-time starter. However, despite finishing second among N.L. shortstops in putouts, assists, and double plays, Jackson continued to struggle in the field, leading all players at his position with 58 errors. He also committed a key error in Game 7 of the World Series, contributing to Washington's victory over the Giants.

Despite missing a significant amount of playing time in each of the next three seasons, Jackson gradually evolved into one of baseball's finest all-around shortstops, further enhancing his offensive game by increasing his run-production and developing into what Casey Stengel called "the greatest bunter I ever saw," while vastly improving himself defensively. A recurrence of an old knee injury he suffered in college limited Jackson to a total of 223 games in 1925 and 1926. Yet, he posted batting averages of .285 and .327, placing among the league's leading hitters in the second of those campaigns. Forced to miss nearly a month of the 1927 season as well after undergoing surgery for appendicitis, Jackson nevertheless batted .318 and established new career highs with 14 home runs and 98 RBIs, en route to earning the first of three straight *Sporting News* All-Star selections and a fifth-place finish in the league MVP voting. He also developed into a much more reliable fielder during that time, improving the accuracy of his throws to the point that he became noted for his powerful throwing arm. Meanwhile, Jackson's quickness and exceptional range earned him the nickname "Stonewall" for his ability to stop balls from going through the infield, in much the same manner that General Thomas "Stonewall" Jackson held Union troops at bay during the Civil War.

Jackson earned *Sporting News* All-Star honors as baseball's best shortstop in 1928 and 1929 as well, concluding the first of those campaigns with 14 homers, 77 RBIs, 73 runs scored, and a .270 batting average, before hitting 21 home runs, driving in 94 runs, scoring 92 times, and batting .294 the following year. He also led all N.L. shortstops in assists both years and compiled the highest fielding percentage among players at his position in 1929.

Despite missing more than a month of the 1930 season with various injuries and a severe case of the mumps, Jackson again posted outstanding numbers, finishing the year with 13 homers, 82 RBIs, and a career-best .339 batting average. He followed that up with another solid season in 1931, driving in 71 runs, scoring 65 times, and batting .310, en route to earning a seventh-place finish in the league MVP balloting.

After being sidelined for much of the next two seasons with various ailments, Jackson appeared in 137 games for the Giants in 1934, enabling him to hit 16 home runs and knock in a career-high 101 runs. In addition to earning a fourth-place finish in the league MVP voting, he started for the National League at shortstop in the second annual MLB All-Star Game.

With the acquisition of veteran shortstop Dick Bartell from Philadelphia prior to the start of the 1935 campaign, Jackson moved to third base, where he spent his final two seasons serving as team captain. After batting .301, driving in 80 runs, and placing second among N.L. third sackers in fielding percentage in his first year at his new position, Jackson suffered through a dismal 1936 season in which he batted a career-low .230. The Giants placed him on waivers at season's end, for the purpose of assigning him to their minor-league affiliate in Jersey City. Jackson spent the next year and a half serving as the team's player-manager before returning to New York as a coach. He concluded his major-league playing career with 135 home runs, 929 runs batted in, 833 runs scored, 1,768 hits, 86 triples, 291 doubles, a .291 batting average, a .337 on-base percentage, and a .433 slugging percentage, continuing to rank among the franchise's all-time leaders in RBIs (6th), hits (7th), doubles (6th), and triples (10th).

Jackson remained a coach in New York until 1941, when he entered a sanitarium after contracting tuberculosis. After recovering from his illness a few years later, he re-joined the Giants as a coach and continued to serve in that capacity until Leo Durocher assumed the managerial reins of the team in 1948. Jackson subsequently managed in the Braves' minor-league system for the next 12 years before retiring from the game at the conclusion of the 1960 campaign.

After leaving the game, Jackson spent the next two decades watching the members of the Hall of Fame Veteran's Committee induct his former teammates George Kelly, Dave Bancroft, Freddie Lindstrom, and Ross Youngs into Cooperstown. He finally received a call informing him that he had been inducted himself in March of 1982. Upon learning the news, Jackson confided, "For a long time I thought, 'Well, I'll be next,' and then I kinda forgot all about the Hall of Fame. The longer you're out, the more time they have to forget, and I've been out a long time. I was really surprised and happy. Anybody who ever played ball wants to go to the Hall of Fame. Don't let any of them kid you."

Jackson lived another five years, eventually losing his battle with Alzheimer's on July 27, 1987, at 83 years of age. Asked a few years earlier about his greatest thrill in the game, Jackson recalled the first time he stood on a professional baseball field: "The first time I stepped on the field I was in awe. It held 4,500 people, or so, and I never saw a park that big. And there I was holding my pants up with a cotton rope."

Career Highlights:

Best Season: Although Jackson posted career-high marks in batting average (.339) and OPS (.915) in 1930, he had his two finest all-around seasons in 1927 and 1929. In addition to placing among the league leaders with 14 home runs and 98 RBIs in the first of those years, Jackson batted .318, compiled an OPS of .849, and led all N.L. shortstops with 444 assists and 85 double plays. However, he posted even better defensive numbers in 1929, when he led all players at his position with 552 assists, 110 doubles plays, and a .969 fielding percentage. Jackson also batted .294, compiled an OPS of .857, knocked in 94 runs, and established career-high marks in home runs (21), runs scored (92), triples (12), walks (64), and total bases (270).

Memorable Moments/Greatest Performances: Jackson led the Giants to a 14–4 win over Cincinnati on August 4, 1923, by going 4-for-5, with a homer, double, and career-high 8 RBIs. Jackson accomplished the rare feat of hitting a grand slam on consecutive days in 1924.

After helping the Giants complete their doubleheader sweep of Philadelphia by driving in 5 runs with a triple and grand slam during a 15–3 win over the Phillies on September 5, he led them to a hard-fought 16–14 victory over the Phillies in the second game of their doubleheader split the very next day by knocking in another 5 runs with a double and a bases-loaded homer.

Jackson had a huge day at the plate on June 15, 1929, when he led the Giants to a 20–15 win over the Pirates in 14 innings by going 4-for-7, with 2 homers, a triple, double, and 7 RBIs.

Jackson had the only 5-for-5 day of his career on July 12, 1931, when he hit safely in each of his five trips to the plate during a 9–4 victory over the Phillies.

Although Jackson batted just .222 against Washington in the 1933 World Series, he helped the Giants take a commanding three-games-to-one lead in the Fall Classic by delivering a key hit in Game Four. With the score tied at

1–1 heading into the 11th inning, Jackson led off the top of the frame with a drag-bunt single, before coming around to score what proved to be the game-winning run. Writing for the *Universal Service* during the Series, Jackson later commented, "I've punched out quite a few hits in my time, but none that have given me greater gladness than the one I punched out yesterday in the 11th to start our rally."

Notable Achievements:

Batted over .300 six times.

Hit more than 20 home runs once (21 in 1929).

Knocked in more than 100 runs once (101 in 1934).

Finished in double-digits in triples three times.

Surpassed 30 doubles once (35 in 1928).

Posted slugging percentage in excess of .500 once (.529 in 1930).

Led N.L. shortstops in: assists four times; fielding percentage twice; and double plays twice.

Ranks among Giants career leaders in: RBIs (6th); hits (7th); extra-base hits (7th); doubles (6th); triples (10th); total bases (7th); games played (6th); at-bats (6th); and plate appearances (8th).

Finished in top five in N.L. MVP voting twice.

Three-time *Sporting News* All-Star selection (1927, 1928 & 1929).

1934 N.L. All-Star.

Four-time N.L. champion (1923, 1924, 1933 & 1936).

1933 world champion.

Elected to Baseball Hall of Fame by members of Veteran's Committee in 1982.

19 BOBBY BONDS

Bobby Bonds surpassed 30 homers and 30 steals in the same season twice while playing for the Giants. *(Courtesy of Mearsonlineauctions.com)*

Despite being best-known these days for being the father of Barry Bonds, Bobby Bonds carved out quite a career for himself in the Major Leagues some two decades earlier. The first player to surpass 30 home runs and 30 stolen bases in the same season more than twice, the elder Bonds possessed an outstanding combination of speed and power that made him one of the most complete players of the 1970s. A true "five-tool" player, Bonds excelled in all facets of the game, retiring at the conclusion of the 1981 campaign with career totals of 332 home runs and 461 stolen bases that made him the only player at that time, other than Willie Mays, to top the 300-mark in both categories. Spending his first seven big-league seasons in San Francisco, Bonds hit more than 30 home runs three times, knocked in more than 100 runs once, batted over .300 once, and stole more than 40 bases and scored more than 100 runs five times each as a member of the Giants, en route to earning two All-Star selections and two top-five finishes in the N.L. MVP voting. The speedy right-fielder also won three Gold Gloves during his time in San Francisco, before personal problems forced him to spend the second half of his career traveling from one city to another. Yet, in spite of his many accomplishments, Bonds is generally considered to be something of a disappointment, never having quite fulfilled the enormous potential he displayed when he first entered the Major Leagues in 1968.

Born in Riverside, California, on March 15, 1946, Bobby Lee Bonds developed a reputation as an exceptional all-around athlete while attending Riverside Polytechnic High School. In addition to starring on the baseball diamond, Bonds earned High School All-America honors in track and field as a senior, en route to being named Southern California High School Athlete of the Year in 1964. After signing with the Giants as an amateur free agent following his graduation later that year, the 18-year-old Bonds began his rapid ascension through the team's minor-league system that ended with his arrival in San Francisco in June of 1968. Appearing in 81 games over the final three months of the campaign, Bonds played well as a rookie, hitting 9 home runs, driving in 35 runs, scoring 55 times, stealing 16 bases, and batting .254, although he also struck out 84 times. Impressed with his new teammate's skill-set, Willie Mays commented, "Bobby has it all . . . He's intelligent, and he wants to learn."

Subsequently billed as the heir apparent to Mays as the Giants' next great outfielder, Bonds did all he could to fulfill that prophecy in 1969, finishing his first full season with 32 home runs, 90 RBIs, 45 stolen bases, and a league-leading 120 runs scored. However, he also batted just .259 and set a new single-season major-league record by striking out 187 times. Bonds hit fewer home runs (26) and knocked in fewer runs (78) the following year, but he improved upon his overall numbers, establishing career-high marks in runs scored (134), hits (200), triples (10), doubles (36), stolen bases (48), and batting average (.302). He also used his exceptional running speed and strong throwing arm to finish among the league's leading right-fielders in putouts

(257), assists (11), and double plays (7). Nevertheless, his strikeouts continued to mount, with Bonds breaking his own single-season mark by fanning 189 times.

Bonds earned his first All-Star selection, his first Gold Glove, and a fourth-place finish in the N.L. MVP voting in 1971, when he finished among the league leaders with 33 home runs, 102 RBIs, 110 runs scored, 26 stolen bases, 178 hits, 32 doubles, 317 total bases, a .512 slugging percentage, and an OPS of .867, while reducing his strikeout total to 137. However, he took a step backwards the following year, concluding the 1972 campaign with 26 homers, 80 RBIs, a .259 batting average, and another 137 strikeouts, although he still managed to place near the top of the league rankings with 118 runs scored and 44 stolen bases.

Despite posting impressive overall numbers in each of his first four full seasons while splitting his time between the leadoff, number three, and cleanup spots in the Giants' batting order, Bonds remained something of an enigma heading into 1973. Blessed with tremendous physical gifts that included superb running speed and a chiseled 6'1", 190-pound frame, the California native seemed destined for greatness as soon as he arrived in San Francisco. But poor mechanics at the plate contributed greatly to his propensity for compiling huge strikeout totals, while a lack of proper focus at times caused him to develop a reputation as a careless base-runner. Bonds also occasionally failed to hustle and frequently missed the cutoff man on throws from the outfield. Meanwhile, off the playing field, he smoked three packs of cigarettes a day and indulged rather heavily in the consumption of alcohol.

Nevertheless, Bonds emerged as one of the best all-around players in the game solely on the strength of his extraordinary physical talent. Sonny Jackson, who spent several years competing against Bonds as a member of the Atlanta Braves, and later coached his son, Barry, after the latter joined the Giants, told *The Press-Enterprise* of Riverside, California, in 2001, "Bobby had that world-class speed. With his quick acceleration, he was going full speed in a heartbeat. He was as fast as anyone I've ever seen. He had great power, and he was a terrific outfielder with better arm strength than Barry."

Bonds finally seemed to put everything together in 1973 when, batting exclusively out of the leadoff spot, he nearly became the first player in major-league history to hit 40 home runs and steal 40 bases in the same season. In addition to hitting 39 homers and swiping 43 bags, the 27-year-old outfielder knocked in 96 runs, batted .283, and led the league with 131 runs scored and

341 total bases, en route to earning a third-place finish in the N.L. MVP balloting, *Sporting News* Player of the Year honors, and the admiration of his peers. Oakland A's third baseman Sal Bando told *Sports Illustrated*, "He's the most dynamic hitter I've ever seen." Dodger second baseman Davey Lopes told that same publication, "Bonds is probably the best outfielder in the majors." Steve Garvey added, "With his individual skills, he can blow a game apart quicker than anyone." Meanwhile, Cincinnati Reds manager Sparky Anderson stated at one point during that 1973 campaign, "As of today, Bobby Bonds is the best ballplayer in America."

However, Bonds failed to perform at the same lofty level in 1974, finishing the year with just 21 homers, 71 RBIs, 97 runs scored, and a .256 batting average. Meanwhile, his inconsistent play, occasional mental lapses, and erratic behavior off the field put him in the respective dog houses of managers Charlie Fox and Wes Westrum at different times during the season, prompting the Giants to part ways with him at the end of the year. Completing a stunning trade with the Yankees on October 22, 1974, the Giants sent the talented but troubled Bonds to New York for star outfielder Bobby Murcer, who earlier in his career had been touted by the Yankees as "the next Mickey Mantle." Bonds left San Francisco with career totals of 186 home runs, 552 RBIs, 765 runs scored, 1,106 hits, 42 triples, 188 doubles, and 263 stolen bases, a .273 batting average, a .356 on-base percentage, and a .478 slugging percentage. He continues to rank among the franchise's all-time leaders in home runs (8th) and stolen bases (tied-9th).

After being dealt to the Yankees, Bonds spent the second half of his career living a nomadic existence that saw him split his final seven seasons between seven different teams. Yet, he continued to post excellent numbers wherever he went, until age and injuries finally began taking their toll on him in 1980.

Despite being hobbled by a knee injury for much of the 1975 campaign, Bonds hit 32 homers, knocked in 85 runs, scored 93 times, stole 30 bases, and batted .270 for the Yankees, earning in the process the last of his three All-Star selections. Traded to the Angels during the subsequent offseason, Bonds spent the next two years back in California, having one of his finest statistical seasons in 1977, when he hit 37 home runs, drove in 115 runs, scored 103 times, stole 41 bases, and batted .264. Bonds then split the next four years between the White Sox, Rangers, Indians, Cardinals, and Cubs, playing his best ball during that stretch of time in 1978, when he surpassed 30 homers and 30 steals for the fifth and final time in his career. Bonds retired at the end of 1981 after appearing in only 45 games for the White Sox. He ended his career with 332 home runs, 1.024 RBIs, 1,258 runs scored, 1,886 hits, 66 triples, 302 doubles, 461 stolen bases, a .268 batting average, a .353 on-base percentage, and a .471 slugging percentage. In addition to topping 30 homers six times, Bonds surpassed 30 steals 10 times and scored more than 100 runs on six separate occasions. His five seasons with more than 30 home runs and 30 stolen bases remain the highest total compiled by any player in major-league history, equaled only by his son, Barry. The elder Bonds also established career (35) and single-season (11, in 1973) MLB records for most times leading off a game with a home run, both of which have since been broken.

Following his playing career, Bonds spent four years serving as hitting instructor for the Cleveland Indians (1984–1987), before returning to San Francisco when his son signed with the Giants as a free agent in 1993. During his second tour of duty with the Giants, Bonds served the club at different times as a coach, scout, and front-office employee, remaining with the organization until he developed lung cancer and a brain tumor that eventually took his life on August 23, 2003, at only 57 years of age.

Looking back at his playing career in 1990, Bonds told *The Los Angeles Times*, "They said I was supposed to be the next Willie Mays. When they told me that, it was an honor. You're talking about a guy who I considered the greatest player to ever wear shoes." Bonds added, "I probably had more success than anyone they ever put that label on.

"You show me another guy who's going to do 30–30 five times. But all the writers kept talking about was potential. 'You haven't reached your potential yet,' they say. Well, unless you win a Pulitzer Prize, you're not living up to your potential either, are you?"

Giant Career Highlights:

Best Season: Although Bonds also compiled outstanding numbers for the Giants in 1970 and 1971, he had his finest all-around season for them in 1973 when, in addition to hitting a career-high 39 home runs, he knocked in 96 runs, amassed 182 hits and 34 doubles, batted .283, stole 43 bases, compiled a career-best OPS of .900, and topped the Senior Circuit with 131 runs scored and 341 total bases. Bonds's 11 leadoff homers established a new single-season major-league record. He also led all N.L. right-fielders with 5 double plays and 347 putouts, with the last figure representing the highest total of his career. In addition to finishing third in the N.L. MVP balloting at season's end, Bonds earned All-Star Game MVP and *Sporting News* N.L. Player of the Year honors and his lone *Sporting News* All-Star selection.

Memorable Moments/Greatest Performances: Bonds literally began his major-league career in grand fashion, becoming just the second player in history to hit a grand slam in his first big-league game when he reached the seats with the bases loaded in the 6th inning of a 9–0 victory over the Dodgers on June 25, 1968.

Bonds homered twice in the same game for the first time a little over two months later, on August 27, 1968, when he led the Giants to an 8–4 home win over the Cubs by driving in 6 runs with a pair of round-trippers. He again reached the seats twice on September 19, when he went 3-for-3, with 2 homers, 3 RBIs, and 4 runs scored during an 11–5 win over the Cardinals.

Bonds had a big day against the Dodgers on July 17, 1969, leading the Giants to a 14–13 victory over their arch-rivals with 3 hits, a pair of homers, 5 RBIs, and 3 runs scored. Bonds again knocked in 5 runs in one game some five weeks later, doing so during a lopsided 13–4 victory over the Phillies in which he hit 2 home runs.

Bonds proved to be the difference in a 4–2 victory over the Mets on July 29, 1970, driving in 3 of the Giants' 4 runs with 4 hits, including a pair of homers.

Bonds had a number of big days at the plate in his banner year of 1973, with one of those coming on May 8, when he went 3-for-3, with 2 home runs, 5 RBIs, and 3 runs scored during a 9–7 win over the Cardinals. Two weeks later, on May 22, Bonds led the Giants to a 7–3 win over Atlanta by collecting 3 hits, including a homer and a double, stealing 3 bases, and scoring 4 runs. He had another huge game against the Pirates on June 6, leading the Giants to a 9–7 victory by going 4-for-4, with a homer, a stolen base, 2 RBIs, and 4 runs scored.

Notable Achievements:

Hit more than 20 home runs six times, surpassing 30 homers on three occasions.

Knocked in more than 100 runs once (102 in 1971).

Scored more than 100 runs five times, topping 120 runs scored on three occasions.

Batted over .300 once (.302 in 1970).

Topped 200 hits once (200 in 1970).

Finished in double-digits in triples once (10 in 1970).

Surpassed 30 doubles three times.

Stole more than 40 bases five times.

Posted slugging percentage in excess of .500 three times.

Surpassed 30 home runs and 30 stolen bases in same season twice (1969 & 1973).

Led N.L. in runs scored twice and total bases once.

Led N.L. outfielders in fielding percentage once and double plays twice.

Led N.L. right-fielders in: putouts twice; fielding percentage once; and double plays three times.

Holds Giants single-season record for most plate appearances (745 in 1970).

Ranks among Giants career leaders in home runs (8th) and stolen bases (tied-9th).

Finished in top five of N.L. MVP voting twice (1971 & 1973).

1973 All-Star Game MVP.

Three-time Gold Glove Award winner (1971, 1973 & 1974).

The Sporting News 1973 N.L. Player of the Year.

1973 *Sporting News* All-Star selection.

Two-time N.L. All-Star (1971 & 1973).

20 GEORGE BURNS

George Burns's total of 62 stolen bases in 1914 represents a 20th-century franchise record. *(Courtesy of Library of Congress)*

An outstanding leadoff hitter who regularly ranked among the N.L. leaders in hits, walks, runs scored, and stolen bases, George Burns spent 11 of his 15 major-league seasons with the Giants, helping them capture three pennants and one world championship during that time. In addition to topping the Senior Circuit in runs scored five times, walks four times, and stolen bases twice as a member of the team, Burns proved to be one of baseball's most consistent hitters, batting over .300 three times and never posting a mark lower than .272 as a regular. An excellent defender as well, Burns did such an exceptional job of patrolling left field at the Polo Grounds that the bleachers in that area of the field came to be known as "Burnsville." Although hardly remembered today, Burns earned the respect of his peers and manager John McGraw, who described him as "one of the most valuable ball players that ever wore the uniform of the Giants."

Born in Utica, New York, on November 24, 1889, George Joseph Burns spent much of his youth playing baseball on the local sandlots, where he usually either pitched or caught "so that I could get as much action as possible," he later recalled. A well-known semipro by 1908, Burns got his start in pro ball with the Utica Harps of the New York State League the following year, gradually transitioning from catcher to the outfield over the course of the next three seasons to take better advantage of his strong throwing arm and outstanding running speed. Discovered playing right field for Utica by John McGraw's old Baltimore Orioles teammate Sadie McMahon in 1911, Burns signed with the Giants and made his major-league debut for them later that year, hitting safely just once in 17 trips to the plate over the final two weeks of the campaign.

With McGraw preferring to bring his younger players along slowly, the 22-year-old Burns spent virtually all of 1912 sitting on the bench alongside his manager, who explained to him during spring training, "You may not play much this year, but I want you with me. You sit next to me on the bench and I'll tell you all I can about the way they play ball up here. And I'll stick you in there now and then to give you some experience. I don't want you to get impatient. Understand?"

Heeding the words of his manager, the soft-spoken rookie, who his teammates nicknamed "Silent George," appeared in only 29 games, compiling a batting average of .294, with 11 runs scored and 7 stolen bases.

Burns opened up the 1913 campaign as New York's starting left-fielder, displacing Josh Devore, who had fallen out of favor with McGraw due to his inability to properly play the Polo Grounds' difficult sun field. Not wishing to incur the wrath of his manager as well, Burns worked extremely hard on his defense, learning the various nuances of his new territory and eventually adopting a special cap with an extra-long bill and blue sunglasses attached to it. Over time, Burns became so adept at playing his position that several of his teammates later described him as the "greatest 'sun-fielder' in the history of the game."

Meanwhile, the right-handed-hitting Burns rapidly emerged as one of the Giants' top offensive threats. After initially batting third in New York's lineup, the 5'7", 160-pound speedster settled into the leadoff spot, where he ended up spending most of his career. Appearing in virtually every game for the Giants for the first of nine straight times, Burns had a solid rookie season, concluding the campaign with a .286 batting average, a .352 on-base percentage, and a team-leading 173 hits, 81 runs scored, 37 doubles, and 40 stolen bases.

Perhaps influenced by Burns's great strength (in spite of his smallish frame, he wielded a 42", 52-oz. bat), John McGraw elected to insert him into the number three-hole in the batting order in 1914. Burns responded by having one of his finest seasons, leading the N.L. with 100 runs scored and a career-high 62 stolen bases, while also placing among the leaders in nine other offensive categories, including hits (170), doubles (35), triples (10), batting average (.303), on-base percentage (.403), and slugging percentage (.417). Although the Giants failed to capture their fourth consecutive league championship, Burns's exceptional performance earned him the first of his four selections to *Baseball Magazine's* N.L. All-America Team and a fourth-place finish in the Chalmers Award balloting (the Chalmers Award served as the precursor to the MVP Award).

Returning to the leadoff spot in New York's lineup the following year, Burns had another solid season, batting .272 and finishing among the league leaders with 169 hits, 83 runs scored, 14 triples, and 27 stolen bases. He also began a string of 459 consecutive games played that established a new record for outfielders.

After batting .279, stealing 37 bases, and leading the league with 105 runs scored in 1916, Burns began an exceptional three-year run during which he earned a spot on *Baseball Magazine's* N.L. All-America Team each season. Burns opened that stretch by batting .302, compiling a .412 on-base percentage, stealing 40 bases, and leading the league with 103 runs scored and 75 bases on balls in 1917. He followed that up by batting .290, scoring 80 runs, and stealing another 40 bases in the war-shortened 1918 campaign, before equaling his career high by batting .303 in 1919, while also leading the league with 86 runs scored, 40 stolen bases, 82 walks, and a .396 on-base percentage.

Burns continued his outstanding play for the Giants in 1920 and 1921, batting .287 and establishing career highs with 6 home runs, 181 hits, and a league-leading 115 runs scored in the first of those campaigns, before batting .299, scoring 111 runs, collecting another 181 hits, and topping the circuit with 80 bases on balls in 1921, after moving to center field to make room in left for Irish Meusel. Nevertheless, the Giants elected to part ways with Burns on December 6, 1921, trading him, along with catcher Mike Gonzalez and

$150,000, to the Cincinnati Reds for third baseman Heinie Groh. Burns left New York with career totals of 34 home runs, 460 RBIs, 877 runs scored, 1,541 hits, 82 triples, 267 doubles, and 334 stolen bases. He also batted .290, compiled a .368 on-base percentage, and posted a .391 slugging percentage as a member of the Giants. Burns continues to rank among the franchise's all-time leaders in runs scored (10th), doubles (8th), steals (4th), bases on balls (6th), and plate appearances (10th).

After joining the Reds, Burns spent most of his time playing center field and right, the two sun fields in Cincinnati. In addition to giving his new team solid play at each position, he remained one of the Senior Circuit's most effective leadoff hitters over the course of the next two seasons, batting .285 and scoring 104 runs in 1922, before compiling a .274 batting average, scoring 99 runs, and leading the league with 101 bases on balls in 1923. Having been relegated to a part-time role in Cincinnati by 1924, Burns joined the Philadelphia Phillies after being placed on waivers by the Reds at season's end. He spent his final big-league season in Philadelphia, posting a batting average of .292 and scoring 65 runs in 88 games with the Phillies in 1925. Burns ended his major-league career with 41 home runs, 613 RBIs, 1,188 runs scored, 2,077 hits, 108 triples, 362 doubles, 383 stolen bases, a .287 batting average, a .366 on-base percentage, and a .384 slugging percentage. His 28 steals of home rank as the third-highest total in baseball history, behind only Ty Cobb and Max Carey.

After leaving Philadelphia at the conclusion of the 1925 campaign, Burns continued his playing career in the minor leagues, appearing in 163 games with Newark of the International League in 1926, before spending the next two seasons serving as player-manager for Williamsport of the New York–Pennsylvania League. Following his retirement as an active player in 1930, Burns spent one year coaching for John McGraw in New York before returning to Gloversville, New York, just outside of Utica, where he ran his father's pool hall for a time, then became payroll clerk at a tannery. He continued to work until 1957, when he retired and lived quietly in Gloversville until his death at age 76 on August 15, 1966.

Giant Career Highlights:

Best Season: Burns had a big year for the Giants in 1917, placing among the N.L. leaders in 12 different offensive categories, including topping the circuit with 103 runs scored and 75 bases on balls. He also performed extremely well in 1919, when he batted a career-high .303 and led the National League with 86 runs scored, 40 stolen bases, 82 walks, and a .396 on-base percentage. And, after the Major Leagues began using a livelier ball the following year, Burns had two of his most productive seasons, batting .287 and establishing career highs with 181 hits and a league-leading 115 runs scored in 1920, before batting .299, amassing another 181 hits, scoring 111 times, and driving in a career-best 61 runs in 1921. Nevertheless, the 1914 campaign would have to be considered his finest all-around season. Spending most of the year hitting third in the Giants lineup, Burns knocked in 60 runs, batted .303, and led the league with 100 runs scored and a 20th-century franchise-record 62 stolen bases. He also finished among the N.L. leaders with 170 hits, 35 doubles, 10 triples, 89 bases on balls, a .403 on-base percentage, and a .417 slugging percentage, establishing career highs in each of the last two categories en route to earning a fourth-place finish in the Chalmers Award balloting.

Memorable Moments/Greatest Performances: Although the Giants lost their May 7, 1915, matchup with the Boston Braves by a score of 11–7, Burns had a huge day, going 4-for-5, with a pair of doubles, 4 RBIs, and 2 runs scored.

Burns hit two home runs in one game for the only time in his career on July 11, 1916, when he led the Giants to an 8–4 win over the Reds in Cincinnati by going 4-for-5, with 2 homers, 4 RBIs, and 2 runs scored.

Burns had his lone 5-for-5 day at the plate on September 17, 1920, when he hit for the cycle, knocked in a run, and scored 3 times during a 4–3, 10-inning victory over the Pittsburgh Pirates.

Nearly three months earlier, on June 28, 1920, Burns homered and drove in a career-high 5 runs, in leading the Giants to a lopsided 18–3 victory over the Philadelphia Phillies.

After struggling at the plate in both the 1913 and 1917 World Series, Burns came up big against the Yankees in the 1921 Fall Classic, helping the Giants capture their first world championship in 16 years by batting .333, with 11 hits in 33 trips to the plate, including a triple and 4 doubles. Helping the Giants overcome an early two-games-to-none deficit in the Series, Burns collected 4 hits in Game 3 before providing the winning margin in the ensuing contest by delivering a two-run double in the top of the 8th inning of the Giants' 4–2 victory.

Notable Achievements:

Batted over .300 three times.

Scored more than 100 runs five times.

Finished in double-digits in triples three times.

Surpassed 30 doubles four times.

Stole at least 40 bases five times, surpassing 60 steals once (62 in 1914).

Compiled on-base percentage in excess of .400 twice.

Led N.L. in: runs scored five times; bases on balls four times; stolen bases twice; and on-base percentage once.

Led N.L. left-fielders in: fielding percentage twice; putouts twice; assists once; and double plays turned once.

Ranks among Giants career leaders in: runs scored (10th); doubles (8th); stolen bases (4th); bases on balls (6th); and plate appearances (10th).

Holds Giants 20th-century single-season stolen base record (62 in 1914).

Hit for cycle vs. Pittsburgh on September 17, 1920.

Finished fourth in 1914 N.L. MVP voting.

Four-time *Baseball Magazine* N.L. All-America Team selection (1914, 1917, 1918 & 1919).

Three-time N.L. champion (1913, 1917 & 1921).

1921 world champion.

21 FREDDIE LINDSTROM

Freddie Lindstrom banged out 231 hits twice while playing for the Giants. *(Courtesy of Library of Congress)*

Dubbed "The Boy Wonder" by Giants fans early in his career for the success he experienced at such a young age, Freddie Lindstrom spent nine years in New York, establishing himself during that time as one of the top offensive threats in manager John McGraw's lineup. An outstanding right-handed line-drive hitter with occasional home-run power, Lindstrom batted over .300 six straight times for the Giants, topping the .350-mark twice. He also hit more than 20 home runs once, knocked in more than 100 runs twice, scored more than 100 runs twice, and surpassed 200 hits on two separate occasions, en route to earning two top-10 finishes in the league MVP voting. A solid defensive player as well, Lindstrom led all N.L. third basemen in assists once and fielding percentage once, before moving to the outfield due to a chronically bad back.

Born on the Southwest Side of Chicago, Illinois, on November 21, 1905, Frederick Charles Lindstrom grew up rooting for the White Sox before suffering the disappointment of having his hero Shoeless Joe Jackson implicated in the *Black Sox* scandal of 1919. After transferring from Chicago's Tilden High School to Loyola Academy in nearby Wilmette, Lindstrom signed with the Giants at only 16 years of age. He spent most of the next two years with the Toledo Mud Hens of the American Association before having his contract purchased by the Giants on September 18, 1923.

Joining the Giants less than five months after celebrating his 18th birthday, Lindstrom spent most of the 1924 campaign serving the team as a utility infielder, compiling a batting average of .253 in 79 official at-bats. Subsequently forced into action in the World Series due to an injury suffered by starting third baseman Heinie Groh, Lindstrom, at 18 years, 10 months, and 13 days old, became the youngest player ever to take part in the Fall Classic. Displaying a tremendous amount of poise for such a young man, Lindstrom acquitted himself extremely well in the seven-game loss to Washington, playing errorless ball in the field and collecting 10 hits in 30 official trips to the plate, for a batting average of .333. Particularly impressive in the Giants' 6–2 victory over Walter Johnson in Game 5 of the Series, when he reached the legendary right-hander for 4 of New York's 13 hits, Lindstrom found himself being praised at the end of the day by Johnson, who described him as "a wonder . . . easily the brightest star in this series."

Lindstrom gradually established himself as the Giants' starting third baseman over the course of the ensuing campaign, finishing the year with 4 home runs, 33 RBIs, and a .287 batting average, in 104 games and just under 400 plate appearances. Rapidly maturing into one of the league's best young players, the 20-year-old infielder then hit 9 homers, drove in 76 runs, scored 90 times, and batted .302 in 1926, en route to earning a ninth-place finish in the N.L. MVP voting. After a similarly productive 1927 season in which he hit 7 home runs, knocked in 58 runs, batted .306, and placed among the league leaders with 107 runs scored and 36 doubles, Lindstrom emerged as one of the Senior Circuit's top batsmen the following year. In addition to hitting 14 home runs and leading the league with 231 hits, he placed near the top of the league rankings with 107 RBIs, 99 runs scored, 39 doubles, 15 stolen bases, 330 total bases, and a .358 batting average. The 5'11", 170-pound Lindstrom also led all N.L. third basemen in assists and fielding percentage, earning in the process a second-place finish to St. Louis first baseman Jim Bottomley in the league MVP balloting.

Lindstrom's stellar play in all phases of the game drew raves from the local media, which sang his praises in the spring of 1929. Sportswriter Pat Robinson wrote in the *New York Daily News*, "Those hands of his are the talk of the baseball world. Sensational playing places him among the greatest in the game."

William Hennigan of the *New York World* gushed, "The best third sacker in the National League, one of the greatest third basemen the game has ever produced."

Ken Smith of the *New York Evening Graphic* added, "Lindstrom hit peaks of third basing never before attained during the final month of last season. An outstanding individual of the game; another Hornsby, Wagner, Cobb, or Speaker, this kid, ace fielder, hitter, thinker, and runner."

Meanwhile, John Kieran reported in his *New York Times* column *Sports of the Times*, "(former Giants pitcher) Arthur Nehf was sitting in the Chicago dugout talking about the Giant hitters. He talked of (Edd) Roush, (Travis) Jackson, (Bill) Terry, and (Shanty) Hogan and then remarked decisively that Freddie Lindstrom was the cleverest of them all at the plate and the hardest man to fool in the clutch."

Despite missing a significant amount of playing time due to injury, Lindstrom had another solid year in 1929, finishing the season with 15 homers, 91 RBIs, 99 runs scored, and a .319 batting average. He followed that up with an exceptional 1930 campaign in which he knocked in 106 runs and placed among the league leaders with 22 home runs, 127 runs scored, 231 hits, 39 doubles, 15 stolen bases, 350 total bases, and a career-high .379 batting average.

Apparently just reaching his peak at only 25 years of age, Lindstrom began experiencing physical problems in 1931 that altered the remainder of his career dramatically. Hampered by a bad back and a broken ankle he suffered while sliding into third base, Lindstrom appeared in only 78 games in 1931, a season in which the Giants shifted him to center field. Although Lindstrom developed into a solid outfielder, finishing first among N.L. center-fielders with 18 assists in 1932, he never again experienced the same level of success at the plate. After hitting 15 home runs, driving in 92 runs, scoring 83 times, and batting .271 in 1932, Lindstrom found himself included in a three-team trade the Giants completed with Pittsburgh and Philadelphia at season's end that sent him to the Pirates. New Giants player-manager Bill Terry, whose relationship with Lindstrom changed after the team reneged on its original promise to have the latter succeed John McGraw as skipper, explained the move by stating, "Fred no longer has that burst of speed he used to have."

Lindstrom spent the next two years in Pittsburgh, batting .310 and scoring 70 runs in 1933, before assuming a part-time role the following year. He subsequently split his final two seasons between the Chicago Cubs and Brooklyn Dodgers, announcing his retirement after being released by Brooklyn prior to the start of the 1937 campaign. Still only 31 years old at the time, Lindstrom ended his playing career with 103 home runs, 779 runs batted in, 895 runs scored, 1,747 hits, 81 triples, 301 doubles, a .311 batting average, a .351 on-base percentage, and a .449 slugging percentage. In his nine years with the Giants, Lindstrom hit 91 homers, knocked in 603 runs, scored 705 times, amassed 1,347 hits, 63 triples, and 212 doubles, batted .318, compiled a .359 on-base percentage, and posted a .462 slugging percentage. His .318 batting average continues to rank as the eighth-best in franchise history.

Following his retirement, Lindstrom spent several years managing in the minor leagues, before coaching the Northwestern University baseball team for 13 seasons. The members of the Veteran's Committee elected him to the Hall of Fame in 1976, five years before he passed away at 75 years of age on October 4, 1981.

Giant Career Highlights:

Best Season: Lindstrom had easily his two best seasons in 1928 and 1930, compiling extremely similar numbers in numerous offensive categories those two years. After hitting 14 home runs, driving in 107 runs, scoring 99 times, amassing 231 hits, 39 doubles, and 330 total bases, stealing 15 bases, batting .358, and posting an OPS of .894 in the first of those campaigns, Lindstrom established career-high marks in home runs (22), runs scored (127), total bases (350), batting average (.379), and OPS (.999) two years later, while once again collecting 231 hits, 39 doubles, and 15 stolen bases. On the surface, it would seem that Lindstrom had the finest season of his career in 1930. However, it must be remembered that the N.L. used a livelier ball that year, resulting in a composite league batting average of .303. Despite hitting .379,

Lindstrom finished just fourth in the N.L. batting race, placing in the league's top five in only two other offensive categories. Meanwhile, he finished among the leaders in five different categories in 1928, topping the circuit in hits, finishing second in total bases, and placing fifth in batting average, RBIs, and doubles. Furthermore, Lindstrom led all N.L. third basemen in assists and fielding percentage, with his 340 assists representing easily the highest total of his career. All things considered, Lindstrom had his finest season in 1928.

Memorable Moments/Greatest Performances: Lindstrom delivered one of the most dramatic hits of his career on June 17, 1926, when, after Pittsburgh's Hal Rhyne put the Pirates out in front by a score of 5–3 in the top of the 13th inning by hitting a two-run homer, Lindstrom countered with a three-run blast in the bottom of the frame, giving the Giants a 6–5 victory.

On June 25, 1928, Lindstrom became the first National League player to collect nine hits in a doubleheader when he went 9-for-11, with 4 RBIs and 4 runs scored, in leading the Giants to 12–4 and 8–2 victories over Philadelphia. He nearly matched that effort later in the year when, on September 11, he went 8-for-10 during a doubleheader sweep of the Boston Braves.

Lindstrom had one of his most productive days at the plate on August 24, 1929, when he helped lead the Giants to a 14–8 win over Pittsburgh by going 4-for-5, with a homer, 2 RBIs, and a career-high 5 runs scored.

Lindstrom accomplished a number of outstanding feats during his exceptional 1930 campaign, at one point putting together a 24-game hitting streak that remains tied for the fourth-longest in franchise history. During the streak, which lasted from July 28 to August 23, Lindstrom hit 6 home runs, knocked in 29 runs, scored 29 times, and collected 50 hits in 105 at-bats, for a batting average of .476. The highlight of the streak proved to be Lindstrom's performance against Boston on August 1, when he led the Giants to a 10–4 victory by going 4-for-5, with 2 homers, a double, 3 runs scored, a stolen base, and a career-high 6 runs batted in. Earlier in the year, on April 26, Lindstrom keyed a 13–2 win over the Phillies by going 5-for-5, with 2 RBIs and 4 runs scored. Nearly two weeks later, on May 8, he hit for the cycle, doing so during a 13–10 victory over the Pirates at Forbes Field. Lindstrom finished the contest 5-for-6, with 3 RBIs and 3 runs scored.

Yet, even though Lindstrom performed extremely well against Washington in the 1924 World Series, batting .333, hitting safely four times against Walter Johnson in Game 5, and establishing a new Series record (since broken) in

Game 2 by recording seven assists at third base, he is perhaps best remembered for a play he didn't make. With the Giants and Senators tied at 3 runs apiece in the bottom of the 12th inning of Game 7, a ground ball headed directly towards Lindstrom hit a pebble, causing it to take a bad hop over his head, and allowing the winning run to score. Lindstrom later recalled, "So they won it. (Giants pitcher) Jack Bentley, who was something of a philosopher, I think summed it up after the game. 'Walter Johnson,' Bentley said, 'is such a loveable character that the good Lord didn't want to see him get beat again.'"

Meanwhile, Heinie Groh, whose injury enabled Lindstrom to start every game of the Series at third base for the Giants, told Lawrence Ritter in *The Glory of Their Times*, "It wasn't Freddie's fault. It could have happened to anybody. He never had a chance to get the ball. It was Fate, that's all; Fate and a pebble."

Notable Achievements:

Batted over .300 six times, topping the .350-mark twice.

Hit more than 20 home runs once (22 in 1930).

Knocked in more than 100 runs twice.

Scored more than 100 runs twice.

Surpassed 200 hits twice.

Finished in double-digits in triples once (12 in 1925).

Surpassed 30 doubles three times.

Compiled on-base percentage in excess of .400 once (.425 in 1930).

Posted slugging percentage in excess of .500 twice.

Led N.L. with 231 hits in 1928.

Led N.L. third basemen in assists once and fielding percentage once.

Led N.L. center-fielders with 18 assists in 1932.

Ranks eighth in Giants history with .318 career batting average.

First N.L. player to collect nine hits in a doubleheader (June 25, 1928 vs. Pittsburgh).

Hit for cycle vs. Pittsburgh on May 8, 1930.

Finished second in 1928 N.L. MVP voting.

Two-time *Sporting News* All-Star selection (1928 & 1930).

1924 N.L. champion.

Elected to Baseball Hall of Fame by members of Veteran's Committee in 1976.

22 GAYLORD PERRY

Gaylord Perry teamed up with Juan Marichal to give the Giants one of the National League's most formidable pitching duos during the 1960s. *(Courtesy of Mearsonlineauctions.com)*

The first pitcher in baseball history to win the Cy Young Award in both leagues, Gaylord Perry posted 314 victories over the course of his Hall of Fame career. Although Perry earned both Cy Youngs and amassed the vast majority of his wins while pitching for other teams, he proved to be a key contributor to the success the Giants experienced from 1964 to 1971, compiling 130 victories for teams that captured one division title and earned five second-place finishes during that time. En route to earning two All-Star selections and one runner-up finish in the Cy Young balloting during his time in San Francisco, Perry surpassed 20 victories twice and won at least 15 games on four other occasions. He also compiled an ERA under 3.00 six times, struck out more than 200 batters four times, and threw more than 20 complete games and 300 innings twice each, combining with Juan Marichal to give the Giants arguably the National League's most formidable pitching duo. Yet, in spite of his many accomplishments, Perry is perhaps remembered more than anything else for his purported used of the spitball, or grease-ball, which embarrassed batters, confounded umpires, and infuriated opposing managers for two decades.

Born in Williamston, North Carolina, on September 15, 1938, Gaylord Jackson Perry grew up on a farm, where he and his older brother, Jim, helped their parents raise animals and grow tobacco, corn, and peanuts. Both Perry brothers attended local Williamston High School, with Gaylord starring in football, basketball, and baseball. After starting out as a third baseman on the diamond, the younger Perry gradually transitioned to the pitcher's mound, where he ended up winning 33 of 38 decisions. Despite being offered dozens of college scholarships in both baseball and basketball, Perry elected to sign with the Giants as an amateur free agent in 1958, giving half of the $60,000 bonus money to his parents, and putting the rest in the bank.

Subsequently assigned to St. Cloud in the Class-C Northern League, the 20-year-old Perry began his long and arduous journey to the big leagues. Splitting the next three years between St. Cloud, Corpus Christi of the Double-A Texas League, and Tacoma of the Pacific Coast League, the 6'4", 210-pound right-hander pitched well wherever he went, prompting the Giants to place him on their 40-man major-league roster for the first time late in 1961. However, as it turned out, Perry was still two years away from earning a permanent spot on the Giants roster. Struggling in a limited number of appearances as a spot starter and reliever in both 1962 and 1963, Perry earned a return trip to Tacoma each year, although he received the endorsement of Hall of Fame pitcher and Giants farm director Carl Hubbell, who, after watching him during the latter stages of the 1962 campaign, commented, "He's gotten around to throwing that good fastball of his more frequently, which makes his other pitches more effective. He's acquiring the stuff which will enable him to win consistently with the big club."

Arriving in San Francisco to stay at the start of the 1964 season, Perry benefited greatly from a seven-player trade the Giants completed during the previous offseason in which they acquired pitcher Bob Shaw and two other players from the Milwaukee Braves. Shaw, who had mastered the art of throwing the spitball over the years, taught Perry how to throw the illegal pitch. With Perry also working with pitching coach Larry Jansen on developing a slider, he gradually incorporated both new offerings into his repertoire of pitches that also included a curveball, change of pace, and excellent fastball.

Armed with his new weapons, the 25-year-old Perry had a solid rookie season, compiling a record of 12–11 and an ERA of 2.75 in his dual role of spot starter/long reliever. However, he took a step backwards in 1965, going just 8–12 with a 4.19 ERA, and drawing the ire of his teammates and new Giants manager Herman Franks by constantly arguing with umpires and complaining about errors made behind him in the field.

Arriving in spring training the following year with a career record of just 24–30 and no definite role on the Giants pitching staff, Perry worked harder than ever before, getting himself into the best shape of his young career. Showing the fruits of his labor, Perry emerged as a top-flight starter, establishing himself as the number 2 man in San Francisco's rotation, behind Juan Marichal, by compiling a record of 21–8, a 2.99 ERA, and 201 strikeouts, while tossing 13 complete games and 255 ⅔ innings. Perry's 21 victories and .724 winning percentage placed him third in the league rankings, earning him his first All-Star selection.

Despite posting an overall record of just 31–32 over the course of the next two seasons, Perry continued to perform well for the Giants. Pitching mostly in hard luck (he lost nine games by one run), the lanky right-hander went just 15–17 in 1967, even though he finished among the league leaders with a 2.61 ERA, 230 strikeouts, 18 complete games, 293 innings pitched, and a WHIP of 1.075. Continuing to receive a lack of run-support the following year, Perry finished just 16–15, although he again placed near the top of the league rankings in ERA (2.45), complete games (19), innings pitched (290 ⅔), and WHIP (1.029).

Perry proved to be more fortunate in 1969, when his 2.49 ERA, 233 strikeouts, 26 complete games, and league-leading 325 ⅓ innings pitched helped him compile a record of 19–14. Thrust into the role of staff ace the following year due to the diminished pitching skills of Juan Marichal, Perry responded by going 23–13, leading all N.L. hurlers in victories in the process. He also compiled an ERA of 3.20, struck out 214 batters, finished second in the league with 23 complete games, and topped the circuit with 5 shutouts and 328 ⅔ innings pitched.

As Perry continued his ascension into the select group of elite N.L. pitchers, he further developed his reputation for doctoring baseballs. Frequently accused of using foreign substances, such as spit, jelly, and grease, to make his pitches move in an atypical manner, Perry became the subject of controversy throughout the league, resulting in numerous accusations and strip-searches on the mound. Perry, though, seemed to revel in the attention, using it to his advantage as a means of creating doubt in the hitter's mind. Fidgeting with his glove and touching his face, uniform, cap, belt, or pockets repeatedly while awaiting the signs from his catcher, Perry toyed with opposing batters, making them believe that he intended to deceive them with every pitch.

Although Perry spent most of his career dodging questions related to his purported use of the spitter, he later provided an account of the way he believed his reputation gave him an edge over opposing hitters, revealing: "Cincinnati had a great team in the late '60s, early '70s, and one day I was watching them take batting practice. I said to myself, 'I have to do something different today.' I went out and I shook Rose's hand, Morgan's hand, Perez, and Griffey Sr. with a handful of Vaseline. They thought about that all the rest of the day. I was pitching against them tomorrow, so, what do you think they were looking for? Maybe I used it, maybe I didn't."

For his part, umpire Bill Haller suggested that he never caught Perry doing anything illegal on the mound, stating, "I watched Gaylord like a hawk. I've never found anything. I'll tell you what he's got: a good curve, a fine fastball, a good change, and a fine sinker. I'll tell you what Perry is: He's one helluva pitcher, and a fine competitor."

Years later, Perry discussed more openly his somewhat devious reputation in his autobiography, which he entitled, *Me and the Spitter*. Although he contended that he rarely threw the spitball, Perry admitted, "I'd always have it (grease) in at least two places, in case the umpires would ask me to wipe one off. I never wanted to be caught out there with anything though . . . it wouldn't be professional." Perry's methods worked since, despite being under constant surveillance, he didn't suffer his first ejection for using an illegal substance until 1982—his 21st big-league season.

Perry remained in San Francisco one more year, compiling a record of 16–12 and an ERA of 2.76 in 1971, before being traded to the Cleveland Indians for hard-throwing southpaw Sam McDowell at season's end. Perry left the Giants with a career record of 134–109, an ERA of 2.96, 1,606 strikeouts in 2,294 ⅓ innings of work, 21 shutouts, 125 complete games, and a WHIP of 1.152.

Perry ended up pitching some of his best ball for the Indians, earning A.L. Cy Young honors in his first year in Cleveland by winning a league-leading 24 games for a team that posted an overall record of just 72–84. He also topped the circuit with 29 complete games and finished among the leaders with a 1.92 ERA, 234 strikeouts, and 342 ⅔ innings pitched. After going 19–19 the following year, Perry returned to top form in 1974, concluding the campaign with a record of 21–13, an ERA of 2.51, 216 strikeouts, 28 complete games, and 322 ⅓ innings pitched.

Looking back at Perry's performance for the Indians over the course of those three seasons, former team President Gabe Paul stated, "Gaylord was fantastic, simply fantastic. His contributions were even better than the records show, and they show plenty. He was such a great influence on the younger players. Perry was far and away the best pitcher in the American League."

Perry spent part of one more season in Cleveland, before tensions between him and player-manager Frank Robinson prompted the Indians to trade him to Texas for three players in June 1975. Perry remained in Texas until the end of 1977, winning 15 games for the Rangers in each of his two full seasons there. Traded back to the National League prior to the start of the 1978 campaign, Perry had a big year for the Padres, leading all N.L. hurlers with 21 wins and a .778 winning percentage, en route to becoming the first pitcher to earn Cy Young honors in both leagues.

Perry didn't prove to be nearly as successful in any of his five remaining big-league seasons, failing to win more than 12 games in any single campaign while splitting his time between the Padres, Rangers, Yankees, Braves, Mariners, and Royals. After posting his 300th victory with the Mariners in 1982, Perry retired one year later, ending his career with an overall record of 314–265, an ERA of 3.11, 3,534 strikeouts in 5,350 innings of work, 53 shutouts, 303 complete games, and a WHIP of 1.181. In addition to compiling the 17th-most wins of any pitcher in MLB history, Perry ranks among the all-time leaders in strikeouts (8th), innings pitched (6th), and starts (9th). Over the course of 22 seasons, he earned five All-Star selections and two top-10 finishes in the league MVP voting.

Following his playing career, Perry retired to his 500-acre farm in Martin County, North Carolina, where he grew tobacco and peanuts. After going bankrupt a few years later, he briefly worked for Fiesta Foods as a sales manager before accepting the position of head baseball coach at the University of South Carolina. Perry remained in that post until 1991, when he retired to private life.

Giant Career Highlights:

Best Season: Perry pitched exceptionally well for the Giants in 1966, earning his first All-Star selection by going 21–8, with a 2.99 ERA, 201 strikeouts, 13 complete games, 255 ⅔ innings pitched, and a WHIP of 1.103. Particularly effective during the month of June, Perry earned N.L. Player of the Month honors by winning all five of his decisions, allowing just 4 earned runs over 38 innings in the process. After getting off to a tremendous start, Perry's record stood at 20–2 on August 20. However, he subsequently slumped down the stretch, dropping six of his final seven decisions, to finish the season with a mark of 21–8. Perry proved to be a bit more consistent in 1970, when he earned All-Star honors and a second-place finish in the Cy Young voting by leading all N.L. hurlers with 23 wins, 5 shutouts, and 328 ⅔ innings pitched. He also placed among the league leaders with a 3.20 ERA, 214 strikeouts, 23 complete games, and a WHIP of 1.144. Finishing the season strong, Perry went 6–0 during the month of September, tossing four consecutive shutouts at one point.

Memorable Moments/Greatest Performances: Perry put together two streaks of 40 consecutive scoreless innings during his time in San Francisco, with the first of those lasting from August 28, 1967, to September 10, 1967. The highlight of that skein proved to be an extraordinary effort on September 1, when he tossed 16 shutout innings against Cincinnati in a game the Giants eventually won by a score of 1–0 in 21 innings. Perry's second such streak lasted from September 1, 1970, to September 23, 1970, a period during which he threw four straight shutouts. Included in that streak was a 3–0 whitewashing of San Diego on September 19 in which Perry allowed just 3 hits, retiring the first 19 Padre batters he faced.

Perry turned in a heroic effort on May 31, 1964, when he came out of the bullpen to work 10 scoreless innings in a game the Giants eventually won by a score of 8–6 in 23 innings over the New York Mets. Entering the contest in the bottom of the 13th, Perry surrendered 7 hits and struck out 9 over the next 10 frames, earning the victory in a game that lasted a record 7 hours and 22 minutes.

Perry tossed a pair of 2-hit shutouts during his time in San Francisco, with the first of those coming on August 8, 1964, when he blanked the Reds by a score of 1–0. Perry again shut out Cincinnati on just 2 hits on June 26, 1966, this time emerging victorious in a much less competitive 10–0 game.

Perry turned in one of his most dominating pitching performances on July 22, 1966, allowing just 2 hits and recording a career-high 15 strikeouts, in defeating the Phillies by a score of 4–1.

Perry shut out Chicago on just 1 hit on August 26, 1968, yielding just a 7th-inning single by Glenn Beckert during a 3–0 win over the Cubs.

Just three weeks later, on September 17, 1968, Perry threw the only no-hitter of his career, defeating Bob Gibson and the Cardinals by a score of 1–0 in a classic pitcher's duel at Candlestick Park. Perry allowed just 2 walks and struck out 9 during the contest. Ironically, St. Louis right-hander Ray Washburn no-hit the Giants the very next day, marking the first time in Major League history that back-to-back no-hitters had been pitched in the same series.

Still, the most memorable moment of Perry's career arguably took place on July 20, 1969, when he connected for his first big-league homer. A notoriously weak hitter, Perry once inspired former Giants manager Alvin Dark to quip, "They'll put a man on the moon before he hits a home run." Perry, who homered during a 7–3 victory over the Dodgers, delivered his blast less than one hour after the Apollo 11 spacecraft carrying Neil Armstrong and Buzz Aldrin landed on the moon.

Notable Achievements:

Won more than 20 games twice, surpassing 15 victories four other times.

Posted winning percentage in excess of .700 twice.

Compiled ERA below 3.00 six times, posting mark under 2.50 twice.

Struck out more than 200 batters four times.

Threw more than 300 innings twice, tossing more than 250 innings four other times.

Threw more than 20 complete games twice.

Led N.L. pitchers in: wins once; shutouts once; starts once; innings pitched twice; assists twice; putouts once; and fielding percentage twice.

Ranks among Giants career leaders in: strikeouts (6th); innings pitched (8th); and games started (8th).

Threw no-hitter vs. St. Louis on September 17, 1968.

Finished second in 1970 N.L. Cy Young voting.

June 1966 N.L. Player of the Month.

Two-time N.L. All-Star (1966 & 1970).

Number 97 on *The Sporting News'* 1999 list of Baseball's 100 Greatest Players.

1962 N.L. champion.

Elected to Baseball Hall of Fame by members of BBWAA in 1991.

23 LARRY DOYLE

Larry Doyle's total of 25 triples in 1911 represents a 20th-century franchise record. *(Courtesy of Library of Congress)*

A key contributor to three straight pennant-winning teams as a member of the Giants, Larry Doyle established himself as the National League's premier second baseman during his time in New York, which covered two tours of duty with the club between 1907 and 1920. Wielding an unusually potent bat for a *Dead Ball Era* second sacker, the lefty-swinging Doyle compiled a .292 batting average over parts of 13 seasons with the Giants, surpassing the .300-mark on five separate occasions. Regularly placing among the N.L. leaders in most major offensive categories, Doyle also topped 10 homers twice, scored more than 100 runs once, stole more than 30 bases five times, and finished in double-digits in triples six times, amassing a 20th century franchise record 25 three-baggers in 1911. Yet, Doyle, who acquired the nickname "Laughing Larry" due to his kindly nature and sunny disposition, is perhaps best remembered for telling noted author and newspaperman Damon Runyon in 1911, "It's great to be young and a New York Giant."

Born in Caseyville, Illinois, on July 31, 1886, Lawrence Joseph Doyle spent five years working alongside his father in the coal mines near his home in Breese, Illinois, 39 miles east of St. Louis, before he quit mining in 1906 to begin a career in professional baseball. Having earlier spent his weekends playing semipro ball, Doyle joined Mattoon, Illinois, of the Kentucky-Illinois-Tennessee League, where he remained one year before advancing to Springfield of the Three-I League. After spending the first half of 1907 playing third base for Springfield, Doyle signed with the Giants for a then-record $4,500 after Hall of Fame first baseman Dan Brouthers provided his old teammate John McGraw with a favorable report on the young infielder.

Doyle's time in New York began in dubious fashion when he arrived late to the team after taking the wrong boat across the Hudson River. As Doyle explained years later, "The train from Springfield dumped me off in Jersey City because Grand Central wasn't even built then. When I got off the ferry, I walked over to a cop. 'How do I get to the Polo Grounds?' I asked. 'See the El over there? Take it to the last stop,' he said. I got off at the last stop and looked around. I didn't see any Polo Grounds. All I saw was the ocean. I was at South Ferry, the wrong end of the line."

Doyle made his debut with the Giants the following day, on July 22, 1907, when, starting at second base for the first time in his pro career, he made an error that allowed the Cubs to score an insurance run in their 2–0 victory over the Giants. Although disappointed in his performance, Doyle subsequently received words of encouragement from manager John McGraw, who patted him on the back and said, "Forget it. When you learn more about second, you won't make mistakes like that."

Doyle ended up batting just .260 and committing 26 errors in the field over the season's final 69 games, prompting the local newspapers to question the wisdom of signing the young infielder to such a hefty contract. One reporter for the *New York Evening Telegram* wrote at the start of spring training in 1908:

> This is the summer of Larry Doyle's prosperity or discontent. Doyle was so streaky last year that it was almost out of the question to get any fixed line on his ability. One day he would be a dead wall which nothing could pass, and the next he wobbled on every hit that came

to him, like a boxcar on a coal railroad. Some days he could hit the ball on both sides of the seams, and on other days he missed all sides. Some baseball men are confident that it is merely a question of time when Doyle will establish himself as a sterling, dependable player.

In spite of the doubts expressed by others, John McGraw retained the utmost confidence in Doyle, naming him team captain prior to the start of the 1908 campaign. Rewarding his manager for the faith he placed in him, Doyle finished third in the N.L. with a .308 batting average, while also placing among the league leaders with a .354 on-base percentage and a .398 slugging percentage.

Singing his own praises for displaying so much confidence in his young second baseman, McGraw declared in early September, "I hung on to Doyle when the New York fans and critics were calling for his scalp, and today I would not trade him for any man playing baseball. Think of it, in the last series at Pittsburgh and Chicago, Doyle got in no less than 18 safe hits. Every time he went to bat he hit the ball clean and hard. There is nothing like having confidence in one's own judgment."

Doyle further ingratiated himself to McGraw the following year by topping the Senior Circuit with 172 hits, placing second in the league with 6 home runs and 239 total bases, and also finishing among the leaders with 86 runs scored, 11 triples, 27 doubles, a .302 batting average, a .419 slugging percentage, and an OPS of .779. He followed that up with a similarly productive 1910 campaign in which he batted .285, knocked in 69 runs, scored 97 times, accumulated 14 triples, posted an OPS of .781, and stole a career-high 39 bases—the second of five straight times he swiped more than 30 bags.

Doyle continued his ascension into stardom in 1911, earning a spot on *Baseball Magazine's* N.L. All-America team and a third-place finish in the Chalmers Award voting by leading the Giants to the first of three consecutive pennants by topping the N.L. with 25 triples and placing among the leaders in nine other offensive categories, including home runs (13), runs scored (102), stolen bases (38), batting average (.310), and OPS (.924). He captured league MVP honors the following year by hitting 10 home runs, scoring 98 times, and establishing career highs with 91 RBIs and a .330 batting average. Doyle's exceptional performance prompted noted sports columnist Hugh Fullerton to write, "Doyle is easily the best ball player on the Giants; a hustling, aggressive,

McGraw style of player, full of nerve, grit and true courage. I think he is gamer than his manager, and, in some respects, a better baseball general."

Yet, in spite of the outstanding offense, leadership, and hustle Doyle brought to the Giants, he never developed into a top-flight defensive player. Possessing somewhat limited range and reportedly having a difficult time fielding slowly hit ground balls, Doyle never finished any higher than third in assists among N.L. second basemen. Meanwhile, he led N.L. second sackers in errors on three separate occasions.

After posting solid offensive numbers again in 1913, Doyle experienced something of an off year in 1914, batting just .260 and compiling an OPS of only .695, despite scoring 87 runs. However, he rebounded the following year, leading the N.L. with a .320 batting average, 189 hits, and 40 doubles. With Doyle subsequently batting just .268 and scoring only 55 runs over the first five months of the 1916 campaign, the Giants elected to include him in a trade they completed with the Chicago Cubs in late August that netted them third baseman Heinie Zimmerman. Doyle spent the rest of 1916 and all of 1917 in Chicago before being reacquired by the Giants prior to the start of the 1918 campaign. He subsequently finished out his career in New York, serving the Giants as a part-time player the next three years before announcing his retirement at the end of the 1920 season. Doyle ended his career with 74 home runs, 794 runs batted in, 960 runs scored, 1,887 hits, 123 triples, 299 doubles, 298 stolen bases, a .290 batting average, a .357 on-base percentage, and a .408 slugging percentage, compiling the vast majority of those numbers as a member of the Giants. He retired as the National League's all-time leader among second basemen in hits, triples, doubles, slugging average, total bases (2,654), and extra-base hits (496). Doyle continues to rank among the Giants' all-time leaders in several offensive categories, including runs scored (9th), hits (8th), triples (4th), doubles (7th), and stolen bases (7th).

Following his retirement as an active player, Doyle continued to work for the Giants in various capacities over the course of the next two decades, including managing their minor-league affiliates in Toronto and Nashville. After contracting tuberculosis in 1942, he entered the Trudeau Sanitarium in Saranac Lake, New York, where he remained until the facility closed its doors in 1954 due to the development of an effective antibiotic treatment. Doyle continued to live in Saranac Lake another 20 years, before passing away at the age of 87 on March 1, 1974.

Giant Career Highlights:

Best Season: Although Doyle had a big year for the Giants in 1915, driving in 70 runs, scoring 86 times, and leading the N.L. with a .320 batting average, 189 hits, and 40 doubles, he actually posted better overall numbers in both 1911 and 1912. En route to winning league MVP honors in the second of those campaigns, Doyle hit 10 homers, scored 98 runs, accumulated 184 hits and 33 doubles, stole 36 bases, compiled an OPS of .864, and established career highs with 91 RBIs and a .330 batting average. Nevertheless, the feeling here is that Doyle had his finest all-around season in 1911, when he earned a third-place finish in the Chalmers Award balloting by hitting 13 home runs, knocking in 77 runs, stealing 38 bases, batting .310, and establishing career highs with 102 runs scored, 277 total bases, a .397 on-base percentage, a .527 slugging percentage, an OPS of .924, and a league-leading 25 triples, which represents the highest single-season total in franchise history since the beginning of the 20th century (George Davis amassed 27 triples in 1893).

Memorable Moments/Greatest Performances: Doyle delivered a number of clutch, game-winning hits during his time in New York, with the first of those coming on September 24, 1910, when his RBI single in the bottom of the ninth inning gave the Giants a 6–5 victory over the Cubs.

Doyle came up big again on September 2, 1912, hitting a game-winning three-run homer in the top of the 12th inning that gave the Giants a 5–2 win in the first game of their doubleheader sweep of the Boston Braves.

Doyle provided further heroics on April 17, 1913, when he collected four hits, including the game-winning safety, during a 3–2, 10-inning victory at Boston.

On July 17, 1914, Doyle ended a 21-inning marathon at Pittsburgh's Forbes Field by hitting a game-winning two-run homer off Pirates starter Babe Adams, who suffered a heartbreaking 3–1 defeat.

Doyle made history on September 18, 1911, when he tied a major-league record by stealing home twice during a 7–2 victory over the Pittsburgh Pirates. The Giants swiped a total of 8 bases during the contest.

Doyle had a huge day against Cincinnati on June 5, 1912, collecting 5 hits and scoring 4 runs during a 22–10 pasting of the Reds. He had a similarly productive afternoon against Brooklyn on April 14, 1915, going 5-for-5, with 2 RBIs and 4 runs scored during a 16–3 win over the Dodgers. Less than three months later, on July 10, 1915, Doyle went 4-for-5, with 2 triples, 4 RBIs, and 2 runs scored, in leading the Giants to a 7–3 victory over Cincinnati.

Although the Giants ended up losing the 1911 World Series to Philadelphia in six games, Doyle helped them stave off elimination with a 4–3 victory in Game 5 by going 4-for-5 and scoring the game-winning run in the bottom of the 10th inning. Doyle's game-winning tally subsequently became known as the "phantom run" since he scored it on a sacrifice fly by Fred Merkle, leaping into the arms of his joyous teammates after crossing home plate, but actually failing to touch the plate, as umpire Bill Klem later admitted.

Notable Achievements:

Batted over .300 five times, surpassing the .320-mark twice.

Scored more than 100 runs once (102 in 1911).

Finished in double-digits in home runs twice.

Finished in double-digits in triples six times, surpassing 20 three-baggers once (25 in 1911).

Topped 30 doubles twice, amassing 40 doubles in 1915.

Stole more than 30 bases five straight times (1909–1913).

Compiled slugging percentage in excess of .500 once (.527 in 1911).

Posted OPS in excess of .900 once (.924 in 1911).

Led N.L. in: batting average once; hits twice; triples once; and doubles once.

Led N.L. second basemen in putouts once and double plays turned once.

Ranks among Giants career leaders in: runs scored (9th); hits (8th); triples (4th); doubles (7th); total bases (8th); stolen bases (7th); walks (9th); extra-base hits (10th); games played (7th); plate appearances (6th); and at-bats (7th).

Holds Giants 20th century record for most triples in a season (25 in 1911).

1912 N.L. MVP.

Two-time *Baseball Magazine* N.L. All-America Team selection (1911 & 1915).

Three-time N.L. champion (1911, 1912 & 1913).

24 BUSTER POSEY

Buster Posey captured N.L. MVP honors in 2012, when he hit 24 homers, knocked in 103 runs, and led the National League with a .336 batting average. *(Courtesy of Dirk Hansen)*

The finest all-around catcher in the game today, Buster Posey has been an integral part of the success the Giants have experienced since 2010. An outstanding hitter, solid defender, and exceptional team leader, Posey has earned four All-Star selections, three Silver Sluggers, and three top-10 finishes in the N.L. MVP voting, winning the award in 2012, when he led the Giants to the second of the three world championships they have captured with him calling the signals for them behind home plate. Along the way, Posey has surpassed 20 homers twice, 100 RBIs once, and the .300-mark in batting four times, becoming in 2012 the first catcher in 70 years to lead the National League in hitting. At the same time, Posey has emerged as a top-flight receiver, with his deft handling of pitchers and expert signal-calling allowing Giant hurlers such as Tim Lincecum, Madison Bumgarner, Matt Cain, and Ryan Vogelsong to flourish. Indeed, in his years with the Giants, Posey has caught three no-hitters, including Cain's 2012 perfect game.

Born in Leesburg, Georgia, about 175 miles south of Atlanta, on March 27, 1987, Gerald Dempsey Posey III acquired the nickname "Buster" from his father, who carried with him through his childhood the same moniker. The younger Posey established himself as a multi-sport star while attending local Lee County High School, excelling in baseball, football, basketball, soccer, and golf. Particularly proficient on the baseball diamond, Posey earned numerous individual accolades as a pitcher and hitter while helping his team win a regional championship, including Georgia Gatorade Player of the Year and Louisville Slugger State Player of the Year honors as a senior. After also being named a *Baseball America* All-American, Posey elected to enroll at Florida State University rather than join the Los Angeles Angels of Anaheim, who selected him in the 50th round of the 2005 MLB Draft.

Posey subsequently earned All-America honors as a freshman shortstop with the Seminoles before moving behind the plate to accommodate the needs of his team. Commenting on the youngster's seamless transition to his new position, FSU baseball coach Mike Martin recalled, "I thought when he put the gear on for the first time he'd walk like a duck. After three pitches, I said, 'You got to be kidding me.' He looked as if he had been catching all his life."

Posey went on to win *Baseball America* College Player of the Year honors and *USA Baseball's* Golden Spikes Award, presented annually to the best amateur player in the country, as a junior in 2008, before choosing to turn pro when the Giants selected him with the fifth overall pick of the 2008 amateur draft.

Advancing rapidly through San Francisco's farm system, Posey made his major-league debut with the Giants a little over one year later, at 22 years of age. Appearing in seven games over the final three weeks of the 2009 campaign, Posey hit safely in 2 of his 17 trips to the plate, giving him a batting average of just .118. After beginning the following season back in the minors, Posey fared much better when he returned to the Giants in late May, earning 2010 N.L. Rookie of the Year honors and an 11th-place finish in the league MVP voting by hitting 18 homers, driving in 67 runs, scoring 58 times, and batting .305. He then helped the Giants win their first world championship since they moved to San Francisco more than five decades earlier by batting .375 against Atlanta in the NLDS, before homering once, driving in 2 runs, and compiling a batting average of .300 during the Giants' five-game victory over Texas in the World Series.

Making an extremely favorable impression on his Giants teammates, Posey drew praise from pitcher Matt Cain, who said, "Everybody heard about him . . . wondered what he was going to do. He just stepped right in and took right over. He did everything at an advanced level for a rookie."

Taking note of Posey's maturity at such a young age, Giants hurler Barry Zito commented, "He cares about what's going on defensively with our team, which is something you can't say for a lot of catchers, especially for a young guy coming up."

Tim Lincecum added, "Buster's just coming up, and, already, you see the hands he has."

Entering the 2011 campaign with the Giants expecting big things from him, Posey unfortunately saw his season end abruptly on May 25 when a collision at home plate with Florida's Scott Cousins left him with a broken leg and torn ligaments in his ankle. Forced to undergo season-ending surgery, Posey finished the year with a .284 batting average, 4 homers, and 21 RBIs.

Fully healthy by the start of the 2012 season, Posey led the Giants to their second pennant in three years by hitting 24 homers, driving in 103 runs, and topping the Senior Circuit with a .336 batting average, en route to earning his first All-Star selection and N.L. MVP and Comeback Player of the Year honors. Although Posey subsequently batted just .200 in the playoffs and World Series, he nevertheless made significant contributions to the Giants' successful run to another world championship, collecting 3 homers and 9 RBIs during the postseason.

Posey followed that up with a solid 2013 campaign in which he hit 15 home runs, knocked in 72 runs, and batted .294, before earning a sixth-place finish in the league MVP balloting in 2014 by hitting 22 homers, driving in 89 runs, and batting .311 for the eventual world champions.

In discussing Posey's rapid ascension into elite status among N.L. hitters, Giants manager Bruce Bochy stated, "He's got great discipline at the plate . . . It's nice to have a hitter like that who you're confident is going to put the ball in play."

Bochy added, "You talk about a catcher hitting cleanup, you think of a Johnny Bench. That's who comes to mind. You just don't see many of these guys."

Meanwhile, Matt Cain preferred to focus on Posey's more intangible qualities, calling him "an ultimate leader" and noting, "He's really worked on growing into being that guy who tries to find ways to get everybody even better."

Posey had another outstanding season in 2015, earning his third All-Star selection, third Silver Slugger, and a ninth-place finish in the league MVP voting by hitting 19 homers, driving in 95 runs, and batting .318. Although the 29-year-old receiver posted less impressive numbers on offense this past season, concluding the 2016 campaign with 14 home runs, 80 RBIs, and a .288 batting average, he nevertheless earned All-Star honors for the fourth time in the last five years. Posey will enter the 2017 season with career totals of 116 home runs, 527 RBIs, 443 runs scored, 1,005 hits, 190 doubles, and 8 triples, a lifetime batting average of .307, a .373 on-base percentage, a .476 slugging percentage, and an excellent chance of eventually claiming a considerably higher spot on this list.

Career Highlights:

Best Season: Although Posey also posted excellent numbers in both 2014 and 2015, he clearly had his best season for the Giants in 2012, when he established career-high marks in virtually every offensive category. In addition to topping the Senior Circuit with a .336 batting average, Posey hit 24 homers, scored 78 runs, and placed among the N.L. leaders with 103 RBIs, 178 hits, 39 doubles, a .408 on-base percentage, and a .549 slugging percentage, en route to earning league MVP honors.

Memorable Moments/Greatest Performances: As a rookie in 2010, Posey went on a ten–game hitting spree from July 1 to July 10 during which he batted .514, with 19 hits, 6 home runs, and 13 RBIs. The highlight of the streak came on July 7, when he led the Giants to a 15–2 mauling of the Milwaukee Brewers by going 4-for-4, with a pair of homers, 3 runs scored, and a career-high 6 RBIs.

Later in the year, on September 21, 2010, Posey gave the Giants a 1–0 victory over the Cubs by hitting an eighth-inning homer off Chicago right-hander Andrew Cashner. Although Posey batted just .217 against Philadelphia in the 2010 NLCS, he had a huge Game 4, leading the Giants to a 6–5 victory by going 4-for-5, with 2 doubles and 2 RBIs. His four safeties made him the first rookie to get four hits in one NLCS game.

Posey experienced one of his greatest moments on June 13, 2012, when he caught Matt Cain's perfect game, stating afterwards that the contest had him feeling "as nervous as I've ever been on a baseball field."

Posey also had a number of big days at the plate in 2012, with one of those coming on July 17, when he paced the Giants to a 9–0 win over Atlanta by going 3-for-5, with a pair of doubles and 5 RBIs. Just four days later, Posey drove in 3 runs and collected 4 hits, including a homer and a double, during a 10-inning, 6–5 victory over the Phillies. Posey continued his hot hitting in August, leading the Giants to a 16–4 pasting of Colorado on August 3 by going 4-for-5, with a homer and 3 RBIs. Posey also proved to be the difference in a 3–2 victory over the Arizona Diamondbacks on September 15, going 3-for-4, with a game-winning two-run homer.

However, Posey got his most memorable hit of the 2012 campaign in Game 4 of the World Series, when his two-run homer off Detroit's Max Scherzer in the top of the sixth inning gave the Giants a 3–2 lead in a contest they ended up winning by a score of 4–3 in 10 innings.

Posey had a hand in making history on July 13, 2014, when, during an 8–4 victory over the Arizona Diamondbacks, he combined with Madison Bumgarner to become the first catcher-pitcher tandem ever to hit grand slam home runs in the same game.

Posey had an outstanding day against the Mets on August 3, 2014, leading the Giants to a lopsided 9–0 victory by going 4-for-5, with a homer, double, and 3 runs batted in. Later that month, on August 26, Posey gave the Giants all the offense they needed to defeat Colorado, homering twice and knocking in all 3 runs during a 3–0 win over the Rockies. Just three days later, Posey went 5-for-5, with 3 RBIs and 3 runs scored, during a 13–2 victory over the Milwaukee Brewers.

On June 19, 2015, Posey helped lead the Giants to a 9–5 win over the Dodgers by going 3-for-4, with a grand slam home run and a stolen base. By homering with the bags full and swiping a base in the same game, Posey became the first Giants catcher since Roger Bresnahan in 1903 to accomplish the feat. Just four days later, during a 6–0 victory over San Diego on June 23, Posey once again homered with the bases loaded.

Posey tied his single-game career-high mark in RBIs on May 28, 2016, when he knocked in 6 runs with a pair of three-run homers during a 10–5 win over the Colorado Rockies.

Notable Achievements:

Has hit more than 20 home runs twice.

Has knocked in more than 100 runs once (103 in 2012).

Has batted over .300 four times.

Has surpassed 30 doubles three times.

Has compiled on-base percentage in excess of .400 once (.408 in 2012).

Has posted slugging percentage in excess of .500 twice.

Has led N.L. in batting average once and sacrifice flies once.

2010 N.L. Rookie of the Year.

2012 N.L. Comeback Player of the Year.

2012 N.L. Hank Aaron Award winner.

2012 N.L. MVP.

2015 Wilson Defensive Player of the Year.

Three-time Silver Slugger winner (2012, 2014 & 2015).

2016 Gold Glove winner.

2012 *Sporting News* All-Star selection.

Four-time N.L. All-Star (2012, 2013, 2015 & 2016).

Three-time N.L. champion (2010, 2012 & 2014).

Three-time world champion (2010, 2012 & 2014).

25 HAL SCHUMACHER

Hal Schumacher helped the Giants win three pennants and one world championship during the 1930s. *(Courtesy of RMYAuctions.com)*

Although a shoulder injury limited Hal Schumacher's period of dominance to just a few short seasons, the hard-throwing right-hander contributed significantly to Giant teams that won three pennants and one world championship during the 1930s. Pitching in the shadow of the great Carl Hubbell for most of his 13 years in New York, Schumacher spent much of his time serving as the Giants' number-two starter. Yet, Schumacher, who the New York media dubbed "Prince Hal," in deference to Hubbell, proved to be nearly the equal of "King Carl" from 1933 to 1935, compiling a composite record of 61–31 over the course of those three seasons, while annually placing among the N.L. leaders in ERA, complete games, and innings pitched. A two-time N.L. All-Star, Schumacher remained an effective pitcher even after he lost much of the steam on his fastball, winning a total of 76 games between 1937 and 1942 before entering the military to serve his country in World War II. By the time he retired at the conclusion of the 1946 campaign, Schumacher had recorded a total of 158 victories, placing him among the Giants' all-time leaders in that category.

Born the son of German immigrants on November 23, 1910, in Hinckley, New York, Harold Henry Schumacher spent most of his youth in the village of Dolgeville, about 25 miles east of his place of birth. An outstanding student and exceptional athlete at Dolgeville High School, Schumacher excelled in baseball, football, and basketball in high school, doubling as the baseball team's pitcher and shortstop. He also began playing semipro ball at only 15 years of age, making such a strong impression on major-league scouts in the area that representatives of the Yankees, Cardinals, and Giants began following him around.

Intent on acquiring a college education, Schumacher enrolled at Saint Lawrence University in Canton, New York, following his graduation from Dolgeville High in 1928. In addition to excelling in the classroom, he spent the next three years starring on the athletic field, prompting New York Giants scout Art Devlin to offer him his first baseball contract. Still seeking to fulfill his wish of earning a college degree, Schumacher signed with the stipulation that the Giants allow him to complete his education, recalling years later, "Don't forget, that was in Depression days. I had to leave school because I didn't have enough money to finish school."

After completing his final year of schooling, Schumacher joined the Giants organization in 1931, spending most of the year in the minors, although he also made a few unimpressive appearances at the major-league level. Schumacher joined the Giants for good in 1932, making 13 starts before being removed from the starting rotation by new manager Bill Terry at midseason. The 21-year-old right-hander spent the remainder of the year working out of the bullpen, perfecting his sinker and learning how to mix it in with his effective overhand curve and "heavy" fastball that hit the catcher's mitt like a cannonball.

Inserted back into the starting rotation at the beginning of the 1933 campaign, Schumacher developed into an elite pitcher, teaming with Carl

Hubbell to give the Giants the Senior Circuit's most formidable pitching duo. In addition to compiling a record of 19–12 that placed him fifth in the league in wins, Schumacher finished third in ERA (2.16), second in shutouts (7) and WHIP (1.094), fifth in complete games (21), and eighth in innings pitched (258 ⅔). His exceptional performance earned him the first of his two All-Star selections and a 12th-place finish in the N.L. MVP voting. Schumacher topped that off by winning Game 2 of the World Series, concluding the Fall Classic with a win, a no-decision, and an ERA of 2.45.

Although the Giants failed to repeat as N.L. champions the following year, Schumacher again pitched exceptionally well, earning a 9th-place finish in the MVP balloting by compiling a record of 23–10 and an ERA of 3.18, completing 18 of his 36 starts, and throwing a career-high 297 innings. He had another big year in 1935, earning All-Star honors for the second time by going 19–9, with a 2.89 ERA, 18 complete games, and 261 ⅔ innings pitched.

However, during the latter stages of that 1935 campaign, Schumacher suffered a shoulder injury that ended up compromising his performance the remainder of his career. Plagued by a sore arm for much of 1936, the 25-year-old right-hander finished just 11–13 with a 3.47 ERA for the pennant-winning Giants. Working with a diminished fastball in subsequent seasons, Schumacher developed a palm ball, which helped keep opposing hitters off balance. Nevertheless, he never regained his earlier form, forcing him to assume a less prominent role on the Giants' pitching staff. After winning 13 games each year from 1937 to 1940, Schumacher posted 12 victories in both 1941 and 1942.

Schumacher joined the U.S. Navy following the conclusion of the 1942 campaign, eventually serving as a lieutenant aboard the 512-foot aircraft carrier Cape Esperance. Returning to the Giants when the war ended, he spent all of 1946 in New York, compiling a record of just 4–4 as a spot-starter/long reliever before being released by the club at season's end. Schumacher subsequently announced his retirement, ending his career with a record of 158–121, an ERA of 3.36, 26 shutouts, 906 strikeouts in 2,482 ⅓ innings of work, 137 complete games, and a WHIP of 1.340. He continues to rank among the Giants career leaders in wins, shutouts, innings pitched, and games started.

Following his retirement, Schumacher returned home to Dolgeville, where he spent the next 20 years working as vice president in charge of sales for the Adirondack Bat Company. Among his other duties with the firm, Schumacher visited spring training camps promoting the company's product. After leaving Adirondack in 1967, Schumacher went to work for the national Little

League headquarters in Williamsport, Pennsylvania, organizing instructional programs. Admitted to the Mary Imogene Bassett Hospital in Cooperstown, New York, in the spring of 1993, Schumacher died of stomach cancer shortly thereafter, passing away at the age of 82, on April 21, 1993.

Career Highlights:

Best Season: It could certainly be argued that Schumacher pitched his best ball for the Giants in 1933, when he finished 19–12 and established career-best marks in ERA (2.16), shutouts (7), complete games (21), and WHIP (1.094). He also pitched exceptionally well in 1935, concluding the campaign with a record of 19–9, an ERA of 2.89, 18 complete games, and a WHIP of 1.166. However, Schumacher had his finest all-around season in 1934 when, in addition to placing among the N.L. leaders with a 3.18 ERA, 18 complete games, and a career-high 23 wins, .697 winning percentage, and 297 innings pitched, he set a new league record for pitchers (since broken) by hitting six home runs.

Memorable Moments/Greatest Performances: Schumacher put together the longest winning streak of his career in 1935, when he posted 11 straight victories. An excellent-hitting pitcher throughout his career, Schumacher had a pair of memorable days at the plate for the Giants, with the first of those coming on April 24, 1934, when he homered twice and knocked in 5 runs during an 11–7 win over Philadelphia.

Schumacher again helped his own cause on July 18, 1937, when he went 4-for-4 with a home run during an 11–0 win over St. Louis.

Schumacher turned in one of the finest pitching performances of his career in one of his first big-league starts, shutting out the Braves, 6–0, on just 2 hits, on April 17, 1932. He tossed another 2-hit shutout on May 7, 1933, allowing just a pair of singles during a 5–0 win over Cincinnati.

Schumacher nearly threw what would have been the only no-hitter of his career on April 28, 1935, when he allowed just a controversial infield single to pitcher Orville Jorgens during a 3–0 win over the Phillies. Jorgens hit a ground ball that Giants shortstop Dick Bartell fielded cleanly. However, he subsequently made an errant throw to first base that pulled Bill Terry off the bag. Although the fans in attendance assumed Bartell had made an error on the play, they later learned that it had been ruled a hit.

Schumacher tossed another one-hitter on April 24, 1938, allowing just a leadoff infield single to Goodie Rosen during a 1–0 Giants win over Dodgers. Schumacher also collected 3 hits during the contest.

Despite winning only 11 games for the Giants in 1936, Schumacher made one of those victories a huge one, clinching the pennant for New York on September 24 by defeating the Braves, 2–1, in 10 innings. Schumacher delivered the game-winning run with an RBI single in the top of the final frame.

Schumacher also turned in a pair of memorable efforts in World Series play, defeating Washington by a score of 6–1 in Game Two of the 1933 Fall Classic, and keeping the Giants alive in the 1936 Series by working all 10 innings of a 5–4 win over the Yankees in Game Five. Despite surrendering 4 runs (3 earned) and 10 hits to the Yankees, Schumacher called his 1936 effort the "best ball game I ever pitched in my life," largely because he escaped a bases-loaded, no-out jam in the third inning by striking out Joe DiMaggio and Lou Gehrig, before inducing Bill Dickey to fly out to right field. Schumacher finished the game with 10 strikeouts.

Yet, Schumacher experienced the most surreal moment of his career on July 25, 1935, when he nearly died on the pitcher's mound. Working the sixth inning of the first game of a doubleheader against the Cardinals, Schumacher suddenly found himself overcome by the 95 degree heat in St. Louis. After finishing the frame, he collapsed on the mound, with no discernible heartbeat. Fortunately, he survived the ordeal when the trainers in attendance packed him in ice and later revived him.

Notable Achievements:

Surpassed 20 victories once (23 in 1934), winning 19 games two other times.

Compiled ERA below 3.00 twice.

Threw more than 20 complete games once (21 in 1933).

Hit six home runs in 1934.

Finished second in N.L. with 23 wins in 1934.

Led N.L. pitchers in assists and fielding percentage in 1935.

Ranks among Giants career leaders in: wins (8th); shutouts (tied-8th); innings pitched (7th); and games started (6th).

Two-time N.L. All-Star (1933 & 1935).

Three-time N.L. champion (1933, 1936 & 1937).

1933 world champion.

26 MADISON BUMGARNER

Madison Bumgarner has compiled the lowest career ERA in World Series play of any pitcher in MLB history. *(Courtesy of Dirk Hansen)*

An outstanding left-handed pitcher who has displayed an uncanny ability to perform extraordinarily well under pressure during his major-league career, Madison Bumgarner has established himself as the best big-game pitcher of his generation since arriving in San Francisco in 2010. Compiling an overall record of 8–3 and an ERA of 2.11 in his four postseason appearances with the Giants, Bumgarner has proven to be particularly dominant in World Series play, winning all four of his decisions while posting a microscopic ERA of

0.25 that ranks as the best in the history of the Fall Classic for hurlers with at least 25 innings of work. Excelling during the regular season as well, Bumgarner has won at least 15 games and compiled an ERA under 3.00 four times each, en route to earning four All-Star selections and two top-five finishes in the N.L. Cy Young voting, with his stellar pitching helping the Giants win two division titles and three world championships in his first seven years with the team.

Born in Hickory, North Carolina, on August 1, 1989, Madison Kyle Bumgarner grew up in a log house that his father built in an area some 10 miles away nicknamed "Bumtown" due to the number of fellow Bumgarners who lived there over the years after their ancestors emigrated from Germany. Starring on the mound while attending South Caldwell High School in nearby Hudson, Bumgarner earned Gatorade North Carolina Player of the Year honors as a senior by leading his team to the 2007 4A State Championship with a record of 11–2 and an ERA of 1.05. Although the young southpaw accepted a scholarship offer from the University of North Carolina following his graduation from South Caldwell, he decided to turn pro after the Giants selected him with the 10th overall pick of the 2007 MLB Draft.

Bumgarner began his minor-league career in the South Atlantic League, where he won the pitcher's version of the Triple Crown in 2008 before splitting the ensuing campaign between two different farm clubs, for whom he compiled an overall record of 12–2. Promoted to the Giants in September 2009, the 20-year-old left-hander appeared in four games over the season's final month, allowing just 2 runs in 10 innings of work without earning a decision. Although Bumgarner began the 2010 season back in the minors, he rejoined the Giants for good in late June, after which he posted a record of 7–6 and an ERA of 3.00 in his 18 starts with the club the remainder of the year. He then gave an early indication of his ability to excel in big games, starting and winning the Game 4 clincher against Atlanta in the NLDS, before allowing no runs and just 3 hits over 8 innings, in defeating Texas in Game 4 of the World Series.

Bumgarner's outstanding pitching during the latter stages of the previous campaign earned him a regular spot in the Giants starting rotation in 2011—a season in which he finished 13–13, with an ERA of 3.21 and 191 strikeouts in 204 ⅔ innings of work. He followed that up by going 16–11, with a 3.37 ERA and 191 strikeouts for the eventual world champions in 2012, before earning the first of four straight All-Star selections in 2013 by compiling a record of 13–9 and placing among the league leaders with an ERA of 2.77 and 199 strikeouts.

Bumgarner continued to expand his pitching repertoire over the course of his first few seasons in San Francisco, eventually reaching a point where he felt comfortable throwing four different offerings at various speeds. Although a 90–93 mph four-seam fastball and an 86–90 mph cutter remain his primary pitches, he also throws an 82–85 mph change-up and a curveball that he releases at two different speeds, with two different types of movement—one with a mostly downward break, and the other with a more exaggerated horizontal break. Adding to Bumgarner's ability to confuse opposing batters is his unique pitching style, which gives hitters the impression that he is about to throw towards first base.

Having developed full confidence in his entire arsenal of pitches, Bumgarner compiled the best numbers of his young career in 2014, earning a fourth-place finish in the N.L. Cy Young voting by going 18–10, with a 2.98 ERA and 219 strikeouts. He subsequently performed magnificently in the playoffs and World Series, leading the Giants to their third world championship in five years by winning four of his five decisions, while allowing only 6 earned runs in a postseason-record 52 ⅔ innings of work. Bumgarner's extraordinary performance earned him NLCS and World Series MVP honors, prompting Bob Nightengale to write in the October 28, 2014, edition of *USA TODAY*, "He's Bob Gibson in black and orange. He's the Sandy Koufax of Northern California. He's the San Francisco Giants' modern-day version of Carl Hubbell. Or maybe we're shortchanging Madison Bumgarner. The way he's pitching, there's absolutely no one like him."

In trying to explain the incredible amount of success he has thus far experienced in postseason play, Bumgarner reveals, "There are some times that nerves start to creep in there. I try to keep them out. There is always some competitive anxiety before you get out there. I keep telling myself, 'Just relax,' and keep thinking that, so it will become second nature."

Bumgarner followed up his memorable postseason performance with an exceptional 2015 campaign in which he went 18–9, with a 2.93 ERA, 234 strikeouts, and a league-leading 4 complete games. He had another excellent year in 2016, finishing the season with a record of 15–9, a WHIP of 1.024, and career-best marks in ERA (2.74), strikeouts (251), and innings pitched (226 ⅔). Bumgarner will enter the 2017 season with a career record of 100–67, a lifetime ERA of 2.99, a WHIP of 1.097, and 1,381 strikeouts in 1,397 ⅔ innings of work. Still only 27 years old as of this writing, Bumgarner figures to advance several places in these rankings before his time in San Francisco comes to an end.

Career Highlights:

Best Season: Bumgarner had an exceptional year for the Giants in 2015 when, in addition to going 18–9 with an ERA of 2.93, he ranked among the N.L. leaders with 234 strikeouts, 218 ⅓ innings pitched, and a career-best WHIP of 1.008. He also pitched extremely well in 2016, going 15–9 with a WHIP of 1.024, and establishing new career bests in ERA (2,74), strikeouts (251), and innings pitched (226 ⅔). Nevertheless, Bumgarner had his finest all-around season in 2014 when, en route to earning N.L. Pitcher of the Month honors twice, he went 18–10, with an ERA of 2.98, 219 strikeouts, a WHIP of 1.090, and 217 ⅓ innings pitched. The 6'5", 250-pound southpaw also had an outstanding season at the plate, hitting 4 home runs and establishing career-high marks in RBIs (15), runs scored (10), batting average (.258), and OPS (.755). Furthermore, Bumgarner's fabulous pitching during the postseason not only earned him NLCS and World Series MVP honors, but also recognition as *Sports Illustrated's* Sportsman of the Year and the *Associated Press* Male Athlete of the Year.

Memorable Moments/Greatest Performances: An excellent hitting pitcher, Bumgarner won consecutive Silver Sluggers in 2014 and 2015. He hit the first of his 14 career home runs during a 6–3 victory over Houston on June 12, 2012, in which he also struck out 12 batters.

Bumgarner homered with the bases loaded for the first time in his career on April 11, 2014, knocking in 5 of the Giants' 6 runs, in leading them to a 6–5 win over the Colorado Rockies. Bumgarner again homered with the bags full on July 13, 2014, helping the Giants record an 8–4 victory over the Arizona Diamondbacks by collecting 2 hits, driving in 4 runs, and scoring twice.

Bumgarner once again displayed his hitting prowess on May 21, 2015, when he became the first pitcher to hit a home run off Clayton Kershaw during a 4–0 win over the Dodgers.

Bumgarner again homered off Kershaw this past season, doing so during an April 9, 2016, contest that the Giants eventually lost to Los Angeles by a score of 3–2 in 10 innings.

Bumgarner helped his own cause on May 22, 2016, when, during a 1–0 victory over the Cubs in which he surrendered just 3 hits over 7 ⅔ innings, he delivered the game's only run with a 5th-inning double off Chicago starter Kyle Hendricks.

Bumgarner again excelled both at the bat and on the mound two starts later, homering, yielding just 4 hits, and recording 11 strikeouts over 7 ⅔ innings, in earning a 6–0 win over Atlanta.

Known far more for his pitching skills, Bumgarner has thrown four one-hitters for the Giants, with the first of those coming on June 28, 2012, when he struck out 8 and allowed just a 6th-inning leadoff single to Ryan Hanigan during a 5–0 shutout of the Cincinnati Reds. Bumgarner proved to be even more dominant on August 26, 2014, striking out 13 and working seven perfect innings before allowing a leadoff double to Justin Morneau in the top of the 8th inning, en route to defeating the Colorado Rockies by a score of 3–0. Bumgarner again approached perfection on September 12, 2015, when he retired the first 23 San Diego batters he faced before surrendering a pinch-hit single to Melvin Upton Jr. with two men out in the bottom of the 8th inning. He subsequently retired the next four batters, giving him a one-hit shutout and an 8–0 victory over the Padres. Bumgarner tossed another one-hitter this past season, yielding just an 8th-inning single to Arizona third baseman Jake Lamb and a leadoff walk in the ensuing frame to left-fielder Rickie Weeks, in earning a complete-game 4–0 win over the Diamondbacks on July 10, 2016. Bumgarner also fanned 14 batters during the contest.

Bumgarner turned in another memorable outing on August 3, 2014, when he allowed just 2 hits, walked one batter, and struck out 10, in defeating the Mets by a score of 9–0.

Although the Giants ended up losing their June 23, 2015, matchup with the Padres by a score of 3–2 in 11 innings, Bumgarner pitched extremely well, surrendering 5 hits and 2 runs in 7 ⅓ innings of work while recording a career-high 14 strikeouts, which tied Atlee Hammaker's franchise record for the most strikeouts in a game by a left-handed pitcher.

Bumgarner tied another Giants record during a 3–1 victory over Houston on August 11, 2015, when he fanned seven straight batters, en route to recording a total of 12 strikeouts on the day.

Bumgarner equaled his own career-high mark for strikeouts in his next start, whiffing 14 batters and allowing just 3 hits during a 5–0 shutout of the Washington Nationals on August 16, 2015.

After earlier struggling in the 2012 playoffs, posting an ERA of 11.25 in his two starts, Bumgarner came up big for the Giants in Game 2 of the World Series, tossing 7 scoreless innings, yielding just 2 hits, and striking out 8 during a 2–0 win over the Detroit Tigers.

However, that performance paled in comparison to the effort he turned in during the 2014 postseason. After throwing a 4-hit shutout against Pittsburgh in the N.L. Wild Card game, Bumgarner pitched relatively well against Washington in Game 3 of the NLDS, allowing 6 hits and 2 earned runs over 7 innings, although the Giants ended up losing the contest by a score of 4–1. He then posted two of San Francisco's four victories over St. Louis in the NLCS, surrendering just 3 runs and 9 hits in 15 ⅔ innings of work, with his 7 ⅔ shutout innings in Game 1 at Busch Stadium giving him the all-time record for most consecutive scoreless innings pitched on the road in postseason play (26 ⅔). Bumgarner followed that up with a remarkable performance against Kansas City in the World Series, leading the Giants to a 7-game victory by going 2–0, with a save and a 0.43 ERA. En route to surrendering just 1 run and 9 hits over 21 innings, Bumgarner pitched the Giants to a 7–1 win in Game 1. He then threw a 4-hit, complete-game shutout in Game 5, before returning to the mound on two days' rest in Game 7 and tossing another 5 scoreless innings in relief.

Bumgarner turned in another dominant performance this past postseason, yielding just 4 hits and 2 walks during a 3–0 complete-game victory over the Mets in the N.L. Wild Card game.

Notable Achievements:

Has surpassed 15 victories four times, winning 18 games twice.

Has compiled ERA below 3.00 four times.

Has struck out more than 200 batters three times.

Has thrown more than 200 innings six times.

Led N.L. pitchers with 4 complete games in 2015.

Holds Giants career record for best strikeouts-to-walks ratio (4.289).

Ranks among Giants career leaders in: WHIP (4th); strikeouts (9th); fewest hits allowed per nine innings pitched (10th); and most strikeouts per nine innings pitched (4th).

Holds MLB record for most innings pitched in a single postseason (52 ⅔ in 2014).

Holds MLB record for lowest career ERA in World Series play (minimum 25 IP—0.25).

Two-time N.L. Pitcher of the Month (May & August 2014).
Two-time Silver Slugger winner (2014 & 2015).
Has finished in top five in N.L. Cy Young voting twice (2014 & 2016).
2014 NLCS MVP.
2014 World Series MVP.
2014 *Sports Illustrated* Sportsman of the Year.
2014 *Associated Press* Male Athlete of the Year.
Four-time N.L. All-Star (2013, 2014, 2015 & 2016).
Three-time N.L. champion (2010, 2012 & 2014).
Three-time world champion (2010, 2012 & 2014).

27 TIM LINCECUM

Tim Lincecum earned N.L. Cy Young honors in back-to-back years while pitching for the Giants. *(Courtesy of Dirk Hansen)*

Nicknamed "The Freak" for his ability to generate tremendous velocity on his pitches in spite of his slender 5'11", 170-pound frame, Tim Lincecum experienced a great deal of success his first few seasons in San Francisco, before falling on hard times more recently. En route to compiling an overall record of 62–36 in his first four full seasons with the Giants, Lincecum won two Cy Young Awards, earned four All-Star selections, and garnered *Sporting News* N.L. Pitcher of the Year honors twice. The National League leader in strike-outs three straight times, Lincecum also topped the Senior Circuit in winning percentage, complete games, and shutouts at various times, while placing sec-ond in the league in wins once and ERA twice. In addition to winning at least 15 games on three occasions, the hard-throwing right-hander compiled an

ERA under 3.00 three times and struck out more than 200 batters four times. Although Lincecum pitched less effectively his last four years in the City by the Bay, he nevertheless made significant contributions to all three Giant world championship teams, posting a composite record of 5–2 and an ERA of 2.40 in postseason play, including World Series marks of 2–0 and 2.25.

Born in Bellevue, Washington, on June 15, 1984, Timothy LeRoy Lincecum attended Liberty Senior High School in nearby Renton, where he played two seasons of varsity baseball, earning State Player of the Year honors as a senior by leading his team to the 2003 3A state championship. Subsequently selected by the Chicago Cubs in the 48th round of the 2003 MLB Draft, Lincecum chose to delay the start of his professional career by accepting an athletic scholarship from the University of Washington instead. Drafted once again two years later, this time by the Cleveland Indians in the 42nd round of the 2005 Draft, Lincecum elected to remain in college for another year, during which time he compiled a record of 12–4 and an ERA of 1.94 for the Huskies, prompting his coach, Ken Knutson, to comment, "He has great stuff with a lot of pitches, and easily is the best player I've coached in 15 years here." Named the winner of the 2006 Golden Spikes Award as the nation's best amateur baseball player, the 22-year-old Lincecum finally decided to turn pro after the Giants selected him with the 10th overall pick of the 2006 MLB Draft, making him the first player from the University of Washington to be taken in the first round.

Spending less than one full season in the minor leagues, Lincecum joined the Giants one month into the 2007 campaign after receiving a ringing endorsement from Colorado Rockies prospect Ian Stewart, who called him "the toughest pitcher (he) ever faced," adding, "Guys on our club who have been in the big leagues said he's the toughest guy they ever faced too . . . I'm not really sure why he's down here (in Triple-A), but, for a guy who was drafted last year, that guy is filthy."

Lincecum ended up making 24 starts for the Giants in 2007, finishing the year with a record of 7–5, an ERA of 4.00, and 150 strikeouts in 146 ⅓ innings pitched. Emerging as the ace of the Giants pitching staff the following year, Lincecum concluded the 2008 campaign with a record of 18–5, an ERA of 2.62, and a league-leading 265 strikeouts in 227 innings of work, earning in the process N.L. Cy Young honors and the first of his four consecutive All-Star selections. The young right-hander's early success prompted veteran teammate Rich Aurilia to proclaim, "In my 13 years in the big leagues, this is the only guy I've seen who is worth the hype; the first one." Lincecum also made a believer out of Houston first baseman Lance Berkman, who said after a May 15, 2008, contest in which the right-hander struck out 10 Astros in six innings, "He's got as good of stuff as I've ever seen. . . . He's got three almost unhittable pitches." Meanwhile, Randy Johnson told *USA Today's* Bob Nightengale, "He's (Lincecum) a dying breed because of the way he just dominates the game. When you think how young he is, and he's certainly light years ahead of where I was, there's no telling what he might do the rest of his career."

Lincecum had another exceptional year in 2009, compiling a record of 15–7, an ERA of 2.48, and a league-leading 261 strikeouts, 4 complete games, and 2 shutouts, en route to earning N.L. Cy Young honors for the second straight time. By once again winning that prestigious award, Lincecum became the first pitcher in MLB history to be so honored in each of his first two full seasons. The 25-year-old right-hander's outstanding performance also prompted *The Sporting News* to name him its N.L. Pitcher of the Year for the second consecutive season.

Lincecum owed much of his success to his somewhat unorthodox pitching motion and outstanding command of his fastball and secondary pitches. Employing an unusually long stride and releasing the ball from an overhand delivery, the slight-of-build right-hander incorporated into his pitching repertoire both a four-seam and two-seam fastball, each of which topped out at 99 mph during the early stages of his career. He also developed a sharp-breaking curveball that broke away from right-handed hitters, an 81–83 mph changeup that tailed away from left-handed batters, and a 79–81 mph slider that broke down and away from right-handed hitters. Lincecum recorded the vast majority of his strikeouts with his changeup, which appeared similar to his fastball for the first 30 feet, before diving down sharply as it approached home plate.

In discussing Lincecum's pitching motion, Giants pitching coach Dave Righetti stated, "Everybody's talking like this is some strange delivery. He's just a wiry kid out there using his body to throw the baseball, which is easier on the arm. To me, that's the way you're supposed to throw . . . He's a miniature (Jim) Palmer—great athlete, leans his head back, same arm action."

Giants General Manager Brian Sabean also praised the ace of his team's pitching staff, saying, "He's a freak of nature. To have that kind of athletic ability, those mechanics, and the sheer strength he has—with his stature—is just unheard of."

Giants manager Bruce Bochy noted, "The way Timmy competes, it picks up the whole ball club. He's used to powering his way through lineups, but now you see him pitching more. He picks up things so fast and makes the adjustments. That's what you need at this level, and he's shown he can do it at an early age."

Meanwhile, sportswriter Tim Keown suggested, "Deep down inside, Lincecum is an old-school baseball guy—Bob Gibson in skater-dude motif."

Lincecum continued his outstanding pitching in 2010, going 16–10, with a 3.43 ERA and a league-leading 231 strikeouts, before helping the Giants capture their first world championship since moving to the West Coast by compiling a postseason record of 4–1, along with a 2.44 ERA and 43 strikeouts in 37 innings of work. Although Lincecum won just 13 of his 27 decisions the following year, he earned a sixth-place finish in the Cy Young voting and N.L. All-Star honors for the fourth straight time by placing among the league leaders with a 2.74 ERA and 220 strikeouts.

Unfortunately, Lincecum subsequently experienced a lack of command and a decrease in velocity on his fastball in 2012, relegating him to a record of just 10–15 and an inordinately high ERA of 5.18, although he still managed to strike out 190 batters in 186 innings of work. Unable to regain his earlier form in either of the next two seasons, Lincecum struggled to an overall mark of 22–23, while compiling an ERA well in excess of 4.00 both years. After starting off the 2015 campaign with a record of 7–4 and an ERA of 4.13, Lincecum spent two months on the disabled list, before finally undergoing season-ending surgery to repair a torn labrum in his hip on September 3, 2015. A free agent at season's end, Lincecum remained on the sidelines for the first two months of the 2016 campaign as he continued to recuperate, before inking a one-year, $2.5 million deal with the Los Angeles Angels of Anaheim in late May. He left the Giants having posted an overall record of 108–83 as a member of the team. Lincecum also compiled an ERA of 3.61, a WHIP of 1.268, and 1,704 strikeouts in 1,643 ⅔ innings of work during his time in San Francisco.

After initially being assigned to the Triple-A Salt Lake Bees, Lincecum made his debut with the Angels on June 18, 2016, working six strong innings, to earn his first victory at the major-league level in almost exactly one year (he won his last game for the Giants on June 16, 2015). However, Lincecum struggled in his next eight starts, going just 1–6 with an ERA of 9.16, prompting the Angels to designate him for assignment on August 6, and leaving us all to wonder if the career of the former two-time Cy Young Award winner has come to a premature end.

Giant Career Highlights:

Best Season: Lincecum pitched exceptionally well for the Giants in 2009, earning his second consecutive N.L. Cy Young Award by going 15–7, leading the league with 261 strikeouts, 4 complete games, and 2 shutouts, and establishing career-best marks in ERA (2.48) and WHIP (1.047). Nevertheless, I elected to go with 2008, a season in which Lincecum posted a WHIP of 1.172, finished second in the league with 18 wins and an ERA of 2.62, topped the circuit with a winning percentage of .783 and a career-high 265 strikeouts, and led the majors with 10.5 strikeouts per 9 innings pitched, a .316 slugging-percentage-against, and a .612 OPS-against.

Memorable Moments/Greatest Performances: Lincecum turned in his first truly dominant performance for the Giants on May 17, 2007, when he worked the first 7 innings of a 2–1, 12-inning victory over the Astros, allowing just 2 hits and no earned runs, while striking out 10.

Lincecum again dominated the opposition some six weeks later, on July 1, 2007, when he surrendered just 3 hits and struck out 12 over 7 innings, in defeating Arizona by a score of 13–0.

Lincecum tossed the first complete-game shutout of his career on September 13, 3008, when he allowed just 4 hits and struck out 12 during a 7–0 win over San Diego.

Lincecum pitched brilliantly en route to earning N.L. Pitcher of the Month honors in June 2009, at one point throwing 30 consecutive scoreless innings from June 23 to July 9. Included in the streak was a 10–0 win over St. Louis on June 29 in which he allowed just 2 hits and struck out 8. Lincecum continued his excellent work into late July, recording a career-high 15 strikeouts during a 4–2 win over Pittsburgh on July 27.

The author of two no-hitters, Lincecum accomplished the feat for the first time on July 13, 2013, when he defeated the San Diego Padres by a score of 9–0, surrendering just 4 bases on balls and striking out 13 during the contest. He duplicated his earlier effort on June 25, 2014, allowing only Chase Headley to reach base on a second-inning walk and striking out 6 during a 4–0 win over the Padres. Lincecum also singled twice and scored 2 runs during the game.

An outstanding postseason performer over the course of his career, Lincecum tossed a 2-hit shutout in his first playoff appearance, recording 14 strikeouts during a 1–0 win over the Atlanta Braves in Game 1 of the 2010 NLDS. He followed that up by out-dueling Roy Halladay in Game 1 of the NLCS, allowing 3 runs and 6 hits over the first 7 innings of a 4–3 Giants win over Philadelphia. Lincecum also struck out 8 batters during the contest. After losing his next start against the Phillies, Lincecum posted two victories over Texas in the World Series, performing particularly well in Game 5, when he worked 8 strong innings, allowing just 3 hits and striking out 10, in leading the Giants to a 3–1 victory that ended their 56-year drought between world championships.

Working primarily out of the bullpen during the 2012 postseason, Lincecum allowed just 1 run and 3 hits over 6 ⅓ innings against Cincinnati in the NLDS, before surrendering only 1 walk and striking out 8 in 4 ⅔ nearly perfect innings against Detroit in the World Series.

Notable Achievements:

Surpassed 15 victories three times, winning as many as 18 games in 2008.

Posted winning percentage in excess of .700 once (.783 in 2008).

Compiled ERA below 3.00 three times, posting mark under 2.50 once (2.48 in 2009).

Struck out more than 200 batters four times.

Threw more than 200 innings four times.

Led N.L. pitchers in: winning percentage once; complete games once; shutouts once; and strikeouts three times.

Ranks among Giants career leaders in: strikeouts (4th); strikeouts-to-walks ratio (6th); and most strikeouts per nine innings pitched (2nd).

Threw two no-hitters (vs. San Diego on July 13, 2013; and vs. San Diego on June 25, 2014).

June 2009 N.L. Pitcher of the Month.

Two-time N.L. Cy Young Award winner (2008 & 2009).

Two-time *Sporting News* N.L. Pitcher of the Year (2008 & 2009).

Four-time N.L. All-Star (2008, 2009, 2010 & 2011).

Three-time N.L. champion (2010, 2012 & 2014).

Three-time world champion (2010, 2012 & 2014).

28 IRISH MEUSEL

Irish Meusel led the National League with 125 RBIs in 1923 while playing for the pennant-winning Giants. *(Courtesy of Library of Congress)*

A hard-hitting outfielder who excelled at driving in runs, Emil "Irish" Meusel spent parts of six seasons in New York, establishing himself during that time as one of the National League's top RBI-men. The right-handed-hitting Meusel, whose younger brother, Bob, starred in New York at the same time for the Yankees, knocked in more than 100 runs four times for the Giants, topping the Senior Circuit with 125 RBIs in 1923, one year after he finished second in the league with a career-high 132 runs batted in. Meusel also hit more than 20 home runs once, scored more than 100 runs twice, surpassed 200 hits once, finished in double-digits in triples three times, and batted well over .300 four times for the Giants, with his .314 mark as a member of the team placing him among the franchise's all-time leaders. Meusel's potent bat and consistent out-field play made him a key contributor to four consecutive pennant-winning teams during the first half of the 1920s.

Born in Oakland, California, on June 9, 1893, Emil Frederick Meu-sel acquired the nickname "Irish" over time because he looked Celtic, even though his ancestors originally emanated from Alsace. After attending Manual Arts High School in Los Angeles, Meusel signed with the Washington Sena-tors, for whom he spent virtually all of the next six years playing in the minor leagues, appearing in only one game with the Nats in 1914. Acquired by the Phillies on September 20, 1917, in that year's Rule 5 Draft, Meusel arrived in Philadelphia the following year, beginning his big-league career in earnest at 24 years of age.

Splitting his time between left field and center, Meusel had a solid rookie campaign, hitting 4 homers, driving in 62 runs, stealing 18 bases, and batting .279 in 124 games. Although Meusel established himself as Philadelphia's pri-mary left-fielder over the course of the next two seasons, he also saw a consid-erable amount of action in right, performing well wherever the Phillies asked him to play. He developed into one of the team's better hitters as well, posting batting averages of .305 and .309 in 1919 and 1920, respectively, while finish-ing second in the league with 14 home runs in the second of those campaigns.

Yet, in spite of the success he experienced in Philadelphia, Meusel gradu-ally fell out of favor with Phillies management due to his somewhat lackadaisi-cal approach to the game. As a result, the Phillies elected to trade him to the Giants for two lesser players and $30,000 on July 25, 1921, even though he batted .353 for them during the first four months of the season.

The acquisition of Meusel proved to be a coup for the Giants, who ben-efited greatly from the outfielder's offensive contributions down the stretch. Continuing his hot-hitting, Meusel batted .329 and drove in 36 runs over the season's final two months, in helping the Giants overcome a 7 ½ game deficit to the Pittsburgh Pirates to capture the first of their four consecutive National League pennants. Meusel concluded the campaign with a composite batting average of .343, along with 14 homers, 87 RBIs, 96 runs scored, and 201 hits, placing him among the league leaders in all five categories. He also finished second among N.L. outfielders with a career-high 28 assists.

Inserted into the cleanup spot in the Giants batting order in 1922, Meusel thrived as never before, batting .331 and establishing new career highs with 16 home runs, 132 runs batted in, 100 runs scored, 204 hits, and 17 triples. He followed that up by batting .297, hitting 19 home runs, scoring 102 times, and leading the league with 125 RBIs in 1923. After a somewhat less productive 1924 campaign in which he batted .310 and knocked in 102 runs, but hit only 6 homers and scored just 75 times, Meusel earned a 12th-place finish in the 1925 N.L. MVP voting by hitting 21 home runs, driving in 111 runs, and batting .328. He also led all N.L. left fielders in assists for the first of two straight times, throwing out 15 runners on the base paths.

Although the 5'11", 178-pound Meusel never hit more than 21 home runs in any single season, he had outstanding extra-base power, finishing among the N.L. leaders in total bases seven times during his career, while also placing near the top of the league rankings in slugging percentage on five separate occasions. A notorious free-swinger, Meusel never walked more than 38 times in a season. However, he hardly ever struck out, fanning only 199 times in more than 5,300 total plate appearances over the course of his career. Meusel also ran well and did an excellent job in the outfield, although he lacked the powerful throwing arm that his brother, Bob, possessed. And, even though Meusel developed a reputation earlier in his career for failing to hustle at times, he always put forth a 100 percent effort under the watchful eye of the cantankerous John McGraw.

Meusel spent one more year in New York, hitting 6 homers, driving in 65 runs, batting .292, and scoring only 51 runs in 1926, before being released by the Giants at season's end. He subsequently signed with the Brooklyn Dodgers, with whom he spent his final season serving as a part-time player before announcing his retirement four months into the 1927 campaign. Meusel ended his career with 106 home runs, 819 runs batted in, 701 runs scored, 1,521 hits, 93 triples, 250 doubles, 113 stolen bases, a .310 batting average, a .348 on-base percentage, and a .464 slugging percentage. In addition to compiling a batting average of .314 as a member of the Giants, he hit 70 home runs, knocked in 571 runs, scored 447 times, collected 931 hits, 64 triples, and 148 doubles, stole 46 bases, compiled a .352 on-base percentage, and posted a .477 slugging percentage in his years with the team.

Following his retirement, Meusel briefly served as a Giants coach before embarking on an acting career that saw him appear in several Hollywood movies with a baseball theme. He later became a security guard at the Santa

Anita race track. Meusel passed away in Long Beach, California, at the age of 69, on March 1, 1963, after suffering a heart attack.

Giant Career Highlights:

Best Season: Although Meusel played extremely well for the Giants in 1923 and 1925, driving in a league-leading 125 runs in the first of those campaigns before compiling a career-high OPS of .912 in the second, he had his finest all-around season in 1922. By hitting 16 home runs, scoring 100 runs, batting .331, posting an OPS of .877, and establishing career-high marks in hits (204), triples (17), total bases (314), and runs batted in (132), Meusel finished among the N.L. leaders in six different offensive categories, placing second in RBIs, triples, and total bases.

Memorable Moments/Greatest Performances: Meusel turned in several of his most notable performances during that 1922 campaign, leading the Giants to a 16–7 victory over the Phillies on May 30 by homering twice, collecting 3 hits, scoring 3 times, and driving in 6 runs. He again knocked in 6 runs a little over a month later on July 10, when he went 4-for-4, with a homer and double, during a 19–2 pounding of the Pirates. Meusel had another big day on August 5, when he contributed 4 hits, 2 RBIs, and 4 runs scored to a 19–7 drubbing of the Cubs. Less than two weeks later, on August 18, Meusel led the Giants to a 17–11 victory over the Cubs by going 5-for-6, with a homer, double, 5 RBIs, and 3 runs scored.

Although the Giants lost their July 26, 1923, matchup with the Cubs by a score of 11–10, Meusel had a huge day at the plate, collecting 3 hits, homering once, and driving in 7 runs.

Meusel had the most productive game of his career on September 2, 1925, when he homered, doubled, collected 4 hits, scored 3 runs, and drove in a career-high 9 runs during a lopsided 24–9 victory over the Phillies.

Meusel excelled in each of three World Series he played against the Yankees and his brother, Bob. Particularly effective in the 1921 and 1922 Fall Classics, the elder of the Meusel brothers homered once and knocked in 7 runs in each of those Series, while posting batting averages of .345 and .250, respectively. After leading the Giants to a 13–5 win in Game 3 of the 1921 Fall Classic by collecting 3 hits and driving in 3 runs, Meusel helped them tie the Series at three games apiece by hitting a two-run homer during their 8–5 victory in Game 6. In the following year's Fall Classic, Meusel hit a three-run homer off Bob Shawkey in the top of the first inning of Game 2, giving the Giants their only runs of a contest that eventually ended in a 3–3 tie.

Notable Achievements:

Hit more than 20 home runs once (21 in 1925).
Knocked in more than 100 runs four times, topping 120 RBIs twice.
Scored more than 100 runs twice.
Batted over .300 four times.
Surpassed 200 hits once (204 in 1922).
Finished in double-digits in triples three times.
Topped 30 doubles once (35 in 1925).
Posted slugging percentage in excess of .500 twice.
Led N.L. with 125 RBIs in 1923.
Led N.L. left-fielders in assists twice.
Ranks ninth in Giants history with .314 career batting average.
Four-time N.L. champion (1921, 1922, 1923 & 1924).
Two-time world champion (1921 & 1922).

29 JEFF TESREAU

Jeff Tesreau ranked among the N.L. leaders in wins and ERA in four of his seven full seasons with the Giants. *(Courtesy of Library of Congress)*

Even though his major-league career lasted less than seven full seasons, Jeff Tesreau earned a prominent place in these rankings by establishing himself as one of the National League's dominant pitchers during his first few years in New York. Making an immediate impact as a rookie in 1912, Tesreau posted 17 victories and compiled a league-leading 1.96 ERA, joining in the process Hall of Fame hurlers Christy Mathewson and Rube Marquard in giving the Giants the Senior Circuit's most formidable starting rotation. The right-handed spitball artist subsequently won a total of 98 games over the course of the next five seasons, surpassing 20 victories twice, before a disagreement with

Giants manager John McGraw caused him to leave the team midway through the 1918 campaign, bringing his career to a premature end at only 30 years of age.

Born in Ironton, Missouri, on March 5, 1888, Charles Monroe Tesreau completed only eight years of school before he set off for nearby Perryville at age 17 to work in a lead mine and pitch for the mining company's team. Before long, Tesreau garnered interest from the independent Perryville team of the Trolley League, with whom he spent all of 1908, winning 37 of the 43 games he started. He subsequently spent 1909 pitching for various teams in the Texas League, impressing everyone with the velocity with which he threw his fastball, but frustrating his managers with his inability to control it. After failing a tryout with the Detroit Tigers due to his lack of control, Tesreau returned to the Texas League in 1910, spending the entire year at Shreveport, where he began to show signs of gaining better command of his pitches. The Giants purchased his contract during the latter stages of the campaign, after which they brought him to New York for a quick look. Although Tesreau didn't appear in any games for the Giants during the season's final month, he caught the eye of sportswriter Bill McBeth, who noticed the 6'2", 220-pound pitcher's resemblance to former heavyweight boxing champion James J. Jeffries and nicknamed him "Jeff."

The Giants returned Tesreau to the minors in 1911, during which time he continued to work on the spitball (still a legal pitch at the time) he learned from Giants special instructor Wilbert Robinson during spring training. After concluding the campaign with a record of 14–9 for Toronto of the Eastern League, Tesreau rejoined the Giants for good the following year, earning the honor of starting the second game of the regular season. Betrayed by his defense, Tesreau ended up losing the contest by a score of 4–2, even though he surrendered just 3 hits and 3 walks to Brooklyn. Tesreau's strong performance prompted the *New York Times* to write, "Tesreau has curves which bend like barrel hoops and speed like lightning. He's just the kind of a strong man (John) McGraw has been looking for."

Tesreau went on to establish himself as one of McGraw's most dependable pitchers, finishing his rookie season with a record of 17–7, 19 complete games, 243 innings pitched, and a league-leading 1.96 ERA. Particularly effective during the latter stages of the campaign, Tesreau put together a seven-game winning streak down the stretch that included a no-hitter against the Philadelphia Phillies on September 6. He subsequently went head-to-head against

Boston staff ace Smoky Joe Wood three times in the World Series, losing their first two matchups but emerging victorious in their third meeting, which tied the Series at three games apiece. Afterwards, Tesreau commented, "It was the worst game I pitched and the only one I won."

Tesreau continued to evolve into one of the Senior Circuit's best pitchers in 1913, concluding his sophomore campaign with a record of 22–13, completing 17 of his league-leading 38 starts, and placing near the top of the league rankings with 167 strikeouts, 282 innings pitched, and an ERA of 2.17. He followed that up with arguably his finest season, going 26–10 in 1914, with a 2.37 ERA, 189 strikeouts, 322 ⅓ innings pitched, and a league-leading 8 shutouts. Tesreau's exceptional performance earned him a sixth-place finish in the Chalmers Award voting.

Tesreau excelled for the Giants his first few seasons even though he continued to struggle with his control at times, placing second in the league in walks in both 1913 and 1914. Able to overcome his occasional lack of command with a devastating spitball, which he threw with the speed of a top fastball, Tesreau finished first in the Senior Circuit in fewest hits allowed per nine innings pitched in each of his first three seasons, holding his opponents to a .223 batting average over the course of his career. Commenting on the pitch Tesreau used most frequently to baffle opposing hitters, Hall of Fame second baseman Johnny Evers said, "That big fellow has the best spitball in the league. I think he is as good with the spitter as (Chicago White Sox Hall of Fame pitcher) Ed Walsh."

Pitching for a last-place Giants team in 1915, Tesreau still managed to compile a respectable 19–16 record, while finishing among the N.L. leaders with a 2.29 ERA, a 1.013 WHIP, 176 strikeouts, 8 shutouts, 24 complete games, and 306 innings pitched. He also reduced his walks total to just 75—down 53 from the previous year. Tesreau put together another solid season in 1916, going 18–14, with a 2.92 ERA, 5 shutouts, 23 complete games, and 268 ⅓ innings pitched, before his skills began to erode somewhat the following year, when he finished just 13–8 with a 3.09 ERA.

The 1917 campaign proved to be Tesreau's last full season in the Major Leagues. Asked by John McGraw to take the pitchers, catchers, and some out-of-shape players down South for some early conditioning prior to the start of spring training the following year, Tesreau complied with his manager's request. However, he later drew the ire of McGraw when he refused to discuss with him the players' evening activities, stating that he considered a man's behavior away from the ballpark to be his own personal business. A feud subsequently developed between the two men, causing Tesreau to leave the team after he got off to a relatively slow 4–4 start. After initially expressing interest in returning to the majors in 1919, he decided to retire for good when McGraw refused to trade or release him. Tesreau ended his career with a record of 119–72, giving him a winning percentage of .623. He also compiled a 2.43 ERA, struck out 880 batters in 1,679 innings of work, threw 123 complete games and 27 shutouts, and posted a WHIP of 1.145. He continues to rank among the Giants career leaders in ERA, shutouts, and WHIP.

Following his retirement as an active player, Tesreau briefly worked at Bethlehem Steel before assuming the position of head baseball coach at Dartmouth College. He continued to serve in that capacity until his death on September 24, 1946, five days after he suffered a stroke during a fishing trip. Only 58 years old at the time of his passing, Tesreau held the school record for victories (348) until 2010, often going up against his old World Series foe, Joe Wood, who spent many years coaching at Yale University.

Career Highlights:

Best Season: Although Tesreau finished just 19–16 for the last-place Giants in 1915, he actually pitched some of his best ball for them that year, compiling an ERA of 2.29, throwing 24 complete games, and placing either second or third in the league in strikeouts (176), shutouts (8), innings pitched (306), and WHIP (1.013). Tesreau also performed extremely well in each of his first two seasons, going 17–7 as a rookie, with 19 complete games and a league-leading 1.96 ERA, before winning 22 games, compiling a 2.17 ERA, striking out 167 batters, and tossing 17 complete games in his sophomore campaign of 1913. However, Tesreau had his finest season in 1914, when, in addition to posting an ERA of 2.37 and a WHIP of 1.135, he established career-high marks in wins (26), strikeouts (189), shutouts (8), complete games (26), and innings pitched (322 ⅓). His 8 shutouts led the National League, while his 26 victories placed him second only to Philadelphia's Grover Cleveland Alexander, who won 27 games for the Phillies.

Memorable Moments/Greatest Performances: On September 6, 1912, Tesreau became the first rookie of the modern era to throw a no-hitter when he defeated the Phillies by a score of 3–0 in the first game of a doubleheader sweep by the Giants.

Tesreau came tantalizingly close to tossing a second no-hitter on May 16, 1914, when Pittsburgh's Joe Kelly singled against him with two men out in the 9th inning to give the Pirates their first hit of the game. Tesreau retired the next batter, finishing with a 2–0, one-hitter.

Tesreau threw a pair of two-hit shutouts in July of 1914, blanking the Reds 5–0 on July 20 before defeating the Pirates 1–0 nine days later. He hurled another gem against Brooklyn on April 26, 1915, allowing just 2 hits and striking out 9 during a 3–0 win over the Dodgers.

Tesreau also engaged in a pair of memorable pitching duels with Philadelphia's Grover Cleveland Alexander in 1913, losing their first matchup by a score of 1–0 on May 1, before defeating the Hall of Fame right-hander by a score of 4–2, in 11 innings, on July 3.

Notable Achievements:

Won more than 20 games twice, surpassing 25 victories once (26 in 1914).

Won at least 17 games three other times.

Compiled ERA below 2.50 five times, finishing with mark under 2.00 once (1.96 in 1912).

Posted winning percentage in excess of .700 twice.

Threw more than 300 innings twice.

Tossed more than 20 complete games three times.

Led N.L. pitchers in: ERA once; shutouts once; and games started twice.

Finished second in N.L. with 26 wins in 1914.

Ranks among Giants career leaders in: ERA (4th); shutouts (tied-6th); and WHIP (tied-10th).

Finished sixth in 1914 N.L. MVP voting.

Three-time N.L. champion (1912, 1913 & 1917).

30 FREDDIE FITZSIMMONS

Freddie Fitzsimmons won a total of 170 games in his 13 years with the Giants. *(Courtesy of LegendaryAuctions. com)*

Nicknamed "Fat Freddie" due to his heavy build, Freddie Fitzsimmons spent his entire 19-year major-league career in the New York metropolitan area pitching for two of baseball's most bitter rivals—the New York Giants and the Brooklyn Dodgers. Although Fitzsimmons never established himself as the ace of either team's pitching staff, he proved to be an extremely effective starter and a consistent winner, posting 217 career victories—the third-highest total compiled by any National League right-hander during the period that extended from 1920 to 1955. Having most of his finest seasons with the Giants, Fitzsimmons won 170 games for them between 1925 and 1937, winning at least 14 games in eight of nine seasons at one point, including five campaigns with at least 17 victories. An agile fielder as well in spite of his large frame, Fitzsimmons led all N.L. hurlers in putouts four times, fielding percentage twice, and assists once, retiring with the eighth most putouts of any pitcher in league history.

Born in Mishawaka, Indiana, on July 28, 1901, Fred Landis Fitzsimmons spent five long years pitching in the minor leagues at Muskegon, Michigan, and Indianapolis, Indiana, before joining the Giants in August of 1925, two weeks after celebrating his 24th birthday. After posting a record of 6–3 and an ERA of 2.65 as a spot-starter over the final two months of the season, Fitzsimmons became a regular member of the Giants' starting rotation the following year, concluding the campaign with a record of 14–10 and an ERA of 2.88 that placed him sixth in the league rankings. He followed that up with another solid performance in 1927, going 17–10 with a 3.72 ERA.

Fitzsimmons emerged as one of the National League's better pitchers in 1928, when he compiled a record of 20–9 and an ERA of 3.68 for a Giants team that finished just two games behind the pennant-winning St. Louis Cardinals. After winning another 15 games the following year, Fitzsimmons had two of his finest seasons, going 19–7 with a league-leading .731 winning percentage in 1930, before compiling a record of 18–11 and placing among the league leaders with a 3.05 ERA in 1931.

Never a particularly hard thrower, Fitzsimmons depended primarily on breaking pitches to retire opposing batters. Known in particular for his mastery of the knuckle-curve, Fitzsimmons also became famous for his unusual wind-up, in which he rotated his pitching arm while twisting his body so that he faced second base before turning to deliver the pitch. In discussing the right-hander's deceptiveness on the mound, Chicago Cubs Hall of Fame catcher Gabby Hartnett stated in the November 1940 edition of *Baseball Magazine*, "When Fitz was good he used to give you two knucklers and then come through with a high fastball. The next time you would look for the fast one he'd throw another knuckler. He was a whiz at giving you the pitch you weren't looking for at that particular time."

A fierce competitor, Fitzsimmons used anything at his disposal to navigate his way past opposing lineups, as sportswriter Joe McGuff suggested when he wrote, "He knocked down line drives with his feet and legs, challenged batters and umpires, and withstood the verbal explosions of John McGraw, the terrible-tempered manager of the New York Giants."

Although listed in the record books at 5'11" and 185 pounds, Fitzsimmons weighed considerably more throughout most of his career. Nevertheless, he fielded his position extremely well, frequently accepting more chances than any other National League hurler.

After finishing just 11–11 with a 4.43 ERA in 1932, Fitzsimmons helped the Giants capture the pennant the following year by posting 16 victories, compiling an ERA of 2.90, and leading all N.L. hurlers with 35 starts. He followed that up by placing among the league leaders with 18 wins, a 3.04 ERA, and a career-high 263 ⅓ innings pitched in 1934, before arm problems limited him to just 15 starts and 4 victories in 1935. Yet, even though Fitzsimmons finished the season with a disappointing 4–8 record, all four of his wins ended up being complete-game shutouts, tying him for the league lead in that category.

Having undergone elbow surgery during the latter stages of the 1935 season, Fitzsimmons made only 17 starts for the Giants the following year, concluding the campaign with a record of 10–7 and an ERA of 3.32. He then won 2 of his first 4 decisions in 1937, before the Giants traded him to the Dodgers for reliever Tom Baker in mid-June. After going just 4–8 for the Dodgers the rest of the year, Fitzsimmons compiled an overall mark of 18–17 over the course of the next two seasons, before having an exceptional 1940 campaign in which he finished 16–2, with a 2.81 ERA and a league-leading .889 winning percentage. Although Fitzsimmons again pitched well for the Dodgers in 1941, compiling a record of 6–1 and an ERA of 2.07, he never again assumed a significant role on their pitching staff, appearing in a total of just 10 games the next two seasons before being released by the club on July 27, 1943—just one day before he turned 42 years of age. Fitzsimmons subsequently announced his retirement, ending his career with a record of 217–146, an ERA of 3.51, 870 strikeouts in 3,223 ⅔ innings of work, 30 shutouts, 186 complete games, and a WHIP of 1.297. In his years with the Giants, Fitzsimmons went 170–114, with a 3.54 ERA, 693 strikeouts in 2,514 ⅓ innings of work, 22 shutouts, 150 complete games, and a WHIP of 1.303.

After retiring as an active player, Fitzsimmons immediately became manager of the Philadelphia Phillies, continuing in that capacity until the middle of the 1945 campaign, when he lost his job after leading the team to an overall mark of just 105–181. Fitzsimmons also served as general manager of the Brooklyn Dodgers in the All-America Football Conference in 1943 and 1944. Following his managerial stint in Philadelphia, Fitzsimmons spent many years coaching with various teams, including his beloved Giants from 1949 to 1955. He ended his coaching career with the Kansas City Athletics in 1966, after which he retired to Yucca Valley, California. Fitzsimmons lived another 13 years, passing away at 78 years of age on November 18, 1979, after suffering a heart attack.

Giant Career Highlights:

Best Season: Fitzsimmons won 20 games for the only time in his career in 1928, when he finished 20–9, with a 3.68 ERA, 16 complete games, 261 ⅓ innings pitched, and a WHIP of 1.259. However, he actually had a slightly better year in 1931, when he ranked among the N.L. leaders with 18 wins, a 3.05 ERA, 4 shutouts, 19 complete games, 253 ⅔ innings pitched, and a WHIP of 1.198 that represented his lowest mark as a full-time starter with the Giants. Furthermore, Fitzsimmons—a relatively good-hitting pitcher throughout his career—had his most productive season at the plate, batting .228 and establishing career highs with 4 home runs, 18 RBIs, and 16 runs scored. Factoring everything into the equation, Fitzsimmons had his finest all-around season in 1931.

Memorable Moments/Greatest Performances: Fitzsimmons often contributed to his own victories on offense, with one of the more notable instances being his July 30, 1930, performance against the Braves, when he went 3-for-5, with a homer, double, and 3 RBIs during a 5–2 Giants win. He had a similarly productive afternoon on June 20, 1931, collecting 3 hits, scoring twice, and hitting a home run during a lopsided 10–0 victory over the Pirates. Fitzsimmons had another big day at the plate on June 4, 1932, contributing to a 10–4 win over the Phillies by going 3-for-3, with a homer and 2 runs scored. Fitzsimmons collected 4 hits in one game for the only time in his career on June 12, 1934, when he went 4-for-5 during a 12–1 Giants win over Cincinnati. On April 29, 1937, just six weeks before being traded to the Dodgers, Fitzsimmons helped the Giants defeat Brooklyn, 9–0, by going 3-for-4, with a homer, double, and 2 runs scored.

Fitzsimmons turned in one of the finest pitching performances of his career on August 18, 1934, when he allowed just 2 hits during a 5–0 shutout of the Reds.

Less than one month later, on September 13, 1934, Fitzsimmons suffered a heartbreaking 2–0 loss to St. Louis when he threw 11 scoreless innings against the Cardinals before allowing them to cross the plate twice in the top of the 12th inning.

Although Fitzsimmons won only 4 games in 1935, he pitched exceptionally well during the month of May, compiling a perfect 3–0 record, tossing three shutouts, and allowing only 3 earned runs in 30 total innings of work. Particularly impressive in his May 30 start, Fitzsimmons shut out the Dodgers, 6–0, on just 2 hits.

Fitzsimmons pitched one of his best games for the Giants on August 28, 1936, when he allowed just 1 run and 6 hits over 13 innings, in defeating the Pirates by a final score of 7–2 in 14 innings.

Notable Achievements:

Won 20 games once, surpassing 17 victories on four other occasions.

Compiled ERA below 3.00 three times.

Posted winning percentage in excess of .700 once (.731 in 1930).

Led N.L. pitchers in: winning percentage once; shutouts once; games started once; putouts four times; assists once; and fielding percentage twice.

Ranks among Giants career leaders in: wins (7th); shutouts (tied-10th); innings pitched (6th); and games started (7th).

Two-time N.L. champion (1933 & 1936).

1933 world champion.

31 RUBE MARQUARD

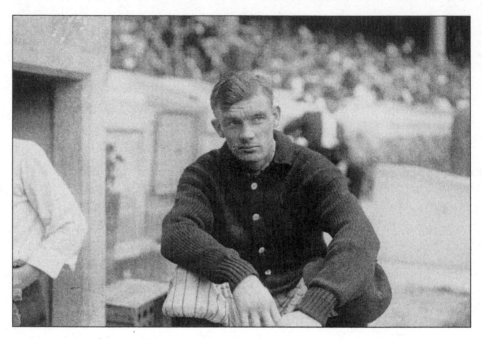

Rube Marquard won a franchise-record 19 straight decisions in 1912. *(Courtesy of Library of Congress)*

Referred to early in his career as the "$11,000 Lemon" due to his inability to fulfill his enormous potential his first few years in New York after being signed to that then-unheard of sum, Rube Marquard ended up giving the Giants a solid return on their investment. After compiling an overall record of just 9–18 from 1908 to 1910, Marquard posted a composite mark of 73–28 over the course of the next three seasons, winning well in excess of 20 games each year, and helping the Giants capture three consecutive National League pennants. Along the way, the lanky left-hander led all N.L. pitchers in wins, winning percentage, and strikeouts one time each, tying a major-league record in 1912 by winning his first 19 decisions. More than 100 years later, no one else has yet been able to match that feat.

Born in Cleveland, Ohio, on October 9, 1886, Richard William Marquard received his initiation into the world of professional baseball as batboy for the hometown Indians, tending to the lumber of such future Hall of Famers as Napoleon Lajoie and Elmer Flick. After later making a name for himself on the Cleveland sandlots, Marquard began his own pro career with Canton in the Central League in 1907, for whom he won 23 of his 36 decisions. Promoted to the American Association the following year, Marquard acquired the nickname "Rube" while pitching for Indianapolis when a newspaper account of one of his starts said, "He is so tall and skinny, he looks like a big number one when he stands on the mound, but he pitches like (Philadelphia A's Hall of Fame left-hander) Rube Waddell."

Purchased by the Giants for a then-record $11,000 after winning 20 games for Indianapolis in 1908, Marquard made his major-league debut during the season's final week, two weeks shy of his 22nd birthday. Beginning his career in ignominious fashion, the 6'3", 180-pound southpaw absorbed his first loss, surrendering 5 runs (2 earned) and 6 hits over 5 innings of work. Marquard fared little better in his rookie campaign of 1909, going just 5–13, although he did manage to compile a very respectable 2.60 ERA. Dropped from New York's regular starting rotation the following year, Marquard finished the season 4–4 with a 4.46 ERA, prompting local newspapers to label him the "$11,000 Lemon."

After working extensively with new Giants assistant coach Wilbert Robinson early in 1911, Marquard finally began to realize his full potential, compiling a record of 24–7, an ERA of 2.50, and a league-leading 237 strikeouts in his breakout season. Putting to rest any doubts about his ability to succeed at the major-league level, Marquard joined Christy Mathewson at the top of the Giants' starting rotation, giving them the best one-two punch in the Senior Circuit. He followed that up with another big year in 1912, concluding the campaign with a record of 26–11 that made him the N.L.'s top winner. Marquard opened up the season with 19 straight victories, tying in the process the league record for most consecutive wins at the start of a season. He also placed among the league leaders in ERA (2.57), strikeouts (175), complete games (22), and innings pitched (294 ⅔). Marquard then capped off his outstanding season by posting another two victories in the World Series, which the Giants eventually lost to Boston in eight games (one game finished in a tie).

Blessed with an exceptional fastball, of which Hall of Fame shortstop Joe Tinker once said, "You can't hit what you can't see," Marquard nevertheless preferred to use his forkball and a screwball he learned from Mathewson as his "out" pitches. In explaining his reasoning, Marquard stated, "Any hitter can hit a fast one. But not many can hit slow ones."

However, Giants manager John McGraw considered Marquard's fastball to be his most effective pitch, stating in his book *My Thirty Years in Baseball*, "When right, Marquard's fastball had a peculiar jump to it that was a complete baffler to opponents. It was in the use of this ball at the right moment that he won his 19 straight games."

Marquard had one more big year for the Giants, going 23–10, with a 2.50 ERA and 20 complete games in 1913, before falling out of favor with McGraw when he finished just 12–22 the following year. Having grown impatient with Marquard after the latter won just 9 of his first 17 decisions in 1915, McGraw elected to place him on waivers in late August. Brooklyn subsequently scooped him up, after which Marquard spent the next five-plus seasons pitching for the Dodgers. Although Marquard never again experienced the same amount of success he had during his three peak years with the Giants, he nevertheless had two very good years for the Dodgers, finishing 13–6, with a career-best 1.58 ERA in 1916, before posting 19 victories for them the following season. After compiling an overall mark of 56–48 for Brooklyn, Marquard spent one season in Cincinnati, going 17–14 in 1921 before joining the Boston Braves, with whom he spent his final four years in the majors, posting a record of just 25–39 during that time. After working mostly out of the Boston bullpen in 1925, Marquard chose to announce his retirement at season's end, concluding his career with a record of 201–177, a 3.08 ERA, 1,593 strikeouts in 3,306 ⅔ innings of work, 197 complete games, 30 shutouts, and a WHIP of 1.237. In his eight years with the Giants, Marquard compiled a record of 103–76, with a 2.85 ERA, 897 strikeouts in 1,546 innings pitched, 99 complete games, 16 shutouts, and a WHIP of 1.197.

Following his retirement as an active player, Marquard spent the next few years managing and scouting for several minor-league teams before eventually working for many years behind the mutual windows at racetracks in Florida and Maryland. Inducted into the Baseball Hall of Fame by the members of the Veteran's Committee in 1971, Marquard passed away nine years later, on June 1, 1980, at the age of 93.

Since his passing, Marquard's induction into Cooperstown has been questioned by many, including baseball historian Bill James, who described him as "probably the worst starting pitcher in the Hall of Fame." Although it is generally believed that the interviews Marquard contributed to the popular baseball book *The Glory of Their Times* had a good deal to do with his election, it has since been learned that most of the stories he "recounted" lacked merit.

Giant Career Highlights:

Best Season: It could easily be argued that Marquard had his best year for the Giants in 1912, when he posted a league-leading and career-high 26 wins that included a record-tying 19 consecutive victories at the start of the season. He also won another two games in the World Series and placed near the top of the league rankings in strikeouts (175), complete games (22), innings pitched (294 ⅔), winning percentage (.703), and ERA (2.57). However, even though Marquard won three fewer games the following year, concluding the 1913 campaign with a record of 23–10, he arguably pitched slightly better ball. In addition to finishing third among N.L. hurlers in wins, Marquard once again ranked among the league leaders in strikeouts (151), complete games (20), innings pitched (288), winning percentage (.697), and ERA (2.50), while also finishing third in the league with a WHIP of 1.031 that represented easily his best mark as a member of the Giants. Nevertheless, Marquard had the most dominant season of his career in 1911, when he compiled a record of 24–7 that gave him a league-best .774 winning percentage. He also compiled an ERA of 2.50 and a WHIP of 1.178, worked 277 ⅔ innings, and established career highs with 22 complete games, 5 shutouts, and a league-leading 237 strikeouts, which remained a National League record for left-handers until Sandy Koufax whiffed 269 batters in 1961.

Memorable Moments/Greatest Performances: Marquard experienced one of his greatest moments on July 8, 1911, when he hit the only home run of his career during a 5–2 victory over the Chicago Cubs. He accomplished another memorable feat in his next start four days later, when he fanned six consecutive batters during a 4–3 win over the Pirates, striking out the side in both the second and third innings.

Marquard tossed a pair of gems in August of 1911, striking out 13 batters during a 3–2, 12-inning victory over Grover Cleveland Alexander and the Phillies on August 14, before fanning 11 and allowing just 2 hits during a 2–1 win over Pittsburgh on the 24th of the month. Before losing to the Cubs in his next start, Marquard continued a pair of extremely impressive winning streaks when he recorded a 2–1 victory over Brooklyn on July 3, 1912. In addition to tying a National League record by posting his 19th consecutive victory that season, Marquard extended the Giants winning streak to 16 games.

Marquard pitched extraordinarily well in the 1912 World Series, defeating the Red Sox twice and compiling an ERA of 0.50 by allowing just 1 earned run over 18 innings.

However, Marquard pitched his two most memorable games for the Giants in his final two seasons in New York, with the first of those coming on July 17, 1914, when he got the best of Pittsburgh's Babe Adams in a 21-inning marathon finally won by the Giants by a score of 3–1 on a two-run home run by Larry Doyle in the final frame. Marquard worked all 21 innings, surrendering 15 hits and just 2 walks. He turned in another extraordinary effort in the second game of the ensuing campaign, tossing a 2–0 no-hitter against Brooklyn on April 15, 1915. Marquard faced 30 batters, needing only one hour and 16 minutes to complete his masterpiece.

Notable Achievements:

Won more than 20 games three times, surpassing 25 victories once (26 in 1912).

Posted winning percentage in excess of .700 twice.

Struck out more than 200 batters once (237 in 1911).

Threw more than 20 complete games three times.

Led N.L. pitchers in: wins once; winning percentage once; and strikeouts once.

Holds share of single-season franchise record by winning 19 straight decisions in 1912.

Holds major-record for most consecutive victories at the start of a season (19 in 1912).

Threw no-hitter vs. Brooklyn on April 15, 1915.

Three-time N.L. champion (1911, 1912 & 1913).

Elected to Baseball Hall of Fame by members of Veteran's Committee in 1971.

32 BOBBY THOMSON

Bobby Thomson is embraced by manager Leo Durocher after hitting the "Shot Heard 'Round the World." *(Courtesy of LegendaryAuctions.com)*

Remembered most for his pivotal role in one of the most iconic moments in American sports history, Bobby Thomson capped a remarkable comeback by the Giants when he put them in the 1951 World Series by hitting a three-run, ninth-inning homer off Brooklyn Dodgers pitcher Ralph Branca in the final game of a three-game playoff between the two teams. Yet, even though Thomson achieved baseball immortality when he delivered his "Shot Heard 'Round the World," he contributed to the Giants in many other ways during his time in New York. En route to earning three All-Star selections and one top-10 finish in the N.L. MVP voting over parts of eight seasons with the Giants, Thomson surpassed 20 home runs six times, 100 RBIs four times, and 100 runs scored once. He also batted over .300 twice and did whatever the Giants asked of him defensively, manning five different positions on the diamond at one point or another as a member of the team. Still, as Thomson later discovered, he will forever be remembered as the man who won the 1951 pennant for the Giants with his decisive blow.

Born in Glasgow, Scotland, on October 25, 1923, Robert Brown Thomson arrived in the United States at the age of 2, settling with his family in Staten Island, New York, where he ironically grew up rooting for the Brooklyn Dodgers. Excelling in soccer and baseball while attending Curtis High School, Thomson signed with the New York Giants the day after he received his diploma. However, after spending just one month in New York's farm system, Thomson entered the Air Force where he trained as a bombardier. Fortunate in that his crew never saw hostile action during the war, Thomson spent his entire three-year tour of duty serving within the continental United States. Nevertheless, he remained away from the game for two years, competing on a semi-professional level only in the summer of 1945 while awaiting his discharge.

Showing few signs of rust after he returned to the minors in 1946, Thomson hit 26 home runs for Triple-A Jersey City, prompting the Giants to summon him to the big leagues in early September. Appearing in 18 games over the final month of the campaign, Thomson began his major-league career by batting .315, hitting 2 homers, and driving in 9 runs, in just over 50 official at-bats.

With Thomson having struggled somewhat defensively in his brief trial at third base the previous year, the Giants elected to take advantage of his outstanding running speed by moving him to center field in 1947. Looking back at his first spring training with the big club, Thomson recalled, "I was a raw rookie in Arizona during spring training in 1947, but I could do three things. I could run. I had a good arm. And I could hit with power."

Earning the starting center-field job early in the year, the right-handed-hitting Thomson had an outstanding rookie season, batting .283, driving in 85 runs, and placing among the N.L. leaders with 29 home runs and 105 runs scored. He also did a solid job in the outfield, finishing second among players at his position in putouts and assists. Splitting his time between center field and left the following year, Thomson posted less impressive numbers on offense, batting just .248, with only 16 homers, 63 RBIs, and 75 RBIs. Nevertheless, he made the N.L. All-Star team for the first time in his career. Shifted back to center field full-time by new Giants manager Leo Durocher in 1949, Thomson had one of his finest all-around seasons, placing among the league leaders in 11 different offensive categories, including home runs (27), RBIs (109), runs scored (99), hits (198), and batting average (.309), en route to earning All-Star honors for the second straight time.

Yet, even though the 6'2", 190-pound Thomson proved to be a tough competitor who served as the Giants' top offensive threat in 1949, he failed to gain the favor of Durocher, who often expressed his feelings towards the outfielder in unattributed viewpoints that appeared in the local newspapers. Durocher, who generally preferred hard-nosed, aggressive players, found Thomson to be too easygoing for his liking, intimating as much to the local writers when he suggested that Thomson had the ability to play like Joe DiMaggio if he drove himself harder.

Still, Durocher found himself leaning heavily on Thomson in each of the next four seasons due to the outstanding offensive production and defensive versatility he offered the Giants. After a slightly subpar 1950 campaign in which he hit 25 homers, knocked in 85 runs, scored 79 times, and batted .252, Thomson helped lead the Giants to the pennant the following year by hitting 32 home runs, driving in 101 runs, scoring 89 times, and batting .293. Equally significant, Thomson agreed to move to third base in order to accommodate rookie center-fielder Willie Mays, who the Giants brought up in late May. Commenting years later on Thomson's unselfish act, Mays stated, "Leo wanted him to move to third base. He didn't have a problem with that. That's class."

With Thomson, Mays, Monte Irvin, and Alvin Dark serving as their primary offensive weapons, and with Sal Maglie and Larry Jansen each winning 23 games, the Giants overcame a 13-game deficit to Brooklyn in mid-August by winning 37 of their final 44 games. After tying the Dodgers on the final day of the regular season, the Giants faced their bitter rivals in a winner-take-all three-game playoff for the National League pennant. Aided by a Thomson two-run homer off Ralph Branca, the Giants won the opener by a score of 3–1. Brooklyn subsequently took Game 2, routing the Giants by a score of 10–0. The Dodgers appeared to be on their way to winning the decisive third contest as well when they took a 4–1 lead into the bottom of the ninth inning.

However, two singles and a double made the score 4–2 and brought Thomson to the plate as the potential winning run. With Branca once again on the mound, this time in relief of Brooklyn starter Don Newcombe, Thomson took the right-hander's first pitch for a strike. However, he jumped on his second offering, driving it deep into the left-field stands for a three-run homer that gave the Giants a 5–4 victory and the N.L. pennant. With the Polo Grounds in a frenzy, Giants play-by-play announcer Russ Hodges immortalized the moment by screaming repeatedly: "The Giants win the pennant! The Giants win the pennant!"

Thomson posted excellent numbers for the Giants in each of the next two seasons as well, earning his third All-Star selection in 1952 by hitting 24 homers, driving in 108 runs, scoring 89 times, batting .270, and leading the league with 14 triples, before hitting 26 home runs, knocking in 106 runs, scoring 80 times, and batting .288 the following year, while splitting his time between third base and the outfield. Nevertheless, he found himself unable to live up to the unrealistically high expectations the fans set for him after he performed so heroically for them in the 1951 playoffs. Anticipating a home run every time Thomson stepped into the batter's box, Giants fans booed him whenever he left men on base. Although Thomson enjoyed the many perks hitting the "Shot Heard 'Round the World" accorded him throughout the remainder of his life, suggesting years later, "It was the best thing that ever happened to me. It may have been the best thing that ever happened to anybody," he also admitted that it may have forced him to put undue pressure on himself. Looking back at the overall impact his pennant-winning blast had on his career, Thomson stated, "In New York, after that famous home run, they expected me to be up there every year. That homer raised me to a high level, with the top guys in the game." Thomson added, "I produced. But sometimes I think I could have produced more."

The return of Willie Mays from the military, the presence of hard-hitting Hank Thompson at third base, and the need for additional starting pitching prompted the Giants to include Thomson in a six-player trade they completed with the Milwaukee Braves on February 1, 1954, that netted them pitchers Johnny Antonelli and Don Liddle, among others. Although still only 30 years old at the time of the deal, Thomson never again performed at the same level he reached during his peak seasons in New York. Appearing in just 43 games with the Braves in 1954 after breaking his ankle while sliding into second base during a spring training game, Thomson finished the year with just 2 homers,

15 RBIs, and a .232 batting average. He spent two more full seasons in Milwaukee, having his best year for the Braves in 1956, when he hit 20 homers and knocked in 74 runs. Traded back to the Giants for second baseman Red Schoendienst midway through the 1957 campaign, Thomson hit 8 home runs, drove in 38 runs, and batted .242 in 81 games with his old team. However, Thomson's return to New York proved to be short-lived, since the Giants dealt him to the Chicago Cubs just prior to the start of the 1958 season. He subsequently spent two years with the Cubs, having his best season for them in 1958 when he hit 21 homers, knocked in 82 runs, and batted .283. Traded to Boston following the conclusion of the 1959 campaign, Thomson appeared in 40 games with the Red Sox, before being released by them at midseason. He then signed with the Orioles, who released him just three weeks later. Choosing to announce his retirement after being cut loose by Baltimore, Thomson ended his career with 264 home runs, 1,026 runs batted in, 903 runs scored, 1,705 hits, 74 triples, 267 doubles, a .270 batting average, a .332 on-base percentage, and a .462 slugging percentage. While playing for the Giants, he hit 189 homers, knocked in 704 runs, scored 648 times, collected 1,171 hits, 56 triples, and 192 doubles, batted .277, compiled a .337 on-base percentage, and posted a .484 slugging percentage.

After leaving baseball, Thomson became a sales executive at a New York City paper products company, stating years later, "I wanted to get a responsible job, stay home more with my wife and daughter, and live a normal life." He lived in Watchung, New Jersey, until 2006, when he moved to Savannah, Georgia, to be near his daughter and grandchildren. Thomson passed away four years later, on August 16, 2010, two months shy of his 87th birthday. Upon learning of Thomson's passing, Baseball Commissioner Bud Selig said on MLB.com: "Bobby Thomson will always hold a special place in our game for hitting one of the signature home runs in baseball history. 'The Shot Heard 'Round the World' will always remain a defining moment for our game, illustrating the timeless quality of the national pastime."

Giant Career Highlights:

Best Season: It could be argued that Thomson had his best year for the Giants in 1951, when he helped lead them to the pennant by knocking in 101 runs, scoring 89 times, and establishing career-high marks in homers (32), on-base percentage (.385), slugging percentage (.562), and OPS (.947). Furthermore, Thomson performed the selfless act of moving to third base in order to make room in center field for Willie Mays, earning in the process an 8th-place finish in the N.L. MVP voting. And, of course, he also clinched the pennant for the Giants with his dramatic game-winning home run against the Dodgers in Game 3 of the playoffs. Nevertheless, the feeling here is that Thomson had his finest all-around season in 1949, when he hit 27 homers, scored 99 runs, compiled an OPS of .873, and established career highs with 109 RBIs, 198 hits, 35 doubles, 10 stolen bases, 332 total bases, and a .309 batting average. In addition to finishing in the league's top 10 in 11 different offensive categories, Thomson led all N.L. center-fielders with 4 double plays and placed second among league outfielders with 488 putouts, which represented easily the highest total of his career.

Memorable Moments/Greatest Performances: Thomson had a huge afternoon against Cincinnati on July 21, 1949, when he led the Giants to a 9–5 victory over the Reds by driving in a career-high 6 runs with 2 homers and a double. Nearly two months later, on September 18, Thomson helped the Giants record a 13–4 win over Pittsburgh by going 4-for-4, with a pair of homers, 5 RBIs, and 4 runs scored.

Thomson equaled his career-high in RBIs on June 6, 1950, when he led the Giants to a lopsided 10–4 victory over the Pirates by driving in 6 runs with 2 homers and a triple.

Thomson, who batted .440 over the final month of the 1951 campaign, had one of his best days at the plate on September 7, when he went 5-for-5 during a 7–3 victory over the Braves.

Thomson displayed a penchant for hitting big home runs over the course of his career, delivering one such blow on June 16, 1952, when his grand slam homer in the bottom of the ninth inning gave the Giants an 8–7 victory over the Cardinals. Thomson again came through in the clutch on April 20, 1953, when he gave the Giants a 1–0 win over the Braves with a one-out homer in the bottom of the ninth.

However, Thomson unquestionably got the biggest hit of his career on October 3, 1951, when he won the pennant for the Giants with his dramatic three-run homer off Brooklyn's Ralph Branca in Game 3 of the National League playoffs. Revealing his thoughts as he stepped up to the plate with the Dodgers holding a 4–2 lead in the bottom of the ninth inning, Thomson recalled, "I kept telling myself: 'Wait and watch. Give yourself a chance to hit.'" After taking Branca's first pitch for a strike, Thomson deposited his second offering into the left-field seats, with Giants announcer Russ Hodges describing the action as follows:

> There's a long drive . . . it's gonna be . . . I believe—the Giants win the pennant! The Giants win the pennant! The Giants win the pennant! The Giants win the pennant! Bobby Thomson hits into the lower deck of the left-field stands! The Giants win the pennant, and they're going crazy, they're going crazy! . . . I don't believe it, I don't believe it, I do not believe it!"

Recalling his emotions at the time, Thomson said, "I can remember feeling as if time was just frozen. It was a delirious, delicious moment."

Notable Achievements:

Hit more than 20 home runs six times, surpassing 30 homers once (32 in 1951).

Knocked in more than 100 runs four times.

Scored more than 100 runs once (105 in 1947).

Batted over .300 twice.

Finished in double-digits in triples once (14 in 1952).

Topped 30 doubles once (35 in 1949).

Posted slugging percentage in excess of .500 four times.

Led N.L. with 14 triples in 1952.

Led N.L. center-fielders in double plays twice.

Ranks seventh all-time on Giants with 189 career home runs.

Three-time N.L. All-Star (1948, 1949 & 1952).

1951 N.L. champion.

33 ALVIN DARK

Alvin Dark, seen here with three U.S. Marines, helped the Giants win two pennants and one world championship during the 1950s. *(Courtesy of Boston Public Library, Leslie Jones Collection)*

Named the greatest shortstop in Giants history by a fan vote taken in 1969, Alvin Dark spent parts of seven seasons in New York, proving to be one of the National League's finest all-around players at his position during that time. A three-time N.L. All-Star, Dark batted over .300 three straight times for the Giants, while also hitting more than 20 homers and scoring more than 100 runs twice each. A solid fielder as well, Dark led all league shortstops in putouts twice, assists once, and double plays twice as a member of the team. Possessing outstanding leadership qualities and a fiery temperament, Dark served as captain of the Giants throughout his tenure in New York, leading them to two pennants and one world championship. And, after his playing career ended, Dark returned to the Giants as manager for four seasons, guiding them to their first pennant since relocating to San Francisco.

Born in Comanche, Oklahoma, on January 7, 1922, Alvin Ralph Dark spent most of his youth in Louisiana, battling malaria and diphtheria as a child. Overcoming his early maladies, Dark developed into an outstanding athlete while attending Lake Charles High School, earning All-State honors as a tailback in football, while also starring in baseball and basketball. Subsequently offered a basketball scholarship by Texas A&M University, Dark instead elected to enroll at Louisiana State University, where he spent the next two years lettering in all three sports. However, with World War II raging in Europe, Dark joined the Marine Corps' V-12 program, through which he transferred to the University of Louisiana at Lafayette, where he continued his education and athletic career for another year. After completing his military training in 1943, Dark spent the next two years serving in Asia before being discharged from the service in 1945.

Selected by the Philadelphia Eagles as a quarterback in the 1945 NFL Draft, Dark chose to pursue a career in professional baseball instead. After signing with the Braves as an amateur free agent in 1946, the 24-year-old Dark arrived in Boston a few months later. Appearing in 15 games for the Braves after making his major-league debut with them on July 14, 1946, Dark collected 3 hits in 13 trips to the plate, for a batting average of .231. He subsequently spent the entire 1947 campaign in the minor leagues before returning to Boston the following year.

Dark played extremely well for the Braves in 1948, helping them win their first pennant in 34 years by scoring 85 runs and placing among the league leaders with 175 hits, 39 doubles, and a .322 batting average, en route to earning Rookie of the Year honors and a third-place finish in the N.L. MVP voting. He followed that up with a solid 1949 season in which he batted .276 and scored 74 runs.

With the Giants desperately seeking to upgrade the middle of their infield, they completed a deal with the Braves on December 14, 1949, that sent four players, including slugging third baseman Sid Gordon, to Boston for Dark and second baseman Eddie Stanky. Immediately named team captain by manager Leo Durocher upon his arrival in New York, Dark had an exceptional first season with his new team. In addition to providing leadership to the

Giants' young starting lineup that also included Bobby Thomson, Don Mueller, Whitey Lockman, and Hank Thompson, the right-handed-hitting Dark batted .279, hit 16 home runs, knocked in 67 runs, and scored 79 times, in helping the Giants improve their record by 13 games.

Dark subsequently proved to be a key figure on the Giants' 1951 pennant-winning ball club, earning his first All-Star nomination and a 12th-place finish in the N.L. MVP balloting by hitting 14 homers, driving in 69 runs, leading the league with 41 doubles, and placing among the leaders with 114 runs scored, 196 hits, and a .303 batting average. He also led all players at his position in assists (465), putouts (295), and double plays (114).

Dark made an extremely favorable impression on Leo Durocher over the course of his first two seasons in New York, with the Giants manager stating on one occasion, "He's a great shortstop—fast, smart, alert, with a fine pair of hands. He's an intelligent, scientific, natural .300 hitter. He's my shortstop, and I wouldn't trade him for any other in the league today."

Although the Giants failed to repeat as N.L. champions in either of the next two seasons, Dark continued to perform well for them at shortstop, once again leading all players at his position in putouts in 1952, while hitting 14 homers, knocking in 73 runs, scoring 92 times, and batting .301. He improved upon those numbers the following year, concluding the 1953 campaign with 23 home runs, 88 RBIs, 126 runs scored, and a batting average of .300. Dark then helped the Giants capture their second pennant in four seasons in 1954 by hitting 20 homers, driving in 70 runs, scoring 98 times, and batting .293, earning in the process a fifth-place finish in the league MVP voting.

The 5'11", 185-pound Dark spent most of his time in New York serving as the number two hitter in the Giants' batting order, doing an excellent job in that role. An outstanding hit-and-run man, Dark excelled at hitting behind runners, pushing the ball to the opposite field, and bunting runners over into scoring position. In discussing the many contributions Dark made to his team on offense, Joe DiMaggio said, "Dark did anything to keep the rally alive and give the fat part of the batting order a chance to come up with men on base."

Dark also possessed unusual power for a shortstop of his day, with his 23 homers in 1953 establishing a new record for N.L. shortstops. At the time of his retirement, he also ranked among the all-time league leaders for players at his position in home runs (3rd) and slugging percentage (7th).

After missing a total of only 4 games in his first five seasons with the Giants, Dark found himself limited to just 115 games in 1955 by a broken rib and an injured shoulder. Nevertheless, he still managed to post decent numbers, finishing the year with 9 homers, 77 runs scored, and a .282 batting average, while also being named the first recipient of the Lou Gehrig Memorial Award, presented annually to the player who best exemplified the Hall of Fame first baseman's character and integrity, both on and off the field.

Yet, in spite of the respect Dark garnered throughout the league for his sportsmanship, he had a dark side that surfaced from time to time. Extremely competitive, Dark brought with him to the playing field the football mentality he acquired during his years in Louisiana, stating on separate occasions, "Friendships are forgotten when the game begins" and, "In this game of baseball, you live by the sword and die by it. You hit and get hit. Remember that."

The most notable example of Dark's more aggressive side could be found in an incident that occurred during a 1955 contest between the Giants and Dodgers. After Jackie Robinson took exception to several close pitches thrown by Sal Maglie, he attempted to exact a measure of revenge against the Giants starter by bunting the ball down the first-base line in an effort to make Maglie either field the ball or cover first base so that he could run him over. However, when Maglie refused to cover the bag, Robinson instead bowled over Giants second baseman Davey Williams, who found himself standing in the path of the infuriated Dodger third baseman. Dark retaliated against Robinson in the ensuing inning, though, not even hesitating as he rounded second base after doubling to left field. Although Robinson received the throw from the outfield in plenty of time to tag out the hard-charging Dark, the latter knocked the ball out of his glove when he arrived at third base, causing Robinson to be charged with an error. While Robinson later said that he admired Dark for defending his teammate, the Giants shortstop called his adversary "a Hitler."

The 1955 campaign ended up being Dark's last full season in New York. With Dark batting .252 with only 17 RBIs in his first 48 games the following year, the Giants included him in a nine-player trade they completed with the St. Louis Cardinals on June 14, 1956, that netted them, among others, Hall of Fame second baseman Red Schoendienst. Dark left the Giants having hit 98 home runs, driven in 429 runs, scored 605 times, collected 1,106 hits, 30 triples, and 205 doubles, batted .292, compiled a .334 on-base percentage, and posted a .439 slugging percentage as a member of the team.

Dark performed well for the Cardinals over the course of the next two seasons, batting .290, knocking in 64 runs, and scoring 80 times in 1957, before being dealt to the Chicago Cubs during the early stages of the ensuing campaign. He spent the better part of the next two seasons starting at third base for the Cubs, before splitting his final year between the Phillies and Braves, assuming a part-time role with both teams. Dark retired at the end of the 1960 season, concluding his career with 126 home runs, 757 RBIs, 1,064 runs scored, 2,089 hits, 72 triples, 358 doubles, a .289 batting average, a .333 on-base percentage, and a .411 slugging percentage. In addition to his three N.L. All-Star selections, he earned one *Sporting News* All-Star nomination and two top-five finishes in the league MVP voting.

Following his retirement, Dark became manager of the Giants, continuing to serve in that capacity from 1961 to 1964, when controversy over some racially insensitive remarks he made forced Giants owner Horace Stoneham to relieve him of his duties. After guiding the Giants to the pennant in 1962, Dark became increasingly frustrated with his team's inability to repeat as league champions in either of the next two seasons, voicing his displeasure to *Newsday* writer Stan Isaacs in a 1964 article that quoted him as saying: "We have trouble because we have so many Negro and Spanish-speaking players on this team. They are just not able to perform up to the white ball players when it comes to mental alertness. You can't make most Negro and Spanish-speaking players have the pride in their team that you get from white players."

Dark attempted to defend himself by claiming that his comments had been taken out of context. Meanwhile, Willie Mays, who Dark earlier named team captain, and Jackie Robinson both spoke on his behalf, with the latter stating, "I have found Dark to be a gentleman and, above all, unbiased. Our relationship has not only been on the ball field, but off it." Nevertheless, with it later surfacing that Dark had ordered his players not to speak Spanish in the clubhouse, Stoneham elected to fire his manager at season's end after the Giants finished fourth in the league.

In spite of the controversy Dark experienced in San Francisco, he ended up having a lengthy managerial career that also included stops in Kansas City (1966–67), Cleveland (1968–1971), Oakland (1974–75), and San Diego (1977), with his 1974 A's team winning the World Series. After leaving baseball, Dark retired to his home in Easley, South Carolina, where he lived until November 13, 2014, when he lost his battle with Alzheimer's at 92 years of age. Upon learning of his former teammate's passing, Monte Irvin stated, "Alvin was our captain. He led us on the field and off the field; just a good guy to have on your team. We had a lot of fun. Baseball will miss Alvin, and I'll miss him."

Giant Career Highlights:

Best Season: Dark had an outstanding year for the Giants in 1954, when he helped lead them to the pennant by hitting 20 home runs, driving in 70 runs, scoring 98 times, collecting 189 hits, and batting .293, en route to earning a fifth-place finish in the N.L. MVP voting. However, he had his finest season one year earlier, concluding the 1953 campaign with a .300 batting average, 194 hits, and career-high marks in home runs (23), RBIs (88), runs scored (126), doubles (41), total bases (316), and OPS (.823).

Memorable Moments/Greatest Performances: Although not known as a home-run hitter, Dark had the ability to hit the long ball, as can be evidenced by his July 4, 1950, performance against the Dodgers, when he homered in both games of a doubleheader split with Brooklyn. After going 2-for-4 with a homer, double, 2 RBIs, and 2 runs scored in the opener, Dark went 2-for-4 with a homer, triple, 3 RBIs, and 1 run scored in the nightcap. Dark flexed his muscles again later in the year, giving the Giants all the runs they needed by hitting a pair of homers during a 2–0 victory over the Dodgers on September 9, 1950.

Dark had a big day at the plate on June 9, 1951, when he helped lead the Giants to a 10–1 rout of the Cubs by going 3-for-5, with 2 homers and 4 RBIs. Dark, though, had the most productive day of his career on August 26, 1953, when he led the Giants to a lopsided 13–4 victory over the Cardinals by going 5-for-5, with a home run, 5 RBIs, and 2 runs scored. He had another big day against St. Louis on June 3, 1954, when he went 4-for-4, with a pair of doubles and 5 runs scored, during a 13–8 Giants win.

An outstanding postseason performer during his time in New York, Dark batted .417, with a homer, 4 RBIs, and 5 runs scored, against the Yankees in the 1951 World Series. He also hit safely in every game of the 1954 Fall Classic, leading the Giants to a four-game sweep of the heavily favored Cleveland Indians by batting .412, with 7 hits and 2 runs scored.

Notable Achievements:

Batted over .300 three times.

Surpassed 20 home runs twice.

Scored more than 100 runs twice, topping 120 runs scored once (126 in 1953).

Surpassed 30 doubles three times, topping 40 two-baggers twice.

Led N.L. in: doubles once; games played once; and at-bats twice.

Led N.L. shortstops in: assists once; putouts twice; and double plays twice.

Finished in top five of N.L. MVP voting twice.

1954 *Sporting News* All-Star selection.

Three-time N.L. All-Star (1951, 1952 & 1954).

1955 Lou Gehrig Memorial Award winner.

Two-time N.L. champion (1951 & 1954).

1954 world champion.

34 PABLO SANDOVAL

Pablo Sandoval helped the Giants win the 2012 World Series by becoming just the fourth player ever to hit three home runs in one Series game. *(Courtesy of Dirk Hansen)*

Known affectionately to his teammates as "Kung Fu Panda," Pablo Sandoval spent his first seven big-league seasons in San Francisco, making significant contributions during that time to three world championship Giant teams. A solid line-drive hitter with occasional home-run power, the switch-hitting Sandoval topped 20 homers twice, knocked in 90 runs once, and batted over .300 three times while playing for the Giants, en route to earning two All-Star selections and one top-10 finish in the league MVP voting. Performing especially well in the postseason, Sandoval displayed a remarkable ability to raise his level of play in the playoffs and World Series, compiling a lifetime batting average of .344 in three postseason appearances with the Giants, including a memorable 2012 Fall Classic in which he batted .500 and became just the fourth player in baseball history to hit three home runs in one World Series game.

Born in Puerto Cabello, Carabobo, Venezuela, on August 11, 1986, Pablo Emilio Sandoval grew up practicing baseball in an empty two-car garage with his older brother, Michael. The younger Sandoval entered the world of professional baseball while still in high school, signing as an amateur free agent with the Giants in 2003 after attending a scouting tournament in the Dominican Republic a few months earlier. Beginning his minor-league career as a catcher with the Arizona League Giants in 2004, Sandoval gradually transitioned to the infield over the course of the next few seasons as he advanced through San Francisco's farm system. Summoned to the big leagues by the Giants for the first time just three days after celebrating his 22nd birthday in August 2008, Sandoval spent the final six weeks of the campaign splitting his time between first base, third base, and catcher, compiling a batting average of .345, with 3 homers and 24 RBIs, in 41 games and 145 official trips to the plate.

A free-swinger when he first joined the Giants, Sandoval soon found himself being tutored by hitting coach Carney Lansford, who said of his pupil, "As much as I try to get him to be disciplined, it's like caging a lion. He leaves the dugout ready to swing the bat. I literally tell him before every at-bat, 'Swing at a strike.'" The 5'11", 255-pound Sandoval also quickly acquired the nickname "Kung Fu Panda" due to his roundish frame, which teammate Barry Zito likened to that of the main character from the movie of the same name.

Armed with his new moniker and a somewhat more patient approach at the plate, Sandoval claimed the Giants starting third-base job in 2009, earning a seventh-place finish in the N.L. MVP voting by hitting 25 homers, driving in 90 runs, scoring 79 times, and finishing second in the league with a .330 batting average.

Perhaps feeling a bit too sure of himself following his strong showing in 2009, Sandoval allowed himself to blow up to nearly 280 pounds by the end of the ensuing campaign, resulting in a subpar performance that saw him hit just 13 homers, knock in only 63 runs, and bat just .268. Benched during the 2010 NLCS, Sandoval finished his first postseason with no homers, 2 RBIs, and only 3 hits in 17 at-bats, for a batting average of just .176, even though the Giants ended up capturing their first world championship since 1954.

Determined to raise his level of play in 2011, Sandoval worked extremely hard during the subsequent offseason, enabling him to shed more than 30 pounds of extra weight. In the best shape of his young career, the 25-year-old third baseman displayed the fruits of his labor by batting .315, hitting 23 homers, and driving in 70 runs, despite missing 41 games after suffering a broken hamate bone in his right wrist in late April. Activated off the disabled list in mid-June, Sandoval went on a 22-game hitting streak that lasted from June 19 to July 14, earning in the process his first All-Star selection and a 17th-place finish in the league MVP balloting.

Sandoval made the All-Star team again in 2012 after starting off the season by hitting safely in the first 20 games, establishing in the process a new franchise record for the longest consecutive hitting streak to begin a season. However, he ended up missing a total of 54 games due to a fractured left hamate bone and an injured left hamstring, reducing his offensive production by season's end to 12 home runs, 63 RBIs, and a .283 batting average. Nevertheless, with Sandoval fully recovered by the start of the postseason, he led the Giants to their second world championship in three years by hitting 3 homers, driving in 9 runs, and batting .320 during the N.L. playoffs, before earning World Series MVP honors by hitting 3 home runs, knocking in 4 runs, and collecting 8 hits in 16 at-bats during his team's four-game sweep of Detroit in the Fall Classic.

Despite spending two weeks on the disabled list with a left foot injury the following season, Sandoval once again posted solid numbers for the Giants, concluding the 2013 campaign with 14 homers, 79 RBIs, and a .278 batting average. He had another good year in 2014, hitting 16 homers, driving in 73 runs, and batting .279 during the regular season, before once again displaying his ability to perform well under pressure in the postseason by batting .366, in helping the Giants capture their third world championship in five years.

A free agent at the end of 2014, Sandoval elected to sign a five-year, $95 million deal with the Boston Red Sox, bringing his time with the Giants to an end. He left San Francisco with career totals of 106 home runs, 462 RBIs, 398 runs scored, 946 hits, 19 triples, and 192 doubles, a batting average of .294, a .346 on-base percentage, and a .465 slugging percentage. Upon signing with the Red Sox, Sandoval said, "It was a tough decision for me. It took me a long time to be sure that I was going to make the right decision . . . But I want a new challenge. I made that choice to be here in Boston because I need a new challenge."

However, Sandoval later proved to be considerably less diplomatic during an interview with *Bleacher Report's* Scott Miller, stating that it "wasn't hard at all" to leave the Giants, and suggesting that he never had any intention of returning to them. Sandoval told Miller, "I knew early in spring training last year I was going to leave. They didn't respect my agent. Contract talks, everything."

Sandoval added, "The Giants made a good offer, but I didn't want to take it. I got five years (and $95 million) from Boston. I left money on the table in San Francisco. It is not about money. It is about how you treat the player."

When asked who he would miss from the Giants, Sandoval replied, "Only Bochy. I love Boch. He's like my dad. He's the only guy that I miss . . . and Hunter Pence; just those guys."

Experiencing very little in the way of success since leaving the Giants, Sandoval had easily the worst season of his career in 2015, when he hit just 10 homers, knocked in only 47 runs, and batted just .245 for the Red Sox. After losing his starting third-base job to youngster Travis Shaw the following spring, Sandoval ended up appearing in only three games before undergoing season-ending surgery to repair a torn labrum in his left shoulder on May 3, 2016. Although Sandoval is expected to make a full recovery by the start of the 2017 campaign, it remains to be seen whether or not he can regain his earlier form, or, for that matter, his starting job at the hot corner.

Giant Career Highlights:

Best Season: Sandoval clearly played his best ball for the Giants in his first full season with the club, establishing career-high marks in virtually every offensive category in 2009 by hitting 25 homers, driving in 90 runs, scoring 79 times, amassing 5 triples, 44 doubles, 189 hits, and 318 total bases, batting .330, compiling an on-base percentage of .387, and posting a slugging percentage of .556. En route to earning his lone top-10 finish in the N.L. MVP voting, Sandoval placed among the league leaders in batting average (2nd), doubles (3rd), hits (4th), total bases (6th), slugging percentage (6th), and OPS (7th).

Memorable Moments/Greatest Performances: Sandoval had his first big day at the plate for the Giants on September 7, 2008, when he doubled twice and knocked in 5 runs during an 11–6 win over the Pittsburgh Pirates.

Sandoval hit a dramatic home run for the Giants on May 12, 2009, when his three-run homer with two men out in the bottom of the 9th inning gave the Giants a 9–7 walk-off win over the Washington Nationals.

Sandoval experienced a memorable moment on July 30, 2009, when, with Willie McCovey in attendance on the 50th anniversary of his major-league debut, the Giants third baseman hit his first home run into McCovey Cove. Sandoval, who also doubled and knocked in 4 runs during the contest, said afterwards, "It's special right now. I hit McCovey Cove and McCovey's here. He talks to me every time he's in the clubhouse."

Some two months later, on September 29, 2009, Sandoval helped lead the Giants to an 8–4 victory over Arizona by going 4-for-4, with a homer, double, 2 RBIs, and career-high 4 runs scored.

Sandoval had a big day at the plate on September 15, 2011, when he hit for the cycle during an 8–5 win over the Colorado Rockies.

Sandoval again tormented Colorado pitchers on September 20, 2012, when, during a 9–2 victory over the Rockies, he became the sixth Giants player to homer from both sides of the plate in the same game.

Sandoval hit his second game-winning walk-off home run against Washington on May 21, 2013, when, despite battling the flu, he delivered a one-on, one-out homer in the bottom of the 10th inning that gave the Giants a 4–2 victory over the Nationals.

Sandoval had a tremendous day at the plate on September 4, 2013, when he led the Giants to a 13–5 victory over San Diego by going 4-for-5, with 3 home runs and a career-high 6 RBIs.

Nevertheless, Sandoval unquestionably experienced the greatest moment of his career in Game 1 of the 2012 World Series, when he led the Giants to an 8–3 victory over Detroit by going 4-for-4, with 3 home runs and 4 RBIs. Sandoval's three round-trippers enabled him to join Babe Ruth, Reggie Jackson, and Albert Pujols as the only players in MLB history to hit three homers in one World Series game. Sandoval went on to collect four more hits during the Fall Classic, setting in the process a new Giants franchise record for most hits in a postseason with 24, which included 6 home runs.

Sandoval also came up big for the Giants in the 2014 postseason, delivering a game-tying RBI double against Washington in the top of the 9th inning of Game 2 of the NLDS, en route to breaking his own franchise record by collecting 26 postseason hits.

Notable Achievements:

Hit more than 20 home runs twice.
Batted over .300 three times, topping the .330-mark twice.
Surpassed 30 doubles twice, topping 40 two-baggers once (44 in 2009).
Posted slugging percentage in excess of .500 twice.

Finished second in N.L. with batting average of .330 in 2009.

Hit for cycle vs. Colorado on September 15, 2011.

Hit three home runs in one game vs. San Diego on September 4, 2013.

Hit three home runs vs. Detroit in Game 1 of 2012 World Series.

Holds Giants record with 26 postseason hits in 2014.

2012 World Series MVP.

Two-time N.L. All-Star (2011 & 2012).

Three-time N.L. champion (2010, 2012 & 2014).

Three-time world champion (2010, 2012 & 2014).

35 JACK CLARK

Jack Clark surpassed 20 home runs five times as a member of the Giants. *(Courtesy of PristineAuction. com)*

A hard-hitting outfielder with a ferocious swing that earned him the nickname "Jack the Ripper," Jack Clark developed a reputation as one of baseball's most dangerous hitters during his time in San Francisco. At his best with the game on the line, Clark proved to be an outstanding clutch hitter who one writer described as the National League's version of Eddie Murray. Spending parts of his first 10 major-league seasons in San Francisco, Clark served as the Giants starting right-fielder in seven of those, surpassing 20 home runs five times and 100 RBIs once, and batting over .300 twice, en route to earning two All-Star selections and two top-10 finishes in the N.L. MVP voting. Yet, in spite of his outstanding production, Clark eventually wore out his welcome in San Francisco with his rebellious nature and constant complaining about the poor playing conditions at Candlestick Park.

Born in New Brighton, Pennsylvania, on November 10, 1955, Jack Anthony Clark signed with the Giants shortly after they selected him in the 13th round of the 1973 amateur draft following his graduation from Gladstone High School in Covina, California. The right-handed-hitting outfielder subsequently advanced rapidly through San Francisco's farm system, spending the rest of 1973 with the Great Falls Giants, before moving on to Fresno the following year and Lafayette in 1975. After hitting a league-leading 23 home runs with Lafayette, Clark received his first call-up to the big leagues in September of 1975, appearing in 8 games with the Giants before being returned to the minors prior to the start of the ensuing campaign. He then spent most of 1976 in the minor leagues before arriving in San Francisco to stay during the latter stages of the season.

After earning the Giants starting right-field job in spring training of 1977, the 21-year-old Clark went on to have a solid rookie season, finishing the year with 13 home runs, 51 RBIs, 64 runs scored, a .252 batting average, and 11 outfield assists. He developed into the Giants' best player the following year, batting .306 and leading the team with 25 homers, 98 RBIs, 90 runs scored, 181 hits, 46 doubles, a .537 slugging percentage, and an OPS of .895, en route to earning his first All-Star selection and a fifth-place finish in the league MVP voting.

Clark continued to play well for the Giants in each of the next two seasons, earning his second straight All-Star nomination in 1979 by hitting 26 homers, driving in 86 runs, scoring 84 times, and batting .273, before hitting 22 home runs, knocking in 82 runs, scoring 77 times, batting .284, and finishing third in the league with a .517 slugging percentage and .900 OPS the following year, despite missing a month after having a bone in his left hand broken by a Mark Bombeck pitch. Rapidly developing into the Giants' team leader, Clark won the first Willie Mac Award in the second of those campaigns for his spirit and leadership. He also established himself as one of baseball's best clutch hitters by leading the National League with 18 game-winning RBIs. And, although Clark lacked outstanding running speed, he did a solid job for the Giants in right field, ranking among the top players at his position in fielding percentage, before eventually going on to lead all

N.L. right-fielders in putouts three times, assists twice, and double plays four times.

Playing the game with a barely controlled fury and a perpetual snarl, Clark intimidated opposing pitchers with his angry expression and rugged appearance. Possessing a lean but muscular 6'2", 195-pound frame, jet black hair, and a vicious swing that earned him his ominous nickname, Clark presented a menacing figure in the batter's box. Coiling his body like an angry cobra, Clark whipped his bat around at tremendous speeds, driving fierce line drives to all fields. And hurlers found the prospect of facing him with the game on the line in the late innings of contests particularly frightening since he seemed to thrive in such situations.

Clark's aggressive approach to his craft initially made a favorable impression on new Giants manager, Frank Robinson, when the latter assumed control of the team in 1981. The two men got along relatively well at first, with Clark hitting 17 homers, driving in 53 runs, and scoring 60 times in their first year together, despite having the season cut short by a player's strike. Clark further endeared himself to Robinson in 1982 by hitting 27 home runs, knocking in 103 runs, scoring 90 times, batting .274, and collecting a league-leading 21 game-winning hits. However, their relationship began to sour somewhat the following year when Clark missed nearly 30 games due to injury, causing his offensive totals to drop to just 20 homers, 66 RBIs, and 82 runs scored. Things completely unraveled between the two men over the course of the ensuing campaign when Robinson began to question Clark's toughness following a lengthy stay on the disabled list. With Robinson expressing the belief that Clark spent far too much time recovering from an injury, he butted heads with Clark, who fumed at his manager's contention. After the local media also questioned Clark's dedication to the team, the latter drove an additional wedge between himself and the hometown fans by voicing his dissatisfaction with the playing conditions at cold and windy Candlestick Park.

Although Clark performed well whenever he took the field in 1984, batting .320, hitting 11 homers, and driving in 44 runs, in only 57 games, his gruff demeanor and rebellious nature prompted the Giants front office to begin fielding offers for him at season's end. The power-starved St. Louis Cardinals proved to be an excellent trading partner, completing a deal with the Giants on February 1, 1985, that sent a package of four players that included David Green, Dave LaPoint, Gary Rajsich, and Jose Uribe for the disgruntled slugger. Clark left San Francisco with career totals of 163 home runs, 595

RBIs, 597 runs scored, 1,034 hits, 30 triples, and 197 doubles, a batting average of .277, an on-base percentage of .359, and a slugging percentage of .477.

Moved to first base after he joined the Cardinals, Clark had a big first year in St. Louis, earning All-Star honors and his first Silver Slugger by finishing near the top of the league rankings with a .393 on-base percentage and a .502 slugging percentage, batting .281, hitting 22 home runs, and driving in 87 runs, despite being limited by injuries to only 126 games and 442 official at-bats. After suffering through an injury-plagued 1986 campaign, Clark returned to top form in 1987, earning his second Silver Slugger, the last of his four All-Star selections, and a third-place finish in the N.L. MVP voting by hitting 35 homers, knocking in 106 runs, scoring 93 times, batting .286, and leading the league with 136 bases on balls, a .459 on-base percentage, and a .597 slugging percentage.

Commenting years later on the impact Clark made in St. Louis in his book, *You're Missin' a Great Game,* former Cardinals manager Whitey Herzog stated, "We'd have never won the 1985 and 1987 pennants without him. He was one of the scariest fastball hitters I ever saw. Some of his shots to the opposite field didn't just scatter the fans—they left the seats in splinters. There wasn't a pitcher in baseball that didn't fear Jack Clark."

Yet, in spite of the tremendous offensive contributions Clark made to the Cardinals, he eventually wore out his welcome in St. Louis as well. After developing a somewhat contentious relationship with star shortstop Ozzie Smith over the course of the three previous seasons, Clark got into a contract squabble with Cardinals management at the conclusion of the 1987 campaign. Displeased with his situation in St. Louis, Clark elected to sign a free-agent deal with the Yankees.

Despite hitting 27 home runs, driving in 93 runs, and walking 113 times in 1988, Clark's .242 batting average and 141 strikeouts made him a huge disappointment in New York. Seeking to rid themselves of his exorbitant contract, the Yankees traded Clark to the San Diego Padres for three players in October of 1988. Always one to speak his mind, Clark expressed his feelings about the time he spent in the American League when he stated, "I hate that damn league. Every game lasts 3 ½ to 4 hours. No wonder the fans are bored over there."

Clark spent the next two years in San Diego, totaling 51 home runs and 156 RBIs during that time, before his caustic personality began to wear thin on the Padres as well. After feuding with Padres manager Greg Riddoch and popular teammate Tony Gwynn, who he called "selfish," Clark signed with the Boston Red Sox when he became a free agent at the end of 1990. He ended up spending two years in Boston, hitting 28 home runs, driving in 87 runs, and batting .249 in the first of those seasons, before assuming a part-time role with the Red Sox the following year. Clark elected to call it quits at the conclusion of the 1992 campaign, ending his career with 340 home runs, 1,180 runs batted in, 1,118 runs scored, 1,826 hits, 39 triples, 332 doubles, a .267 batting average, a .379 on-base percentage, and a .476 slugging percentage. Following his playing career, Clark ended up being driven into bankruptcy by his appetite for luxury cars. Yet, he eventually got back on his feet, returning to baseball, first as a coach for the Los Angeles Dodgers, and later as a minor-league manager. More recently, Clark assumed a position as co-host of a radio sports talk show in St. Louis, where he continued to create controversy by accusing Albert Pujols of using performance-enhancing drugs during his time with the Cardinals. Upon learning of Clark's accusations, Pujols threatened him and the radio station with a defamation lawsuit, causing the station to cut ties with Clark after only seven shows. Clark later apologized and retracted his allegations against Pujols, stating that he had "no knowledge whatsoever" that Pujols ever used PEDs, and adding, "During a heated discussion on air, I misspoke." In return, Pujols dropped the lawsuit.

Giant Career Highlights:

Best Season: Clark had a big year in 1982, earning a 7th-place finish in the N.L. MVP balloting by hitting 27 homers, driving in 103 runs, scoring 90 times, and batting .274. However, he had his finest all-around season for the Giants in 1978, when he earned his lone *Sporting News* All-Star selection as a member of the team and a 5th-place finish in the MVP voting by placing among the league leaders with 25 home runs, 98 RBIs, 90 runs scored, 181 hits, 8 triples, 46 doubles, a .306 batting average, a .537 slugging percentage, and an OPS of .895. Clark also stole a career-high 15 bases, collected 16 outfield assists, and led all N.L. right-fielders with 5 double plays and a career-best 328 putouts. Meanwhile, his 26-game hitting streak, which lasted from June 30 to July 25, remains the longest by any Giants player since 1900.

Memorable Moments/Greatest Performances: Although the Giants dropped both ends of a doubleheader to the Braves on June 30, 1978, Clark began his 26-game hitting streak in impressive fashion, homering twice in the 10–9 loss in the opener before reaching the seats once more in the nightcap, which the Giants lost by a score of 10–5.

Clark had the only 5-for-5 day of his career on July 22, 1983, when he hit safely in all 5 trips to the plate during a 5–3 win over the Pirates.

Clark had a number of big days at the plate for the Giants in 1982, with the first of those coming on May 28, when he homered twice and drove in 5 runs during a 10–5 victory over the Pirates. Clark again tormented Pittsburgh's pitching staff the very next day, hitting another 2 homers and knocking in 6 runs, in leading the Giants to a 9–5 win over the Pirates. Clark homered twice in the same game again on August 6, with his second round-tripper tying the score with Houston at 6–6 in the bottom of the 9th inning. Reggie Smith followed Clark's blast with one of his own, enabling the Giants to beat the Astros in walk-off fashion by a score of 7–6. Less than two weeks later, on August 18, Clark led the Giants to a 16–9 pounding of Pittsburgh by going 4-for-5, with a homer, double, 6 RBIs, and 2 runs scored. Clark, though, experienced his most memorable moment of the 1982 campaign on September 4, when he reached Cardinals closer Bruce Sutter for a 2-out, three-run homer in the bottom of the 9th inning, to give the Giants a 5–4 win over St. Louis.

Notable Achievements:

Surpassed 20 home runs five times.

Knocked in more than 100 runs once (103 in 1982).

Batted over .300 twice.

Surpassed 30 doubles twice, topping the 40-mark once (46 in 1978).

Compiled on-base percentage in excess of .400 once.

Posted slugging percentage in excess of .500 three times.

Led N.L. outfielders in assists once and double plays three times.

Led N.L. right-fielders in: putouts three times; assists twice; and double plays four times.

Holds longest hitting streak by any Giants player since 1900 (26 games in 1978).

May 1978 N.L. Player of the Month.

1978 *Sporting News* All-Star selection.

Two-time N.L. All-Star (1978 & 1979).

36 JO-JO MOORE

Jo-Jo Moore served as the leadoff hitter for three pennant-winning Giants teams during the 1930s. *(Courtesy of Boston Public Library, Leslie Jones Collection)*

An underrated member of Giant teams that won three pennants and one world championship during the 1930s, Jo-Jo Moore spent his entire career in New York, patrolling left field at the Polo Grounds for the better part of 10 seasons. Nicknamed the "Gause Ghost" due to his slender build and place of birth, Moore proved to be one of the National League's premier leadoff hitters in his years with the Giants, earning six All-Star nominations and one top-five finish in the league MVP voting. En route to compiling a lifetime batting average of .298, Moore topped the .300-mark five times. He also scored more than 100 runs three times and surpassed 200 hits twice. A solid outfielder as well, Moore possessed one of the strongest throwing arms of his era, leading all players at his position in assists on three separate occasions.

Born in Gause, Texas, some 85 miles northeast of Austin, on December 25, 1908, Joseph Gregg Moore spent three years playing in the minor leagues before the Giants purchased his contract from San Antonio of the Texas League towards the tail end of the 1930 campaign. Arriving in New York City at the height of the Depression, Moore recalled years later, "I saw street corner after street corner where they had soup kitchens, and the people would be four abreast, and the lines would run for several blocks."

Joining the Giants for the final two weeks of the 1930 season, Moore appeared in only three games, garnering five plate appearances, and collecting his first hit as a major leaguer. Subsequently relegated to Newark and Jersey City of the International League by John McGraw, who considered him too thin to succeed at the major-league level, the 5'11", 155-pound Moore spent virtually all of 1931, and much of 1932, in the minors, before finally being rescued by new Giants skipper Bill Terry after the latter assumed control of the team midway through the 1932 campaign.

Taking over as the Giants starting left-fielder and leadoff hitter shortly after he rejoined the team, Moore ended up having a solid rookie season, batting .305 and scoring 53 runs in 86 games and 361 official at-bats. Assuming the same roles the following year, Moore helped lead the Giants to the pennant by batting .292, scoring 56 runs finishing second among N.L. outfielders with 19 assists, and leading all left-fielders in the league with 5 double plays. Although the Giants failed to repeat as N.L. champions in 1934, Moore earned his first of five straight All-Star selections and a third-place finish in the MVP balloting by hitting 15 home runs, driving in 61 runs, and placing among the league leaders with 106 runs scored, 192 hits, 37 doubles, and a career-high .331 batting average. He also performed exceptionally well in each of the next two seasons, batting .295, hitting another 15 homers, knocking in 71 runs, scoring 108 times, and collecting 201 hits in 1935, before batting .316, hitting 7 home runs, driving in 63 runs, and reaching career-high marks in runs scored (110) and hits (205) the following year.

Surpassed only by Chicago's Stan Hack among N.L. leadoff hitters throughout the period, the left-handed swinging Moore proved to be Hack's equal as an offensive player in most areas, posting a similar batting average and possessing more power and comparable base-running ability. However, Moore, a notorious first-ball hitter, lacked Hack's patience at the plate, walking more than 50 times just once his entire career. In fact, Moore became so well known for swinging at first pitches that opposing managers occasionally levied fines against their pitchers if they placed their first offerings to him too close to the middle of the plate. On the other hand, Moore rarely struck out, whiffing only 247 times in almost 6,000 total plate appearances over the course of his career.

Primarily a slap hitter when he first joined the Giants, Moore gradually developed a solid line-drive stroke that produced a significant number of extra-base hits. Early in his career, he also learned from veteran teammate Lefty O'Doul how to pull the ball into the short right-field stands at the Polo Grounds. Moore often waited until the last possible moment to start his swing, revealing that New York Yankees catcher Bill Dickey, who faced him in the 1936 and 1937 World Series, once told him, "I've caught behind lots of guys, but I've never had anybody hit the ball right out of my mitt the way you do."

Though known more for his powerful throwing arm on defense, Moore did an excellent job of covering left field at the Polo Grounds as well, using his outstanding speed to consistently rank among the top players at his position in putouts. Doing an expert job of handling the ballpark's difficult sun field, Moore once claimed, "I never once lost a fly ball in the sun."

Moore continued his string of five straight All-Star selections in 1937 and 1938, concluding the first of those campaigns with 6 homers, 57 RBIs, 89 runs scored, and a .310 batting average, before hitting 11 home runs, driving in 56 runs, scoring 76 times, and batting .302 the following year. Although he subsequently experienced something of a drop-off in offensive production the next three seasons, failing to bat any higher than .276 or drive in more than 47 runs, he remained a solid player for the Giants, leading all N.L. left-fielders in assists and fielding percentage in 1939, and earning his last All-Star nomination in 1940.

After Moore batted .273, knocked in 40 runs, and scored only 47 times in 1941, the Giants sold him to the Cincinnati Reds. However, he never appeared in a single game with the Reds, instead spending all of 1942 and 1943 with the minor-league Indianapolis Indians of the American Association. The 35-year-old Moore retired at the end of the 1943 season, ending his major-league career with 79 home runs, 513 RBIs, 809 runs scored, 1,615 hits, 53 triples, 258 doubles, a .298 batting average, a .344 on-base percentage, and a .408 slugging percentage.

Following his retirement, Moore returned to his hometown of Gause, where he raised cattle. He lived until the ripe old age of 92, passing away on April 1, 2001, in Bryan, Texas.

Career Highlights:

Best Season: Moore played his best ball for the Giants from 1934 to 1936, averaging 199 hits and 108 runs scored over the course of those three seasons. En route to earning the second of his five consecutive All-Star nominations in 1935, Moore batted .295, hit 15 home runs, scored 108 times, amassed 201 hits, and knocked in a career-high 71 runs. In addition to batting .316 the following year, Moore drove in 63 runs and established career-high marks in runs scored (110) and hits (205). However, he had his finest all-around season in 1934, when he earned a third-place finish in the N.L. MVP voting by hitting 15 home runs, knocking in 61 runs, scoring 106 times, collecting 192 hits, and establishing career highs with 37 doubles, a .331 batting average, and an OPS of .856.

Memorable Moments/Greatest Performances: Moore put together three impressive hitting streaks during his time in New York, hitting safely in 20 straight games in both 1932 and 1937, and compiling a career-long 23-game hitting streak in 1934.

Moore had his biggest day as a rookie on September 7, 1932, when he led the Giants to a 7–5 win over Cincinnati by going 5-for-5, with a homer, double, and 3 runs batted in.

Moore again went 5-for-5 during a 6–5 victory over Pittsburgh on July 21, 1933, finishing the game with 2 RBIs and 2 runs scored. He had another huge day nearly two weeks later, on August 2, leading the Giants to an 18–1 mauling of Philadelphia by collecting 5 hits, including 3 doubles, driving in 2 runs, and scoring 4 times.

Moore hit two home runs in one game for the only time in his career on July 13, 1934, when he led the Giants to a 7–6 win over Pittsburgh by going 4-for-5, with 2 RBIs and 4 runs scored. Exactly three years later, on July 13, 1937, he collected 5 hits and knocked in 4 runs during an 11–10 victory over the Phillies.

Moore delivered arguably the most memorable hit of his career on August 23, 1934, when his three-run homer off Paul Dean in the top of the 9th inning turned a 3–2 deficit to the Cardinals into a 5–3 Giants win.

Moore tied a World Series record in the sixth inning of Game 2 of the 1933 Fall Classic when he reached Washington starter Alvin Crowder for a pair of singles during a 6-run Giants outburst.

Although the Giants lost the 1937 World Series to the Yankees in five games, Moore performed exceptionally well, batting .391 and tying a record for the most hits in a five-game Series by collecting 9 hits in his 23 trips to the plate.

Notable Achievements:

Batted over .300 five times.

Scored more than 100 runs three times.

Surpassed 200 hits twice.

Finished in double-digits in triples once (10 in 1937).

Topped 30 doubles three times.

Led N.L. with 681 at-bats in 1935.

Led N.L. left-fielders in: assists three times; fielding percentage once; and double plays twice.

Holds Giants single-season record for most official at-bats (681 in 1935).

Ranks among Giants career leaders in: hits (9th); doubles (9th); total bases (tied-10th); and at-bats (10th).

Finished third in 1934 N.L. MVP voting.

Six-time N.L. All-Star (1934, 1935, 1936, 1937, 1938 & 1940).

Three-time N.L. champion (1933, 1936 & 1937).

1933 world champion.

37 HOOKS WILTSE

Hooks Wiltse established a new major-league record in 1904 by winning the first 12 decisions of his career. *(Courtesy of Library of Congress)*

A key contributor to five pennant-winning teams and one world championship ball club as a member of the Giants, George "Hooks" Wiltse spent his entire 11-year National League career in New York, before spending one final season with Brooklyn of the short-lived Federal League. Overshadowed by the incomparable Christy Mathewson his entire time in New York, Wiltse rarely received the credit he deserved for being one of the Senior Circuit's premier left-handers. Nevertheless, the slender southpaw posted a total of 126 wins for the Giants between 1904 and 1911, surpassing 20 victories on two separate occasions. Wiltse also did an excellent job whenever John McGraw asked him to come out of the Giants bullpen, annually placing among the league leaders in saves. A consummate team player, Wiltse even filled in at other positions from time to time, distinguishing himself in Game Two of the 1913 World Series with his outstanding defense at first base.

Born on his family's farm in Pecksport, New York, on September 7, 1879, George LeRoy Wiltse got his start in baseball by joining his older brother Lewis in using the barn door for target practice. After moving with his family to Syracuse, Wiltse eventually began his career in pro ball with Scranton of the independent Pennsylvania State League in 1902, before the league disbanded midway through the campaign. After returning to Syracuse, he signed with Troy of the New York State League, with whom he spent the remainder of the year pitching and playing the outfield. Having compiled an unimpressive 7–15 record for Troy in his dual role, Wiltse concentrated solely on pitching when he rejoined the team in 1903. Improving his mark to 20–8, Wiltse subsequently drew interest from the Giants, who purchased his contract at season's end.

Joining the Giants in 1904, Wiltse spent the first part of the campaign working in relief before gradually earning a spot in the starting rotation. Excelling in each role, the six-foot, 185-pound southpaw got off to a tremendous start, setting a record that stood for 73 years by winning the first 12 decisions of his career. Although Wiltse tailed off a bit late in the year, losing three of his final four decisions, he still ended up compiling an outstanding 13–3 record, along with a 2.84 ERA and 14 complete games.

Spending most of the ensuing campaign working as a spot-starter and long reliever, Wiltse continued to pitch well for the Giants, posting a record of 15–6 and an ERA of 2.47, striking out 120 batters in 197 innings of work, and completing 18 of his 19 starts. Yet, in spite of the success Wiltse experienced during the regular season, he failed to make a single appearance in the 1905 World Series since Christy Mathewson (3) and Joe McGinnity (2) started and finished all five games for the Giants.

It was during the early stages of his career that Wiltse acquired the nickname "Hooks," which, ironically, came neither from his ability to curve a baseball, nor from his hooknose, but, rather, from his outstanding fielding ability. One story credits Giants catcher Frank Bowerman with applying the moniker to him when he yelled, "That's hooking them, George," everytime Wiltse reached out with his long right arm to snare line drives and high bounders headed back through the box. Still another report claims that Wiltse acquired the nickname even earlier, during his days in Syracuse, when a manager told him he had hooks for hands after watching him work out at first base.

Assuming a more prominent role on the Giants pitching staff in 1906, Wiltse finished 16–11, with a 2.27 ERA, 4 shutouts, 21 complete games, and a career-high 6 saves, which placed him second in the N.L. rankings. After another solid season in 1907 in which he won 13 games and compiled an outstanding 2.18 ERA, Wiltse replaced the aging Joe McGinnity as the number two man in the Giants starting rotation the following year. In perhaps his finest season, Wiltse concluded the 1908 campaign with a record of 23–14, an ERA of 2.24, and career-high marks in shutouts (7), complete games (30), and innings pitched (330). He followed that up with another big year in 1909, going 20–11, with a 2.00 ERA, 4 shutouts, 20 complete games, and 269 ⅓ innings pitched.

Unable to maintain the same heavy workload in subsequent seasons, Wiltse developed a reputation as a cold-weather pitcher who tended to wear down during the hot summer months. After finishing 14–12, with a 2.72 ERA, 18 complete games, and 235 ⅓ innings pitched in 1910, Wiltse never again worked more than 200 innings. Still, he remained a valuable member of the Giants pitching staff during their pennant-winning years of 1911, 1912, and 1913. Returning to his earlier role of spot-starter/long reliever in the first of those campaigns, Wiltse compiled a record of 12–9, with a 3.27 ERA, 4 shutouts, and 11 complete games. He then went 9–6 with a 3.16 ERA in 1912, before going 0–0 with a 1.56 ERA in 1913 while working almost exclusively out of the bullpen.

Wiltse made 20 relief appearances for the Giants in 1914 before they released him on August 29. He ended his time in New York with a record of 136–85, an ERA of 2.48, 948 strikeouts in 2,053 innings, 27 shutouts, 151 complete games, 28 saves, and a WHIP of 1.137. After beginning 1915 with Jersey City of the International League, Wiltse finished out his major-league career later in the year with the Federal League's Brooklyn Tip-Tops. He subsequently pitched, managed, and played first base in the minor leagues through 1924, before briefly serving as pitching coach for the Yankees. Wiltse retired from baseball in 1926, after which he returned to Syracuse to sell real estate. He later got involved in politics as well, serving as a Syracuse alderman from 1932 to 1933 and as deputy assessor from 1933 to 1944. Wiltse lived until January 21, 1959, when he died from emphysema at age 79 in Long Beach, New York.

Giant Career Highlights:

Best Season: Wiltse pitched extremely well for the Giants in 1909, concluding the campaign with a record of 20–11 and an ERA of 2.00 that represented his lowest mark as a starter. However, he had his finest season one year earlier, when he compiled an ERA of 2.24 and established career-best marks in wins (23), starts (38), innings pitched (330), complete games (30), shutouts (7), and WHIP (1.027), placing among the league leaders in all six categories.

Memorable Moments/Greatest Performances: Wiltse made his second major-league start a memorable one, tossing a 3-hit shutout in defeating Brooklyn by a score of 11–0 on June 19, 1904.

On September 15, 1904, Wiltse won his 12th straight game when he defeated Boston by a score of 3–2 at the Polo Grounds. In so doing, he set a new major-league record for the most consecutive victories at the start of a career, one that San Diego Padres relief pitcher Butch Metzger ended up tying 72 years later.

Wiltse became just the second pitcher of the modern era to strike out 4 batters in an inning on May 15, 1906, when a third-strike error by Giants catcher Roger Bresnahan forced him to face an extra Cincinnati batter in the fifth inning. Wiltse also struck out the side in the previous frame, making him the only pitcher in major-league history to fan 7 batters over two consecutive innings. He finished the game with 12 strikeouts, in defeating the Reds by a score of 4–1.

Wiltse turned in one of his finest performances on May 4, 1907, when he defeated Brooklyn by a score of 10–0, allowing just one hit in 8 innings of work.

Wiltse hurled a number of gems in 1908, with his first such effort coming on June 24, when he tossed a two-hit shutout against Boston to give the Giants a 4–0 win in the first game of their doubleheader sweep of the Braves. Ten days later, Wiltse celebrated the fourth of July by pitching a 10-inning no-hitter against the Philadelphia Phillies. He actually had a perfect game going with two men out in the ninth inning, before hitting George McQuillan with a 1–2 pitch, just one offering after home plate umpire Charles Rigler called a ball on a pitch he later admitted should have been called a strike. The Giants ended up scoring a run in the ensuing frame, giving them a 1–0 victory. Wiltse's 10-inning no-hitter remains a major-league record. Wiltse turned in another epic performance on July 28, when he battled Pittsburgh starter Vic Willis for 16 innings before umpires finally called the game because of darkness with the score tied at 2–2.

Yet, ironically, Wiltse is remembered equally for the outstanding glove work he displayed at first base in Game 2 of the 1913 World Series. After being used sparingly on the mound during the regular season, Wiltse entered Game 2 in the third inning when injuries to Fred Merkle and Fred Snodgrass left Giants manager John McGraw without anyone else to play first base. With Hall of Fame pitchers Christy Mathewson and Eddie Plank engaged in a 0–0 pitcher's duel in the bottom of the ninth inning, the Athletics threatened to take a two-games-to-none lead in the Series when they put runners on second and third with nobody out. However, Wiltse squelched the rally by throwing out both men at home plate when the next two batters hit hard ground balls towards him. The Giants subsequently evened the Fall Classic at a game apiece when they scored three runs in the ensuing frame, although they eventually lost the Series in five games.

Notable Achievements:

Surpassed 20 victories twice, winning at least 15 games two other times.

Compiled ERA below 2.50 six times, finishing with mark under 2.00 once (1.56 in 1913).

Posted winning percentage in excess of .700 twice.

Threw more than 300 innings once (330 in 1908).

Completed at least 20 of his starts three times, tossing 30 complete games in 1908.

Ranks among Giants career leaders in: wins (10th); ERA (6th); shutouts (tied-6th); complete games (10th); and WHIP (8th).

Set major-league record in 1904 by winning first 12 decisions of career.

Threw 10-inning no-hitter vs. Philadelphia on July 4, 1908.

Five-time N.L. champion (1904, 1905, 1911, 1912 & 1913).

1905 world champion.

38 J. T. SNOW

J. T. Snow won four straight Gold Gloves for his exceptional work at first base for the Giants. *(Courtesy of PristineAuction.com)*

Known primarily for his outstanding defense at first base, J. T. Snow won six consecutive Gold Gloves over the course of his career, the last four of which he earned while playing for the Giants. The unofficial captain of the Giants infield, Snow provided direction to his infield mates, using his knowledge of opposing hitters, his excellent instincts, and his quickness and soft hands to make the other players around him better. A good hitter as well, Snow hit more than 20 home runs twice during his time in San Francisco, while also driving in more than 90 runs three times and batting over .300 once. Snow's solid all-around play helped the Giants capture three division titles and one National League pennant in his nine years with the club.

The son of former Pro Bowl wide receiver Jack Snow, who spent his entire 11-year NFL career with the Los Angeles Rams, Jack Thomas Snow was born in Long Beach, California, on February 26, 1968. A multi-sport star at Los Alamitos High School, Snow began concentrating exclusively on baseball after he enrolled at the University of Arizona. Subsequently selected by the Yankees in the fifth round of the 1989 amateur draft, Snow spent the next four years advancing through New York's farm system, during which time he found his path to the big leagues blocked by Don Mattingly. After finally making his major-league debut during the latter stages of the 1992 campaign, Snow received his big break that offseason when the Yankees included him in a package of three players they sent to the California Angels for left-handed pitcher Jim Abbott.

Snow struggled somewhat at the plate in his first two seasons with the Angels, posting batting averages of .241 and .220, while totaling only 24 home runs and 87 RBIs in a part-time role. However, the 26-year-old first baseman developed into a solid hitter in 1995, concluding the campaign with 24 homers, 102 RBIs, and a .289 batting average. He also won the first of his six straight Gold Gloves with his outstanding work around the bag. But, when Snow hit just 17 home runs, knocked in only 67 runs, and batted just .257 the following year, the Angels elected to trade him to the Giants for pitchers Allen Watson and Fausto Macey at season's end.

Snow had a big first year in San Francisco, establishing career highs with 28 home runs, 104 RBIs, 36 doubles, and 96 bases on balls, while also scoring 81 runs, batting .281, and compiling an OPS of .898. However, he proved to be far less productive in 1998, hitting 15 homers, driving in 79 runs, scoring 65 times, and batting just .248. Snow's lack of success at the plate over the course of that 1998 campaign convinced him to abandon the idea of switch-hitting, turning him into strictly a left-handed batter for the remainder of his career.

Despite posting only modest numbers against southpaws in future seasons, Snow performed extremely well for the Giants in both 1999 and 2000, finishing the first of those years with 24 home runs, 98 RBIs, 93 runs scored, and a .274 batting average, before hitting 19 homers, knocking in 96 runs, scoring 82 times, batting .284, and leading the National League with 14 sacrifice flies the following year. But, it was with his glove that Snow truly excelled.

Although the advanced numbers used by sabermetricians to determine a player's overall defensive value would seem to indicate that Snow had only marginal defensive skills, he possessed an outstanding throwing arm, displayed superb instincts on bunts and ground balls, excelled at digging throws out of the dirt and completing the 3–6–3 double play, and made any necessary strategic decisions regarding the team's infield defense. After acquiring Snow during the latter stages of the first baseman's career, Boston Red Sox manager Terry Francona told the *Hartford Courant*, "I've known J. T. for a long time. He's about as good defensively as you're ever going to see in the game. That's how good he is."

Unfortunately, Snow's offense failed to keep pace with his defense from 2001 to 2003—a period during which he missed a significant amount of time due to injury. Batting over .270 just once over that three-year stretch, Snow totaled only 22 home runs and 138 RBIs during that time, although his leadership helped the Giants advance to the World Series in 2002.

Despite appearing in only 107 games in 2004, Snow rebounded to hit .327, with 12 home runs, 60 RBIs, and 32 doubles. Particularly effective during the season's second half, Snow batted .387 after the All-Star break, which placed him second only to Ichiro Suzuki among major-league players.

Snow remained in San Francisco just one more year, hitting 4 home runs, driving in 40 runs, and batting .275 in 2005, while sharing time at first base with the right-handed-hitting Lance Niekro. With the Giants subsequently choosing not to offer him salary arbitration at season's end, Snow signed as a free agent with the Red Sox, bringing to an end his time in San Francisco. He left the Giants having hit 124 home runs, driven in 615 runs, scored 561 times, collected 1,043 hits, 15 triples, and 228 doubles, batted .273, compiled a .369 on-base percentage, and posted a .438 slugging percentage as a member of the team.

After joining the Red Sox, Snow saw very little playing time over the first three months of the 2006 campaign, prompting him to ask for his unconditional release. Officially released by the Red Sox on June 19, Snow announced his retirement, ending his playing career with 189 home runs, 877 runs batted in, 798 runs scored, 1,509 hits, 19 triples, 293 doubles, a .268 batting average, a .357 on-base percentage, and a .427 slugging percentage.

Following his retirement, Snow began working as a color commentator on Giants radio broadcasts alongside play-by-play announcer Dave Flemming. While serving in that capacity, he signed a one-day contract with the Giants on September 24, 2008, so that he could retire as a member of the team. Snow has since become a special assistant to Giants General Manager Brian Sabean. He also serves as a roving minor-league instructor for the team.

Giant Career Highlights:

Best Season: Snow performed very well for the Giants in 1999, hitting 24 home runs, driving in 98 runs, scoring 93 times, and batting .274. However, he had his finest season two years earlier, concluding the 1997 campaign with career-high marks in home runs (28), RBIs (104), and doubles (36), scoring 81 runs, batting .281, and compiling an OPS of .898, which represented easily the highest figure he posted in any season in which he accumulated more than 500 official at-bats.

Memorable Moments/Greatest Performances: Snow helped lead the Giants to a 9–1 victory over Cincinnati on August 4, 1997, by hitting a pair of homers, knocking in 5 runs, and scoring 3 times.

Snow had a big day at the plate on April 29, 1999, when he went 4-for-5, with a triple and 4 RBIs, during a 6–5 win over the Expos.

Snow had an extremely productive afternoon against the Brewers on May 21, 2000, when he collected 3 hits, including a homer and double, drove in 5 runs, and scored 4 times during a 16–10 victory over Milwaukee. He again knocked in 5 runs on July 17 of that year, leading the Giants to a 10–8 win over Texas by going 3-for-4, with a pair of homers. Less than one month later, on August 15, 2000, Snow again homered twice during a 9–7 win over the Expos, driving in a career-high 6 runs in the process.

On April 20, 2002, Snow helped lead the Giants to a 13–9 win over the Houston Astros by going 4-for-5, with a homer and 5 RBIs.

Snow had a hand in all 8 runs the Giants scored on September 15, 2004, when he homered, doubled, knocked in 5 runs, and scored 3 times during an 8–1 victory over the Milwaukee Brewers. However, he had the biggest day of his career one month earlier, when he hit 3 home runs, drove in 4 runs, and scored 5 times during a 16–6 win over the Phillies on August 13.

Snow delivered arguably the biggest hit of his career in Game 2 of the 2000 NLDS, when he hit a three-run pinch-hit homer off New York Mets reliever Armando Benitez in the bottom of the 9th inning that tied the contest at 4 runs apiece. Unfortunately, New York won the game in the ensuing frame before going on to eliminate the Giants in four games.

Nevertheless, Snow experienced the most memorable moment of his career in Game 5 of the 2002 World Series, when he helped avert potential disaster by scooping up by the back of the jacket and carrying off to safety 3-year-old batboy, Darren Baker. The young son of then-Giants manager Dusty Baker, oblivious to the events transpiring around him, wandered into the home plate area to collect the bat of Kenny Lofton following the latter's triple. In what turned into a touching scene, Snow acted alertly, saving the young boy from serious harm by hauling him to safety just as teammate David Bell barreled home with another run.

Notable Achievements:

Hit more than 20 home runs twice.
Knocked in more than 100 runs once (104 in 1997).
Surpassed 30 doubles once (36 in 1997).
Compiled on-base percentage in excess of .400 once (.429 in 2004).
Posted slugging percentage in excess of .500 twice.
Led N.L. with 14 sacrifice flies in 2000.
Led N.L. first basemen with .999 fielding percentage in 1998.
Hit three home runs in one game vs. Philadelphia on August 13, 2004.
Four-time Gold Glove winner (1997, 1998, 1999 & 2000).
2002 N.L. champion.

39 JIM RAY HART

Jim Ray Hart topped 30 homers twice for the Giants during the 1960s. *(Courtesy of Dexter Press)*

A powerful right-handed batter who came up through the Giants' farm system during the early 1960s, Jim Ray Hart began his major-league career in promising fashion, earning a second-place finish in the 1964 N.L. Rookie of the Year voting by hitting 31 home runs, driving in 81 runs, and batting .286. Hart continued to establish himself as an elite hitter in each of the next three seasons, averaging 28 homers, 96 RBIs, and 92 runs scored from 1965 to 1967, while batting a combined .291 over that three-year stretch. However, the hard-hitting third baseman's star faded just as quickly as it rose due to a number of factors that included a series of injuries, an aversion to playing the hot corner, and a fondness for alcohol. No longer much of a factor by 1969, Hart spent his final four seasons in San Francisco serving the Giants primarily as a part-time player before moving on to New York, where he finished out his career fulfilling the same role with the Yankees. Nevertheless, Hart's one All-Star selection, three top-20 finishes in the N.L. MVP balloting, and significant offensive contributions to Giant teams that finished second in the National League four straight times ended up earning him a spot in these rankings.

Born in Hookerton, North Carolina, on October 30, 1941, James Ray Hart signed with the Giants as an amateur free agent in 1960, after which he spent the next three years advancing through a farm system that had earlier produced standout players such as Orlando Cepeda, Willie McCovey, Felipe Alou, Matty Alou, Juan Marichal, and Gaylord Perry in rapid succession. After being promoted to the Giants in July of 1963, Hart began his career ignominiously by having his shoulder blade broken by a Bob Gibson fastball in just his second major-league at-bat. Following Hart's return to the lineup, Curt Simmons beaned him, forcing him to sit out the rest of the season after appearing in a total of only seven games.

Awarded the starting third-base job at the beginning of the ensuing campaign, the 22-year-old Hart provided additional offensive firepower to a lineup that already included Mays, McCovey, and Cepeda, earning a runner-up finish to Philadelphia's Richie Allen in the Rookie of the Year voting by batting .286, knocking in 81 runs, and placing among the league leaders with 31 home runs and a .498 slugging percentage. On the flip side, Hart struggled in the field, committing 28 errors at the hot corner—the second-highest total of any National League third baseman. Hart compiled outstanding offensive numbers again in 1965, concluding the campaign with 23 home runs, 96 runs batted in, 91 runs scored, and a .299 batting average. He followed that up by hitting a career-high 33 homers, driving in 93 runs, scoring 88 times, and batting .285 in 1966, earning in the process his lone All-Star selection. However, Hart's defensive woes continued, as he led the National League with 34 errors in 1965, before committing another 26 miscues in the field the following year.

Possessing limited range and not the surest of hands, Hart expressed his disdain for playing third base when he said, "It's just too damn close to the hitter." In discussing Hart in his book, *The New Bill James Historical Abstract*, the noted baseball historian ranked Hart as the 74th-best third baseman of all-time, writing about him, "A better hitter than 59 of the 73 men listed ahead of him at third base. This should tell you all you need to know about his defense."

Yet, the Giants had to find a way to keep Hart's powerful bat in the lineup, prompting them to accord him a significant amount of playing time in left field in each of the next two seasons. Splitting his time almost equally between third base and left field in 1967, Hart turned in one of his finest offensive performances. In addition to batting .289, he finished among the N.L. leaders with 29 home runs, 99 RBIs, 98 runs scored, and a .509 slugging percentage. Although his production fell off somewhat the following year, Hart had another solid season, hitting 23 homers, knocking in 78 runs, and batting .258.

Unfortunately, Hart never again approached those numbers. A shoulder injury in 1969 helped contribute to his rapid decline, limiting him to just 95 games, 236 official plate appearances, 3 home runs, 26 RBIs, and a .254 batting average. Garnering virtually the same amount of playing time the following year, Hart increased his offensive production somewhat, concluding the campaign with 8 homers, 37 RBIs, and a .282 batting average. But, with the already stocky Hart, who spent his first few years in San Francisco playing at 5'11" and close to 195 pounds, sporting an ever-increasing waistline, his playing time continued to diminish in subsequent seasons.

Contributing further to Hart's fall from grace was an ever-increasing dependence on alcohol, which he discussed in a June 1991 article in *Baseball Digest*. Hart admitted that he spent much of the second half of his career waiting for his paycheck to arrive so that he could use it for drinking money. Focusing far more on his alcoholic consumption than on playing the game, Hart often arrived at the park hung over or drunk, preventing him from maximizing his once enormous potential. As a result, he appeared in a total of only 55 games in 1971 and 1972, before the Giants sold him to the Yankees shortly after the 1973 regular season got underway.

Serving the Yankees exclusively as a part-time DH in 1973, Hart experienced a moderate amount of success, finishing the season with 13 homers, 52 RBIs, and a .254 batting average. However, when he got off to a slow start the following year, the Yankees released him on June 7, bringing to an end his days as a major-leaguer. Hart ended his career with 170 home runs, 578 RBIs, 518 runs scored, 1,052 hits, 29 triples, 148 doubles, a .278 batting average, a

.345 on-base percentage, and a .467 slugging percentage, compiling the vast majority of those numbers while playing for the Giants.

Following his release by the Yankees, Hart spent two years playing in Mexico before retiring from baseball in 1976. He subsequently entered into a dark period of his life, during which time his addiction to alcohol drove him to poverty and despair. Hart's wake-up call came when he passed out on a flight to Toronto for an old-timer's game. After entering and successfully completing a rehab program in San Mateo, Hart joined the Teamsters as a Warehouseman for Safeway Stores in Richmond, California, and later, Tracy, California, when operations moved there in 1992. Hart remained in that post until 2006, when he retired from Safeway. Following his retirement, Hart lived another 10 years, passing away at 74 years of age on May 19, 2016, following a lengthy battle with an unspecified illness.

Giant Career Highlights:

Best Season: Hart made the N.L. All-Star team for the only time in his career in 1966, when he hit 33 homers, knocked in 93 runs, scored 88 times, batted .285, and posted an OPS of .853. However, he compiled slightly better overall numbers the following year, when he hit 29 home runs, batted .289, posted a slugging percentage of .509, and established career-high marks in RBIs (99), runs scored (98), triples (7), bases on balls (77), on-base percentage (.373), and OPS (.882). Particularly effective during the month of July, Hart earned N.L. Player of the Month honors for July 1967 by batting .355, with 13 homers and 30 RBIs.

Memorable Moments/Greatest Performances: Hart scored 4 runs in one game twice in his career, doing so for the first time on August 5, 1965, when he helped lead the Giants to a lopsided 18–7 victory over the Reds by going 3-for-5, with a homer, double, and 2 runs batted in. Hart again crossed the plate four times against Cincinnati on July 12, 1968, when he went 4-for-5, with a pair of homers and 5 RBIs, during an 11–4 win over the Reds.

Hart highlighted his exceptional July 1967 with an especially outstanding performance on the 8th of the month, homering twice, knocking in 5 runs, and scoring 3 times during an 8–4 win over the Dodgers.

Hart had a huge game against the Phillies on June 6, 1968, hitting a pair of homers and driving in 6 runs, in leading the Giants to a 7–2 victory.

However, Hart had his biggest day at the plate on July 8, 1970, when he hit for the cycle and knocked in a career-high 7 runs during a 13–0 win over the Atlanta Braves. By hitting a three-run homer and a three-run triple in the fifth inning, Hart became one of the few players in MLB history to amass 6 RBIs in one inning.

Notable Achievements:

Hit more than 20 home runs five times, surpassing 30 homers twice.
Knocked in more than 90 runs three times.
Scored more than 90 runs twice.
Topped 30 doubles once (30 in 1965).
Posted slugging percentage in excess of .500 twice.
Hit for the cycle on July 8, 1970.
July 1967 N.L. Player of the Month.
1966 N.L. All-Star.

40 KEVIN MITCHELL

Kevin Mitchell earned N.L. MVP honors in 1989 by leading the Giants to the pennant. *(Courtesy of PristineAuction.com)*

Acquired by the Giants in a multi-player trade with the San Diego Padres on July 5, 1987, Kevin Mitchell went on to become the most prominent figure included in the deal, establishing himself as one of the most feared right-handed batters in the National League over the course of the next few years. Spending parts of five seasons in San Francisco, Mitchell surpassed 30 homers, 90 RBIs, and 90 runs scored two times each, en route to earning a pair of All-Star selections and one Silver Slugger. The enigmatic outfielder reached the apex of his career in 1989, when he led the Giants to their first pennant in 27 years by topping the Senior Circuit in five different offensive categories, including home runs (47) and RBIs (125), en route to earning league MVP honors. Unfortunately, Mitchell's number of peak seasons proved to be few since his indifferent attitude and unpredictable behavior off the field prevented him from maximizing his full potential. As a result, the Giants ended up parting ways with him after only 4 ½ years, precluding him from earning a higher place in these rankings.

Born in San Diego, California, on January 13, 1962, Kevin Darnell Mitchell used baseball to escape the violent streets of his hometown. The product of a broken home, Mitchell grew up on the south side of San Diego, roaming his neighborhood with a gang called the Pierules. Raised by his grandmother, Mitchell dropped out of Clairemont High School and spent four years doing, in his own words, "a lot of bad stuff" as a member of the Pierules. Yet, through it all, he continued to play baseball, even as he developed a reputation for being able to knock out people with one punch.

Mitchell's sordid past followed him to the minor leagues after the New York Mets signed him as an amateur free agent in 1980, with his gruff demeanor and volatile disposition often overshadowing his obvious talent. Still, even though his 1981 brawl with teammate Darryl Strawberry during a pickup basketball game raised the eyebrows of many within the organization, Mitchell advanced slowly but surely through New York's farm system, finally arriving in the big leagues to stay in 1986. Recalling Mitchell's earliest days in New York, former Mets hitting coach Bill Robinson said, "He was a tough kid. He had talent and a terrible attitude."

The 5'11", 210-pound Mitchell incurred the wrath of many of his teammates as a rookie by cutting the sleeves off their expensive suits and burning their shoes. He also twice drew fines from the league office for brawling on the field. Looking back at his first big-league season, Mitchell stated, "I didn't listen. It was the way I grew up. I was always protecting my back, always threatening to go home."

Nevertheless, the 24-year-old rookie proved to be an asset to New York's world championship ball club, hitting 12 home runs, driving in 43 runs, and batting .277, in 108 games and 328 official at-bats, while manning five different positions on the diamond. But, when the Padres made disgruntled outfielder Kevin McReynolds available at season's end, the Mets didn't hesitate to include Mitchell in the package of players they sent to San Diego to acquire his services.

Initially unhappy over returning to his hometown since doing so reminded him of his raucous youth, Mitchell later said, "I get evil every time I go back there." Performing erratically on the field for the Padres, Mitchell hit just 7 homers, knocked in only 26 runs, and batted just .245 over the first half of the campaign, before the Giants acquired him and pitchers Dave Dravecky and Craig Lefferts for a package of four nondescript players.

Mitchell balked at the idea of going to San Francisco at first, revealing years later, "I had been traded two times, and that was tough. I called my grandmother and told her I was coming home for good." However, Mitchell's grandmother advised him otherwise, telling him, "Kevin, look where you came from and how hard you worked. That's your gift. Why give it away?"

Ultimately choosing to join the Giants, Mitchell posted solid numbers over the second half of the 1987 campaign, hitting 15 home runs, driving in 44 runs, scoring 49 times, and batting .306 in his 69 games with the N.L. West champs. He regressed somewhat the following year, though, finishing the 1988 season with 19 homers, 80 RBIs, 60 runs scored, and a .251 batting average.

After undergoing arthroscopic surgery on his ailing right knee during the subsequent offseason and donning contact lenses for the first time, Mitchell really came into his own in 1989. Ably assisted by Giants batting coach Dusty Baker, who worked extensively with him on his mechanics at the plate, Mitchell emerged as an offensive force, leading the league with 47 home runs, 125 RBIs, 345 total bases, a .635 slugging percentage, and a 1.023 OPS, while also scoring 100 runs, batting .291, and compiling an on-base percentage of .388. Mitchell, who spent most of the previous two seasons playing third base, also did a solid defensive job in left field for the Giants, placing second among players at his position in putouts, and finishing third in assists. Mitchell's outstanding all-around play earned him the first of two straight All-Star selections, the only Silver Slugger of his career, N.L. MVP honors, and recognition as the Major League Player of the Year.

Mitchell carried with him to the plate the same aggressive attitude that helped him survive on the mean streets of San Diego as a youth, stating on one occasion, "I get two strikes on me and I tell myself, 'The pitcher, he's trying to take something from me.' I'm ready to fight him."

Yet, at the same time, Mitchell realized how far he had come, proclaiming at one point during his MVP campaign, "Ain't no telling where I would have gone without baseball. I'd probably be in jail or somewhere dead. Everyone in my neighborhood thought I was going to be the bad guy, because I was always in trouble and in the gang fights. But now kids can see me and say, 'There's something else we can do. Just look at Mitch.'"

Unfortunately, Mitchell's time at the top proved to be short-lived. After following up his MVP season by driving in 93 runs, scoring 90 times, batting .290, and placing among the league leaders with 35 home runs and a .544 slugging percentage in 1990, he appeared in only 113 games in 1991 due to injury. Mitchell performed relatively well whenever he found his name written on the lineup card, hitting 27 homers, driving in 69 runs, and batting .256, in 371 official at-bats. However, he once again began to experience problems off the field, being arrested on suspicion of rape (the charges were later dropped), and being accused by an unnamed teammate of being "stone drunk" at 2 o'clock in the morning following a Saturday night game in Los Angeles.

Growing increasingly weary of Mitchell's erratic behavior and new indifferent demeanor on and off the field, the Giants elected to trade him and pitcher Mike Remlinger to the Seattle Mariners for pitchers Dave Burba, Bill Swift, and Mike Jackson on December 11, 1991. In attempting to explain the move, Giants General Manager Al Rosen stated, "Headaches, stomachaches—it's always something with this guy." Mitchell left the Giants having hit 143 home runs, driven in 411 runs, scored 351 times, collected 614 hits, 17 triples, and 109 doubles, batted .278, compiled a .356 on-base percentage, and posted a .536 slugging percentage as a member of the team.

Despite being limited to just 99 games in 1992 by injuries to his ribs and foot, Mitchell posted solid numbers for the Mariners, concluding the campaign with 67 RBIs and a .286 batting average. But he brought his poor attitude with him to Seattle, prompting the Mariners to trade him to Cincinnati for pitcher Norm Charlton at season's end.

Once again plagued by injuries his first year in Cincinnati, Mitchell appeared in only 93 games in 1993. However, he experienced something of an emotional rebirth as a member of the Reds, displaying a tenacity he lacked since his MVP season of 1989. Agreeing to receive several cortisone injections over the course of the campaign to quell the pain in his ailing shoulder so that he might play, Mitchell finished the year with 19 home runs, 64 RBIs, and a .341 batting average. He followed that up by hitting 30 homers, driving in 77 runs, and batting .326 during the strike-shortened 1994 season, en route to earning a 9th-place finish in the N.L. MVP voting.

The 1994 campaign proved to be Mitchell's last season of note in the Major Leagues. After spending all of 1995 playing in Japan, Mitchell returned to the United States the following year to begin a three-year stint during which he served as a part-time player with the Red Sox, Reds, Indians, and Athletics.

Released by the A's in August 1998, Mitchell ended his playing career with 234 home runs, 760 RBIs, 630 runs scored, 1,173 hits, 25 triples, 224 doubles, a .284 batting average, a .360 on-base percentage, and a .520 slugging percentage.

Since retiring as an active player, Mitchell has run afoul of the law on numerous occasions, with the first such instance occurring late in 1998, when police arrested him for assaulting his father during an argument. Although Mitchell eventually got his life back on track by serving as a big brother to inner city youths and as the designated hitter for the independent Western League's Sonoma County Crushers, his dark side resurfaced once again in August 2000, when he earned a nine-game suspension for punching the opposing team's owner in the mouth during a bench-clearing brawl. More recently, Mitchell was arrested in 2010 for alleged misdemeanor battery at the Bonita Golf Club in Bonita, California. He currently lives in San Diego and plays in the San Diego Adult Baseball League for the San Diego Black Sox.

Giant Career Highlights:

Best Season: Was there ever any doubt? Mitchell had easily the best season of his career in 1989, when he earned N.L. MVP honors by batting .291, scoring 100 runs, amassing 34 doubles, and topping the Senior Circuit with 47 homers, 125 RBIs, 345 total bases, a .635 slugging percentage, and a 1.023 OPS. He continued his outstanding play in the NLCS, helping the Giants advance to the World Series for the first time since 1962 by batting .353, with 2 home runs, 7 RBIs, and 5 runs scored.

Memorable Moments/Greatest Performances: Although best known for his slugging at the plate, Mitchell made a rather remarkable defensive play during the early stages of his MVP campaign of 1989. Sprinting toward the left-field foul line in St. Louis's Busch Stadium in pursuit of a high fly off the bat of Ozzie Smith, Mitchell overran the ball, but reached back with his bare hand to make a circus catch.

Mitchell made his debut with the Giants a memorable one, hitting a pair of homers and driving in 4 runs during a 7–5 victory over the Chicago Cubs on July 5, 1987. Some five weeks later, on August 13, Mitchell led the Giants to a 7–6 win over Houston in 11 innings by going 4-for-6, with a homer and 4 RBIs.

Mitchell got one of his most memorable hits for the Giants on May 11, 1988, when his solo homer in the top of the 16th inning proved to be the difference in a 5–4 victory over the Cardinals. Later in the year, on July 9, Mitchell helped lead the Giants to a 21–2 pounding of St. Louis by going 4-for-5 at the plate, with a homer, 4 RBIs, and 4 runs scored.

Mitchell hit 3 home runs during a doubleheader split with Cincinnati on June 6, 1989, homering once in the 4–3 loss in Game 1 before reaching the seats twice in the 3–2 win in the nightcap. He finished the afternoon having driven in 5 of the 6 runs the Giants scored on the day.

Mitchell helped pace the Giants to a lopsided 16–2 victory over Houston on April 13, 1991, by going 3-for-3, with a pair of homers, 4 RBIs, and 4 runs scored.

Mitchell, though, had the biggest day of his career on May 25, 1990, when he homered three times and knocked in 5 runs during a 9–8 victory over the Pirates in Pittsburgh.

Notable Achievements:

Hit more than 20 home runs three times, topping 30 homers twice and 40 homers once (47 in 1989).

Knocked in more than 100 runs once (125 in 1989).

Scored 100 runs in 1989.

Batted over .300 once (.306 in 1987).

Surpassed 30 doubles once (34 in 1989).

Posted slugging percentage in excess of .500 four times, topping .600-mark once (.635 in 1989).

Compiled OPS in excess of 1.000 once (1.023 in 1989).

Led N.L. in: home runs once; RBIs once; total bases once; slugging percentage once; and OPS once.

Ranks among Giants career leaders in slugging percentage (4th) and OPS (8th).

Hit three home runs in one game vs. Pittsburgh on May 25, 1990.

1989 N.L. MVP.

1989 Major League Player of the Year.

1989 Silver Slugger winner.

1989 *Sporting News* All-Star selection.

Two-time N.L. All-Star (1989 & 1990).

1989 N.L. champion.

41 ROBB NEN

Robb Nen amassed more saves than any other reliever in Giants history. *(Courtesy of Julio Cesar Martinez)*

A hard-throwing right-hander with a devastating slider nicknamed "The Terminator," Robb Nen spent five years in San Francisco, establishing himself during that time as the greatest closer in Giants history. A three-time All-Star, Nen led all N.L. relievers in saves once and games finished twice as a member of the Giants, en route to compiling a franchise record 206 saves. Dominating opposing batters to such an extent that Giants fans came to rename the ninth inning the "Nenth," Nen amassed at least 37 saves in each of his five seasons in San Francisco, while also posting an ERA under 2.00 twice and striking out more than one batter per inning each year. Unfortunately, Nen's sense of self-sacrifice, which helped the Giants advance to the playoffs twice and the World Series once, led to him further damaging his already torn rotator cuff, bringing his career to a premature end.

Born in San Pedro, California, on November 28, 1969, Robert Allen Nen grew up around baseball, as the son of former major-league first baseman Dick Nen. After attending Los Alamitos High School, where he played both varsity football and baseball with future Giants teammate J. T. Snow, Nen decided to forego a college education and pursue a career in baseball when the Texas Rangers selected him in the 32nd round of the 1987 amateur draft. He then spent six long years in the minors before finally earning a spot on the Rangers roster at the start of the 1993 campaign. Nen's stay in Texas proved to be short-lived, though, since his lack of success on the mound over the course of the next three months prompted the Rangers to trade him and pitcher Kurt Miller to the Marlins for fellow hurler Cris Carpenter in mid-July.

Nen continued to struggle after he arrived in Florida, finishing his rookie season with a composite ERA of 6.75. However, he began to flourish after he assumed a more prominent role in the Marlins bullpen the following year, finishing the season with 15 saves and a 2.95 ERA after taking over as the team's closer. Nen subsequently amassed a total of 93 saves for the Marlins from 1995 to 1997, performing particularly well in the second of those campaigns, when he went 5–1, with a 1.95 ERA and 35 saves. Nevertheless, after Nen helped Florida win the World Series in 1997 by saving two games in the Fall Classic, the Marlins elected to include him in the "fire sale" they conducted at season's end in which they traded away most of their best players in order to minimize team payroll.

Dealt to the Giants for Mike Villano, Joe Fontenot, and Mick Pageler, Nen began an extremely successful five-year run in San Francisco by posting 7 victories, 40 saves, and a 1.52 ERA in 1998, while also striking out 110 batters and surrendering only 59 hits in 88 ⅔ innings of work, en route to earning the first All-Star selection of his career. Nen followed that up with another 37 saves and his second straight All-Star nomination in 1999, even though he pitched less effectively, winning only 3 of his 11 decisions and compiling an ERA of 3.98. Nen returned to top form in 2000, earning a fourth-place finish in the N.L. Cy Young voting by going 4–3, with a 1.50 ERA and 41 saves, which represented the third-highest total in the Senior Circuit. He performed extremely well again the following year, posting 4 victories, an ERA of 3.01, and a league-leading 45 saves, while also striking out 93 batters in 77 ⅔ innings of work, allowing only 58 hits, and topping the circuit with a career-high 71 games finished.

Known for his unusual delivery in which he tapped his toe on the ground before releasing the ball, Nen featured a splitter, a fastball that typically hit the upper 90s on the radar gun, and a superb slider that looked like a fastball until it broke straight down as it neared home plate at a velocity of up to 92 mph. Nen also had a great deal of heart, which he exhibited during the latter stages of the 2002 campaign, when he continued to pitch with a partially torn rotator cuff, knowing that doing so put his career in jeopardy.

After earning his final All-Star selection and helping the Giants advance to the playoffs by going 6–2, with a 2.20 ERA and 43 saves in 2002, Nen spent the entire postseason pitching in pain, well aware that doing so put him at further risk. Nevertheless, he performed extremely well throughout the playoffs, saving 7 of the Giants' 10 victories, before eventually faltering against the Angels in Game 6 of the World Series.

Forced to undergo three different shoulder surgeries the next two years, Nen received high praise during his absence from teammate Marquis Grissom, who said in the March 3–9, 2004, edition of *USA Today Sports Weekly*, "I hope he (Nen) does his thing because we need him. People don't understand what a big part of the team he is. If you're going to do well, having a closer like Robb is everything."

Nen finally gave up hope of mounting a comeback early in 2005, announcing his retirement on February 20 of that year. Upon learning of Nen's decision, Giants assistant general manager, Ned Colletti, said, "He really died on the sword for the club and his teammates. As much as we missed him closing games, we really missed his presence, and who he is."

Nen left the game with a career record of 45–42, an ERA of 2.98, 314 saves, 793 strikeouts in 715 innings pitched, and a WHIP of 1.213. In addition to saving 206 games in his five years with the Giants, Nen went 24–25 with a 2.43 ERA, struck out 453 batters in 378 ⅓ innings of work, and posted a WHIP of 1.084.

As a way of showing their appreciation to Nen, the Giants held a special ceremony before their July 9, 2005, game against the Cardinals during which they honored him with a plaque commemorating his 300th career save. The plaque is now located on the public walkway behind the right-field wall of AT&T Park, not far from McCovey Cove.

Following his retirement, Nen accepted a position in the Giants front office, where he serves as a special assistant to General Manager Brian Sabean.

Giant Career Highlights:

Best Season: Nen pitched brilliantly in his first year in San Francisco, concluding the 1998 campaign with a record of 7–7, an ERA of 1.52, 40 saves, and career-high marks in strikeouts (110) and innings pitched (88 ⅔). He also allowed only 59 hits and walked just 25 batters, en route to compiling a WHIP of 0.947. However, Nen proved to be even a bit more dominant in 2000, when he finished 4–3, with a 1.50 ERA, 41 saves, and 92 strikeouts in 66 innings of work. By surrendering only 37 hits and 19 bases on balls to the opposition, Nen posted a career-best WHIP of 0.848, earning in the process a fourth-place finish in the Cy Young voting and a 12th-place finish in the MVP balloting. Particularly effective during the month of July, Nen set a new major-league record by recording 14 saves over the course of the month.

Memorable Moments/Greatest Performances: Nen made his debut with the Giants a resounding one, working 2 perfect innings and striking out 5 of the 6 batters he faced, in helping his new team record a 9–4 extra-inning win over Houston on Opening Day of 1998. Nen turned in another dominant performance on June 4, 1999, when he allowed just a single and struck out 5 batters over 2 innings of work during a 4–3 win over Oakland in 15 innings. Although the Giants eventually lost their July 8, 2001, matchup with the Milwaukee Brewers by a score of 6–4 in 13 innings, Nen performed magnificently during the latter stages of the contest, retiring all 9 batters he faced in the 10th, 11th, and 12th innings, while striking out 4. As noted earlier, Nen performed heroically throughout the 2002 postseason when, despite pitching with a torn rotator cuff, he saved 7 of the Giants' 10 wins, working a total of 9 innings, allowing 9 hits and 3 walks, striking out 8, and surrendering just 1 earned run.

Notable Achievements:

Surpassed 40 saves four times, topping 30 saves on one other occasion.
Compiled ERA below 2.50 three times, posting mark under 2.00 twice.
Struck out more than 100 batters once (110 in 1998).
Posted WHIP under 1.000 twice.
Led N.L. pitchers in saves once and games finished twice.
Holds Giants career record for most saves (206).
Finished fourth in 2000 N.L. Cy Young voting.
Three-time N.L. All-Star (1998, 1999 & 2002).
2002 N.L. champion.

42 ROGER BRESNAHAN

Roger Bresnahan compiled a career on-base percentage of .403 that ranks as the third best in Giants history. *(Courtesy of Library of Congress)*

An extremely versatile player who manned every position on the diamond at one point or another during his major-league career, Roger Bresnahan established himself as the *Dead Ball Era's* most famous catcher with his unique skill set and innovations in protective equipment. Bresnahan's keen batting eye and unusual speed for a catcher enabled him to become one of the few receivers in baseball history to regularly bat leadoff for his team—a spot in the Giants lineup he maintained for much of his seven seasons in New York. Batting over .300 twice, posting a mark in excess of .280 four other times, and placing among the N.L. leaders in bases on balls four times as a member of the Giants, Bresnahan finished near the top of the league rankings in on-base percentage six times, placing second on two separate occasions. A solid receiver as well, Bresnahan led all N.L. catchers in putouts once and caught-stealing percentage once, developing a special rapport with Giants ace Christy Mathewson, who generally pitched his best ball with Bresnahan behind home plate. Still, it is his contributions to the development of playing equipment for which Bresnahan is perhaps remembered most.

Born in Toledo, Ohio, on June 11, 1879, to Irish immigrants who arrived in this country nine years earlier, Roger Phillip Bresnahan developed his love of baseball while attending Catholic grade school in his hometown. After spending the previous year playing with a semipro team from Manistee, Michigan, the 17-year-old Bresnahan began his career in professional baseball with Lima of the Ohio State League, shortly after graduating from Toledo's Central High School in 1896. Signed by the National League's Washington Senators primarily as a pitcher after just one full season at Lima, Bresnahan compiled a perfect 4–0 record in his six appearances with the Senators in 1897, tossing a six-hit shutout against the St. Louis Browns in his first major-league start, before being released by the club the following spring after demanding more money. He subsequently spent the next two seasons honing his catching skills with Toledo of the Interstate League and Minneapolis and Buffalo of the Western League before resurfacing in the National League with the Chicago Orphans late in 1900. Bresnahan arrived in the Major Leagues to stay the following year, spending the 1901 campaign serving as a catcher and utility man under player-manager John McGraw on the newly formed American League's Baltimore Orioles. When McGraw and several Oriole teammates jumped to the National League's New York Giants midway through the following campaign, Bresnahan went with them, batting .287 in his first 51 games in New York, while splitting his time primarily between the outfield and catcher.

Although Bresnahan also saw some action at first base, third base, and catcher in 1903, he played mostly center field his first full season with the Giants. Possessing speed that belied his stocky 5'9", 200-pound frame, Bresnahan ended up doing a solid job in the outfield, accumulating 14 assists and having a hand in six double plays. He excelled even more on offense, though, scoring 87 runs and finishing among the league leaders with 34 stolen bases, 61 walks, a .350 batting average, a .443 on-base percentage, a .493

slugging percentage, and a .936 OPS. Continuing to spend most of his time in the outfield the following year, Bresnahan contributed greatly to the Giants' pennant-winning campaign by collecting another 14 assists, finishing third among N.L. outfielders with 9 double plays, hitting a career-high 5 home runs, scoring 81 times, batting .284, and placing among the league leaders with a .381 on-base percentage and a .410 slugging percentage from his lead-off spot in the batting order.

Even though he continued to see some action at other positions in his remaining years in New York, Bresnahan became the Giants' regular starting catcher in 1905, a season in which he helped lead them to the world championship by batting .302 and compiling a .411 on-base percentage. More importantly, he emerged as Christy Mathewson's most trusted receiver, helping the ace of the Giants pitching staff compile a brilliant 31–9 record and a magnificent 1.28 ERA.

In speaking of the qualities that made Bresnahan the favorite catcher of most Giant pitchers, Manager John McGraw stated, "Bresnahan had a memory almost as good as Mathewson or (Joe) McGinnity. He never had to be told twice. Once we had discovered a weak spot in the opposition and had discussed a plan for attacking it, I could depend absolutely on Bresnahan to carry it out. He did not forget. His whole mind was concentrated on winning that particular game, and it was rarely that he overlooked anything."

Bresnahan also became a favorite of McGraw, who saw a lot of himself in the compact, hot-tempered, and fiercely competitive catcher. Described by one reporter as "highly strung and almost abnormally emotional," Bresnahan excelled at umpire-baiting, causing him to be ejected, fined, and suspended on numerous occasions. Equally hard on teammates who failed to put forth a 100 percent effort, Bresnahan, wrote noted baseball historian Bill James, "was one of those guys that, if you were on his team and played hard, he was as nice to you as could be, but, if you got on his bad side, you'd think he was the Breath of Hell."

As much as anything, though, Bresnahan became known for the innovations in catcher's equipment that he introduced to Major League Baseball. After discovering in a home-plate collision that Red Dooin of the Phillies wore papier-mâché protectors under his stockings, Bresnahan showed up on Opening Day 1907 wearing a huge pair of shin guards modeled after a cricketer's leg pads. Although opponents and fans alike initially objected to Bresnahan's added protection, most teams adopted a less bulky version of his equipment within two years. Bresnahan also developed the first batting helmet and introduced the idea of wearing a padded face-mask while catching.

Bresnahan remained the Giants' regular receiver three more years, performing particularly well in 1906 and 1908. After scoring 69 runs, batting .281, and compiling a .419 on-base percentage in the first of those campaigns, Bresnahan concluded his time in New York by scoring 70 runs, batting .283, and walking a league-leading 83 times in 1908, en route to posting an on-base percentage of .401. Not wishing to stand in Bresnahan's way when the Cardinals subsequently expressed an interest in acquiring him to be their player-manager, the Giants traded the veteran catcher to St. Louis for three players on December 12, 1908, bringing to an end his seven-year stay in New York. During his time with the Giants, Bresnahan batted .293, compiled a .403 on-base percentage, and posted a .393 slugging percentage. He also hit 15 home runs, knocked in 291 runs, scored 438 times, stole 118 bases, and collected 731 hits, including 35 triples and 135 doubles.

Bresnahan served as player-manager in St. Louis for four years, failing to lead the Cardinals to any higher than a fifth-place finish, while never appearing in more than 88 games, although he continued to post solid batting averages and on-base percentages. After clashing repeatedly with new Cardinals owner Helene Robison Britton during the 1912 campaign, Bresnahan was sold to the Chicago Cubs, with whom he spent his final three seasons serving as a part-time player before being released by the club at the end of 1915. The 36-year-old Bresnahan subsequently chose to announce his retirement, ending his career with 26 home runs, 530 RBIs, 682 runs scored, 1,252 hits, 71 triples, 218 doubles, 212 stolen bases, a .279 batting average, a .386 on-base percentage, and a .377 slugging percentage.

Following his retirement as an active player, Bresnahan purchased the minor league Toledo Mud Hens, who he owned until 1924, when he assumed a coaching position with the Giants under his old friend John McGraw. After four years in New York, Bresnahan spent two years serving as a coach for the Detroit Tigers, before the stock market crash of 1929 forced him to assume a number of less-glamorous jobs that included working as a manual laborer for the forerunner of the WPA and serving as a guard at the Toledo Workhouse. Bresnahan lived until the age of 65, passing away after suffering a heart attack at his home in Toledo on December 4, 1944. The members of the Old Timers Committee elected him to the Baseball Hall of Fame the following year, making him just the second catcher to be so honored (the same committee inducted Buck Ewing six years earlier).

The induction of Bresnahan to Cooperstown has drawn criticism from various quarters through the years, with Bill James writing that the catcher "wandered into the Hall of Fame on a series of miscalculations," and suggesting that "the Hall of Fame had, for the first time, selected a player who clearly had no damn business being there."

Yet, John McGraw held a very different opinion, stating in the May 1919 edition of *Baseball Magazine*, "Roger Bresnahan was the greatest catcher I ever saw, always excepting Buck Ewing."

Giant Career Highlights:

Best Season: Spending most of the year patrolling center field for the Giants, Bresnahan clearly had his best season in 1903 when, in addition to hitting 4 home runs, driving in 55 runs, and amassing 8 triples, he established career highs with 87 runs scored, 142 hits, 30 doubles, 34 stolen bases, a .350 batting average, a .443 on-base percentage, and a .493 slugging percentage, placing in the league's top five in five different offensive categories in the process.

Memorable Moments/Greatest Performances: Bresnahan homered twice in the same game for the only time in his career on June 6, 1904, when he accomplished the rare feat of hitting two inside-the-park home runs during an 11–0 win over the Pittsburgh Pirates. Bresnahan hit another inside-the-park homer a few weeks later, on July 21, 1904, when his ninth-inning blow broke a 3–3 tie with the Cubs, giving the Giants a 4–3 victory.

However, the 1905 World Series undoubtedly proved to be the highlight of Bresnahan's playing career. Starting all five games behind the plate for New York, Bresnahan caught three complete game shutouts by Christy Mathewson, and another by Joe McGinnity, in helping the Giants defeat the Philadelphia Athletics, four-games-to-one. Bresnahan also led both teams with a .313 batting average and a .500 on-base percentage.

Notable Achievements:

Batted over .300 twice, reaching .350-mark once (.350 in 1903).
Surpassed 30 doubles once (30 in 1903).
Stole more than 20 bases twice, topping 30 steals once (34 in 1903).
Compiled on-base percentage in excess of .400 four times.

Posted OPS in excess of .900 once (.936 in 1903).

Led N.L. with 83 walks in 1908.

Finished second in N.L. in on-base percentage twice.

Led N.L. catchers in putouts once and caught stealing percentage once.

Ranks third all-time on Giants in career on-base percentage (.403).

Two-time N.L. champion (1904 & 1905).

1905 world champion.

Elected to Baseball Hall of Fame by members of Old Timers Committee in 1945.

43 LARRY JANSEN

Larry Jansen posted a league-leading 23 victories for the 1951 pennant-winning Giants. *(Courtesy of LegendaryAuctions.com)*

The fact that Larry Jansen first arrived in the Major Leagues just three months shy of his 27th birthday prevented him from having as lengthy a career as many of the other pitchers included in these rankings. Nevertheless, the right-hander proved to be one of the Giants' most dependable starters throughout much of his tenure in New York, surpassing 20 victories twice between 1947 and 1951, en route to posting an overall record of 96–57 during that five-year period. Possessing outstanding control, Jansen consistently finished among the N.L. leaders in fewest walks allowed per nine innings pitched, leading the league in that category once and placing second three other times. A key figure in the Giants' historic comeback of 1951 that saw them overcome a 13-game deficit to the Dodgers in the season's final seven weeks, Jansen topped all N.L. hurlers with 23 victories that year, earning in the process one of his two All-Star selections. He also earned MVP consideration four times, placing seventh in the voting in 1947, when he finished second in the Rookie of the Year balloting as well.

Born in Verboort, Oregon, on July 16, 1920, Lawrence Joseph Jansen attended Forest Grove High School, during which time he also began playing semipro baseball. Following his graduation in 1938, Jansen signed with the Salt Lake City Bees—a minor-league affiliate of the Boston Red Sox at that time. However, after two years in Salt Lake City, Jansen became a free agent when Baseball Commissioner Kenesaw Mountain Landis ruled that the Red Sox mishandled his contract. Jansen subsequently joined the Pacific Coast League's San Francisco Seals, with whom he spent all of 1941, before the minor leagues suspended play for the next two seasons due to the nation's involvement in World War II. Returning to Oregon, Jansen spent those two years working on his family's dairy farm and playing semipro ball, before rejoining the Seals in 1944. Eventually establishing himself as the PCL's top pitcher, Jansen became the last AAA hurler to win 30 games in 1946 when he compiled a record of 30–6 and an ERA of 1.57. Taking note of Jansen's outstanding performance, the New York Giants purchased his contract and summoned him to the big leagues the following year.

After beginning the 1947 season working out of the Giants bullpen, Jansen soon earned a regular spot in the starting rotation, posting three straight wins before dropping his next three decisions. The rookie right-hander then went on an exceptional run that saw him lose just two more games the rest of the year, concluding the campaign with a record of 21–5 that gave him the league's best winning percentage. Jansen also finished among the league leaders with a 3.16 ERA, 20 complete games, and 248 innings pitched, earning in the process a 7th-place finish in the N.L. MVP voting and a runner-up finish to Jackie Robinson in the Rookie of the Year balloting.

Featuring an outstanding overhand curve, a good fastball, and excellent control, Jansen established himself as the ace of New York's pitching staff his first year in the league, making a strong impression on Giants manager Mel Ott, who told *Baseball Magazine*, "His (Jansen's) other talents were glossed over, and, by the time he reached the Polo Grounds, people had him marked as a control pitcher only. But, as a matter of fact, he is quite fast. He has a good deal of speed." Meanwhile, commenting on Jansen's impeccable control after one of his more impressive starts, Giants catcher Walker Cooper stated, "I don't believe he missed the target by more than two inches all day."

Jansen had another good year in 1948, compiling a record of 18–12 and an ERA of 3.61, and placing among the league leaders with 15 complete games, 277 innings pitched, 4 shutouts, and 126 strikeouts. With the Giants posting a losing record in 1949, Jansen finished just 15–16, although he still managed to place near the top of the league rankings with 17 complete games, 259 ⅔ innings pitched, and 113 strikeouts. Jansen rebounded the following year, though, earning his first All-Star selection by going 19–13, with a 3.01 ERA, 21 complete games, 275 innings pitched, 161 strikeouts, and a league-leading 5 shutouts and 1.065 WHIP.

Jansen subsequently assumed a prominent role in the miraculous comeback the Giants waged in 1951, winning six games in the final month of the regular season, en route to compiling a record of 23–11 that tied him with teammate Sal Maglie for the league lead in victories. Jansen also finished among the league leaders with a 3.04 ERA, 18 complete games, 278 ⅔ innings pitched, 145 strikeouts, and a WHIP of 1.112.

Looking back at the pressures he faced each time he took the mound that summer, Jansen told Thomas Kiernan in *The Miracle at Coogan's Bluff*, "I'd finish a game and I'd be so exhausted, so drained, I couldn't sleep at all that night. The next night, I'd get a few hours, but then the pressure would begin to build to the next start two days away, and I wouldn't sleep for two nights. By the time I got out on the mound, I'd be pitching from memory. But, by God, it must have worked, because that was one of my best years."

The 1951 campaign proved to be Jansen's last year as a top-flight starter. Plagued by a sore arm in each of the next two seasons, the veteran right-hander posted a composite record of just 22–27 in 1952 and 1953, before being relegated to coaching duties midway through the 1954 campaign. Hoping to make a comeback, Jansen spent the following year pitching in the minor leagues, after which he signed with the Cincinnati Reds. Jansen ended his career in Cincinnati in 1956, making just 8 appearances for the Reds before announcing his retirement at season's end. He concluded his career with a record of 122–89, an ERA of 3.58, 17 shutouts, 842 strikeouts in 1,756 ⅔ innings of work, 107 complete games, and a WHIP of 1.224, compiling virtually all those numbers while pitching for the Giants.

Following his retirement, Jansen spent the next few seasons coaching and managing in the Pacific Coast League before returning to the Giants as pitching coach in 1961—their fourth year in San Francisco. He remained in that post for the next 11 years, helping to develop the pitching skills of future Hall of Famers Juan Marichal and Gaylord Perry during that time. Jansen joined the coaching staff of the Chicago Cubs in 1972, after which he spent the next two years serving under his former Giants manager, Leo Durocher, as pitching coach. After retiring from baseball, Jansen returned to his hometown of Verboort, Oregon, where he became a real estate salesman. Jansen spent the remainder of his life in Verboort, dying in his sleep at the age of 89 on October 10, 2009.

Giant Career Highlights:

Best Season: Despite finishing just 6 games over .500 with a record of 19–13 in 1950, Jansen pitched some of his best ball for the Giants that year, ranking among the N.L. leaders in virtually every major statistical category for pitchers. He also placed near the top of the league rankings in most statistical categories the following season, when he helped the Giants capture the pennant by recording a career-high 23 victories. Nevertheless, the feeling here is that Jansen had his best all-around year in 1947, when, pitching for a Giants team that finished fourth in the Senior Circuit with a record of 81–73, he compiled a mark of 21–5 that gave him a league-best .808 winning percentage. The rookie right-hander also finished among the N.L. leaders with 20 complete games, 248 innings pitched, a 3.16 ERA, and a WHIP of 1.202, earning in the process his only top-10 finish in the league MVP voting.

Memorable Moments/Greatest Performances: Jansen pitched extremely well in his first major-league start, throwing a complete-game 6-hitter in defeating the Braves by a score of 2–1 on May 10, 1947.

Jansen pitched one of his best games for the Giants on July 7, 1948, surrendering just 2 hits during a 7–0 victory over the Phillies in Philadelphia. Jansen turned in another memorable performance a little over two months later, on September 11, when he went the distance in defeating Brooklyn by a score of 2–1 in 13 innings. He allowed 7 hits to the Dodgers, while walking 4 and striking out 6.

Jansen again performed brilliantly on April 14, 1949, when he tossed another 2-hit shutout against the Phillies, this time defeating them by a score of 1–0. Jansen finished the game with 8 strikeouts and no walks.

Jansen put together an extremely impressive streak in June of 1950, throwing three straight shutouts and 30 consecutive scoreless innings, before surrendering a pair of second-inning runs to the Dodgers during a 10–3 Giants win on June 27.

Jansen hit the only home run of his career on July 28, 1950, reaching the seats against St. Louis starter Al Brazle during an 8–3 victory over the Cardinals.

Jansen tossed the third and final 2-hit shutout of his career on September 18, 1950, when he allowed just a pair of doubles during a 13–0 win over the Cardinals.

Notable Achievements:

Won more than 20 games twice, surpassing 18 victories on two other occasions.

Posted winning percentage in excess of .800 once (.808 in 1947).

Threw more than 250 innings four times.

Tossed at least 20 complete games twice.

Led N.L. pitchers in: wins once; winning percentage once; shutouts once; WHIP once; putouts three times; and fielding percentage once.

Two-time N.L. All-Star (1950 & 1951).

1951 N.L. champion.

44 ART FLETCHER

Art Fletcher manned shortstop for the Giants for parts of 12 seasons. *(Courtesy of Library of Congress)*

A hard-nosed player known for his brashness and feistiness, Art Fletcher proved to be an extension of his pugnacious manager John McGraw on the playing field during his 12 years in New York. Serving as the Giants starting shortstop from 1911 to 1919, Fletcher quarreled with opposing players, umpires and fans alike, establishing himself in the process as the leader of a cantankerous New York squad that captured four National League pennants in his nine years as a starter. A pretty fair player as well, the right-handed-hitting Fletcher compiled a .275 batting average as a member of the Giants, topping the .300-mark once and batting over .280 on four other occasions. Known equally for his solid defense, Fletcher led all N.L. shortstops in assists four times and fielding percentage twice.

Born in Collinsville, Illinois, on January 5, 1885, Arthur Fletcher went against his parents' wishes by pursuing a career in professional baseball. After obtaining a degree in stenography from a business college in St. Louis, Fletcher began his pro career playing shortstop for Staunton, Illinois, in 1906, before spending the following year with the Collinsville Reds. Offered a chance to try out for Dallas of the Texas League in 1908, Fletcher made the most of his opportunity, exhibiting a tremendous amount of confidence in a series of exhibition games the Dallas squad played against the New York Giants. Refusing to be intimidated by his National League opponents and their contentious manager John McGraw, Fletcher slid into the major leaguers, spikes high, crowded the plate when their pitchers threw at him, and responded in kind when they taunted him verbally. Fletcher's brash behavior so impressed McGraw that the Giants manager reportedly said of him, "That's my kind of ball player," prompting him to purchase the young infielder's contract for $1,500.

After spending the entire 1908 campaign with Dallas, Fletcher joined the Giants the following year. He subsequently spent the next two seasons serving as a utility infielder, appearing in a total of only 84 games and posting batting averages of just .214 and .224. During that time, Fletcher had a collar sewn on his uniform that he wore turned up to hide the jutting chin that often served as a source of amusement to his opponents.

Fletcher's playing time increased dramatically after he replaced Al Bridwell as the starter at shortstop in May of 1911. Although Giants fans initially expressed their displeasure towards Fletcher after he took over at short for the popular Bridwell, he eventually won them over with his solid hitting, strong defense, and aggressive style of play. Appearing in 112 games over the course of the campaign, Fletcher ended up batting a career-high .319, scoring 73 runs, and stealing 20 bases, in helping the Giants capture the first of three straight National League pennants. He also began a string of 10 straight seasons in which he ranked among the league leaders in times-hit-by-pitch, finishing first in that category a total of five times.

Rapidly establishing himself as the leader of one of the *Dead Ball Era's* finest infields that also included Fred Merkle at first base, Larry Doyle at second, and Buck Herzog at third, Fletcher continued his rise to prominence in 1912, batting .282, driving in 52 runs, and scoring 64 times from his number eight spot in the batting order. Fletcher increased his offensive production after manager McGraw moved him to the middle of the lineup the following year, finishing the season with 71 RBIs, 76 runs scored, and a .297 batting average, en route to earning a 12th-place finish in the Chalmers Award balloting. He followed that up with a similarly productive 1914 campaign in which he drove in 79 runs, scored 62 times, and batted .286.

However, even as Fletcher gradually developed into one of the Giants' better offensive players, he remained a notorious free-swinger who rarely walked and typically compiled extremely mediocre on-base percentages. Over the course of 13 major league seasons, Fletcher drew as many as 30 bases on balls and posted an on-base percentage in excess of .350 just once. Furthermore, even though Fletcher often drew praise for his defensive work, being compared at times to defensive standouts Honus Wagner and Joe Tinker, he regularly finished among the league leaders in errors, committing as many as 63 miscues in 1914. It should be noted, though, that he also had outstanding range, leading all N.L. shortstops in assists on four separate occasions.

Those negatives notwithstanding, Fletcher made a tremendous impact on the Giants with his leadership and aggressiveness on the playing field. Led by Fletcher and the equally combative John McGraw, the Giants became the National League's most hated team during the second decade of the 20th century, as sportswriter Frank Graham noted when he wrote, "There was fighting everywhere they went, and Fletcher always was in the thick of it. He fought enemy players, umpires, and fans. He was fined and suspended frequently."

At the same time, Graham paid tribute to Fletcher when he added, "If there be one among the gamesters of baseball who is gamer than the rest, that man be Fletcher."

After two more solid seasons, Fletcher helped lead the Giants to another pennant in 1917, the year that McGraw named him team captain. In addition to driving in 56 runs and scoring 70 times, Fletcher led all league shortstops in fielding percentage for the first of two straight times. He remained in New York two more years, posting batting averages of .263 and .277, before being traded to the Philadelphia Phillies for future Hall of Fame shortstop Dave Bancroft on June 7, 1920. Fletcher finished out the 1920 campaign in Philadelphia, batting .296 for the hapless Phillies, before sitting out the entire 1921 season following the death of his brother and father. Returning to the Phillies in 1922, Fletcher batted .280 and hit a career-high 7 home runs, in only 110 games, before announcing his retirement at season's end to become manager of the team. He concluded his career with 32 home runs, 670 RBIs, 684 runs scored, 1,534 hits, 77 triples, 238 doubles, 160 stolen bases, a .277 batting average, a .319 on-base percentage, and a .365 slugging percentage. During Fletcher's time in New York, he hit 21 home runs, knocked in 579 runs, scored 602 times, collected 1,311 hits, 65 triples, and 193 doubles, stole 153 bases, batted .275, compiled an on-base percentage of .318, and posted a slugging percentage of .356.

After managing the Phillies for four years following his retirement as an active player, Fletcher accepted a coaching position with the New York Yankees and his old friend from the National League, Yankees manager Miller Huggins. Fletcher continued to serve in that capacity until heart problems forced him to retire in 1945, long after Joe McCarthy replaced Huggins as manager of the team. During his time with the Yankees, Fletcher served on the coaching staffs of 10 American League pennant-winners and nine world championship teams, earning in the process more than $75,000 in World Series checks. When Fletcher died of a heart attack in Los Angeles at the age of 65 on February 6, 1950, the wire services reported that he had cashed more Series checks than anyone else in baseball history.

Giant Career Highlights:

Best Season: Fletcher arguably played his best ball for the Giants in his first year as a starter, concluding the 1911 campaign with 20 stolen bases, 73 runs scored, and career-high marks in walks (30), batting average (.319), on-base percentage (.400), and slugging percentage (.429). However, he appeared in only 112 games, limiting him to just 326 official at-bats, 104 hits, and 37 RBIs. Fletcher actually posted better overall numbers in both 1913 and 1914, finishing the second of those seasons with 62 runs scored, 147 hits, a .286 batting average, an OPS of .711, and a career-high 79 RBIs. Fletcher, though, performed slightly better in 1913, when he knocked in 71 runs, batted .297, compiled an OPS of .735, and established career highs in runs scored (76), hits (160), triples (9), and stolen bases (32).

Memorable Moments/Greatest Performances: Fletcher had one of his biggest days at the plate for the Giants on May 28, 1915, when he led them to an 11–4 victory over the Cardinals by going 4-for-4, with a homer, 4 RBIs, and 2 runs scored. He had a similarly productive afternoon against Brooklyn on

June 1, 1920, just six days before being dealt to Philadelphia, going 4-for-5, with 4 RBIs, during a 10–9 Giants loss. Fletcher turned in another four-hit performance against Boston on September 24, 1919, leading the Giants to a 6–1 win in the first game of their doubleheader split with the Braves by going 4-for-5, with a pair of doubles.

However, Fletcher experienced arguably the most memorable moment of his career on August 14, 1917, when, in the second game of a doubleheader split with the Robins, he engaged in an all-out brawl with Brooklyn outfielder Casey Stengel that resulted in both men being ejected from the contest.

Notable Achievements:

Batted over .300 once (.319 in 1911).

Surpassed 20 stolen bases twice, topping 30 steals once (32 in 1913).

Posted on-base percentage of .400 in 1911.

Led N.L. in times hit by a pitch five times.

Led N.L. shortstops in assists four times and fielding percentage twice.

Holds Giants career record for most times hit by a pitch (132).

Four-time N.L. champion (1911, 1912, 1913 & 1917).

45 MONTE IRVIN

Monte Irvin spent nearly a decade starring in the Negro Leagues before finally signing with the Giants in 1949. *(Courtesy of LegendaryAuctions.com)*

Had Monte Irvin joined the Giants earlier in his playing career, he undoubtedly would have finished much higher in these rankings. Irvin, though, spent most of his peak seasons competing in the Negro Leagues, robbing him of an opportunity to ply his skills against major-league players until he reached 30 years of age. A true "five-tool player" who excelled in every aspect of the game, Irvin received the following review from Negro League legend Cool Papa Bell: "Most of the black ballplayers thought Monte Irvin should have been the first black in the Major Leagues. Monte was our best young ballplayer at the time. He could hit that long ball, he had a great arm, he could field, and he could run. He could do everything." Meanwhile, Roy Campanella, who competed against Irvin in the Negro Leagues, said, "Monte was the best all-round player I have ever seen."

Irvin went on to spend parts of seven seasons with the Giants, performing particularly well for them in 1951, when he earned a third-place finish in the N.L. MVP voting by leading them to their first pennant in 14 years. Nevertheless, the fact remains that Giants fans never got to see the best of Monte Irvin.

Born in Haleburg, Alabama, on February 25, 1919, Montford Merrill Irvin grew up in East Orange, New Jersey, where he established himself as one of the greatest all-around athletes the state ever produced. Earning 16 varsity letters in four different sports while attending East Orange High School, Irvin starred in baseball, football, basketball, and track, setting a state record for the javelin throw in the last sport. While still in high school, Irvin also began playing baseball for a semipro team known as the Orange Triangles.

Following his graduation from high school, Irvin received a scholarship offer to play football at the University of Michigan. However, he turned it down since he did not have enough money to move to Ann Arbor. Choosing instead to enroll at Lincoln University in Pennsylvania, Irvin simultaneously began playing professional baseball with the Newark Eagles of the Negro Leagues under the assumed name "Jimmy Nelson" to protect his amateur status.

The New York Giants first learned of Irvin's talents in 1938, when one of his teachers wrote to Giants owner Horace Stoneham, telling him, "We've got a player here you would not even believe." After dispatching a pair of scouts to watch Irvin play, Stoneham received a glowing report of the young man's abilities, revealing to Irvin years later, "They told me that you were the next Joe DiMaggio."

However, with the unwritten rules of the day being what they were, Stoneham chose not to sign Irvin, telling him many years later, "I only wish I had been braver than that." As a result, Irvin remained in school while continuing to further his reputation as one of the finest young talents in Negro-League baseball.

Irvin performed brilliantly while playing for Newark from 1939 to 1942, starring in the field, at the bat, and on the base paths. Although he spent most of his time at shortstop, Irvin did an excellent job wherever the Eagles put him, claiming in his typically understated fashion that he played the outfield like Willie Mays. An exceptional hitter as well, Irvin hit for both power and average, batting .400 against the highest level of competition in 1941, before compiling a mark of .397 and hitting 20 home runs in just 63 games in the Mexican League the following year.

Irvin temporarily put his playing career on hold when he entered the military late in 1942, after which he spent the next three years serving his country during World War II. Approached by Branch Rickey about the possibility of signing with the Dodgers when he returned to the States in 1946, Irvin expressed concerns over his ability to perform at an elite level so soon after leaving the service. Complicating matters even further, Newark Eagles business manager Effa Manley refused to allow Rickey to sign Irvin without receiving compensation. Since Rickey did not respect the Negro Leagues as a fully organized entity, he chose not to do so, leaving the task of integrating Major League Baseball squarely on the shoulders of Jackie Robinson. Looking back at the events that transpired at the time, Manley said:

> Monte was the choice of all Negro National and American League club owners to serve as the No. 1 player to join a white major league team. We all agreed, in meeting, he was the best qualified by temperament, character, ability, sense of loyalty, morals, age, experience and physique to represent us as the first black player to enter the white majors since the Walker brothers back in the 1880s. Of course, Branch Rickey lifted Jackie Robinson out of Negro ball and made him the first, and it turned out just fine.

Returning to the Eagles in 1946, Irvin spent three more years playing in the Negro Leagues before finally signing with the Giants at 30 years of age in 1949 after Horace Stoneham paid Manley the $5,000 he requested. During his time in Newark, Irvin appeared in five East-West All-Star Games. Reflecting back on his years with the Eagles, Irvin stated, "For me, there was nothing like my time with the Eagles—ever. We were young, and the world was new to us. It was the happiest time of our lives. They wouldn't let us play in their big leagues, but we had this game of ours . . . this marvelous, blessed game . . . and we just went out and played it."

Although the 6'1", 195-pound Irvin still possessed a considerable amount of talent when he signed with the Giants in 1949, he commented at the time,

"This should have happened to me 10 years ago. I'm not even half the ball-player I was then."

Assigned to Jersey City of the International League, Irvin compiled a batting average of .373, before being called up to New York in early July. Assuming a part-time role with the Giants the remainder of the year, Irvin batted just .224 and knocked in only 7 runs, in 36 games and 93 total plate appearances, before being returned to the minor leagues at season's end. However, after the right-handed-hitting Irvin got off to a torrid start in 1950, batting .510 and hitting 10 home runs in only 51 at-bats, the Giants recalled him in mid-May, beginning his major-league career in earnest. Splitting his time between the outfield and first base the rest of the year, Irvin appeared in 110 games, batting .299, hitting 15 homers, and driving in 66 runs, in only 374 official at-bats.

Although Irvin continued to play some first base in 1951, he gradually established himself as the Giants regular left-fielder over the course of the campaign. Proving to be a key factor in New York's successful run to the N.L. pennant, Irvin hit 24 homers, scored 94 runs, batted .312, and led the league with 121 runs batted in, en route to earning a third-place finish in the MVP voting. Combining with Hank Thompson and Willie Mays to form the first all-black outfield ever to play in the Major Leagues, Irvin served as a mentor to both men, proving to be particularly influential in the development of the 20-year-old Mays, who manager Leo Durocher asked him to take under his wing. Reflecting back on his earliest days with the Giants, Mays later recalled, "In my time, when I was coming up, you had to have some kind of guidance. And Monte was like my brother . . . I couldn't go anywhere without him, especially on the road . . . It was just a treat to be around him. I didn't understand life in New York until I met Monte. He knew everything about what was going on, and he protected me dearly."

Upon learning of Mays' comments, Irvin quipped, "I did that for two years and, in the third year, he started showing me around."

Despite being sidelined for much of the 1952 campaign by a broken ankle he suffered in April, Irvin earned his lone National League All-Star selection. Appearing in only 46 games, he hit 4 home runs, knocked in 21 runs, and batted .310. Healthy again for most of 1953, Irvin rebounded by hitting 21 homers, driving in 97 runs, and batting .329, even though he missed much of August after re-injuring his ankle.

Irvin's leadership and outstanding play made a strong impression on teammate Bobby Thomson, who later said, "I always respected Monte Irvin as much as any player I played with. He would show up and do the job every day; one of the strong guys on the ball club."

Hampered by a bad ankle and slowed by Father Time, Irvin never again put up big numbers for the Giants. After hitting 19 home runs, knocking in 64 runs, and batting .262 in 1954, Irvin got off to a slow start the following year, prompting the Giants to send him down to the minor leagues. He spent the remainder of the year with the Minneapolis Millers, before signing with the Chicago Cubs prior to the start of the ensuing campaign. Irvin ended his playing career with the Cubs in 1956, hitting 15 homers, driving in 50 runs, and batting .271 in 111 games, before announcing his retirement at season's end. Over parts of eight seasons in the big leagues, Irvin hit 99 home runs, knocked in 443 runs, scored 366 times, collected 731 hits, 31 triples, and 97 doubles, batted .293, compiled a .383 on-base percentage, and posted a .475 slugging percentage, compiling virtually all those numbers as a member of the Giants.

Following his retirement, Irvin briefly scouted for the New York Mets, before spending 17 years serving as a public relations specialist under Baseball Commissioner Bowie Kuhn. During his time in that position, Irvin gained induction into the Hall of Fame, being elected by the members of the Committee on Negro League Baseball in 1973. He later served as a member of that body, as well as the Hall of Fame Veteran's Committee. Irvin spent much of the last three decades educating the public on the history of the Negro Leagues, before passing away of natural causes six weeks shy of his 97th birthday on January 11, 2016.

In discussing his love of the game, Irvin once said, "Baseball is a game you'd play for nothing. And I am so happy the Lord gave me a little ability, because it allowed me to meet a lot of good people and see so many exciting places." Irvin then added, "My only wish is that major-league fans could've seen me when I was at my best."

Giant Career Highlights:

Best Season: Although Irvin established career-high marks in batting average (.329), slugging percentage (.541), and OPS (.947) in 1953, he clearly had his best season for the Giants two years earlier. In addition to leading the N.L. with 121 RBIs in 1951, Irvin placed among the league leaders with 24 home runs, 94 runs scored, 174 hits, 11 triples, a .312 batting average, a .415 on-base percentage, and a .514 slugging percentage. He also drew 89 bases on balls and struck out only 44 times, went 12-for-14 in stolen base attempts, including 5 steals of home, and committed just one error in the outfield, giving him a fielding percentage of .996 that placed him second in the league rankings. Irvin's exceptional all-around performance earned him a third-place finish in the N.L. MVP balloting, with only Roy Campanella and Stan Musial garnering more votes. Irvin later called that season "the high point of my life."

Memorable Moments/Greatest Performances: Irvin exhibited his ability to contribute to his team in any number of ways during a doubleheader split with the Braves on April 19, 1951, beginning the afternoon by going 1-for-2, with 3 walks, 2 runs scored, and a steal of home in the Giants' 4–2 win in the opener. Although Boston won the nightcap by a score of 13–12 in 10 innings, Irvin hit a grand slam homer and knocked in 6 runs.

During a 7–3 Giants win over Boston on September 7, 1951, Irvin hit one of the longest home runs in the history of Braves Field, driving a Phil Paine offering an estimated 500 feet. He finished the day 2-for-5, with 3 RBIs. Nearly three weeks later, on September 26, Irvin nearly hit for the cycle, going 3-for-5, with a homer, triple, double, 4 RBIs, and 2 runs scored, in leading the Giants to a lopsided 10–1 victory over the Phillies.

Irvin turned in another outstanding all-around effort against Philadelphia on July 6, 1953, going 4-for-5, with a double, 3 RBIs, 1 run scored, and a stolen base during a 6–0 blanking of the Phillies. Just two days later, on July 8, Irvin led the Giants to an 11-inning, 10–7 win over the Pirates by knocking in a career-high 7 runs. After driving in the game's first 3 runs with a bases-loaded double in the top of the first inning, Irvin again came through with the bags full in the final frame, delivering the game's decisive blow with a grand slam home run. Although the Giants lost their matchup with the Dodgers four days later by a score of 4–3 in 10 innings, Irvin continued his hot-hitting, going 4-for-5, with a homer, triple, and 2 RBIs.

Irvin also performed exceptionally well against the Yankees in 1951 World Series, leading all players on both teams with 11 hits and a .458 batting average. After leading the Giants to a 5–1 victory in the Series opener by collecting 4 hits and stealing home, Irvin hit safely in his first three trips to the plate in Game 2, giving him 7 consecutive hits over two games.

Notable Achievements:

Hit more than 20 home runs twice.

Knocked in more than 100 runs once (121 in 1951).

Batted over .300 three times.

Finished in double-digits in triples once (11 in 1951).

Compiled on-base percentage in excess of .400 twice.

Posted slugging percentage in excess of .500 twice.

Led N.L. with 121 RBIs in 1951.

Led N.L. left-fielders in fielding percentage once.

Tied for ninth in Giants history with .389 career on-base percentage.

Finished third in 1951 N.L. MVP voting.

1952 N.L. All-Star.

Two-time N.L. champion (1951 & 1954).

1954 world champion.

Elected to Baseball Hall of Fame by members of Negro League Committee in 1973.

46 DON MUELLER

Don Mueller finished second to teammate Willie Mays in the 1954 N.L. batting race. *(Courtesy of Mearsonlineauctions.com)*

Nicknamed "Mandrake the Magician" because of the frequency with which his hits found holes in the opposing infield's defense, Don Mueller spent parts of 10 seasons in New York, serving as the Giants starting right-fielder in each of his last eight years with the team. A solid left-handed hitter with little power but a remarkable ability to consistently put the ball in play, Mueller batted over .300 four times for the Giants, finishing a close second to teammate Willie Mays in the 1954 batting race with a mark of .342. A steady defensive player as well, Mueller led all N.L. right-fielders in fielding percentage three times, while also topping all league outfielders in assists once. Mueller's consistent play earned him two All-Star selections and helped lead the Giants to two pennants and one world championship during the 1950s.

Born in the St. Louis suburb of Creve Coeur, Missouri, on April 14, 1927, Donald Frederick Mueller received his earliest batting lessons from his father, Walter J. Mueller—a backup outfielder for the Pittsburgh Pirates from 1922 to 1926. Looking back at the manner in which his father instructed him, Mueller recalled, "He taught me an awful lot. He showed me how to grip the bat, to use pressure on one hand or the other to hit where you want to hit. He also had me focus on the ball by pitching corn kernels that I would hit with a broomstick. Concentrating on such a small object improved my depth perception."

Mueller attended Christian Brothers High School in Richmond Heights, Missouri, where he developed into such an outstanding baseball player that he received offers from several major-league teams, including the Chicago Cubs. Rejecting Chicago's bid because he said, "My dad didn't like the contract they offered me," Mueller instead chose to sign with the New York Giants, whose player-manager, Mel Ott, had been his childhood hero.

After signing with the Giants as a 17-year-old amateur free agent in 1944, Mueller spent most of the next four seasons playing for New York's Triple-A affiliate in Jersey City, while also serving in the Merchant Marines for the first two years. Summoned to New York after batting .348 and hitting 10 home runs at Jersey City during the first half of the 1948 campaign, Mueller made his major-league debut with the Giants on August 2, compiling a batting average of .358 in 36 games and 81 at-bats over the season's final two months. Returned to the minor leagues at the start of the ensuing campaign, Mueller re-joined the Giants for good later in the year, batting just .232 in his 56 official at-bats with the club.

With Leo Durocher having replaced Mel Ott as Giants manager two years earlier, Mueller won the starting right-field job early in 1950. In discussing the events that facilitated his insertion into the starting lineup, Mueller explained, "The team did not have a good won-loss record. Leo got rid of the home-run hitters. He wanted base hits, with good pitching. I got the job because I was his kind of ballplayer: hit, advance the runner."

Mueller played well in his first full season in New York, overcoming an early-season slump to finish the campaign with a .291 batting average, 7 homers, and a career-high 84 RBIs. With the vast majority of Mueller's hits being line drives and soft singles just beyond the reach of opposing infielders, sportswriters dubbed him "Mandrake the Magician" after a popular comic strip character of the time.

Despite being known primarily as a singles hitter in subsequent seasons, Mueller showed increased power at the plate in 1951, hitting a career-high 16 home runs, while also driving in 69 runs and batting .277. He followed that up by hitting 12 homers, knocking in 49 runs, and batting .281 in 1952, before beginning an outstanding three-year run during which he batted well over .300 each season. After hitting 6 home runs, driving in 60 runs, and batting .333 in the first of those campaigns, Mueller earned All-Star honors for the first of two straight times in 1954 by batting .342, knocking in 71 runs, scoring 90 times, and leading the league with 212 hits. He performed well again in 1955, finishing the year with 8 homers, 83 RBIs, and a .306 batting average.

In addition to the fact that Mueller possessed little in the way of power, his biggest fault as a hitter proved to be the lack of patience he displayed at the plate. Failing to walk more than 34 times in any single season, Mueller compiled a lifetime on-base percentage of just .322. On the other hand, he rarely struck out, fanning only 146 times in almost 4,600 plate appearances over the course of his career. Factoring into the equation Mueller's strikeouts and walks, he put the ball in play an amazing 93 percent of the time.

Mueller began to experience a precipitous drop-off in offensive production in 1956, batting just .269, while totaling only 5 homers, 41 RBIs, and 38 runs scored. After he followed that up by batting .258, driving in 37 runs, and scoring 45 times in 1957, the Giants sold him to the Chicago White Sox prior to the start of the ensuing campaign. Mueller left New York with career totals of 65 home runs, 504 RBIs, 492 runs scored, 1,248 hits, 37 triples, and 134 doubles, a batting average of .298, an on-base percentage of .323, and a .394 slugging percentage.

Assuming a backup role in Chicago in 1958, Mueller batted .253 before being released by the White Sox early in 1959 after he made just 4 pinch-hitting appearances for them. He subsequently announced his retirement, ending his career with virtually the same numbers he compiled during his time in New York. Following his playing days, Mueller retired to the family farm in Chesterfield, Missouri, where he raised cattle. He also spent a few years scouting for the Giants in Missouri and Illinois, before beginning a lengthy career as an insurance company investigator. Mueller lived until December 28, 2011, passing away at the age of 84, just six months after he lost his wife of 62 years.

Career Highlights:

Best Season: Mueller performed well for the Giants in 1955, earning N.L. All-Star honors by batting .306, collecting 185 hits, and driving in 83 runs. Nevertheless, there is little doubt that he had his finest all-around season one year earlier, when he knocked in 71 runs and reached career-high marks in hits (212), runs scored (90), triples (8), doubles (35), batting average (.343), and OPS (.807). In addition to finishing a close second to teammate Willie Mays in the N.L. batting race, Mueller topped the Senior Circuit in hits. He also led all league outfielders with 14 assists, en route to earning a 12th-place finish in the N.L. MVP voting.

Memorable Moments/Greatest Performances: Mueller helped lead the Giants to an 11–6 win over Cincinnati in the first game of their doubleheader split with the Reds on August 27, 1950, by going 5-for-6, with 3 RBIs and 3 runs scored.

Although Mueller developed a reputation over the course of his career for being primarily a singles hitter, he experienced a brief power surge during the latter stages of the 1951 campaign, hitting 5 home runs over a two-day period. After reaching the seats three times and knocking in 5 runs during an 8–1 Giants victory over the Dodgers on September 1, Mueller led his team to an 11–2 win over Brooklyn the very next day by hitting 2 more homers and driving in another 5 runs. Making things even sweeter, he hit his last home run just moments after learning he had become a new father.

Despite being overshadowed by Stan Musial, who hit 5 home runs on the day, Mueller turned in another outstanding effort on May 2, 1954, in helping the Giants gain a split of their doubleheader with the Cardinals. After Musial led St. Louis to a 10–6 victory in the opener by hitting 3 homers and driving in 6 runs, the Cardinals great added another 2 round-trippers in the nightcap. However, Mueller went 5-for-5, with a double, triple, 2 RBIs, and 3 runs scored, in leading the Giants to a 9–7 win.

Mueller had another exceptional day at the plate a little over two months later, when he hit for the cycle during the Giants' 13–7 victory over Pittsburgh on July 11, 1954. Completing his cycle in his final at-bat by hitting his first home run of the year into the right field stands at the Polo Grounds against

Pirates southpaw Dick Littlefield, Mueller later revealed, "Normally, I didn't try to pull left-handers. I took them the other way. But I was a situation hitter, and this was a situation. So I pulled him over the right-field wall for a home run." Mueller finished the game 4-for-5, with 4 RBIs.

Mueller concluded his banner year by recording 7 hits in 18 at-bats against Cleveland in the 1954 World Series, en route to compiling a .389 batting average that helped lead the Giants to a four-game sweep of their American League counterparts.

Mueller had his last big game for the Giants on August 25, 1957, when he led them to a 10–1 victory over Cincinnati by going 4-for-4, with a pair of homers, 3 RBIs, and 4 runs scored.

Notable Achievements:

Batted over .300 four times, topping the .330-mark on three occasions.

Surpassed 200 hits once (212 in 1954).

Topped 30 doubles once (35 in 1954).

Led N.L. with 212 hits in 1954.

Led N.L. in At-Bats-Per-Strikeout Ratio five times.

Finished second in N.L. with .342 batting average in 1954.

Led N.L. outfielders with 14 assists in 1954.

Led N.L. right-fielders in fielding percentage three times and double plays once.

Two-time N.L. All-Star (1954 & 1955).

Two-time N.L. champion (1951 & 1954).

1954 world champion.

47 RICH AURILIA

Rich Aurilia holds the Giants' single-season record for most home runs by a shortstop (37 in 2001). *(Courtesy of Christopher M. Matthews)*

A native New Yorker who spent virtually his entire career playing on the West Coast, Rich Aurilia served as the Giants starting shortstop for seven seasons, establishing himself during that time as one of the National League's top offensive players at his position. The right-handed-hitting Aurilia surpassed 20 home runs three times as a member of the Giants, setting a franchise record for shortstops by hitting 37 round-trippers in 2001, en route to earning his lone All-Star selection and Silver Slugger. Aurilia also batted over .300 once, accumulated more than 200 hits once, knocked in more than 80 runs twice, and scored more than 100 runs once during his time in San Francisco, helping the Giants capture three division titles and one league championship in the process.

Born in Brooklyn, New York, on September 2, 1971, Richard Santo Aurilia attended local Xaverian High School before enrolling at St. John's University in Queens, where he represented the Red Storm as an All-Big East selection in 1992. Selected by the Texas Rangers in the 24th round of the 1992 Major League Baseball Draft, Aurilia spent the next two years in Texas's farm system before being traded to the Giants for pitcher John Burkett on December 22, 1994. Summoned to the big leagues by the Giants for the first time during the latter stages of the 1995 campaign, Aurilia made an extremely favorable impression in the nine games in which he appeared, hitting 2 homers, driving in 4 runs, and batting .474.

Originally expected to inherit the starting shortstop job in San Francisco following the trade of Royce Clayton at the conclusion of the 1995 season, Aurilia instead found himself sharing playing time with Shawon Dunston and José Vizcaíno in 1996 and 1997, respectively. Appearing in a total of only 151 games those two years, Aurilia hit just 8 homers and knocked in only 45 runs, while compiling batting averages of .239 and .275.

Aurilia finally established himself as the Giants starting shortstop in 1998, finishing the season with 9 home runs, 49 RBIs, 54 runs scored, and a batting average of .266, before emerging as an offensive threat the following year, when he hit 22 homers, drove in 80 runs, scored 68 times, and batted .281. At the same time, though, Aurilia proved to be something of a liability in the field, leading all N.L. shortstops with 28 errors in the second of those campaigns.

Aurilia posted solid offensive numbers again in 2000, hitting 20 home runs, knocking in 79 runs, scoring 67 times, and batting .271, while committing 7 fewer errors in the field. However, he compiled easily the most impressive stat-line of his career in 2001 after he assumed the number-two spot in the Giants batting order, immediately in front of Barry Bonds. With opposing pitchers not wishing to face Bonds with men on base, Aurilia saw more good pitches to hit than ever before, enabling him to hit 37 homers, drive in 97 runs, score 114 times, bat .324, and lead the league with 206 hits. He also had a good year in the field, leading all N.L. shortstops in putouts and double plays. Aurilia's strong all-around performance earned him All-Star honors for the only time and a 12th-place finish in the league MVP voting.

The 2001 campaign turned out to be a career-year for Aurilia, who never again approached those lofty offensive numbers. Yet, even though he didn't prove to be nearly as productive at the plate in future seasons, he gradually developed into a solid defensive shortstop in spite of his somewhat limited range, committing only 11 miscues in the field in 2002, en route to leading all players at his position with a .980 fielding percentage.

After totaling 28 home runs and 119 RBIs for the Giants in 2002 and 2003, while posting batting averages of .257 and .277, Aurilia signed as a free agent with the Seattle Mariners when the Giants refused to meet his salary demands. He subsequently spent less than one full season in Seattle, returning to the National League later in 2004 after being dealt to the San Diego Padres. Aurilia then spent two productive seasons in Cincinnati, having his best year for the Reds in 2006, when he hit 23 homers, knocked in 70 runs, and batted an even .300.

A free agent again at the end of 2006, Aurilia elected to return to the Giants, with whom he spent the remainder of his career. Upon announcing Aurilia's signing, Giants Senior Vice President & General Manager Brian Sabean stated, "He (Aurilia) clearly is a highly productive player who can fill many infield needs, while his character and desire to win are unquestioned."

Plagued by various injuries in 2007, Aurilia appeared in only 99 games for the Giants, hitting just 5 homers, knocking in only 33 runs, and batting just .252, while splitting his time between all four infield positions. Playing mostly first and third base the following year, Aurilia rebounded somewhat to hit 10 home runs, drive in 52 runs, and bat .283. However, after batting just .213 in a utility role in 2009, he chose to announce his retirement, ending his career with 186 home runs, 756 RBIs, 745 runs scored, 1,576 hits, 22 triples, 301 doubles, a .275 batting average, a .328 on-base percentage, and a .433 slugging percentage. In his years with the Giants, Aurilia hit 143 homers, knocked in 574 runs, scored 574 times, collected 1,226 hits, 17 triples, and 232 doubles, batted .275, compiled a .327 on-base percentage, and posted a .431 slugging percentage. No other National League shortstop hit as many home runs as the 79 Aurilia totaled from 1999 to 2001. Following his playing career, Aurilia became a member of Comcast SportsNet Bay Area.

Giant Career Highlights:

Best Season: There is little doubt that Aurilia had his finest season in 2001, when he established career highs in virtually every major offensive category, including home runs (37), RBIs (97), runs scored (114), triples (5) doubles (37), batting average (.324), on-base percentage (.369), slugging percentage (.572), and hits (206), leading the league in the last category.

Memorable Moments/Greatest Performances: Aurilia's first start for the Giants proved to be a memorable one, with the shortstop going 4-for-5, with a homer, double, 2 RBIs, and 3 runs scored during a 12–4 victory over the Rockies on September 28, 1995.

Aurilia helped key a 10–3 win over the Angels on June 14, 1997, by hitting the first-ever grand slam in interleague play.

Aurilia had a huge day at the plate against Atlanta on May 3, 1998, leading the Giants to a 12–8 victory over the Braves by going 4-for-5, with a pair of homers, 4 RBIs, and 3 runs scored.

Aurilia helped lead the Giants to a 15–2 pounding of the Colorado Rockies on June 16, 1999, by going 3-for-4 with 5 RBIs.

Although the Giants lost to the Dodgers by a score of 14–8 on June 26, 2001, Aurilia had a big game, going 4-for-5, with a homer, double, 4 RBIs, and 2 runs scored. Just a little over one month later, on July 28, Aurilia homered twice, knocked in 5 runs, and scored 3 times during an 11–4 win over the Diamondbacks. He had another big day at the plate on August 5, going 4-for-5, with a homer, double, and 5 RBIs during an 8–4 victory over the Phillies.

Still, Aurilia may well be remembered by Giants fans more than anything for his exceptional performance during the 2002 postseason. After hitting 2 homers and driving in 7 runs against Atlanta in the NLDS, Aurilia homered twice, knocked in 5 runs, and batted .333, in helping the Giants defeat the Cardinals in 5 games in the NLCS. Particularly outstanding in Game 2 against St. Louis, Aurilia helped give the Giants a 2–0 Series lead by homering twice and driving in 3 runs during San Francisco's 4–1 win. Aurilia continued his hot hitting against the Angels in the World Series, hitting 2 home runs and knocking in 5 runs, although the Giants ended up losing to their interstate rivals in 7 games. Aurilia concluded the postseason with 6 home runs, 17 RBIs, 13 runs scored, a .265 batting average, and a .588 slugging percentage.

Notable Achievements:

Hit more than 20 home runs three times, topping 30 homers once (37 in 2001).

Scored more than 100 runs once (114 in 2001).

Batted over .300 once (.324 in 2001).

Topped 200 hits once (206 in 2001).

Surpassed 30 doubles twice.

Posted slugging percentage in excess of .500 twice.

Led N.L. with 206 hits in 2001.

Led N.L. shortstops in: putouts once; fielding percentage once; and double plays once.

2001 Silver Slugger winner.

2001 *Sporting News* All-Star selection.

2001 N.L. All-Star.

2002 N.L. champion.

48 ROD BECK

Rod Beck's 48 saves in 1993 represent a single-season franchise record. *(Courtesy of LegendaryAuctions.com)*

Nicknamed "The Shooter" for the gunfighter's mentality he brought with him to the pitcher's mound each time he entered a game in the late innings to secure a victory for his team, Rod Beck spent 13 years in the Major Leagues, earning the respect and admiration of players, coaches, and fans wherever he went. Playing in four different cities, the hard-throwing right-hander spent most of his finest seasons with the Giants, amassing more than 30 saves in four of his seven years as a member of the team. Intimidating opposing batters with his intensity and fierce competitiveness, Beck proved to be one of the National

League's top closers for nearly a decade, before arm problems brought his period of dominance to an end.

Born in Burbank, California, on August 3, 1968, Rodney Roy Beck grew up in Southern California, where he spent his formative years as a baseball fan rooting for the Los Angeles Dodgers. Starring on the mound for Grant High School, in nearby Van Nuys, Beck led his school to its only city baseball title as a senior by winning all four playoff games in the City Section baseball tournament, including the final game at Dodger Stadium, when Grant defeated Granada Hills. Commenting years later on the impression Beck made on him at the time, former Granada Hills Coach Darryl Stroh, who managed his team to five city titles, recalled, "Probably, of all the pitchers I had an opportunity to face, he was the most dominant. He was almost unbeatable. He had such great command. He was very confident, and with good reason."

After being selected by the Oakland Athletics in the 13th round of the 1986 amateur draft following his graduation from Grant High, Beck spent two years in Oakland's farm system, during which time he remained a starting pitcher. However, Oakland dealt him to the Giants for minor-league hurler Charlie Corbell on March 23, 1988, after which Beck gradually transitioned into the bullpen. Arriving in San Francisco early in 1991, Beck ended up posting decent numbers as a rookie, making 31 appearances, compiling a record of 1–1 and an ERA of 3.78, and recording 38 strikeouts in 52 ⅓ innings of work.

Replacing Dave Righetti as the Giants closer over the course of the ensuing campaign, Beck thrived in his new role, finishing the 1992 season with a record of 3–3, an exceptional 1.76 ERA, and 17 saves, while striking out 87 batters and allowing only 62 hits over 92 innings. He followed that up by going 3–1, with a 2.16 ERA and 48 saves in 1993, finishing second in the league to Chicago's Randy Myers in the last category. Beck also struck out 86 batters and surrendered just 57 hits in 79 ⅓ innings of work, en route to earning the first of his three All-Star selections and a 12th-place finish in the N.L. MVP voting.

The 6'1", 215-pound Beck gradually established himself as one of baseball's most intimidating closers his first few seasons with the Giants, creating angst in opposing batters as he leaned in to glare at them with a menacing stare, his long hair blowing in the wind as his pitching arm swung like a pendulum by his side. Although his fastball hardly ever reached 90 mph, he made up for a lack of velocity with outstanding location and excellent use of his sinker, slider, and splitter.

Barney Nugent, who served as the Giants assistant athletic trainer during Beck's time in San Francisco, remembered, "He had that Fu Manchu, that menacing glare, the stare, the dangling right arm; that mullet blowing in the Candlestick breeze all the time. . . . It was, 'Me against you, and I'll tell you, I'm going to win. There's no way that I'm gonna lose.' That was Shooter, and everybody could respond to it."

Yet, in spite of Beck's frightening appearance, he remained remarkably friendly and approachable off the field, with his blue-collar attitude and affable nature making him extremely popular with teammates, reporters, and fans. Trevor Hoffman, who later spent two years working alongside Beck in San Diego's bullpen, revealed, "It was hard to get through that exterior of what he looked like, but it took about 1 ½ minutes to realize that's all it was. He was a teddy bear."

Tim Wakefield, a teammate of Beck's for three years in Boston, added, "His image was not something he was. He had a huge heart and was so humble. He was so full of life."

Beck earned his second straight All-Star selection during the strike-shortened 1994 campaign by amassing 28 saves, compiling a 2.77 ERA, and leading all N.L. pitchers with 47 games finished. He subsequently suffered through a subpar 1995 season in which he posted a 4.45 ERA, although he still managed to finish third in the league with 33 saves. Despite saving 35 games and lowering his ERA to 3.34 the following year, Beck continued to struggle somewhat, losing all nine of his decisions and blowing seven save opportunities.

Beck spent one more year in San Francisco, earning the last of his three All-Star nominations by going 7–4, with a 3.47 ERA and 37 saves, before opting for free agency at season's end. After signing with the Chicago Cubs prior to the start of the 1998 campaign, Beck had a bounce-back year, amassing a career-high 51 saves, while finishing first in the Senior Circuit with 70 games finished. However, that proved to be his last year as a dominant closer. After getting off to a slow start the following year, Beck spent two months on the DL following surgery to remove bone chips from his pitching shoulder. Returning to the Cubs sooner than expected, Beck found his closer's role filled by the newly-acquired Rick Aguilera, making him expendable. Chicago subsequently dealt Beck to the Red Sox for two players on August 31, bringing to an end his relatively brief stay in the Windy City.

Beck ended up spending a little over two years in Boston, posting an overall record of 9–5 and saving 9 games for the Red Sox, before undergoing

Tommy John surgery at the conclusion of the 2001 campaign. He then missed all of 2002 and spent the first two months of 2003 in the minor leagues, before signing as a free agent with San Diego on June 2, 2003. Filling in for an injured Trevor Hoffman, Beck assumed the role of closer for the Padres over the final four months of the season, earning N.L. Comeback Player of the Year honors by saving 20 games and compiling a 1.78 ERA. Unfortunately, Beck's arm gave out the following year, prompting the Padres to release him in mid-August. He subsequently announced his retirement, ending his career with a record of 38–45, an ERA of 3.30, 286 saves, 644 strikeouts in 768 innings of work, and a WHIP of 1.164. In his seven seasons with the Giants, Beck compiled a record of 21–28, an ERA of 2.97, and 199 saves, struck out 393 batters in 463 innings of work, and posted a WHIP of 1.073. His total of 199 saves places him second only to Robb Nen in franchise history.

Following his retirement, Beck continued to battle the personal demons that plagued him during the latter stages of his career, frequently turning to drugs as a means of getting the same adrenalin rush he received from being a major-league closer. Unfortunately, Beck's addiction ended up costing him his life, with police discovering cocaine in the bedroom of his suburban Phoenix home when they found him dead on June 23, 2007. Beck was only 38 years old at the time of his passing.

In remembering his former teammate, Giants shortstop Rich Aurilia said, "He was a great teammate and a great competitor. You talk to everybody; they'll have nothing but good things to say. He's somebody that Giants' fans will always remember."

Giant Career Highlights:

Best Season: Beck pitched extremely well for the Giants in 1992 after he assumed the closer's role from Dave Righetti, saving 17 games, striking out 87 batters in 92 innings of work, and posting career-best marks in ERA (1.76) and WHIP (0.837). Particularly effective down the stretch, he finished the season by allowing just one earned run in 28 ⅓ innings pitched over his last 22 appearances. However, Beck had the most dominant season of his career the following year, concluding the 1993 campaign with a 3–1 record, a 2.16 ERA, 48 saves, 86 strikeouts over 79 ⅓ innings, and a WHIP of 0.882. Beck's total of 48 saves remains a franchise record. He also established a new major-league mark (since broken) by converting 24 consecutive save opportunities.

Memorable Moments/Greatest Performances: Although the Giants lost their September 30, 1991, matchup with Houston by a score of 2–0, Beck turned in the first truly dominant performance of his career, working the final 2 innings, and striking out 4 of the 6 batters he faced.

Although he didn't get the save, Beck held Philadelphia's offense at bay on May 13, 1992, working 2 ⅔ perfect innings and striking out 4 during a 5–3 Giants win over the Phillies.

Beck again pitched brilliantly on July 12, 1992, striking out 4 of the 6 batters he faced during a 4–0 win over the Expos.

Beck turned in a pair of dominant performances early in 1993, working 2 scoreless innings and recording 5 strikeouts during an 11-inning, 13–12 victory over the Braves on April 18, before fanning 4 of the 5 batters he faced during a 10-inning, 9–8 loss to the Phillies on April 26.

Beck pitched magnificently during the latter stages of that 1993 campaign as the Giants strove to overtake Atlanta for the division title, working 8 times over a 9-day stretch in late September and early October, and picking up a win and 6 saves.

Yet, Beck turned in the most dramatic performance of his career on September 18, 1997, when he helped propel the Giants to their first division title in 8 years by working the final three frames of a 12-inning, 6–5 victory over the Dodgers. Beck's outing began ominously, when, after entering the contest in the top of the 10th inning with the score tied at 5–5, he loaded the bases with no one out by surrendering three straight singles to Dodger batsmen. However, he subsequently struck out Todd Zeile and got Eddie Murray to hit into an inning-ending double play. Tim Keown later wrote in *The Chronicle*, "Beck stormed off the mound like a grizzly. The crowd roared down at Beck, and Beck pumped his fist against his glove and roared right back at it." The Giants won the game two innings later when backup catcher Brian Johnson hit a walk-off homer in the bottom of the 12th. Beck earned the victory, working 3 scoreless innings, striking out 2, and allowing just those 3 singles. The victory tied the Giants with the Dodgers for first place in the division, which San Francisco eventually won by a two-game margin.

Notable Achievements:

Saved more than 30 games four times, topping 40 saves once (48 in 1993).

Compiled ERA below 3.00 three times, posting mark under 2.00 once (1.76 in 1992).

Posted WHIP under 1.000 twice.

Led N.L. pitchers in games finished three times.

Finished second in N.L. in saves three times.

Holds Giants single-season saves record (48 in 1993).

Ranks second in Giants history in career saves (199).

1994 N.L. Rolaids Relief Man of the Year.

Three-time N.L. All-Star (1993, 1994 & 1997).

49 JOHNNY ANTONELLI

Johnny Antonelli posted a win and a save during the Giants' four-game sweep of Cleveland in the 1954 World Series. *(Courtesy of T. Scott Brandon)*

Despite being surrounded by controversy for much of his 12-year major-league career, Johnny Antonelli proved to be one of the National League's premier left-handers during the 1950s. Resented in Boston for accepting the huge sum of money the Braves offered him when he signed with them right out of high school, Antonelli received a similarly cool reception in New York after the Giants acquired him for 1951 playoff hero Bobby Thomson prior to the start of the 1954 campaign. However, Antonelli soon ingratiated himself to Giants fans by posting 21 victories in his first year in New York, helping his new team capture the world championship in the process. And, after the Giants experienced a fall from grace in subsequent seasons, Antonelli remained one of the team's few bright spots, surpassing 20 victories twice and 16 wins another two times between 1954 and 1959, en route to earning five All-Star selections. Nevertheless, the forthright Antonelli eventually left the Giants a hated man after expressing his dissatisfaction with the team, the city of San Francisco, and the local media.

Born in Rochester, New York, on April 12, 1930, John August Antonelli attended local Jefferson High School, where he starred in baseball, football, and basketball. Particularly proficient in the first of those sports, Antonelli became a top pitching prospect in high school by tossing five no-hitters, earning him praise from none other than Hall of Fame pitcher Carl Hubbell, who, after scouting the young southpaw for the Giants, said that Antonelli had the best all-around stuff he had ever seen.

Although several other teams expressed interest in signing Antonelli after he graduated from Jefferson High, the Boston Braves ended up acquiring his services after they offered him a then-record $65,000 bonus on the recommendation of scout Jeff Jones, who told club president Lou Pirini, "He's by far the best big-league prospect I've ever seen. He has the poise of a major league pitcher right now and has a curve and fastball to back it up. I think so much of this kid's chances that, if I had to pay out the money myself, I wouldn't hesitate to do it—if I had the money."

After signing with the Braves as an amateur free agent in June of 1948, the 18-year-old Antonelli arrived in Boston one month later amid a considerable amount of controversy. With the rules of the day requiring the Braves to keep him on their major-league roster for at least two years due to the exorbitant amount of his contract, Antonelli found himself sitting on the bench, taking up a valuable roster spot for a team seeking to win its first pennant in 34 years. Johnny Sain, whose 24 victories helped lead the Braves to their first league championship since 1914, expressed the feelings of many of his teammates when he stated that he considered an unproven pitcher such as Antonelli to be undeserving of such a huge signing bonus. In fact, Sain, who earned just $21,000 in 1948, threatened to walk out on his contract.

Relegated mostly to pitching batting practice over the final three months of the 1948 campaign, Antonelli ended up working a total of just four innings. Disrespected by the coaching staff, which left him off the World Series roster,

Antonelli also incurred the wrath of his teammates, who failed to award him even a fraction of a World Series share. Although Antonelli saw a bit more action in each of the next two seasons, he proved to be mostly ineffective, compiling an overall record of just 5–10, while remaining persona non grata in the clubhouse.

After entering the military in 1951 to serve his country during the Korean War, Antonelli ended up resurrecting his career while stationed at Fort Myer, Virginia. Pitching for his Army team, Antonelli compiled a record of 42–2, proving what he could do with regular work. Inserted into the Braves starting rotation when he returned to the team in 1953, Antonelli finished 12–12, with a 3.18 ERA, 11 complete games, and 2 shutouts.

Taking note of Antonelli's improved performance, the pitching-starved Giants completed a six-player trade with the Braves on February 1, 1954 that sent Antonelli and three others to New York for Bobby Thomson and backup catcher Sam Calderone. Although Antonelli later called the deal "the best break of my career," he initially found himself being treated with disdain by Giants fans, who expressed, through their shabby treatment of him, their dismay over losing Thomson. However, Antonelli soon turned the boos into cheers by helping the Giants capture the N.L. pennant. Immediately establishing himself as the ace of his new team's pitching staff, Antonelli earned his first All-Star selection and a third-place finish in the N.L. MVP voting by going 21–7, with a league-leading 2.30 ERA, 6 shutouts, and .750 winning percentage. He continued his success in the World Series, leading the Giants to a four-game sweep of the heavily-favored Cleveland Indians by posting a win, a save, and an ERA of 0.84.

Pitching for a Giants team that finished only 6 games over .500 the following year, Antonelli concluded the 1955 campaign with a record of just 14–16. Nevertheless, he still managed to place among the league leaders with a 3.33 ERA, 143 strikeouts, 14 complete games, 235 ⅓ innings pitched, and a WHIP of 1.224. Antonelli returned to top form in 1956, when, despite pitching for a team that finished just 67–87, he earned a 14th-place finish in the MVP balloting by compiling a record of 20–13. In addition to finishing second in the league in wins, Antonelli placed among the leaders in ERA (2.86), strikeouts (145), shutouts (5), complete games (15), innings pitched (258 ⅓), and WHIP (1.161). Although Antonelli made the N.L. All-Star Team for the third of five times in 1957, he pitched less effectively, winning only 12 of his 30 decisions and compiling an ERA of 3.77.

Antonelli improved upon his performance dramatically after the Giants moved to San Francisco in 1958, posting a composite record of 35–23 over the course of the next two seasons. Particularly impressive in 1959, the 29-year-old southpaw earned All-Star honors for the final time by going 19–10, with a 3.10 ERA, 17 complete games, a league-leading 4 shutouts, and a career-high 282 innings pitched and 165 strikeouts.

Still, even though Antonelli pitched extremely well in 1959, rumors of his dissatisfaction with the Giants, the local media, and San Francisco in general began to surface. Playing on the West Coast, in foreign surroundings, Antonelli, like many of his Giants teammates, had a difficult time adjusting to his new environment. Things only worsened in 1960 when the Giants moved from Seals Stadium into windy Candlestick Park, the team struggled to a fifth-place finish, and Antonelli got off to a slow start, causing him to be demoted to the bullpen. Blamed for many of the team's failures by the local media, Antonelli exacerbated the situation by complaining about the poor playing conditions at the Giants' new home ballpark. Subsequently vilified by Giants fans, who came to view him as a transplanted New Yorker, Antonelli spent his remaining time in San Francisco being booed unmercifully by the hometown fans.

After Antonelli finished just 6–7 with a 3.77 ERA in 1960, the Giants put an end to his misery on December 3 of that year by trading him and promising young outfielder Willie Kirkland to the Cleveland Indians for former A.L. batting champion Harvey Kuenn. Antonelli subsequently split the 1961 campaign between the Indians and the Milwaukee Braves, before announcing his retirement at season's end after being purchased by the expansion New York Mets. He concluded his career with a record of 126–110, an ERA of 3.34, 1,162 strikeouts in 1,992 ⅓ innings of work, 25 shutouts, 102 complete games, and a WHIP of 1.283. In Antonelli's seven seasons with the Giants, he went 108–84, with a 3.13 ERA, 919 strikeouts in 1,600 ⅔ innings pitched, 21 shutouts, 86 complete games, and a WHIP of 1.228.

Following his playing career, Antonelli returned to his hometown of Rochester, New York, where he ran a chain of tire stores bearing his name before eventually retiring from the business world.

Although Antonelli perhaps never quite lived up to the enormous potential he displayed in high school, he developed into a very good major-league pitcher and a consistent winner in his years with the Giants. In discussing Antonelli in his book *Stan Musial: The Man's Own Story*, the legendary Hall of Famer said, "Johnny Antonelli was a good pitcher with great control for several years. In his 20-game peak he came up with a terrific change of pace that made him outstanding."

Giant Career Highlights:

Best Season: Despite pitching for rather mediocre Giant teams, Antonelli performed extremely well in both 1956 and 1959, posting win totals of 20 and 19, respectively. Nevertheless, the 1954 campaign would have to be considered his signature season. Winning 11 straight games at one point, Antonelli finished the year with a record of 21–7 that gave him a league-best .750 winning percentage. He also led all N.L. hurlers with a 2.30 ERA and 6 shutouts, tossed a career-high 18 complete games, placed second in the league with a WHIP of 1.171, and finished among the leaders with 152 strikeouts and 258 ⅔ innings pitched, en route to earning a third-place finish in the N.L. MVP voting and *Sporting News* Pitcher of the Year honors.

Memorable Moments/Greatest Performances: Antonelli turned in one of his finest all-around performances of the 1954 campaign on April 25, when he surrendered just 3 hits and went 2-for-4 at the plate during a 5–0 victory over the Phillies.

Antonelli went on an exceptional run from May 25 to August 1, 1954, posting 11 consecutive wins over that nine-week span without suffering a loss. Standout games included back-to-back shutouts against Cincinnati and Milwaukee in early June, a 10–0, 3-hit shutout of the Phillies on July 5, and a 13-inning, complete game 2–1 win over the Reds on July 20.

Antonelli pitched one of his most memorable games on May 1, 1955, when he worked all 16 innings of a 2–1 victory over Cincinnati. Antonelli surrendered just 6 hits to the Reds, while striking out 11. He had arguably the finest all-around game of his career later in the year, on September 13, when he allowed 6 hits during a 9–1 victory over the Braves and went 4-for-5 at the plate, with a homer, double, 4 RBIs, and 2 runs scored.

Antonelli turned in his most dominant pitching performance on August 15, 1956, when he shut out the Dodgers by a score of 1–0, surrendering just 2 hits and striking out 11 during the contest.

Yet, Antonelli will always be remembered most fondly by Giants fans for his performance in the 1954 World Series. After striking out 9 Cleveland Indian batters during a 3–1 Giants victory in Game 2 of the Fall Classic,

Antonelli returned to the mound two days later to record the final 5 outs of a 7–4 Giants win that made them world champions. He finished the Series with a win, a save, an ERA of 0.84, and 12 strikeouts in 10 ⅔ innings of work.

Notable Achievements:

Won at least 20 games twice, surpassing 16 victories on two other occasions.

Posted winning percentage in excess of .700 once (.750 in 1954).

Compiled ERA under 3.00 twice.

Threw more than 250 innings three times.

Led N.L. pitchers in: winning percentage once; ERA once; and shutouts twice.

Finished second among N.L. pitchers in wins twice.

Finished third in 1954 N.L. MVP voting.

1954 *Sporting News* Pitcher of the Year.

Two-time *Sporting News* All-Star selection (1954 & 1959).

Five-time N.L. All-Star (1954, 1956, 1957, 1958 & 1959).

1954 N.L. champion.

1954 world champion.

50 SAL MAGLIE

Sal Maglie compiled the highest career winning percentage of any pitcher in Giants history. *(Courtesy of Mearsonlineauctions.com)*

One of only 14 players to wear the uniforms of all three New York City teams before the Giants and Dodgers moved to the West Coast, Sal Maglie gradually acquired the nickname "Sal the Barber" due to his propensity for giving opposing batters close shaves with pitches up and in, just under their chins. A frightening figure on the mound who stared down hitters with an angry look made even more menacing by his dark features and razor-stubble beard, Maglie earned a number 1 ranking from Hall of Fame hurler Nolan Ryan in his book, *Kings of the Hill*, in the category of "intimidators." Yet, the 6'2", 180-pound right-hander depended on more than just intimidation to thwart opposing batters, relying equally on his superb curveball and excellent command of the strike zone to establish himself as one of the National League's top pitchers of the early-1950s. Having most of his finest seasons for the Giants, Maglie compiled a composite record of 59–18 from 1950 to 1952, en route to posting an overall mark of 95–42 as a member of the team that gives him a franchise-best .693 career winning percentage. Maglie's stellar pitching helped lead the Giants to two pennants and one world championship, earning him in the process a pair of All-Star selections and two top-10 finishes in the N.L. MVP voting.

Born the son of Italian immigrants in Niagara Falls, New York, on April 26, 1917, Salvatore Anthony Maglie mystified and angered his parents with his love of baseball, forcing him to constantly sneak out of the house to play as a youngster. After graduating from Niagara University, Maglie initially spent some time working at various local chemical plants, before beginning his pitching career with a semipro team out of Buffalo, New York. Subsequently offered an opportunity to compete in the minors, Maglie failed to distinguish himself over the course of the next three seasons. Nevertheless, with the vast majority of major leaguers entering the service during World War II, Maglie received an offer to sign with the New York Giants in 1942 after the U.S. military deemed him unfit for service due to a chronic sinus condition.

Experiencing little in the way of success in his one year in New York's farm system, Maglie chose to resign, after which he spent the next two years working as a pipe fitter in a defense plant. Still, Maglie did not completely abandon his dream of playing in the Major Leagues, continuing to sharpen his pitching skills with various Canadian amateur teams. Having regained his confidence, Maglie returned to professional baseball in 1945, spending most of the year in the minor leagues, before making his debut with the Giants at 28 years of age, on August 9, 1945. Appearing in 13 games over the final two months of the campaign, Maglie made a favorable impression, compiling a record of 5–4 and an ERA of 2.35.

Apparently on the verge of establishing himself as a legitimate major-league pitcher, Maglie chose to join several other players in jumping to the Mexican League in order to make more money. With MLB Commissioner Happy Chandler subsequently banning all players who jumped leagues,

Maglie spent the next four years in exile, unable to return to the Giants until Chandler lifted the ban in 1950.

Still, Maglie's years in Mexico ended up doing wonders for his career. Reconnected with *Dead Ball Era* pitching star Dolf Luque, with whom Maglie first became familiar when the former served as pitching coach for the Giants, Maglie developed an exceptional curve ball, which became his best pitch. Luque, who originally convinced Maglie to sign with the Mexican League, taught his protégé how to deliver the curve from three different release points: overhand, sidearm, and underhand. In addition to causing his signature pitch to move differently under different conditions, Maglie's various arm angles served as a source of confusion to opposing batters. Luque also stressed to Maglie the importance of pitching inside and frequently brushing back hitters as a means of taking control of a game.

Armed with his new weapon and a more aggressive mindset, an older and wiser Maglie returned to the Giants in 1950. Employing all the lessons he learned from Luque during his time in Mexico, the 33-year-old Maglie gradually worked his way into New York's starting rotation after beginning the year in the bullpen. Appearing in a total of 47 games and making 16 starts, Maglie concluded the campaign with a record of 18–4, 12 complete games, and a league-leading .818 winning percentage, 2.71 ERA, and 5 shutouts. He followed that up by posting a brilliant 23–6 record for the pennant-winning Giants in 1951, tying teammate Larry Jansen for the league lead in victories in the process. Maglie also finished among the league leaders with a 2.93 ERA, 146 strikeouts, 3 shutouts, 22 complete games, 298 innings pitched, and a WHIP of 1.141, en route to earning his first All-Star selection and a fourth-place finish in the N.L. MVP voting.

Maglie again performed exceptionally well for the Giants in 1952, earning All-Star honors once more by compiling a record of 18–8 that placed him second among N.L. pitchers in wins. He also posted an ERA of 2.92 and finished third in the league with 5 shutouts. Maglie's excellent work prompted Arthur Daley of the *New York Times* to write at one point during the season, "The experts will tell you that Maglie has the best curve ball in the big leagues, and now he knows what to do with it, and how to control it."

Meanwhile, as Maglie established himself as one of the Senior Circuit's premier hurlers, he also developed a reputation as arguably the most intimidating pitcher in all of baseball. Taking with him to the mound before each start an attitude he described when he stated, "When I'm pitching, I own the plate," Maglie struck fear into opposing batters with his glowering appearance and tendency to knock them down with his high hard one. Nicknamed "Sal the Barber" by *New York Daily News* baseball reporter Jim McCulley for the manner in which he "shaved the batters" chins by throwing up and in to them, Maglie expressed his disdain for hitters when he told Dodgers beat writer Roger Kahn, "The hell with all the hitters . . . the hell with all of them." Maglie added, "When I'm pitching, I figure the plate is mine, and I don't like anyone getting too close to it."

In describing the unnerving experience of batting against Maglie, Cincinnati's Danny Litwhiler revealed, "He scares you to death. He's scowling and gnashing his teeth, and if you try to dig in on him, there goes your Adam's apple. He's gonna win if it kills you and him both."

In paying tribute to his longtime teammate, Alvin Dark once remarked, "He is the only man I've ever seen pitch a shutout on a day when he had absolutely nothing. Maglie got by on meanness."

Yet, in spite of his ferocious mound presence, Maglie remained kind, courteous, and good-natured off the field, with one reporter writing, "When Maglie spoke, he sounded like a priest in a confessional."

Unfortunately, back problems began plaguing Maglie in 1952, preventing him from ever again being a dominant pitcher for the Giants. Limited to only 24 starts in 1953, Maglie concluded the campaign with a record of just 8–9 and an uncharacteristically high 4.15 ERA. He rebounded somewhat the following year, though, compiling a mark of 14–6 for the pennant-winning Giants, and finishing among the league leaders with a 3.26 ERA.

The 1954 season proved to be Maglie's last full year with the Giants. After the 38-year-old right-hander went 9–5 with a 3.75 ERA over the first four months of the ensuing campaign, the Giants placed him on waivers, ending his lengthy association with the organization. Subsequently claimed by the Indians, Maglie spent the rest of 1955 in Cleveland, losing both his decisions, before being sold to the Brooklyn Dodgers early the following year. Inserted into the Dodgers' starting rotation, Maglie experienced a remarkable renaissance in Brooklyn, earning a second-place finish in the N.L. MVP voting by compiling a record of 13–5 and an ERA of 2.87 for the pennant-winning Dodgers. After Maglie posted a mark of 6–6 over the first five months of the 1957 campaign, Brooklyn sold him to the Yankees, with whom he spent the remainder of the year. Maglie then split the 1958 season between the Yankees and Cardinals, going a combined 3–7, before announcing his retirement when St. Louis released him just prior to the start of the 1959 season. Maglie ended his career with a record of 119–62, giving him an outstanding .657 winning percentage. He also compiled an ERA of 3.15, struck out 862 batters in 1,723 innings of work, threw 25 shutouts and 93 complete games, and posted a WHIP of 1.250. In addition to going 95–42 as a member of the Giants, Maglie compiled an ERA of 3.13, amassed 654 strikeouts over 1,297 ⅔ innings, tossed 20 shutouts and 77 complete games, and posted a WHIP of 1.272.

Following his playing days, Maglie spent one year scouting for the Cardinals, before doing two tours of duty as pitching coach for the Red Sox (1960–62; 1966–67). He then served as pitching coach for the Seattle Pilots in 1969—their only year in existence. After baseball, Maglie worked as a wholesale liquor salesman and a coordinator for the Niagara Falls Convention Bureau until he suffered a brain aneurysm in 1981. Although Maglie made a full recovery, his health gradually deteriorated over time, causing him to pass away at 75 years of age, on December 28, 1992, due to complications from pneumonia.

Giant Career Highlights:

Best Season: Maglie performed brilliantly for the Giants in 1950, at one point posting 11 straight wins en route to compiling an overall record of 18–4 that gave him a league-leading .818 winning percentage. He also led all N.L. pitchers with an ERA of 2.71 and 5 shutouts. Nevertheless, Maglie pitched his best ball for the Giants the following year, when, in addition to leading the league with 23 victories, he finished second in ERA (2.93), winning percentage (.793), and complete games (22), third in strikeouts (146) and innings pitched (298), and fourth in WHIP (1.141), establishing career-best marks in four of the seven categories. Particularly effective down the stretch, Maglie won 8 of his last 9 decisions, in helping the Giants overtake the Dodgers for the 1951 N.L. pennant.

Memorable Moments/Greatest Performances: Maglie had a memorable afternoon against the Braves on June 19, 1953, surrendering just 4 hits and going 3-for-5 at the plate, with 4 RBIs and 2 runs scored, during a 15–1 Giants win in Milwaukee.

Maglie went undefeated from July 21 to September 21, 1950, going a perfect 11–0 over that two-month stretch. Especially dominant from August

26 to September 9, Maglie threw four straight complete-game shutouts during that time, en route to tossing a total of 45 ⅔ consecutive scoreless innings.

Maglie turned in one of his most dominant pitching performances for the Giants on May 4, 1951, when he allowed just a leadoff triple to Pete Castiglione during a 5–1, one-hit victory over the Pittsburgh Pirates. Maglie turned in another brilliant effort three weeks later, on May 27, when he surrendered just 2 hits in defeating the Phillies by a score of 2–0. Maglie continued his excellent pitching against the Dodgers on June 26, when he shut out the Giants' arch-rivals by a score of 4–0, allowing just 3 hits during the contest.

On April 20, 1952, Maglie recorded the first shutout by a visiting pitcher at Ebbets Field since 1949 when he blanked the Dodgers, 6–0, on just 2 hits.

Yet, perhaps the most memorable performance of Maglie's Giants career took place on April 30, 1954, when he worked all 14 innings of a 4–2 victory over the Cubs that ended with a two-run homer by Willie Mays in the final frame.

Notable Achievements:

Surpassed 20 victories once (23 in 1951), winning 18 games two other times.

Posted winning percentage in excess of .700 three times.

Compiled ERA under 3.00 four times.

Threw more than 250 innings once (298 in 1951).

Tossed more than 20 complete games once (22 in 1951).

Led N.L. pitchers in: wins once; winning percentage once; ERA once; and shutouts once.

Holds Giants career record for highest winning percentage (.693).

Finished fourth in 1951 N.L. MVP voting.

1951 *Sporting News* All-Star selection.

Two-time N.L. All-Star (1951 & 1952).

Two-time N.L. champion (1951 & 1954).

1954 world champion.

SUMMARY

Having identified the 50 greatest players in New York/San Francisco Giants history, the time has come to select the best of the best. Based on the rankings contained in this book, the members of the Giants all-time team for each city are listed below. Our squads include the top player at each position, along with a pitching staff that features a five-man starting rotation, a set-up man, and a closer. The closer for the New York team and the fifth starter for the San Francisco squad are players who just missed making it into the top 50. Following the two separate squads, I have listed the members of the Giants all-time team for both cities combined.

New York Giants Starting Lineup:

Player/Position:
George Burns LF
Frankie Frisch 2B
Bill Terry 1B
Willie Mays CF
Mel Ott RF
Freddie Lindstrom 3B
Travis Jackson SS
Roger Bresnahan C

New York Giants Pitching Staff:

Christy Mathewson SP
Carl Hubbell SP
Joe McGinnity SP
Hal Schumacher SP
Jeff Tesreau SP
Hooks Wiltse SU
Hoyt Wilhelm CL

San Francisco Giants Starting Lineup:

Player/Position:

Bobby Bonds RF
Buster Posey C
Barry Bonds LF
Willie Mays CF
Willie McCovey 1B
Jeff Kent 2B
Matt Williams 3B
Rich Aurilia SS

San Francisco Giants Pitching Staff:

Juan Marichal SP
Gaylord Perry SP
Madison Bumgarner SP
Tim Lincecum SP
Jason Schmidt SP
Rod Beck SU
Robb Nen CL

New York/San Francisco Giants Starting Lineup:

Player/Position:
Frankie Frisch 2B
Travis Jackson SS
Barry Bonds LF
Willie Mays CF
Willie McCovey 1B
Mel Ott RF
Matt Williams 3B
Buster Posey C

New York/San Francisco Giants Pitching Staff:

Christy Mathewson SP
Juan Marichal SP
Carl Hubbell SP
Joe McGinnity SP
Gaylord Perry SP
Rod Beck SU
Robb Nen CL

GLOSSARY

Abbreviations and Statistical Terms

AVG. Batting average. The number of hits divided by the number of at-bats.

CG. Complete games pitched.

CL. Closer.

ERA. Earned run average. The number of earned runs a pitcher gives up, per nine innings. This does not include runs that scored as a result of errors made in the field and is calculated by dividing the number of runs given up, by the number of innings pitched, and multiplying the result by 9.

HITS. Base hits. Awarded when a runner safely reaches at least first base upon a batted ball, if no error is recorded.

HR. Home runs. Fair ball hit over the fence, or one hit to a spot that allows the batter to circle the bases before the ball is returned to home plate.

IP. Innings pitched.

OBP. On-base percentage. Hits plus walks plus hit-by-pitches, divided by plate appearances.

RBI. Runs batted in. Awarded to the batter when a runner scores upon a safely batted ball, a sacrifice or a walk.

RUNS. Runs scored by a player.

SB. Stolen bases.

SLG PCT. Slugging percentage. The number of total bases earned by all singles, doubles, triples and home runs, divided by the total number of at-bats.

SO. Strikeouts.

SP. Starting pitcher.

SU. Set-up reliever.

WHIP. Walks and hits allowed per inning pitched. The total number of bases on balls and hits allowed by a pitcher, divided by his total number of innings pitched.

WIN PCT. Winning percentage. A pitcher's number of wins divided by his number of total decisions (i.e. wins plus losses).

BIBLIOGRAPHY

Books:

DeMarco, Tony, et al., *The Sporting News Selects 50 Greatest Sluggers*. The Sporting News, a division of Times Mirror Magazines, Inc., St. Louis, MO., 2000.

Shalin, Mike, and Neil Shalin, *Out by a Step: The 100 Best Players Not in the Baseball Hall of Fame*. Diamond Communications, Inc., Lanham, MD, 2002.

Thorn, John, and Palmer, Pete, eds., with Michael Gershman, *Total Baseball*. HarperCollins Pub., Inc., New York, 1993.

Williams, Ted, with Jim Prime, *Ted Williams' Hit List*. Masters Press, Indianapolis, IN, 1996.

Videos:

Sports Century: Fifty Greatest Athletes—Willie Mays. ESPN, 1999.

The Glory of their Times. Cappy Productions, Inc., 1985.

The Sporting News' 100 Greatest Baseball Players. National Broadcasting Co., 1999.

Websites:

The Ballplayers, online at BaseballLibrary.com (http://www.baseballlibrary.com/baseballlibrary/ballplayers).

Bio Project, online at SABR.org (http://www.sabr.org/bioproj/person).

Historical Stats, online at MLB.com (http://www.mlb.com/stats.historical/individual stats player).

The Players, online at Baseball-Reference.com (http://www.baseball-reference.com/players).

The Players, online at Retrosheet.org (http://www.retrosheet.org/boxesetc/index.html/players)

The Teams, online at Baseball-Reference.com (http://www.baseball-reference.com/teams).

TSN-All-Stars, online at BaseballChronology.com (http://www.baseballchronology.com/Baseball/Awards/TSN-AllStars.asp).

ACKNOWLEDGMENTS

I would like to express my gratitude to the grandchildren of Leslie Jones, who, through the Trustees of the Boston Public Library, Print Department, supplied many of the photos included in this book.

I also wish to thank Troy R. Kinunen of MEARSonlineauctions.com, Jeffrey Marren of LegendaryAuctions.com, Richard Albersheim of Albersheimsstore.com, Kate of RMYauctions.com, Pristineauction.com, Aaron Frutman of DGA Productions, George A. Kitrinos, Dirk Hansen, T. Scott Brandon, Jude Seymour, Julio Cesar Martinez, and Christopher M. Matthews, each of whom generously contributed to the photographic content of this work.